KNOWING REALITY

A Guided Introduction to Metaphysics and Epistemology

Dwayne Moore

broadview press

BROADVIEW PRESS – www.broadviewpress.com
Peterborough, Ontario, Canada

Founded in 1985, Broadview Press remains a wholly independent publishing house. Broadview's focus is on academic publishing; our titles are accessible to university and college students as well as scholars and general readers. With over 800 titles in print, Broadview has become a leading international publisher in the humanities, with world-wide distribution. Broadview is committed to environmentally responsible publishing and fair business practices.

Library and Archives Canada Cataloguing in Publication

Title: Knowing reality : a guided introduction to metaphysics and epistemology / Dwayne Moore.
Names: Moore, Dwayne, 1975- author.
Description: Includes bibliographical references and index.
Identifiers: Canadiana (print) 20230439640 | Canadiana (ebook) 20230439675 | ISBN 9781554815302 (softcover) | ISBN 9781460408186 (EPUB) | ISBN 9781770488823 (PDF)
Subjects: LCSH: Metaphysics. | LCSH: Knowledge, Theory of.
Classification: LCC BD111 .M66 2023 | DDC 110—dc23

Broadview Press handles its own distribution in North America:
PO Box 1243, Peterborough, Ontario K9J 7H5, Canada
555 Riverwalk Parkway, Tonawanda, NY 14150, USA
Tel: (705) 743-8990; Fax: (705) 743-8353
email: customerservice@broadviewpress.com

For all territories outside of North America, distribution is handled by Eurospan Group.

Canada  Broadview Press acknowledges the financial support of the Government of Canada for our publishing activities.

Edited by Michel Pharand
Book design by Em Dash Design

PRINTED IN CANADA

This book is made of paper from well-managed FSC®- certified forests, recycled materials, and other controlled sources.

Contents

Additional Resources

Visit this book's companion resources for additional materials, including video content and an automated tool for planning argumentative essays.

sites.broadviewpress.com/knowing

Preface

I did not want to write this textbook: it was too much work! But I did anyway. Why? I have taught introductory metaphysics and epistemology on many occasions—at four different universities over the past fifteen years, often multiple courses per year—but was never fully satisfied with the textbooks available for use. Some focused exclusively on metaphysics, so an additional textbook on epistemology was needed. That was too expensive for students. Others added sections on ethics and political philosophy, none of which was relevant to my course. What I needed was a textbook that focused on both metaphysics and epistemology, and nothing else.

I found some, but new issues arose. Some textbooks were exclusively anthologies, which is nice because it exposes students to primary sources, letting them read the works of some of the greatest minds in history. But first contact with primary sources is difficult for introductory students, and these sources were under-explained, or insufficiently contextualized within the range of philosophers and positions on the issues. Other textbooks were single-authored readers, which is nice for clearly explaining difficult and different views, while explaining the relative merits and demerits of each position relative to other views. But I wanted students to be exposed to multiple voices on a topic, and be exposed to the primary sources that first shaped the discussion.

I tried guided anthologies for a while, textbooks which guide the reader through the primary sources. One was too long. It contained lengthy excerpts from numerous primary sources per topic, and included more topics than could be covered in one term. My courses were twelve weeks long, so I needed twelve chapters, each chapter exactly as long as the expected amount of reading per week. Another anthology focused only on historical texts and issues, whereas I wanted something more current. I wanted something that begins with the history but ends at the cutting edge of the contemporary scene, especially to capture the diversity present in that scene. Still another was too text-centric. The authors provided the historical context and argumentative summary of the primary sources, but did not lay out the broader topics under discussion. I needed a text that maps out the logical space of an issue, locates each philosopher on the map, and evaluates the peaks and valleys of each position on the map. Another problem, I regret to say, is that the eyes of my introductory students glazed over when I asked text-centric questions such as 'What is Plato's theory of forms' or 'What is Hume saying here in *An Enquiry Concerning Human Understanding*.' But those same students were suddenly interested when I asked topic-centric questions such as 'Do humans have free will?' and 'Does God exist?' Those same students would excitedly approach me after class to see if I had seen the latest episode of *Black Mirror*, since it addresses issues from my lecture.

I needed something more interesting, engaging, and relevant to students, as they were interested in doing philosophy. I just had to figure out how to bring out its natural appeal. I started adding thought experiments to class, to pique student interest in the topic. When one thought experiment was well received, I used it the following year. If another flopped, I dropped it. I started adding examples from films, which also elicited substantial engagement. But now my class lectures were diverging too much from the textbook I was using. I needed the text itself to make the issues relevant and interesting. I found a few popular philosophy texts, such as *The Good Place and Philosophy* and *The Office and Philosophy*, but those texts lacked the academic rigour and depth of a university course. I needed a textbook that was as engaging and interesting as these pop philosophy books, but maintained the academic rigour of a textbook anchored to historical issues and sources.

I could not find any of these. So, I wrote one myself. This textbook seeks to achieve all these goals at once. A textbook devoted to both (and only) metaphysics and epistemology. A guided reader that also exposes students to primary sources. A twelve-chapter book, covering twelve topics, taking the typical twelve academic weeks in a term to finish. A book that is long enough to stand on its own as the only required reading for the course, but short enough to not place undue expectations on first-year students. A textbook that begins with historical issues and philosophers, but ends at the cutting edge of the diverse cast comprising the contemporary scene of each issue. A textbook that centers each chapter on an engaging issue, and visually maps out the logical terrain on that issue, locating each philosopher on the map for a visual sense of the conceptual space. A textbook that maintains its academic rigour while simultaneously beginning each chapter with a thought experiment that stimulates interest in the topic and scatters other relevant examples throughout.

In sum, this textbook is the culmination of fifteen years of continuously tweaking the teaching content in my introductory metaphysics and epistemology courses. In one sense, it is lamentable that it took me fifteen years to come up with course content I am satisfied with. Most instructors probably get there sooner. However, for those who are still looking for an appropriate textbook, and for those who are just starting out and want a 'no assembly required' text for first time use, this textbook may be for you. It is, after all, vetted by the crowd-sourcing of ten thousand leery students. As such, I would like to dedicate this textbook to all my former students for contributing in some way to its content, either by rolling their eyes at just the right time, or by pointing me to some relevant movie, or by engaging more wholeheartedly in certain conversations than others.

Chapter 1

Philosophy and Sophistry

THOUGHT EXPERIMENT 1
Michael's Job Interview

On the TV series *The Office*, Michael Scott is a bumbling but sometimes effective office manager. In one episode (Season 3: "The Job"), Michael is being interviewed for a promotion. During the interview, he is asked to state his three greatest strengths and weaknesses. Michael has to decide whether to be honest and state actual weaknesses that may lead the boss away from hiring him, or cleverly avoid having to state his actual weaknesses in an attempt to secure the promotion. Michael chooses the latter, and responds: "I work too hard, I care too much, and sometimes I can be too invested in my job ... my weaknesses are actually strengths." He does not choose the honest path of knowing his own weaknesses and expressing them (he has plenty to choose from); rather, he chooses to say whatever he thinks will advance his career. Did Michael answer well? How would you answer this question, knowing that you should be honest, but also knowing that a job is on the line?

Imagine you are in a job interview and the employer asks you to name your greatest weakness. What do you say? You could be honest and say, "I'm a bit lazy at times." But you know that the employer will not hire you if you say that. You could be cunning and say, "I am too dedicated to my work." It isn't honest, but the employer will hire you if you say that. Imagine a professor asks you to write a five-page paper about some controversial topic. Do you regurgitate the arguments the professor made, thinking it will get you a better grade? Or do you express your honest views? Imagine you are constructing an online dating profile and you need a picture. Do you dress up, borrow a puppy to pose with, and apply the best filter to the picture, knowing these will land you more dates? Or do you post the normal version of you with a nice smile, knowing this is the real you, despite losing out on a couple of dates? We constantly face the following dilemma: do we choose the truth though it may not be advantageous, or do we choose the advantageous though it may not be the truth?

Part of the answer to these questions involves analyzing how important the truth is to us. Consider some additional questions on this issue: do we go to university for the sake of getting a job, or for the sake of increasing our knowledge of the world? Do we listen to news for the sake of getting the whole truth on an issue, or do we listen to the news stations that just report (on) stories that confirm our political view? Do we follow the religious beliefs (or the lack of religious beliefs) of our parents because that is simply what we were taught, or do we search for the truth about God (or the lack of a God)? In each case, one of these options emphasizes a concern for the truth, while the other option minimizes the quest for the truth.

It is possible to imagine a spectrum, where on one side are those with a deep concern for the truth (even to the point of sacrificing personal gain), and on the other side are those who care little for the truth but instead aim for personal gain. The earliest philosophers all stand on the left side of the spectrum, showing a strong commitment to figuring out the truths of nature and the truths about the best way to live, even to the point of suffering for the sake of the truth. By looking at two of these earliest philosophers, Thales and Socrates, we will get a sense of what philosophy is.

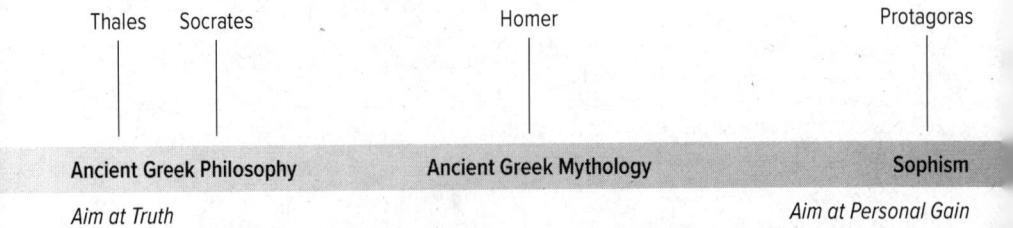

Spectrum 1: The Truth vs. Personal Gain[1]

Before looking at them, let us begin with a brief definition of philosophy. The word **philosophy** comes from two Greek words, *philos* = love and *sophia* = wisdom, so philosophy means the love of wisdom. According to this classic definition, philosophers care for the truth, as they love wisdom. Here is a more contemporary definition: philosophy is the reasoned investigation of life's most important questions. There are several matters to consider here.

First, why a *reasoned* investigation? Physicists use colliders to analyze their subject matter (i.e., particles), biologists use microscopes to analyze their subject

---

1 This chapter, like every chapter in this book, is organized around a spectrum of positions on an issue. The purpose of the spectrum is to provide a visual representation of central differences between the popular positions on an issue that are emphasized in the chapter, and then locate the approximate positions of the philosophers discussed in the chapter on this spectrum. The various available positions on an issue, and the locations of philosophers on a spectrum, are in fact more complex than the analysis represented in each spectrum. However, each chapter follows one central strand of reasoning that explains why these different philosophers are located where they are on a particular spectrum.

matter (i.e., cells), archaeologists use pickaxes to analyze their subject matter (i.e., ruins), and philosophers use reasoning to analyze their subject matter (i.e., life's important questions). This means that philosophers arrive at conclusions through reasoning and evidence, and evaluate whether beliefs are well supported or not based on the quality of the reasoning used. We will look at some of these methods for evaluating and constructing reasoned arguments below.

Second, the emphasis is on an *investigation* into life's important questions, rather than on a *solution* to those questions. While philosophers aim to answer life's important questions, it is sometimes the case that they develop several viable answers, and it is also sometimes the case that answers elude their grasp. The emphasis is on the *attempt* to answer the questions and the attempt to arrive at the best conclusions and beliefs possible.

Lastly, what are life's most important questions? There are unimportant questions: why do we nail down coffin lids? Would you rather see an elephant the size of a frog or a frog the size of an elephant? There are important questions that philosophers do not investigate: how can we predict earthquakes? What causes cancer? There are important philosophical questions that philosophers normally investigate but that we will not investigate in this textbook. Some of these questions are in the realm of political and moral philosophy: what is the best form of government? Is equality or freedom more important? What is the best way to live life? Is abortion acceptable? Should cloning be allowed? But last come the important philosophical questions that we will investigate in this textbook. Here are some questions in **metaphysics**, or the study of the nature of reality, that we will investigate: what are objects made of? What are persons and do they stay the same despite changing? Do we have a soul? Do we have free will? Why does the universe exist? Does God exist? Here are some questions in **epistemology**, or the study of the nature of knowledge, that we will investigate: what is truth? What is knowledge? Can humans know truth? Are we living in a computer simulation? How do we reason well enough to win arguments? Does science lead to truth? How do we have self-knowledge? Should we trust religious experience?

1.1 Ancient Greek Mythology

There are various philosophical traditions: the African philosophical tradition, the Chinese philosophical tradition, the Indian philosophical tradition, and so on, each with its own rich history. Most European and North American philosophers study Western Philosophy, which has its historical roots in Ancient Greece, starting in the year 585 BCE. What happened then? Prior to this date, Greek myths were passed down orally from generation to generation until authors such as Homer and Hesiod wrote them down. These writings speak of many Greek gods, including Zeus, Ares, Hades, Apollo, Athena, and Hermes, to name but a few. All of these gods possess various powers and diverse agendas, and sporadically intervene (or, refrain from intervening) in the world of human affairs.

This left the Greek people living in a confusing world where beliefs in various gods at different times would influence human affairs in conflicting ways for reasons humans could not fathom. In Homer's *Iliad*, for example, several gods argue about whether or not to create havoc for the city of Troy before finally deciding to send Minerva to hatch a plot against the city. She descends from Mount Olympus as a meteor to carry out the wishes of the gods; the humans below notice the meteor but do not know whether it means peace or war:

> The sire of gods and men heeded her words, and said to Minerva, "Go at once into the Trojan and Achaean hosts, and contrive that the Trojans shall be the first to break their oaths and set upon the Achaeans." This was what Minerva was already eager to do, so down she darted from the topmost summits of Olympus. She shot through the sky as some brilliant meteor which the son of scheming Saturn has sent as a sign to mariners or to some great army, and a fiery train of light follows in its wake. The Trojans and Achaeans were struck with awe as they beheld, and one would turn to his neighbour, saying, "Either we shall again have war and din of combat, or Jove the lord of battle will now make peace between us."[2]

Notice that the Trojans do not know about the mischief of the gods, nor did they know whether a meteor was a sign of peace or war. The ancient Greeks lived in confusion about the workings of the world, as the unknown whims of a pantheon of moody gods with differing agendas dictated the events of the world. Thus the world, to the ancient Greeks, was unknowable, unexplainable, and unpredictable. Will a drought kill the crops this year? It depends on the whims of the gods, not on trackable weather patterns. Will Phoebe fall in love with me? It depends on whether she is struck by Cupid's arrow, not on whether there is a natural attraction. Will the villager conceive a child? It depends on whether Aphrodite (the goddess of love) is angry, not on whether the sperm enters the egg. Will the sick child survive? It depends on whether Asclepius (the god of medicine) heals her or not, not on what the diagnosis and treatment is. Of course we enjoy reading the Greek myths and feel that they sometimes embody valuable outlooks and lessons. But the view that nature is influenced by a plurality of gods with unknown motives makes it difficult for us to come to an understanding of the basic structures of our lives and of the universe.

1.2 Ancient Greek Philosophy

Ancient Greek philosophers reject this mythological view that the world is unknowable, unexplainable, and unpredictable. Rather, they say the world is a **cosmos**, which means an orderly arrangement, just as putting on cosmetics is

---

2   Homer, *The Iliad*, Book IV, trans. S. Butler (The Floating Press, 2008), 84–85.

the orderly arranging of one's face. Operating behind all the moving parts of the cosmos is a **logos**, or a logic or reason. If the events of the world are ordered, patterned, and logical, it is possible for humans to understand, explain, and predict the world and human affairs. This idea set in motion the scientific spirit of explaining events in the natural world and also brought about the philosophical spirit of theorizing about the fundamental nature of the world.

Thales (625–545 BCE) is widely considered the first philosopher and scientist. On the assumption that the universe is an orderly cosmos with a system of logic or repeating patterns, Thales used astronomy to track solar eclipses and used mathematics to predict that a solar eclipse should occur in 585 BCE. Thales predicted correctly! As Herodotus reports,

> On one occasion [the Medes and the Lydians] had an unexpected battle in the dark, an event which occurred after five years of indecisive warfare: the two armies had already engaged and the fight was in progress, when day was suddenly turned into night. This change from daylight to darkness had been foretold to the Ionians by Thales of Miletus, who fixed the date for it within the limits of the year in which it did, in fact, take place.[3]

Rather than looking to the sky and seeing a comet, and wondering which god had sent it, and whether it was an omen of war or peace, Thales looked to the sky and noticed the patterns in nature and predicted that an eclipse would occur, and it did. Thales did not credit sorcery or divination for this prediction, but astronomy and mathematics. This event is often considered the inaugural moment of philosophy. Thales went on to document the summer and winter solstices, and calculate that a year comprises 365 days, once again focusing on the cycles and patterns of nature. As we will see in Chapter 3.1, he forms a grand theory of how the universe works as well. Other philosophers advanced contrasting theories of how the universe works, but an attempt to explain the universe is common to all these early philosophers.

Thales' search for answers to the truth about how the world works sometimes led to personal harm. Plato recounts the following story: "They say that once when Thales was gazing upwards while doing astronomy, he fell into a well, and that a witty and charming Thracian serving-girl made fun of him for being eager to know the things in the heavens but failing to notice what was just behind him and right by his feet."[4] Thales also lived a life of some poverty. He did not use his mind to acquire wealth and personal gain, but rather to seek answers to how the world works. Thales embodies the philosophical spirit of a deep interest in investigating life's most important questions.

Plato (427–347 BCE) was one of the most influential philosophers of all time. In fact, Alfred North Whitehead once quipped that "The safest general

---

3 Herodotus, *The History of Herodotus* I.74, trans. H. Cary (London: Henry Bohn, 1848), 32.
4 Plato, *Theaetetus* 174a, in *Readings in Ancient Greek Philosophy: Fourth Edition*, ed. Mark Cohen, Patricia Curd, and C.D.C. Reeve (Indianapolis: Hackett, 2011), 11.

characterization of the European philosophical tradition is that it consists of a series of footnotes to Plato."[5] In other words, Plato introduces almost all of the difficult puzzles that later philosophers grapple with. Plato's writings consist of dialogues where his teacher **Socrates** (470–399 BCE) wanders around asking citizens for answers about important life questions, such as the true nature of piety, beauty, love, or friendship.

The **Socratic Method**, or the way in which Socrates practised philosophy, involves asking another person for their answers to a question, and then pointing out the implications and problems with their replies. Some find this strategy annoying, as it often makes the respondent look foolish. Others appreciate the strategy, as it gives the respondent the chance to get to the heart of their thinking.

Typically, the citizen that Socrates is speaking with provides a quick answer to Socrates' question, but Socrates finds problems with that answer. For example, in one dialogue Socrates wonders about the nature of temperance. The person he is speaking with, Charmides, suggests that temperance may be quietness of soul, but Socrates protests that an energetic attitude is better for learning. Charmides then suggests that temperance may involve modesty, but Socrates points out that boldness is sometimes needed. The discussion goes on and no suitable answer is found. Socrates' discussions with citizens had two results. First, they showed that Socrates was deeply concerned about uncovering answers to life's important questions, usually moral questions about the best way to live life. Second, the citizens grew angry with Socrates. Socrates made a fool of them when he pointed out errors in their answers, and he often left the discussion without a proper resolution. Eventually, a number of powerful Athenians arrested him and tried to have him executed. The following dialogue recounts Socrates' defence before his jury at his trial for impiety and corruption of the youth:

Apology (Plato, 4th Century BCE)[6]

And you know how Chaerephon was, how zealous he was about whatever he pursued, and so for example when he went to Delphi he was so bold as to ask this—and, as I say, don't interrupt, gentlemen—he asked if there was anyone wiser than me. The Pythia then replied that no one was wiser. And his brother here will bear witness to you about these things, since he himself has died.

---

5   Alfred North Whitehead, *Process and Reality*, ed. David Ray Griffin and Donald W. Sherburne (New York: The Free Press, 1978), 39.
6   Plato, *Apology* 21a–21d; 29c–30b, 38a, in *The Apology and Related Dialogues*, ed. Andrew Bailey, trans. Cathal Woods (Broadview Press, 2016).

Think about why I am bringing this up: it's because I'm going to teach you where the prejudice against me came from. Because when I heard this I pondered in the following way: "Whatever does the god mean? And what riddle is he posing? For I am not aware of being wise in anything great or small. What in the world does he mean, then, when he says that I am wisest? For certainly he does not lie; he is not permitted to." And for a long time I puzzled over his meaning. Then, very reluctantly, I embarked on a sort of trial of him. I went to one of the people who are thought to be wise, hoping to refute the oracle there if anywhere, and reply to its pronouncement: "This man here is wiser than me, though you said I was." So, scrutinizing this fellow—there's no need to refer to him by name; he was one of the politicians I had this sort of experience with when I examined him, men of Athens—in talking with him it seemed to me that while this man was considered to be wise both by many other people and especially by himself, he was not. And so I tried to show him that he took himself to be wise, but was not. As a result I became hated by this man and by many of those present.

And so, as I was going away, I was thinking to myself, "I am at least wiser than this man. It's likely that neither of us knows anything worthwhile, but whereas he thinks he knows something when he doesn't know it, I, when I don't know something, don't think I know it either." ...

So if you now acquitted me—rejecting Anytus, who said that either I should not have been brought here to trial in the first place, or, now that I have, executing me is unavoidable, and who tells you that if I were acquitted, your sons, practicing what Socrates teaches, will at once be thoroughly corrupted—if, referring to this, you said to me, "Socrates, we are not at present persuaded by Anytus and we acquit you but on the following condition, namely that you no longer spend your time on this quest and search for wisdom, and that if you are caught still doing this, you will die"—if, as I was saying, you were to acquit me on these conditions, I would say to you, "I cherish and love you, men of Athens, but I am more obedient to the god than to you, and so long as I have breath and am able I will not cease seeking wisdom and appealing and demonstrating to every one of you I come across, saying my customary things: Best of men, you are an Athenian, of the greatest and most renowned city in regard to wisdom and power. Are you not ashamed that you care about how you will acquire as much money as possible, and reputation and honor, while you do not care or worry about wisdom and truth and how your soul might be as good as possible?" And if one of you disputes this and says that he does care, right away I will not let him go or leave him but will question and cross-examine and refute him, and if he does not appear to possess virtue, but he says he does, I will reproach him for considering the most valuable things to be of the least importance and the most worthless to be of the greatest importance....

For I go around doing nothing other than persuading you, both young and old, not to care for your wealth and your bodies ahead of, or as intensely as, caring for how your soul might be as good as possible, saying that virtue does not come from wealth, but from virtue come wealth and all other human goods, both private and public....

If instead I say that in fact this is the greatest good for a man, to talk every day about virtue and the other things you hear me converse about when I examine both myself and others, and that the unexamined life is not worth living for a man, you would believe this even less if I said it.

In this passage,

1. *Socrates explains his practice of approaching citizens of Athens to investigate important questions. He cares about getting the correct answer, so he points out any errors in their thinking. This makes him unpopular, but he is only pursuing wisdom.*
2. *Socrates argues that philosophers investigate truth, wisdom, and how the soul can be in the best condition. The way to attain truth, wisdom, and the best condition for the soul is to discuss important issues every day.*
3. *Socrates argues that we should not devote all our attention to pursuing wealth and honour, but we should devote more attention to caring for the soul and pursuing virtue.*

In the end, Socrates was sentenced to death. He had a chance to renounce his philosophical attitude of investigating life's important questions, but he refused to do so, so he was put to death. This is an extreme example of how the philosopher cares about learning the truth more than devoting his mental energy towards monetary or honorific gain.

What would Socrates or Thales tell Michael Scott to say at his job interview? They might tell him to investigate himself so that he knows his own soul, so he knows his weaknesses and develops strategies for overcoming them. They might tell him to care for the truth, and that he should be honest and explain his weaknesses, though he should also discuss his strengths and argue for why he should be promoted. They might tell him not to be careless about the truth, not to say whatever needs to be said to land the job.

Objection: No Practical Value

One classic objection to the practice of philosophy is that it has no practical value, that it does not help improve life. This issue is evident in the case of Thales and Socrates. Thales, while he discovered some truths about the heavenly bodies, lived in relative poverty and fell into a well. Socrates, while he discovered some truths about the best way to live, ended up losing his life because of it. In today's age, if Michael tells the truth about his many weaknesses, he may not get the job, but the job is important. If we study philosophy in university, it may not lead to gainful employment, but a job is important. In an episode of *That '70s Show* called "Thanksgiving," Laurie announces, "I've decided to major in philosophy." Eric sarcastically replies, "That's good because they just opened up that big philosophy factory in Green Bay." Eric's point is that there is no such thing as a philosophy factory, philosophy rarely leads to a job, and more generally, practising philosophy does not help us get the things we want in life. Philosophy is a nice hobby, like playing the piano, but it cannot help us achieve a successful life. Sophism, on the contrary, which we turn our attention to now, focuses entirely on using our minds for practical gain, so perhaps sophism can solve this problem?

1.3 Sophism

At the same time as philosophy was developing in Greece, a parallel movement called **sophism** arose. Whereas 'philosophy' comes from the Greek words 'philos' and 'sophia,' which means *love of wisdom*, 'sophism' simply comes from the Greek word 'sophia,' which means *wisdom*, so the sophist is the wise one. Whereas the philosopher loves wisdom, the sophist loves being seen as wise; thus 'sophist' has a negative connotation—so you're a wise guy, are you? Today we may imagine a similar distinction between a lover of wines—a true connoisseur of flavours and tannins—and a wino who simply drinks a lot of wine.

Sophists, like philosophers, aim at wisdom, engage in debate, and, like philosophers, can excel at the art of argumentation. But unlike philosophers, sophists grew so good at debating that they toured Greece and charged money to wealthy citizens to teach their children how to win arguments. The Greeks began to despise sophism, for though sophists were very intelligent and used their intelligence to win debates, in the end it was all mere *sophistry*; that is, they relied on subtle and deceptive logical tricks to manipulate listeners. What is worse, sophists didn't even believe in their own arguments: they just wanted to win the argument for the sake of winning the argument. For example, sophists were commonly accused of "making the weaker argument the stronger argument." This means that they picked an obviously false position and argued so persuasively for it that people came to agree with the false view. Imagine picking a view nobody endorses—that the Earth is flat—and deliberately attempting to convince people it is true, just to see if you can do it! For example, a sophist named Hippias made it a practice to stand in front of crowds and ask them to pick an issue, then asked them to choose which side of the debate he should argue. He then made an impassioned speech in support of the side the crowd had chosen.

Sophistry is rampant in the world today. Some lawyers are modern-day sophists: they are hired by one side to present that side of a case. The lawyer's job is not to seek the truth about whether their client committed the crime or not; rather, their

McDonald's ads show Big Macs with large hamburger patties neatly topped with generous portions of melted cheese and sauce, but the actual Big Mac often comes with thin patties and sloppily arranged cold cheese.

job is to convince the jury that their client did not commit the crime. They use intricate argumentation and only the evidence that supports their case to get their client off the hook; they do not aim at uncovering the truth.

Some politicians are modern-day sophists as well. They use their powers of persuasion to win your vote or turn you toward their narrative and against their opponent's. They avoid the truth in numerous ways: they do not take difficult questions, or, if they do, they dodge the issue and return to their own talking points. Whenever new economic data are published or a new law is passed, they put their spin on that data or law—which means that they interpret the new data or law in a way that aligns best with the views they already hold. They regularly deploy incorrect but persuasive reasoning techniques called logical fallacies (some of which are discussed below).

News media has, for the most part moved away from aiming at truth and toward convincing the viewer of the narrative they endorse. News media chooses not to report stories that do not support their perspective, or they choose to interview only those guests that represent one side of the debate, or they negatively characterize their opponents' actions. Advertisers do not aim at truth either, but at getting viewers to purchase their product. Beer commercials show beautiful people drinking at a lavish party, but the truth may be that people drink beer alone in their basement while watching TV.

In all of these cases, care for truth is minimal, so reasoning is not used for the purpose of investigating and expressing what is actually true. Rather, lawyers or politicians or advertisers devote their mental energies and verbal skills to figuring out how to get the listener to agree with them or buy their product. In other words, lawyers, politicians, and advertisers are sophists rather than philosophers.

Why did sophists use their intelligence to find clever logical tricks to manipulate people into agreeing with them? As the writings below suggest, they were **relativists**. We will look in detail at relativism in Chapter 2.4, but for now suffice

Herodotus (484–425 BCE) recounts a famous example of relativism: "[Darius, King of Persia] called into his presence certain Greeks who were at hand, and asked: 'What he should pay them to eat the bodies of their fathers when they died?' To which they answered, that there was no sum that would tempt them to do such a thing. He then sent for certain Indians, of the race called Callatians, men who eat their fathers, and asked them, while the Greeks stood by ... 'what he should give them to burn the bodies of their fathers at their decease?' The Indians exclaimed aloud, and bade him forbear such language."[7]

How one disposes of the dead may be a matter of cultural preference. But are all truths relative? Can you think of a truth that is true for everyone?

---

7 Herodotus, *The Historians of Greece: Volume II*, trans. G. Rawlinson (New York: The Tandy-Thomas Company, 1909), 86.

it to say that relativists do not think humans can know the truth. Since sophists do not think humans can know the truth, an investigation into the truth about life's important questions becomes pointless—why try to find an answer when humans cannot find an answer? What remains is a bunch of intelligent people with reasoning skills but with no devotion to using these skills to uncover truths. So, they use their reasoning skills to win arguments and achieve personal gain, either through charging money for teaching others how to win arguments, or through getting others to see things their way. Here are some excerpts from some famous sophists of the time, including **Protagoras**, Prodicus, Hippias, and Antiphon.

Sophist Writings (Protagoras, Prodicus, Hippias, Antiphon, 5th Century BCE)[8]

Concerning the gods I [Protagoras] am unable to know either that they are or that they are not or what their appearance is like. For many are the things that hinder knowledge: the obscurity of the matter and the shortness of human life.

[Protagoras says] what may or may not fittingly be done, of just and unjust, of what is sanctioned by religion and what is not; and here the theory may be prepared to maintain that whatever view a city takes on these matters and establishes as its law or convention, is truth and fact for that city. In such matters, neither any individual nor any city can claim superior wisdom.

[Protagoras says] a person is the measure of all things—of things that are, that they are, and of things that are not, that they are not.

[Protagoras] was the first to use in dialectic the argument of Antisthenes that attempts to prove that contradiction is impossible.

Protagoras was the first to declare that there are two mutually opposed arguments on any subject.

Protagoras made the weaker and stronger argument and taught his students to blame and praise the same person.

[Protagoras says] my boy, if you associate with me, the result will be that the very day you begin you will return home a better person, and the same will happen the next day too. Each day you will make constant progress toward being better ... [Protagoras teaches a young man] good counsel concerning his personal affairs, so that he may best manage his own

---

8   *Readings in Ancient Greek Philosophy*, 105–06, 113–15.

household, and also concerning the city's affairs, so that as far as the city's affairs go he may be most powerful in acting and in speaking.

There is a reference to the paradoxical view of Prodicus that contradiction is impossible. What does this mean? It goes against everyone's judgment and opinion. For in both practical and intellectual matters we are constantly conversing with people who contradict us. He says dogmatically that contradiction is impossible, because if two people contradict one another they are both speaking, but they cannot both be speaking with reference to the same fact. He says that only the one who speaks the truth is reporting the fact as it is, while the person who contradicts him does not state the fact.

[Prodicus] says that the gods worshipped by men neither exist nor have knowledge, but that the ancients exalted crops and everything else that is useful for life.

[Hippias says] How can anyone suppose that laws are a serious matter or believe in them, since it often happens that the very people who make them repeal them and substitute and pass others in their place?

[Antiphon says] Justice is a matter of not transgressing what the laws prescribe in whatever city one is a citizen. A person would make most advantage of justice for himself if he treated the laws as important in the presence of witnesses and treated the decrees of nature as important when alone and with no witnesses present.

[Antiphon says] However convincing the accusation is on behalf of the accuser, the defense can be just as convincing. For victory comes through speech.

In these passages,

1. *several sophists argue for relativism. Protagoras says "humans are the measure of all things." If one human says she feels cold, then it is cold to her, while it may be hot to a polar bear. Morals are also relative, as are the gods and customs. Even reasoning is relative, as reasoning can be used to support any claim. We explore the issues of relativism and truth in Chapter 2.*
2. *several sophists argue that we should focus our minds on delivering what is useful for life. Protagoras teaches household management and how to develop powerful cities; Prodicus says that religion is embraced if it is useful for life; Antiphon suggests that laws need not be followed if no one is watching, while he adds that victory in court as well as life comes through speech.*

What advice would the sophist have for Michael Scott during his job interview? They might say that Michael should say whatever is needed to secure a promotion. Getting the job is important, so if telling an employer what they wish to hear is what it takes to achieve this goal, that's fine.

Objection: Insincere

There is debate about the origin of the English word 'sincere.' On one unlikely but interesting account, 'sincere' comes from the Latin words *sine* = without and *cerae* = wax. According to this account, Roman pillars were made of marble, and when cracks appeared some dishonest repairmen simply put wax over the cracks so that the pillars looked nice but lacked structural integrity. Other repairmen promoted their work as being sincere, or, not patching over the cracks with wax but actually fixing the pillar. The moral of this account is that dishonest craftsmen and slick used car salesperson who practise sophistry may profit in the short term, but there are two costs. First, they sacrifice their integrity or sincerity, which is a substantial character flaw. Second, in the long run people realize the dishonesty and no longer trust the sophist, which actually results in personal loss for the sophist. If a used car salesperson gains a reputation for being sleazy, he will lose customers. If a politician, a news source, or even ourselves gain the reputation for being manipulative, then trust erodes—to the detriment of the sophist. This happened with the sophists of ancient Greece, as the term 'sophistry' took on a negative connotation. Aristotle aptly summarizes Protagoras' method and its reception: "This is making the weaker argument stronger. And people were rightly annoyed at Protagoras' promise."[9]

1.4 The Upside of Philosophy

It is important to distinguish sophistry (or bull-crap) from philosophy for several reasons. First, as we have seen, the sophist uses reason not to attain truth but to obtain personal gain, whereas the philosopher uses reason to attain truth rather than obtain personal gain. Whereas the sophist is exemplified by the ambulance-chasing lawyer or the cunning politician or a shrewd marketing campaign, the philosopher is exemplified by the intrepid reporter devoted to uncovering the truth no matter if she upsets powerful people in the process, or the detective seeking the murderer despite numerous dangers, or the jury member willing to put his life on pause in order to see that justice is done. Second, as we will consider now, the distinction leads us to consider the objection to practising philosophy. Namely, the sophist shows us how to use our mind for personal gain, whereas philosophy is accused of being of no personal

---

9   Aristotle, *Rhetoric* 1402a24–26, in *Readings in Ancient Greek Philosophy*, 106.

benefit. So, are there any personal benefits to studying philosophy? Yes there are and here are some of them.

Philosophy and Self-Awareness: People typically want to know themselves, or become self-aware. Imagine having butterflies in your stomach whenever Genevieve walks by, but not taking the time to figure out if this means you like her or are afraid of her. Imagine having a gut reaction against some viewpoint your friend raises, but not knowing why you disagree, or whether you are right or not. We typically want to get to the bottom of our feelings and beliefs. Socrates agrees: he says the unexamined life is not worth living. The philosopher wants us to examine ourselves, figure out why we have the emotional responses we do, and determine which beliefs we hold and why.

Philosophy and the Good Life: Socrates thinks that philosophy helps us live the best life possible. How so? What a person believes influences their lives. If you believe that you do not want to have children, you will probably take measures to avoid having children. If you believe that you do want to have children, you will probably take measures to try to have children. The list of how our beliefs influence our actions is endless. However, this means that having bad beliefs will likely result in taking bad actions, which will eventually result in having a bad life. Stanley, a character on *The Office*, says, "It's like I used to tell my wife, I do not apologize unless I think I'm wrong, and if you don't like it you can leave, and I say the same thing to my current wife, and I'll say it to my next one too." Stanley has a bad belief: that refusing to apologize is more important than preserving a marriage. This is negatively affecting his life: he is getting divorced and not getting along with others. Wouldn't it be nice to have a way to edit ourselves, to spot our damaging beliefs and refine them so we don't end up having a bad life?

Philosophy helps with this. Philosophers value self-awareness not just for the sake of knowing ourselves, but also so that we can figure out if we have damaging beliefs or not, so we can abandon our bad beliefs, so we can end up having a good life. Philosophy is simply the practice of investigating our beliefs, and using good reasoning to evaluate whether they are good or not. If we develop philosophical skills of evaluating our beliefs, we are more likely to have good beliefs, which leads to having a good life. There is no downside to self-examination. If we examine our beliefs and reactions and conclude there are good

Imagine that you have never been able to ask anyone out on a date, and as a result you miss a lot of dating opportunities. Wouldn't it be good to analyze why you don't ask anyone out? If you examine your motives, you may find you should just be more confident, or more willing to take risks, or more willing to make the first move.

reasons to change them, then our lives will improve. If we examine our beliefs and reactions and conclude they are already good, then we grow more confident in our beliefs. Either way, we win.

Philosophy and Following the Crowd: Lemmings are rodents who, according to popular lore, follow each other so closely during mass migration that if one of them jumps off a cliff, the others will jump to their doom as well. This sounds odd, but people tend to follow the crowd as well. We are social creatures and we value fitting in and sharing common beliefs and traditions, so we often feel pressure to follow the crowd. This is fine if the crowd is going in the right direction, for this means we will be going in the right direction as well. If your friends are all studying hard for exams and exercising a lot, it is good to feel pressure to study hard and work out as well. But what if the crowd is walking off a cliff? What if your friends are all telling you to slack off at university, and you feel pressure to do what they do in order to fit in, but you don't really want to do those things? Our **conformity bias**, or the pressure we naturally feel to go along with the crowd, is problematic if the crowd is telling us to do wrong things, or if it believes false things. This tendency to follow the crowd is also problematic when we think a belief is good just because the crowd is doing it— this is the fallacy of appeal to popularity, a mistaken form of reasoning that we will discuss below. And why would we just want to obey what the crowd tells us to do anyway? Why wouldn't we prefer to do what we tell ourselves to do?

Philosophy helps with this. Socrates went to the crowds to see what they believed, and evaluated whether the things they were saying made sense or not. Philosophers invite us to investigate and examine the beliefs and practices that other people are telling us to take part in. If those beliefs and practices make sense, then we can go along with them, but if they are unreasonable, then we should not follow them. In this way, philosophy is like a computer virus scanner. A virus scanner checks each incoming email attachment and program that seeks entrance onto the computer to see if it will harm the computer or not. If an email attachment is bad, the scanner does not grant it access to the computer; if an email attachment is trustworthy, the scanner grants it access. Likewise, different beliefs bombard our minds every day, seeking entry into our consciousness. Philosophy helps us scan whether these beliefs are good or not, letting the good beliefs in while rejecting the bad ones.

Philosophy and Originality: It is good to be original. Not only does everyone want to stand out in some unique way, but professors insist that you come up with your own ideas in essays and technology develops through innovating new gadgets and apps. But how do we come up with original thoughts, or thoughts that are our own? If we always follow the crowd, then our thoughts will only be the recycled thinking of other people, and our passions will only be their quotations. But if we take the time to examine and evaluate our beliefs, and the ideas coming into our minds from others, then we make the ideas our own. They are our own because now we assent to them. If we hear someone else say "War is bad," this is their belief, but it is not our belief yet. If we consider the arguments for and against going to war, and we come to our own conclusion that war is bad, then "War is bad" is now our belief: we own it because we assent to it. Bertrand Russell explains: "The man who has no tincture of philosophy goes through life imprisoned in ... prejudices ... habitual beliefs ... and convictions which have grown up in his mind without the co-operation or consent of his deliberate reason."[10] Without philosophy, foreign ideas from others take root in our minds without our consent. These ideas are not our own, and we have not evaluated them enough to rationally assent to them for our own reasons. But with philosophy we examine our beliefs and the beliefs of others, and weed out the bad ideas, and embrace the good ideas, so now we consent to the ideas in our minds: they are our own; we have our own beliefs. Not only are our ideas "our own" when we assent to them, but the more we examine our beliefs, the more we are likely to come up with new and interesting thoughts of our own, which increases our originality as thinkers. As an added bonus, when our ideas become our own, then our actions become self-governed or **autonomous** as they are caused by our own ideas now, and most people crave autonomy as well.

A famous inspector of counterfeit money said the secret to spotting a fake bill is to study the real bill so well that you will immediately notice the fake. Similarly, if we study good reasoning, we will immediately spot fallacies as we hear or read them.

Philosophy as Bull-Crap Detector: No one likes to be manipulated, no one likes the wool pulled over their eyes, no one likes to play the fool. But there is a lot of sophistry or bull-crap out there. It would be nice to be able to detect bull-crap when we hear it so we don't fall for it. Philosophy can help with that. Philosophers use reasoning to aim at the truth, and they develop systems of logic that reveal whether or not conclusions are properly derived from good reasons. Philosophers notice the common tricks that sophists and bull-crappers use to fool people and label them **fallacies**, which are persuasive but ultimately poor patterns of reasoning that do not reach true conclusions, but do trick people into believing those conclusions nonetheless. In the next section we will look at many specific examples of good reasoning and fallacious reasoning. The strategy is to become so familiar with good and bad reasoning that we can immediately spot bad reasoning when we hear it, and as a result not fall for the tricks of people trying to manipulate us into agreeing with them.

Philosophy and Not Being Stupid: Humans have many moments of genius and creative inspiration that catapult society forward in many different ways.

---

10 Bertrand Russell, *The Problems of Philosophy* (1912) (Oxford: Oxford University Press, 2001), 91.

Unfortunately, humans are also susceptible to astounding lapses in reasoning that lead us to believe the most foolish of things. Psychologists notice numerous cognitive **biases**, or patterns of mistaken reasoning baked into our minds, that prevent us from seeing reality as it is and from believing the truth. For example, we've discussed our tendency to follow the crowd rather than follow the facts. As another example, we are not emotionless, invulnerable, logical calculating machines; rather, we reason using a mind that is also filled with deep concerns, egoistic motivations, emotional impulses, and worries, all of which cloud our judgement. One example of many: do you think you are a better driver or worse driver than others your age? Ola Svenson did a study that revealed that 93% of people put themselves in the top 50% of drivers—which is mathematically impossible.[11] This is an example of the better-than-average bias that humans are susceptible to. We are not disinterested judges of our driving abilities (or of any of our other abilities); rather, we care more about ourselves than we care about others.

Seven birds are sitting on a wire, the farmer shoots $(5 - 2 \times 2)$ of them. How many birds are left sitting on the wire? Most people get caught up in figuring out whether to subtract or multiply first in the mathematical puzzle, but fail to notice that if the farmer shoots at the birds, they will all fly away and none will be left on the wire. We are all imperfect reasoners.

Philosophy helps us avoid falling for these cognitive biases that fool us into making incorrect assessments. Philosophy teaches self-examination, which means that we examine why we believe as we do. By being reflective we stand a better chance of noticing the self-interest or bias in our reasoning patterns. Philosophy also teaches that we should care for the truth, which includes finding out the truth about who we are and who we are not. It is common to think more highly of ourselves than is correct, and our insecurities even make it common to think more poorly of ourselves than is correct in other ways. But to see ourselves exactly as we are: that is a rare feat that philosophy can help with.

---

11 Ola Svenson, "Are We All Less Risky and More Skillful Than Our Fellow Drivers?" *Acta Psychologica* 47, no. 2 (1981): 143–48.

1.5 How to Win an Argument

Not only does consideration of good reasoning and poor reasoning help us avoid falling for bad reasoning, but it also helps us make a good case for our ideas in discussions with others. In other words, it helps us win arguments. Who doesn't want to win an argument? Imagine the next time you are in a disagreement with your parents, or partner, or friend, and when it is your turn to speak you say the exact right thing to get them to see things your way. Who wouldn't want that? The aim is not really just to figure out how to win any argument—that would be sophism. Rather, the aim is to inspect good and bad reasoning patterns so we can learn how to make a better case for our side of the story, learn how to avoid falling for bad arguments from the other side, but also learn how to respect and embrace good arguments from the other side.

1.5.1 Arguments

Let us begin with the basics of an argument. The term 'argument' appears to have negative connotations: for example, Julie and Sam got into an argument, which may imply they were at odds with each other. However, this is not what the term 'argument' means in philosophy. In philosophy, an **argument** is a series of statements, where some statements serve as evidence or support for another statement, the one that is put forward as true. The evidential or supporting statements are called premises. **Premises** are statements used in an argument as support or evidence for a further statement that is put forward as true, which is called the conclusion. **Conclusions** are statements in an argument that, as intended, are supported by the premises.

Consider this argument: 'Strawberries are fruits, and there are strawberries on this cake, so this cake has fruit on it.' First, this is an argument because there are several statements assembled together in a way intended to prove a conclusion. The first two statements, 'Strawberries are fruits' and 'There are strawberries on this cake,' are the premises. They serve as proof for the conclusion. If we ask "How do you know this cake has fruit on it," the answer is: "Because the premises prove it." The conclusion is the point the arguer is trying to make, namely, that the cake has fruit on it.

There are good arguments and bad arguments. In a good argument, (1) all the premises are true and (2) the reasoning leading from the premises to the conclusion is good as well; therefore (3) the conclusion is proven true by the good reasoning from the true premises.

Requirement (1) assumes that a premise can be true or false. We will spend Chapter 2 discussing the nature of truth, and whether humans can know the truth or not. For now, let us simply grant that premises can be true or false, and a true premise states how things are while a false premise states something other than how things are. If the premise is 'There are strawberries on the cake,' and there really are strawberries on the cake, then this premise is true. If the premise is 'There are strawberries on the cake' but there are actually only raspberries on the cake, then this premise is false. Note that *all* the premises in the argument must be true. If one premise is true, but the other premise is false, then the conclusion is not established. Consider the following argument: 'strawberries are animals, and there are strawberries on this cake, so this cake has animals on it.' One of the premises is true: there are strawberries on this cake. But this is not enough to establish the conclusion. The other premise is false, and one false premise is enough to sink the entire argument.

A good argument needs more than merely all the premises in the argument being true. Consider the following argument: 'Strawberries are fruits, and the sun is larger than the Earth, so Friday is one of the days of the week.' In this argument all the premises are true, but these premises do not provide evidence for the conclusion. After all, these premises have nothing to do with the conclusion, so how could they possibly provide support for it? What is missing from this argument is (2): there must be good reasoning from the premises to the conclusion as well. **Reasoning** is the logical connection between different statements.

It is also worth noting that if an argument has a true conclusion, this does not guarantee that it is a good argument. Consider this argument: 'Spiders are fruits, and fruits spin webs, so spiders spin webs.' The conclusion is true, but this is not a good argument because (3) was not established: the conclusion was not proven true *by* the good reasoning from *the true premises*, since the premises were false. Rather, the conclusion happens to be true even though the premises are false, and so they do not prove the conclusion true. Now consider this argument: 'Strawberries are fruits, and sugar is in the cake, so the cake has fruits on it.' In this case the premises and conclusions are all true, but the conclusion was not proven true *by the good reasoning* from the true premises, since the logical connection from the premises to the conclusion is missing.

1.5.2 Deductive Reasoning

Humans engage in different types of reasoning patterns. We will look at two forms of reasoning, as they will both be important later in the book. **Deductive reasoning** structures the logical connections between statements in a way that *guarantees* the truth of the conclusion. In deductive reasoning, if the premises are all true, and the reasoning is good (good reasoning in a deductive argument is called **valid** reasoning), then the conclusion is inescapably true. With deductive reasoning, the argument is considered **sound** if all its premises are true and its reasoning is valid, which is like saying the argument is structurally sound, or well-constructed in every way. Here is an example: 'The sun is a star, and all stars shine light, so the sun shines light.' Can you notice how, since the premises are true, the valid logic sets things up in a way that makes the conclusion inescapable? There is no way for the sun to not shine light, given that the sun is a star and all stars shine light! Poor reasoning in a deductive argument is called **invalid** reasoning. If the premises are all true, but invalid reasoning is used, the deductive argument is **unsound**. For example: 'The sun is a star, and the sun is in our solar system, so all stars are in our solar system.' While both

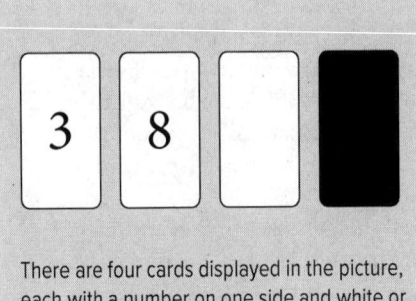

There are four cards displayed in the picture, each with a number on one side and white or black on the other side. Which card(s) must be turned over in order to test the truth of the rule 'If a card shows an even number on one side, then its opposite side is white'?

premises are true, the reasoning is invalid since the true premises only guarantee that one star, our sun, is in our solar system, not that all stars are in our solar system.

We will encounter two specific forms of deductive reasoning in this book. To introduce them both, try the logic puzzle in the side box called the called the **Wason Selection Task**, developed by Peter Wason in 1966. There are four cards displayed in the picture, each with a number on one side and a colour on the other side. You must answer: which card(s) must be turned over in order to test this rule, 'If a card shows an even number on one side, then its opposite side is white.' Less than ten per cent of people get the correct answer. Most people correctly discern that eight must be turned over. After all, if we need to confirm that even numbered cards have white on the back, we had better check the even-numbered card. This part of the test relates to the valid deductive reasoning pattern called **modus ponens**: if P then Q, P, therefore Q. For example: 'If the lion bites the antelope's head off then the antelope will die, and the lion did bite the antelope's head off, so the antelope will die.' Can you notice how there is no way for the antelope to stay alive, given that the lion bit his head off, and given that whenever lions bite antelope heads off the antelopes die?

Returning to the test, most people miss the fact that the only other card that must be turned over is the black card. We must check black because if we find an even number on the other side of that black card, then it is false that even numbers have white backs; after all, this revealed an even number that has a black back. This part of the test relates to the valid deductive reasoning form called **modus tollens**: if P then Q, but it's not the case that Q, so it's not the case that P. Modus tollens is valid reasoning, but is typically harder to grasp, as is evident from the test performed above. Here is an intuitive example of modus tollens: 'If the lion bites the antelope's head off then the antelope will die, but the antelope isn't dead, so the lion did not bite the antelope's head off.' Of course, if the lion biting off the head of the antelope must lead to the antelope's death, but the antelope isn't dead, it must be the case that the lion didn't bite his head off (yet).

Deductive reasoning is profitable because it allows us to be certain of the conclusion, and it forces any disputant to agree with the conclusion as well, assuming they agree that the premises are true. Deductive reasoning is also commonly used in mathematics and in certain forms of computer programming where programs receive input, then follow a set of strict logical rules to arrive at an output.

1.5.3 Inductive Reasoning

Inductive reasoning is another form of reasoning, but in this case the logical connections between statements are not structured in such a way as to guarantee the truth of the conclusion, but only render the conclusion probably true. With inductive reasoning, if the premises are all true or probably true, and the reasoning is good (good reasoning in an inductive argument is called **strong** reasoning), then the conclusion is probably true. Here is an example: 'Eighty per cent of Canadians prefer hockey to ping pong, Nina is a Canadian, so Nina prefers hockey to ping pong.' Can you notice how, even assuming the premises are true, the logic sets things up in a way that makes the conclusion only probably true. Given the true premises, it is probably true that Nina prefers hockey, but there is still a chance she will not be among the eighty per cent that prefer hockey, so it is not certainly true that Nina prefers hockey. Poor reasoning in an inductive argument is called **weak** reasoning. For example: 'Fifty-three per cent of Canadians prefer hockey to soccer, Nina is a Canadian, so Nina prefers hockey to soccer.' Assuming both premises are true, the reasoning is weak since the premises only show that it is fifty-three per cent likely that Nina prefers hockey, so there is a fair chance the conclusion will be wrong. It's still slightly more likely that Nina prefers hockey, but this is a much weaker argument than the earlier one.

We will encounter two types of inductive reasoning in this text. First, **inference to the best explanation**, where something happens, or some fact exists, but you do not know how or why it occurs. For example, you come home from school to find your garage door is wide open. You weren't home, so you don't know how this happened. You could choose to stay confused forever at this mystery or you could do what humans normally do, and use our reasoning skills to figure it out: an event X happened, the possible explanations of X are A, B, or C, but A makes the most sense of those possibilities, so A is probably the explanation of X. The garage door is open, which can be explained by a burglar, a garage door opener malfunction, or your forgetful roommate. The best explanation is your forgetful roommate, so your forgetful roommate probably left the garage door open.

The second form of inductive reasoning we will encounter is arguing from **analogy**, where a thing X has properties A, B, and C, and another thing Y has properties A and B, so it is probable that Y has C as well. For example, soccer is a game played with a team and a ball and has scores, and cricket is a game played with a team and a ball, so knowing nothing else about cricket, you can reason that cricket probably has scores as well. Humans reason inductively more often than they reason deductively. Every time a child is learning a word, say 'ball,' they compare the round objects that their parents called a ball before with some new round object they see and guess "ball?" That is reasoning by analogy, which is inductive reasoning. Every time we think our car will start when we turn the ignition, we are using induction. We are predicting that, since the car started one hundred times in a row, and this moment is similar to those moments, the car will probably start now as well. Newer forms of computer programming called machine learning also use inductive reasoning. For example, a computer, having been fed no information distinguishing dogs and cats, is fed a large number of dog and cat pictures, and its responses, initially merely guesses about what the picture represents, gradually become more accurate as it develops more effective theories about the differences.

1.5.4 Logical Fallacies

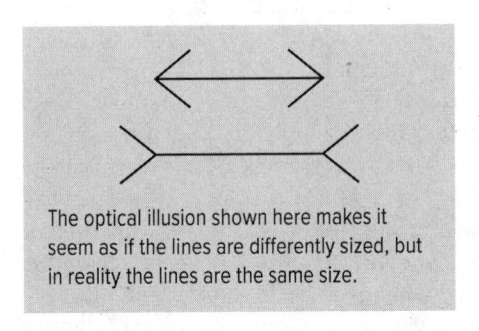

The optical illusion shown here makes it seem as if the lines are differently sized, but in reality the lines are the same size.

The philosopher's aim at truth not only helps us arrive at evidence-based conclusions through good reasoning, but also exposes numerous persuasive, yet mistaken, forms of reasoning. These mistaken forms of reasoning are called **logical fallacies**. Logical fallacies are persuasive—they do convince. But they are mistaken forms of reasoning, so they do not work in securing legitimate evidence for the truth of the conclusion. This is why fallacies are dangerous: they have the power to convince people that their conclusions are true even though the reasoning does not lead to the truth of the conclusion. They are like optical illusions for the intellect. Let us now look at several logical fallacies that we will encounter later in this text.

The **Straw Person** fallacy is probably the most common fallacy. A straw person or scarecrow is a mannequin that looks human enough to fool animals into thinking the farmer is present, but is actually a weak and incorrect version of the real farmer. Likewise, a straw person fallacy occurs when we re-construct a philosophical view (usually one we disagree with) so that it looks enough like the real view to fool some people into thinking this is the view, but is actually a weakened version of the real view. For example, Tessa says war is acceptable if a country is attacked first. Jada, who despises war at all times, responds: "Did you hear Tessa? She thinks we should always be marching off to war!" Jada commits the straw person fallacy here, as she misrepresents Tessa's view. The straw person fallacy is tempting to commit because we either intentionally want to make the opposing viewpoint look crazy so no one will accept it, or our repulsion at the other side of the argument prevents us from seeing the actual viewpoint as it is. In either case, the straw person fallacy is a mistake in reasoning because presenting and then refuting a weak version of the opposition argument does nothing to refute the actual opposition argument. To return to the example: Tessa will no doubt reply, "I didn't say *that*; Jada can't even understand me!" We overcome the straw person fallacy by presenting an opposing argument as accurately as possible.

The **Appeal to Popularity** fallacy occurs when we argue that a claim is true merely because a substantial number of people believe it. For example:

McDonald's says the Big Mac is the most eaten burger of all time with over 99 billion served, so it must be the best burger. Or: most Canadians believe in the monarchy, so the monarchy must be good. As discussed above, it is tempting to follow the crowd, so if everyone agrees with one particular belief system, it is tempting to do so as well. But the popularity of a belief does not make it true. Everyone used to think the Earth was flat, or that the sun revolved around the Earth, but that didn't make these beliefs true. Rather than believing a conclusion because it is popular, we should believe a conclusion because it is supported by good reasoning from true premises.

The **Illicit Appeal to Authority** is a fallacy that occurs when we incorrectly appeal to authorities or experts on an issue. It is appropriate to appeal to experts when there is an issue that we are not expert on but someone else is: Deshaun rolls his ankle playing soccer and he is not a health professional, so he follows the advice of his physiotherapist during rehab. But even in this case, we should not act based on expert opinion itself: we should act based on the evidence that experts have access to. We should not appeal to authorities who are not experts on the issue under consideration. LeBron James is an expert on everything related to basketball, but he is not an expert on which soft drink is the best. So, when Sprite hires him to say that Sprite is the best, we should not defer to him on this issue. We should also not appeal to authorities when expert opinion is split on an issue: half the experts say Coke is unhealthier than Diet Coke, and the other half say Diet Coke is unhealthier than Coke. If the experts are divided, then the evidence is mixed, so we should believe the evidence is mixed.

The **Question Begging** fallacy occurs when we assume the truth of the conclusion in one of the premises that support the conclusion. For example: Milo is guilty of the crime, after all he's in jail, and innocent people don't go to jail! Or again: God exists because the Bible and Quran say God exists, and these holy books can't be wrong because they were inspired by God! In the first example, the question we are asking is this: "Is Milo, the person in jail, guilty or not?" The premise assumes that Milo is guilty since he is in jail, and uses this premise to prove that Milo is guilty. It is tempting to commit this fallacy because we are often so convinced of our view that we do not notice we are using our assumptions as reasons for the conclusion: Ahmed is so convinced that the Quran was inspired by God that he doesn't notice this is just his assumption, and the skeptic will not grant this as evidence.

The **Appeal to Emotion** fallacy occurs when we use emotions as the premise for the conclusion instead of using good reasons as premises for the conclusion. For example: if candidate X gets elected, the country will be ruined forever! Or again: the pet shelter commercial shows a sad-looking puppy while playing soft music as it asks you to donate money. It is tempting to appeal to emotion, as it works in getting others to do what we want—people will be scared enough to not vote for candidate X, and they will feel sympathy enough to donate to the shelter. But emotions are not evidence of the truth of conclusions. If I scream in anger "The sky is green dammit!" my screaming does not suddenly make the conclusion true. If emotions did provide support for conclusions, every argument would be resolved by the side that shouts the loudest or shames the most. The appeal to emotion is a classic example of the distinction between the sophist and philosopher. Appeal to emotion does get others to agree with you, so sophists are eager to use it; but appeal to emotion does not increase the chance that a conclusion is true, so philosophers only use emotion to accentuate the reasons given in support of a conclusion, not as the reason for that conclusion.

The **Ad Hominem** fallacy occurs when we criticize the person making the claim rather than criticizing the claim itself. For example: 'Imelda thinks young people shouldn't have sex until they are married, but she's just a boring old prude,' or 'Chanel thinks young people should explore their sexuality, but she's just immoral and promiscuous.' It is tempting to commit the ad hominem fallacy because we think that discrediting the speaker will discredit his or her argument, but it does not. An argument is evaluated as sound or unsound based on considering the reasons for the conclusion, and independently of who states the argument. The claim that 'nuclear weapons should be banned for the safety of the species' is equally plausible whether Hitler or Einstein says it. We avoid the ad hominem fallacy when we criticize the argument rather than the person: 'Imelda thinks young people shouldn't have sex until they are married, but it seems like young couples should be able to explore their sexual compatibility before getting married to each other.'

A **False Analogy** occurs when we incorrectly argue from analogy, usually by comparing items that are similar in irrelevant ways. Here is a good argument from analogy: Birds have wings and can fly, planes have wings, so they can probably fly. This is a good argument from analogy because the item being compared (i.e., wings) is relevant to the conclusion drawn (i.e., having wings is relevant to whether you can fly or not). Here is a false analogy: 'Birds have two eyes and can fly, humans have two eyes, so they can probably fly.' This is a false analogy because what is compared (i.e., having eyes) is not relevant to the conclusion drawn (i.e., having eyes is not relevant to whether you can fly or not).

The **Fallacy of Composition** occurs when we argue that what is true of the parts of something must be true of the whole thing. For example: 'One beer can't get you drunk, so twenty-four beers won't get you drunk,' or 'Each monthly installment of $300 for the car is cheap enough, so the car is cheap enough.' It is tempting to commit the fallacy of composition because we mistakenly assume that, since the parts make up the whole, what is true of the parts must be true of the whole—each diamond in the ring is expensive, so the whole ring must be expensive! But this is not always the case, as evidenced by the examples above. We avoid the fallacy of composition by carefully considering each part/whole–relation on its own merits—while the parts and whole of the ring are both expensive, the parts don't fit on a finger but the whole does.

The **Fallacy of Equivocation** occurs when we equivocate, or, use the same word in two different senses in different premises of the argument. For example: 'Soup is better than nothing, and nothing is better than sex, so soup is better than sex.' This appears to be valid reasoning, but actually the word 'nothing' is being used in different ways. In premise one, 'nothing' means 'not having anything.' In premise two 'nothing' means 'no such thing.' When we plug in these precise meanings, the conclusion no longer follows: 'Soup is better than not having anything, and there is no such thing that is better than sex,' which does not lead to the view that soup is better than sex.

A **Reductio ad Absurdum** occurs when we argue that the truth of some claim would lead to an absurd result, so the original claim cannot be true. A reductio ad absurdum can be valid reasoning, as it follows the modus tollens: if claim X is true, then result Y would follow, but Y is absurd, so X cannot be true. But a fallacy is committed when the connection between X and Y is not established, which renders the first premise of the modus tollens false. For example: 'If we decriminalize marijuana, then everyone will soon be smoking crack, but as we do not want everyone to smoke crack, we should not decriminalize marijuana.' As the consequences that allegedly follow from decriminalizing marijuana have not been established as true consequences, this is poor reasoning.

The burden of proof is the job that someone has of proving the claim. In the legal system, the burden of proof is on the prosecution in criminal cases— the defendant is presumed innocent until proven guilty, so the prosecution has the burden of proving they are guilty. In philosophy the burden of proof rests on the person making the claim. All claims should be supported by reasons, so we should all be able to provide reasons for the beliefs we hold. The fallacy of **Shifting the Burden of Proof** occurs when the person who has the job of proving the claim shifts this burden onto their opponent. For example, 'I believe rats have no emotions, and I don't need a reason for believing that; I can keep believing rats have no emotions until someone disproves it.' Or, 'I believe rats have emotions, and I don't need a reason for believing that; I can keep believing rats have emotions until someone disproves it.' It is tempting to shift the burden of proof because we tend to think our beliefs should be the default truth and that other views must be established. We overcome this temptation by accepting the philosopher's task to have reasons for all of our beliefs.

While there are many more types of logical fallacies, these specific fallacies will appear later in this text, so it is worth describing them in detail. Fallacies are persuasive in some way, and near to correct reasoning, but they fail to provide good reasons for their conclusions. The use of fallacies is, therefore, yet one more way in which it is possible for sophists to trick us into agreeing with them without actually delivering any truth. Our best defence against these tactics is familiarity with logical fallacies, so we notice the fake argument structure when we hear it.

Summary

In this chapter we defined philosophy as the reasoned investigation into life's important questions. In so doing, philosophers aim to know the truth about the world and life, which leads us to evaluate the beliefs of ourselves and others, to make sure we all have true beliefs. Philosophy is contrasted with sophism, where the sophist does not care for the truth but instead uses tricks of reasoning to fool others into agreeing with them. We discussed various benefits of philosophy before looking at the philosopher's primary tools: arguments and reasoning. It is good to keep these argumentation structures and reasoning patterns in mind, as we will be making use of them throughout the remainder of the text.

Key Terms in Chapter 1: Philosophy and Sophistry		
Philosophy	Autonomous	Reductio ad Absurdum
Metaphysics	Bias	Analogy
Epistemology	Argument	Straw Person
Cosmos	Premise	Appeal to Popularity
Logos	Conclusion	Illicit Appeal to
Thales	Reasoning	Authority
Plato	Deductive Reasoning	Question Begging
Socrates	Valid/Invalid Reasoning	Appeal to Emotion
Socratic Method	Sound/Unsound	Ad Hominem
Sophism	Argument	Fallacy of Composition
Relativism	Wason Selection Task	Fallacy of Equivocation
Protagoras	Modus Ponens	Shifting the Burden of
Logical Fallacy	Modus Tollens	Proof
False Analogy	Inductive Reasoning	Inference to the Best
Conformity Bias	Strong/Weak Reasoning	Explanation

Philosophy on TV: Philosophy and Sophistry

Sherlock (2010–17)

The BBC series *Sherlock*, along with the American version *Elementary* (2012–19) and several films including *Sherlock Holmes* (2009) and *Sherlock Holmes: A Game of Shadows* (2011), follows the famous fictional detective Sherlock Holmes as he solves various crimes. Sherlock represents the philosophical spirit of caring for the truth, as he devotes his life to solving crimes, using reasoned investigation to identify criminals. The philosophical spirit of seeking truth at all costs is represented in various other ways as well, from truth-seeking reporters such as Zoe Barnes in *House of Cards* (2013–18), who dangerously tries to uncover the criminal deeds of a powerful politician, to lawyers and agents uncovering conspiracies at their own peril, such as in *Erin Brockovich* (2000) and *The X-Files* (1993–2018).

Thank You for Smoking (2005)

In *Thank You for Smoking*, Nick Naylor is a smooth-talking lobbyist for tobacco companies who uses rhetorical tricks and research funded by tobacco companies to convince people that smoking is not harmful. He is a classic example of a bull-crap artist, as he repeatedly uses arguments and logic for the purpose of getting people to agree with him, rather than for the sake of pursuing truth. *Chicago* (2002) is another example of a movie with a sophistical character, a lawyer named Billy, who manipulates the press and court evidence in order to acquit a woman who committed murder. Many shows highlight how politicians spin arguments and logic for the purpose of manipulating the voter, including *Spin City* (1996–2002) and the novel *1984*, where the Ministry of Truth is tasked with broadcasting propaganda to the citizens and blocking the free flow of information.

Vice Life Hacks: **Season 1, Episode 1: "The Shed at Dulwich" (2019)**
In this episode Oobah Butler decides to create a fake restaurant in London, England called the Shed at Dulwich, and then writes fake reviews on Trip Advisor about how good the restaurant is. Before long the restaurant becomes the top-rated restaurant in London, even though the reviews reveal that its rustic elegance is actually just a shed, and the photos reveal that such appealingly worded menu items as 'warmed beef tea' are actually disgusting. The episode is a classic example of bull-crap—that online reviews can be faked, that clever wording can turn disgusting food into fine dining—that people fall for.

Additional Resources

Visit this book's companion resources for additional materials, including video content and an automated tool for planning argumentative essays.

sites.broadviewpress.com/knowing/chapter-1

Chapter 2

Truth and Relativism

THOUGHT EXPERIMENT 2.1

He said, she said ...

Jackie and Hyde are two characters on *That '70s Show* who end up in a relationship. In one episode (Season 5, Episode 2: "I Can't Quit You Babe"), the question is raised about how they hooked up. According to Jackie, Hyde invited her over to check out a new ABBA album and then politely tried to make the first move, saying "May I kiss you my lady?" Hyde rejects this story, and says that what actually happened is that Jackie just showed up, obviously wanting him, and came on to him. Jackie rejects this story. Their friends are left wondering what actually happened. How do we know which story is actually true when two or more different stories describing the same situation are told? We assume that they can't both be true. Is that assumption correct? Is there something about *truth* that justifies that assumption? What is truth, anyway?

It is quite common to hear two drastically different sides to the same story. Two children get into a fight, and they both explain how the other is at fault and insist they are innocent. A couple breaks up, and they both have different interpretations, supported by their own sets of facts, about what went wrong and who is to blame. The same event is called a peaceful protest for social justice by some politicians, and violent rioting aimed at destroying America by other politicians. The same person is called a heroic freedom fighter by some, but a cowardly terrorist by others. Who is right? What is the truth of the matter? Do we choose to listen to, and believe, just one side, namely, the side that we want to be true? Do we choose to listen to both sides, then make up our minds based on the evidence? Is there one truth about what happened, or are there only the different perspectives of the one event? These questions lead to other questions about the nature of truth itself. What do we mean by 'truth'? Can humans know the truth? Is there more than one truth?

The question of truth was briefly introduced in Chapter 1.2 and 1.3, where the contrast between philosophers and sophists was drawn, whereby philosophers care about the truth even if it does not provide practical gain, but sophists care about practical gain since they are relativists who do not believe humans can know the truth. In this chapter we consider various models of truth, each of which provide different answers to the question about whether humans can know the truth. These models, along with the philosophers who endorse them, can be placed along the following rough spectrum. On the left side of the spectrum are those views claiming that one objective truth exists and that humans are capable of knowing this truth. On the right side of the spectrum are those views claiming that truth does not exist, or that humans cannot know the truth.

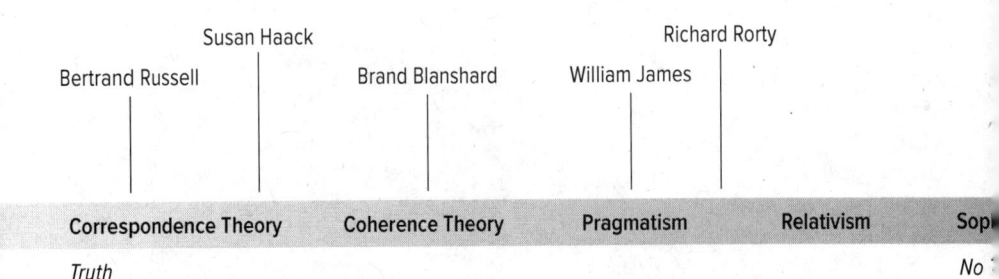

Spectrum 2: Truth Theories

Let us begin our discussion on the left side of the spectrum, with the correspondence theory of truth, as it is often considered the common-sense view of truth that most people start with.

2.1 Correspondence Theory

Here are some true beliefs: "Some people keep dogs as pets," "The Beatles were a rock band," and "The Earth rotates around the sun." But what do we mean when we say "It is *true* that the Beatles were a rock band"? What does it mean for a belief or statement to be *true*? According to the **correspondence theory** of truth, a statement is true when it **corresponds** with, or aligns with, or is in agreement with, the way things actually are. Aristotle provides an early description of this intuition when he says, "To say of what is that it is not, or of what is not that it is, is false, while to say of what is that it is, and of what is not that it is not, is true."[1] To say 'This bird is a blue jay' when the bird *is* a blue jay, is to say something true. To say 'This bird is an eagle' when the bird is a blue jay, is to say something false.

This definition of truth has several parts to it. First, truth pertains to **beliefs** (or statements of those beliefs), where beliefs are the thoughts we have that we agree with (as opposed to doubt or disbelief, which are thoughts we have that

---

1   Aristotle, *Metaphysics* 1011b25.

we disagree with). It is the belief "This bird is a blue jay" that is true (or, false). Beliefs are the **truth-bearer**, which means that beliefs are the things that bear or carry the truth. Second, what exists outside of our minds is what makes beliefs true or false—**reality**, or the way things actually are. Reality is **mind-independent**, which means that its existence, and the way it is, is independent of beliefs or experiences about that reality. Since reality is mind-independent, there exists an **objective truth**, which is a truth that remains true regardless of whether we agree or disagree with it. *Cups fall when dropped* is an objective truth, which means that even if we do not want that to be true, even if we do not believe that to be true, it is still true: that is just the way reality is. The view that there exists a mind-independent objective reality is called **realism**. While reality makes our beliefs true or false, it is not all of reality as a whole that makes particular beliefs true or false. The belief "This bird is a blue jay" is made true by a particular

An object is something that exists regardless of whether we agree that it is there or not. That is, an object, by definition, is not subjective (i.e., it does not depend on subjects to agree that it exists); it is objective (i.e., it just exists). The tree exists, and even if you drive toward it while convincing yourself it is not really there, you will still bump into it. Likewise, objective truth is a truth that is still true regardless of whether we agree with it or not.

slice of reality called a **fact**, which is a relevant object, event, or state of affairs that exists in reality. The particular fact that makes a belief true is called the **truth-maker** of the belief. The true belief "This bird is a blue jay" is made true by the fact that the bird is a blue jay.

Beliefs have **truth-value**, which is to say that beliefs are the types of things that can be true or false. A belief has the truth-value of *true* when there is some fact of reality that this belief aligns with, and this fact makes the belief true. A belief is false, or, has the truth-value of *false*, if there is no fact of reality that this belief aligns with, so there is no corresponding fact to make it true. The belief "This bird is a wasp" has the truth-value of *false*, since the fact is that the bird is a blue jay, so the belief does not line up with the facts. Here is a passage from British philosopher **Bertrand Russell** (1872–1970), one of the leading proponents of the correspondence theory of truth:

The Problems of Philosophy (Bertrand Russell, 1912)[2]

There are three points to observe in the attempt to discover the nature of truth, three requisites which any theory must fulfil. (1) Our theory of truth must be such as to admit of its opposite, falsehood.... (2) It seems fairly evident that if there were no beliefs there could be no falsehood, and no truth either, in the sense in which truth is correlative to falsehood. If we imagine a world of mere matter, there would be no room for falsehood in such a world, and although it would contain what may be called 'facts,' it would not contain any truths, in the sense in which truths are things of the same kind as falsehoods. In fact, truth and falsehood are properties of beliefs and statements: hence a world of mere matter, since it would contain no beliefs or statements, would also contain no truth or falsehood.

(3) But, as against what we have just said, it is to be observed that the truth or falsehood of a belief always depends upon something which lies outside the belief itself. If I believe that Charles I died on the scaffold, I believe truly, not because of any intrinsic quality of my belief, which could be discovered by merely examining the belief, but because of an historical event which happened two and a half centuries ago. If I believe that Charles I died in his bed, I believe falsely: no degree of vividness in my belief, or of care in arriving at it, prevents it from being false, again because of what happened long ago, and not because of any intrinsic property of my belief. Hence, although truth and falsehood are properties of beliefs, they are properties dependent upon the relations of the beliefs to other things, not upon any internal quality of the beliefs. The third of the above requisites leads us to adopt the view—which has on the whole been commonest among philosophers—that truth consists in some form of correspondence between belief and fact....

Thus although truth and falsehood are properties of beliefs, yet they are in a sense extrinsic properties, for the condition of the truth of a belief is something not involving beliefs, or (in general) any mind at all, but only the objects of the belief. A mind, which believes, believes truly when there is a corresponding complex not involving the mind, but only its objects. This correspondence ensures truth, and its absence entails falsehood. Hence we account simultaneously for the two facts that beliefs (a) depend on minds for their existence, (b) do not depend on minds for their truth.

We may restate our theory as follows: If we take such a belief as "Othello believes that Desdemona loves Cassio," we will call Desdemona and Cassio the object-terms, and loving the object-relation. If there is a complex unity "Desdemona's love for Cassio," consisting of the object-terms related by the object-relation in the same order as they have in the belief, then this complex unity is called the fact corresponding to the belief.

---

2   Bertrand Russell, *The Problems of Philosophy*, 186.

Thus a belief is true when there is a corresponding fact, and is false when there is no corresponding fact.

In this passage,

1. *Russell argues that a belief is true if there is a corresponding object or relation between objects that makes the belief true.*
2. *Russell argues that the fact that exists in reality that makes the belief true is extrinsic, which is another way of saying that the object is mind-independent or exists outside the belief that is true. Russell says that facts usually involve objects and relations between objects in the world.*

What would the correspondence theory say about Jackie and Hyde hooking up? There is a fact of the matter, or a "what really happened," independently of their biased accounts. As the show continues, it turns out that Jackie and Hyde were watching TV together and got bored, so they both turned to each other and started making out. This is the truth of what happened. Jackie's story does not correspond with these facts, so her story is false. Hyde's story does not align with these facts either, so his account is also false.

Objection 1: Comparison Problem

On the correspondence theory, the truth/falsity of a belief can only be detected by comparing a belief with a fact, to see if they are in agreement with each other. If they agree, then the belief is true; if they do not agree, then the belief is false. In order to compare two things, however, we must first of all have access to both things. We can compare apples to oranges because we can hold an apple in one hand and an orange in another, and look at them. But we cannot compare apples to the rocks on Pluto because we have no access to the rocks on Pluto. Since facts are mind-independent, they exist beyond minds. They exist beyond our beliefs, and they exist beyond our experience of them, since our beliefs and experiences depend in part on our minds. Since facts are mind-independent, our minds cannot access them. Since we cannot access facts, we cannot compare our beliefs with the facts, so we cannot prove that our beliefs correspond to the facts. The German philosopher Carl Hempel (1905–97) summarizes: "Statements are never compared with a 'reality,' with 'facts.' None of those who support a cleavage between statements and reality is able to give a precise account of how a comparison between statements and facts may possibly be accomplished."[3] Hence the correspondence theory renders it impossible to establish the truth of beliefs, which is the **comparison problem.**

---

3   Carl Hempel, "On the Logical Positivists' Theory of Truth," *Analysis* 2, no. 4 (1935): 50–51.

The British philosopher George Berkeley (1685–1753) says: "An idea can be like nothing but an idea; a colour or figure can be like nothing but another colour or figure. If we look but ever so little into our thoughts, we shall find it impossible for us to conceive a likeness except only between our ideas." Does the fact that a belief is not similar to physical reality mean that a belief cannot correspond to physical reality?[4]

Objection 2: The Matching Problem

The correspondence theory takes true beliefs (or statements of true beliefs) to correspond with, or match, facts. But beliefs are mental states that have consciousness and intentionality to them. Statements of true beliefs are words in a language. Facts are, presumably slices of physical reality that have matter and spatial location. How can beliefs or statements of beliefs correlate with facts when, as we will emphasize in Chapter 5.1, beliefs have such different natures from physical facts? As the German logician Gottlob Frege (1848–1925) worries, "A correspondence, moreover, can only be perfect if the corresponding things coincide and are, therefore, not distinct things at all. It is said to be possible to establish the authenticity of a banknote by comparing it stereoscopically with an authentic one. But it would be ridiculous to try to compare a gold piece with a twenty-mark note stereoscopically."[5] Beliefs and statements are mental or linguistic, which are so distinct from physical facts that it is difficult to imagine how they match one another. Correspondence theories depend on the idea that there is a particular feature of the world that corresponds with each true belief. This seems to suggest some sort of similarity between the belief and its corresponding world-feature. But how can this be? Some correspondence theorists, including Russell in the passage above, resolve this problem by structuring facts in a manner that resembles language. Hence the statement 'Jennie jogged at noon' corresponds with the object Jennie, who has the property *jogged*, at noon. But critics worry that this move imposes the grammar of our language onto reality.

2.2 Coherence Theory

Whereas the correspondence theory says that a belief is true if it corresponds with an objective fact, the **coherence theory** says that a belief is true if it is coherent with a set of other beliefs. A belief is **coherent** with a set of other beliefs if it is logically consistent with that set of other beliefs, or if it implies or

---

4 George Berkeley, *A Treatise Concerning the Principles of Human Knowledge* (1710), ed. C. Krauth (Philadelphia: Lippincott, 1874), 198.
5 Gottlob Frege, "The Thought: A Logical Inquiry," *Mind* 65, no. 259 (1956): 291.

is implied by the other beliefs. Blythe believes that all war causes suffering, and any suffering is wrong, so her additional belief, "War is wrong," coheres with her other beliefs, since they are logically consistent with these other beliefs. A belief is false if it fails to cohere with (i.e., is logically inconsistent with) a set of beliefs. Blythe believes that the first Iraq war was justified, but this belief is inconsistent with her other beliefs about war, so it is false. The coherence theory assumes the truth of the **law of non-contradiction**, which is a fundamental law of logic that says that a sentence and its denial cannot both be true (in the same sense, at the same time). For example, it cannot be the case that this bird that is an eagle is not an eagle. Since it is impossible for a thing to be what it is not, if we believe both "The bird is an eagle" and "The bird is not an eagle," one of those beliefs must be false. When one of them is supported by a large number of other beliefs with which it is consistent, we should reject—count as false— the other one. So that's all there is for a belief to be true or false: coherence or incoherence with the preponderance of our other beliefs.

The coherence theory offers a possible solution to both of the problems facing the correspondence theory. First, the correspondence theory faces the difficulty in comparing beliefs with facts, since facts are mind-independent, hence inaccessible to minds. The coherence theory avoids this problem by saying that beliefs are true if they cohere with other beliefs, and we have access to our other beliefs, so we can compare whether our beliefs are coherent or not. The correspondence theory also faces the difficulty of matching beliefs up with physical facts, since they are so different in nature. The coherence theory only aligns beliefs with other beliefs, which are similar in nature, so it is possible to bring our beliefs into logical alignment. The principle of comparison here is consistency; and it's easy to see how we can know that the two are consistent.

The coherence theory has a certain popular appeal. Imagine this case: Santiago is pressured by his classmates and teachers to vote in a certain way, but he does not want to. Santiago's friend Isabella counsels him to remain true to himself, so he votes as he sees fit. In this case, Santiago's vote is true in the coherence sense of the term, since the way he votes coheres with, or is consistent with, his political beliefs. Years later, Santiago gets betrothed to Isabella, claiming "I will be true to you" (where, incidentally, the term 'betrothed' is rooted in the words 'be true'), which means that he will keep his promises, or his actions will remain consistent with his promises. Imagine, years later, that Santiago and Isabella get into an argument about the morality of eating meat. They decide that vegetarianism is true for Santiago but need not be true for Isabella. They are not saying that "vegetarianism is acceptable" corresponds to an objective fact; rather, they are saying that the belief in vegetarianism is what is consistent with Santiago's other beliefs about animals and harm and the environment, but belief in eating meat is consistent with Isabella's other beliefs about humans being similar to other omnivorous animals in nature. Here is another example: while politicians are accused of lying when they say something that goes against a fact, they are also accused of being fake or not truthful when they say something that hides or distorts their actual views. In the former

Two people are arguing over a financial matter. They can't agree, so they decide to take their dispute to the Rabbi. The first person makes her case, and the Rabbi says, "You're right!" The second person makes her case, and the Rabbi says, "You're also right." The Rabbi's assistant, who was standing by listening, protests: "But Rabbi, they can't both be right." The Rabbi considers this for a minute, then says, "You're right too."

case their statements are false in the sense that they do not correspond to reality, but in the latter case their statements are false in the sense that they are not being consistent with their background beliefs.

While the coherence theory can be interpreted as meaning that truth is consistency with one's personal beliefs, or even that truth is remaining true to one's culture and traditions, these versions of the coherence theory are open to several objections, as we will see. For this reason, most coherence theorists have a more precise claim in mind. They usually argue that a belief is true if it coheres with an *ideal* and *completed* set of true beliefs. Here is how American philosopher **Brand Blanshard** (1892–1987) explains this version of the coherence theory:

The Nature of Thought (Brand Blanshard, 1921)[6]

That view is that reality is a system, completely ordered and fully intelligible, with which thought in its advance is more and more identifying itself. We may look at the growth of knowledge, individual or social, either as an attempt by our own minds to return to union with things as they are in their ordered wholeness, or the affirmation through our minds of the ordered whole itself. And if we take this view, our notion of truth is marked out for us. Truth is the approximation of thought to reality. It is thought on its way home … The degree of truth of a particular proposition is to be judged in the first instance by its coherence with experience as a whole, ultimately by its coherence with that further whole, all-comprehensive and fully articulated, in which thought can come to rest.

But it is time we defined more explicitly what coherence means … Fully coherent knowledge would be knowledge in which every judgement entailed, and was entailed by, the rest of the system. Probably we never find in fact a system where there is so much of interdependence. What it means may be clearer if we take a number of familiar systems … Do we find then in organic bodies the highest conceivable coherence? Clearly not. Though a human hand, as Aristotle said, would hardly be a hand when

6 Brand Blanshard, *The Nature of Thought: Vol. 2* (Norwich: Jarrold and Sons Limited, 1921), 264–76.

detached from the body, still it would be something definite enough; and we can conceive systems in which even this something would be gone ... A completely satisfactory system would have none of these defects. No proposition would be arbitrary, every proposition would be entailed by the others jointly and even singly, no proposition would stand outside the system ...

Because if one holds that truth is correspondence, one cannot intelligibly hold either that it is tested by coherence or that there is any dependable test at all. Consider the first point. Suppose that we construe experience into the most coherent picture possible, remembering that among the elements included will be such secondary qualities as colours, odours, and sounds. Would the mere fact that such elements as these are coherently arranged prove that anything precisely corresponding to them exists 'out there'? I cannot see that it would ... But then the second difficulty arises. If truth does consist in correspondence, no test can be sufficient. For in order to know that experience corresponds to fact, we must be able to get at that fact, unadulterated with idea, and compare the two sides with each other. And we have seen in the last chapter that such fact is not accessible ...

We come now to an objection more frequently made than any we have been considering. Granting that propositions, to be true, must be coherent with each other, may they not be coherent without being true? Are there not many systems of high unity and inclusiveness, which nevertheless are false? ... a novel, or a succession of novels such as Galsworthy's *Forsyte Saga*, may create a special world of characters and events which is at once extremely complex and internally consistent; does that make it the less fictitious? ... This objection, like so many other annihilating criticisms, would have more point if anyone had ever held the theory it demolishes. But if intended to represent the coherence theory as responsibly advocated, it is a gross misunderstanding. That theory does not hold that any and every system is true, no matter how abstract and limited; it holds that one system only is true, namely the system in which everything real and possible is coherently included.

The objection gains point, however, when it goes on to inquire whether all that is actual might not be embraced in more than one system. When a murder is committed, there may be two theories of the crime which do complete and equal justice to all the known facts and yet are inconsistent with each other ... Now we might reply that such a contingency, though possible, is highly improbable. In the case of the murder, every new bit of evidence narrows the range of available hypotheses, and it does not even occur to us that if we knew all the relevant facts we might find ourselves at the end with conflicting theories ...

> **In this passage,**
> 1. *Blanshard says the correspondence theory suffers from the comparison problem.*
> 2. *Blanshard argues that a belief (he uses the term 'proposition'—more on the comparison between beliefs and propositions in Chapter 7.1) is true when it coheres with a complete and final set of beliefs. Every true belief is logically connected to a complete and ideal set of beliefs. The belief "Rain falls from clouds" is true if it coheres with other beliefs such as "Clouds are water drops floating in the sky" and "Falling occurs when things approach the Earth" and "Rain is water falling from the sky."*

What would the coherence theorist say about Jackie and Hyde hooking up? Jackie's story coheres with certain beliefs she has, namely, that she is very attractive and that Hyde wants her. But her story also conflicts with other beliefs she has, namely, she knows that Hyde would never listen to ABBA. So, she is being partly true to her beliefs and partly fake. At the same time, Hyde's story is consistent with his background beliefs that he is attractive and Jackie wants him. The contradiction between the two accounts can be resolved by the fact that they are each only presenting a part of the information. Since neither story is consistent with all of the information, neither story is entirely true. But once all of the information is revealed, once the complete and final set of statements is presented, those statements will cohere together, so there is a truth of the matter.

Objection 1: Coherence without Truth

It seems possible for a set of beliefs to rationally cohere together, yet all be false. A story expresses an internally consistent set of statements about fictional characters and events. For example: Josie loves Ming, but Ming is married to Li Xiu, and Li Xiu is friends with Josie. These characters are fictitious, but there are no contradictions in the story, so we have coherence without truth, which shows that coherence is not the proper definition of truth. A related concern is that the coherence theory seems to allow numerous different accounts of the same event to all be true. Consistent with one perspective, it is true that Hassim is a hero, since he heroically martyred himself to liberate Iraq from American occupiers. But consistent with another perspective, it is false that Hassim is a hero, since he performed the cowardly act of suicide bombing which murdered innocent American liberators. But how can Hassim be both a hero and not a hero? Doesn't this violate the law of non-contradiction? It may not be possible for these conflicts to be eliminated once we all have ideal, all-inclusive belief sets.

Objection 2: Idealism vs. Materialism

Whereas the coherence theorist says that the correspondence model fails since beliefs cannot correlate with a mind-independent world, those endorsing a correspondence model argue that the coherence theory fails since beliefs then only correlate with other beliefs, leaving the physical world out of the picture, and resulting in a world where only beliefs and ideas exist. This leads to a contrast between the **materialist**, who emphasizes a mind-independent *physical* world, and the **idealist**, who emphasizes the mental realm of ideas. We consider these contrasting views of reality in Chapter 3. It is worth noting here, however, that the correspondence theorist tends to link beliefs up with the physical world of the materialist, while the coherence theorist tends to link beliefs up with the mental realm of the idealist. Insofar as the material world appears to exist, it seems appropriate to check our beliefs against this mind-independent world, as the correspondence theorist maintains. As Canadian philosopher Paul Thagard (1950–) explains, "if there is a world independent of representations of it, as historical evidence suggests, then the aim of representation should be to describe the world, not just to relate to other representations."[7]

2.3 Pragmatic Theory

The pragmatic theory of truth is rooted in an emphasis on what is **pragmatic**, or on what is practical or works well. As an example, pragmatic politicians are sometimes contrasted with ideologically driven politicians. The pragmatic politician passes the emergency bill that benefits the state even if the bill does not further her political creed, whereas the ideologue refuses to pass the emergency bill that benefits the state because it goes against her political creed. With respect to truth, the pragmatist asks: does the belief that Smith holds work well for Smith, is it beneficial for his life, or is it actually harming him? The **pragmatic theory of truth** says that a belief is true, or reliable, or trustworthy, if that belief has proven itself to be useful or helpful in life. Asuka's parents told her that she has to study hard in school. After narrowly getting into graduate school, Asuka marvels at how true those words proved to be.

The pragmatic theory is often motivated by weakening the correspondence theory, which then renders a pragmatic approach more reasonable. Shaun and Mindy love each other, but they get into a bad argument. They are both so convinced that they are right that they break up with each other because they both refuse to apologize. They end up missing each other, but never get back together. Their stubborn beliefs that they are right is what is destructive, and their convictions may not even be correct, given that there are two totally different interpretations of what happened. The pragmatist says they should both stop arrogantly thinking they are right, and instead do what works, namely, both should apologize to each other and reconnect. Later on, Shaun visits a counsellor, and he explains his conviction that any partner he has must apologize to him when his feelings are hurt. The counsellor asks: "Is that belief working well

---

7   Paul Thagard, "Coherence, Truth and the Development of Scientific Knowledge," *Philosophy of Science* 74, no. 1 (2007): 29.

for you?" Shaun realizes it is not—his relationships all end poorly because he insists on too much apologizing. By weakening his conviction that his belief is absolutely true, he can begin to see how his beliefs are actually harming himself. If it is possible that the belief is false anyway, why hold onto that belief if it is causing damage?

The pragmatic theory expands on the correspondence theory in several ways. Whereas the correspondence theory says that true beliefs correspond to facts, the pragmatic theory focuses on the usefulness of holding beliefs that correspond to reality. Amare correctly believes he is standing in front of a cliff, but getting this belief correct is important because it keeps him from walking off the edge to his doom. Likewise, there are facts of the universe that are entirely useless— like the temperature of some distant star—that have never been believed as true simply because they are useless to even contemplate. What does it mean for our beliefs to correspond to reality? Perhaps this means that our beliefs enable us to negotiate reality well—to get on well in the world.

The pragmatic theory expands on the coherence theory as well. Whereas the coherence theory says that true beliefs are consistent with a wider set of beliefs, the pragmatic theory notes that survival, happiness, and flourishing are among the wider set of goals that humans possess. Thus, a harmful belief is not consistent with these other beliefs and goals, so this sort of inconsistency constitutes its falsehood. On a smaller scale, the pragmatist can endorse the coherence test for truth: after all, beliefs including a contradiction guide us in two opposite directions, which is not useful for us. Here is a passage from American philosopher and psychologist **William James** (1842–1910), one of the leading historical proponents of the pragmatic model of truth:

Pragmatism (William James, 1904)[8]

Lecture II. ... The true is the name of whatever proves itself to be good in the way of belief, and good, too, for definite, assignable reasons. Surely you must admit this, that if there were no good for life in true ideas, or if the knowledge of them were positively disadvantageous and false ideas the only useful ones, then the current notion that truth is divine and precious, and its pursuit a duty, could never have grown up or become a dogma. In a world like that, our duty would be to shun truth, rather. But in this world, just as certain foods are not only agreeable to our taste, but good for our teeth, our stomach and our tissues; so certain ideas are not only agreeable to think about, or agreeable as supporting other ideas that we are fond of, but they are also helpful in life's practical struggles. If there be any life that it is really better we should lead, and if there be any idea which, if believed

---

8   William James, from *Pragmatism: A New Name for Some Old Ways of Thinking* (1907), in *William James: Writings 1902–1910*, ed. Bruce Kuklick (New York: The Library of America, 1988), Lectures II and VI.

in, would help us to lead that life, then it would be really better for us to believe in that idea, unless, indeed, belief in it incidentally clashed with other great vital benefits. 'What would be better for us to believe'! This sounds very like a definition of truth ...

Lecture VI ... The popular notion is that a true idea must copy its reality. Like other popular views, this one follows the analogy of the most usual experience. Our true ideas of sensible things do indeed copy them. Shut your eyes and think of yonder clock on the wall, and you get just such a true picture or copy of its dial. But your idea of its 'works' (unless you are a clock-maker) is much less of a copy, yet it passes muster, for it in no way clashes with the reality. Even tho it should shrink to the mere word 'works,' that word still serves you truly; and when you speak of the 'time-keeping function' of the clock, or of its spring's 'elasticity,' it is hard to see exactly what your ideas can copy.

You perceive that there is a problem here. Where our ideas cannot copy definitely their object, what does agreement with that object mean? Some idealists seem to say that they are true whenever they are what God means that we ought to think about that object ... Pragmatism, on the other hand, asks its usual question. "Grant an idea or belief to be true," it says, "what concrete difference will its being true make in anyone's actual life? How will the truth be realized? What experiences will be different from those which would obtain if the belief were false? What, in short, is the truth's cash-value in experiential terms?" ...

'The true,' to put it very briefly, is only the expedient in the way of our thinking, just as 'the right' is only the expedient in the way of our behaving. Expedient in almost any fashion; and expedient in the long run and on the whole of course; for what meets expediently all the experience in sight won't necessarily meet all farther experiences equally satisfactorily. Experience, as we know, has ways of boiling over, and making us correct our present formulas. The 'absolutely' true, meaning what no farther experience will ever alter, is that ideal vanishing-point towards which we imagine that all our temporary truths will someday converge.... Meanwhile we have to live today by what truth we can get today, and be ready tomorrow to call it falsehood. Ptolemaic astronomy, Euclidean space, Aristotelian logic, scholastic metaphysics, were expedient for centuries, but human experience has boiled over those limits, and we now call these things only relatively true, or true within those borders of experience. 'Absolutely' they are false ...

In this passage,

1. *James argues against the correspondence theory by saying that our ideas can only vaguely copy experience, which renders it important to consider whether our ideas are useful to us. James also argues*

> *against the coherence theory by saying that our beliefs are not just consistent with God's ideas, but also must be consistent with whatever is useful to us.*
>
> 2. *James argues that true beliefs are whatever it is best for us to believe, whatever is most expedient to believe, and whatever belief helps us most in life's practical struggles.*
>
> 3. *James considers the objection, raised below, that pragmatism leads to believing in useful falsehoods such as Santa Claus. He responds that we will likely not believe in useful falsehoods, as those beliefs would then clash with other useful beliefs we hold, such as the belief that others would ridicule us for believing in things that are considered fictitious.*

What would the pragmatic theory say about Hyde and Jackie? They would not be surprised that their human interests, in this case self-confidence and fear of rejection, would weaken the likelihood that their views are accurate. It is useful for them both to believe the other made the first move, which explains why they hold those views. But if their interpretations begin to damage their relationship, they should abandon those beliefs, as they are now harmful.

Objection 1: Useful Falsehoods

Critics contend that pragmatism leads to believing in useful falsehoods. Bertrand Russell provides the example of Santa Claus. It is useful for kids to believe in Santa Claus, since Santa brings presents and spreads Christmas joy. Since it is more expedient to believe in Santa than believe Santa does not exist, the pragmatic model leads to the view that 'Santa exists' is true. James himself provides the example of Ptolemaic astronomy, according to which the Earth lies at the centre of the solar system. This was a useful theory for centuries, as many boats safely navigated to shore by following the theory, so James suggests it was true *at that time*. But it was never true that the Earth is at the centre of the solar system.

In later chapters we will consider more serious examples of believing in something for the sake of its usefulness rather than its accuracy. In Chapter 6.1 we consider the possibility that people should believe in free will, not because it is true, but because rejecting free will leads to moral decay. In Chapter 9.6 we consider the possibility that rationality is defined as doing what is useful rather than true. In Chapter 10.6–10.7 we consider the possibility that science itself should be shaped by our own interests rather than the simple pursuit of

Your friend loves her new haircut, but you think it looks awful! She asks what you think of her haircut. Should you lie in order to make her feel good, or tell the truth even though it would hurt her feelings? What is more important: the truth or what works best?

truth. In Chapter 12.6.2 we consider the possibility of believing in God because it is useful rather than true, while in Chapter 12.7 we consider the possibility of having faith in ourselves or others because it is useful rather than true. Chapter 1 has already contrasted sophism (i.e., saying whatever works) with caring for the truth. The pragmatic approach lies at the root of all of these attempts to substitute the objective truth for whatever works best for us. The core question, as discussed in Chapter 1, is: is it better to care for the truth or to care for whatever is beneficial? Perhaps everyone believing and saying what they think works best to get what they want actually doesn't work very well, since no one will trust anyone anymore, or be honest with themselves or others anymore, which will not lead to a happy life or well-functioning society. So, oddly, perhaps pragmatism should be rejected on the pragmatic grounds that it doesn't work very well in the long run.

Objection 2: Useless or Harmful Truths

There is also a category of statements that are useless or harmful, but nevertheless true. Here are some useless but true statements: 'Alpha Centauri is slightly older than our sun'; 'several people were born in Philadelphia in 1942'; 'the 1000th digit of pi is 8.' There are also harmful statements that are damaging to believe, such as 'You will die' and 'You will not get all you are working for in life.' These beliefs can be damaging to people, but they nevertheless are true. These considerations show that the uselessness or even harmfulness of a belief does not make it false. The last objection showed the usefulness of a belief does not make it true. So, the truth of a belief seems to be detached from its usefulness, which goes against the pragmatist view.

2.4 Relativism

The correspondence theory maintains that there exists one objective truth, namely, reality and all its facts. The goal of the correspondence theory is for our beliefs to correspond to this objective truth, then we will know the (capital T) Truth. The coherence model also says that humans can know truth; they just say that humans possess truth when their statements are consistent with each other. The pragmatic model likewise says that humans can know truth; they just say that humans possess truth when their statements are useful over the long run. But both the coherence model and the pragmatic model open up the possibility that there may be multiple different truths. The coherence model opens up the possibility that different sets of beliefs can both be internally consistent—being a vegetarian is what is consistent with Santiago's beliefs, but eating meat is consistent with Isabella's beliefs. The pragmatic model opens up the possibility that different beliefs can be useful for different people—believing in vegetarianism works best for Santiago's life, but believing in eating meat works best for Isabella's life.

Some, including the sophists in Chapter 1.3, go one step further by saying that there is no definitive criterion for truth, neither a correspondence criterion, nor a coherence criterion, nor a pragmatic criterion. Instead, different people will believe different things for different reasons, none of which are true in any rigid sense, and none of which should be imposed on others who disagree. This view is called **anti-realism**, as it is the rejection of realism, or, the rejection of the view that there exists an objective truth that corresponds with a mind-independent reality. In place of there being an objective standard of Truth that applies to all is the doctrine of **relativism**, according to which truth is relative to an individual or a group.

There are several different types of relativism. First, there is **local relativism**, according to which there is no objective truth in one domain (one system of beliefs and attitudes), but there may be objective truth in another domain. For example, personal preferences about beer flavours or personal opinions about the best baseball team may be relative to personal tastes or geographical region, but there are still truths about whether electrons exist or not that are true for everyone. This is not to say that everyone agrees on these objective truths! There is also **global relativism**, according to which there is no objective truth in any domain. Scientific theories, personal tastes, theological claims, moral values, even beliefs about the ordinary every-day matters, are never true for all people, but are only true for some people, relative to their interests, perspectives, and background assumptions.

Subjective relativism is the view that truth is relative to an individual: Santiago believes that eating meat is wrong, so relative to, or in comparison with, his own beliefs, it is wrong for him to eat meat, but Santiago does not consider it wrong for Isabella to eat meat, because her eating habits must be compared to her own beliefs, and she believes that eating meat is fine. **Cultural relativism** is the view that truth is relative to one's culture or social group. We encountered a famous example from Herodotus in Chapter 1.3, where the Greeks burned their dead, so it was wrong for them to eat their dead. But the Indians that Darius interviewed eat their dead, so it is wrong for them to burn their dead. Probably both cultures think it wrong to bury the dead, though many contemporary cultures consider that the right thing to do.

Almost everyone believes that beer or team preferences are subjective, but how about cases like this: Shaun and Mindy are having an argument, and Shaun says, "The minute I said no, you gave me THAT LOOK." Mindy says, "I did not! You imagined it." Could it be that on questions like this there is also no real truth of the matter?

Relativism is supported by noticing the traditional difficulties with correspondence theories of truth. Our sense experience of reality is delivered to us by our own perceptual faculties, which each present reality to us in different ways, so we cannot access a mind-independent reality to compare our beliefs with. This issue will occupy us in Chapter 7. Moreover, we interpret our sense experience through a conceptual lens supplied by our culture and personal upbringing, so we cannot access a reality that is unadulterated by our own ideas. This issue will occupy us in Chapter 10.6 and 10.7. Since we cannot step outside of our minds and see what reality really looks like, since we cannot get a God's eye view, or a **view from nowhere**, of reality, we are left with personal truths or cultural truths.

It may be tempting to opt instead for a coherence model or a pragmatic model of truth, if the correspondence model fails. But relativists argue these models of truth are themselves influenced by cultural norms and assumptions. The coherence theorist thinks logical consistency is the criterion for truth, but this simply shows that those who espouse the coherence theory value logical consistency—those darn philosophers pushing logic all the time—where other peoples may value emotion or poetry over logical consistency. For them, there is more truth in a deeply felt emotion, or an inspiring sonnet, than in cold logical consistency. The pragmatic theory is susceptible to similar criticisms. The pragmatic theory values believing what is useful or what works best, but this just reveals a cultural or personal value for utility. Why should utility be the ultimate goal? Religious folk may replace utility with piety, while environmentally conscious folk may replace utility with harmony with nature, while warriors may replace utility with power. To them, pious devotion to a deity, or respect for nature, or control over others, is more important than calculating how useful the belief is. Relativists often add that their view enhances **tolerance** for other views, where tolerance is the value of respecting the different values that different people hold, since acknowledging that our own views are not objectively true enables us to respect other belief systems as well. Here is a passage from American philosopher **Richard Rorty** (1931–2007), a leading contemporary relativist who also had pragmatic tendencies:

"Solidarity or Objectivity" (Richard Rorty, 1991)[9]

There are two principal ways in which reflective human beings try, by placing their lives in a larger context, to give sense to those lives. The first is by telling the story of their contribution to a community ... The second way is to describe themselves as standing in immediate relation to a nonhuman reality. This relation is immediate in the sense that it does not derive from a relation between such a reality and their tribe, or their nation, or their imagined band of comrades. I shall say that stories of the former kind exemplify the desire for solidarity, and that stories of the latter kind

---

9   Richard Rorty, "Solidarity or Objectivity," in *Objectivity, Relativism, and Truth: Philosophical Papers, Volume 1* (Cambridge: Cambridge University Press, 1991), 21–34.

exemplify the desire for objectivity ... Those who wish to ground solidarity in objectivity—call them 'realists'—have to construe truth as correspondence to reality.... By contrast, those who wish to reduce objectivity to solidarity—call them 'pragmatists'—do not require either a metaphysics or an epistemology ... From a pragmatist point of view, to say that what is rational for us now to believe may not be true, is simply to say that somebody may come up with a better idea. It is to say there is always room for improved belief, since new evidence, or new hypotheses, or a whole new vocabulary, may come along. For pragmatists, the desire for objectivity is not the desire to escape the limitations of one's community, but simply the desire for as much intersubjective agreement as possible, the desire to extend the reference of 'us' as far as we can. Insofar as pragmatists make a distinction between knowledge and opinion, it is simply the distinction between topics on which such agreement is relatively easy to get and topics on which agreement is relatively hard to get.

'Relativism' is the traditional epithet applied to pragmatism by realists. Three different views are commonly referred to by this name.... The third is the view that there is nothing to be said about either truth or rationality apart from descriptions of the familiar procedures of justification that a given society—ours—uses in one or another area of inquiry. The pragmatist holds the ethnocentric third view ... He thinks his views are better than the realists, but he does not think that his views correspond to the nature of things. He thinks the very flexibility of the word 'true'—the fact that it is merely an expression of commendation—insures its univocity ... So he feels free to use the term 'true' as a general term of commendation in the same way as his realist opponent does—and in particular to use it to commend his own view ... So when the pragmatist says there is nothing to be said about truth save that each of us will commend as true those beliefs he or she finds good to believe, the realist is inclined to interpret this as one more positive theory about the nature of truth: a theory according to which truth is simply the contemporary opinion of a chosen individual or group. Such a theory would, of course, be self-refuting. But the pragmatist does not have a theory of truth, much less a relativistic one. As a partisan of solidarity, his account of the value of cooperative human inquiry has only an ethical base, not an epistemological or metaphysical one. Not having any epistemology, *a fortiori* he does not have a relativistic one ...

The pragmatists' justification of toleration, free inquiry, and the quest for undistorted communication can only take the form of a comparison between societies that exemplify these habits and those that do not, leading up to the suggestion that nobody who has experienced both would prefer the latter. It is exemplified by Winston Churchill's defense of democracy as the worst form of government imaginable, except for all the others that have been tried so far. Such justification is not by reference to a criterion, but by reference to various detailed practical advantages. It is circular only in that the terms of praise used to describe liberal societies will be drawn from the vocabulary of the liberal societies themselves. Such praise has to be in some vocabulary, after all, and the terms of praise current in primitive or theocratic or totalitarian societies will not produce the desired result. So the pragmatist admits that he has no ahistorical standpoint from which to endorse the habits of modern democracies he wishes to praise. These consequences are just what partisans of solidarity expect. But among partisans of objectivity they give rise, once again, to fears of the dilemma formed by ethnocentrism on the one hand and relativism on the other. Either we attach a special privilege to our own community, or we pretend an impossible tolerance for every other group. I have been arguing that we pragmatists should grasp the ethnocentric horn of this dilemma. We should say that we must, in practice, privilege our own group, even though there can be no noncircular justification for doing so.

In this passage,

1. *Rorty contrasts those who seek objectivity (i.e., the correspondence theorist) with those who seek solidarity. Those seeking solidarity seek connectedness with one's community and its interests and values, rather than a detached or mind-independent truth.*

2. *Rorty says that solidarity involves accepting that truth and rationality are relative to one's culture. On this view, the word 'true' is used to commend or applaud certain beliefs. To say 'the sky is blue is true' is to express agreement with the view that 'the sky is blue,' or to express solidarity with those who believe that the sky is blue. The goal is for more and more people to achieve agreement on beliefs, since that extends the scope of the community.*

3. *Rorty provides an example of democracy. Democracy is not correct because it is the objectively correct method of governance. Rather, democracy is correct because a set of countries have found democracy useful, so want to get others to embrace democracy as well, and Rorty, since he was raised in a democracy, agrees with the project of democratization. Others, raised in non-democratic cultures, may think that democracy is worthless, and they will likewise attempt to increase the community of countries that reject democracy.*

What would the relativist say about Hyde and Jackie? They would be quick to point out that Hyde and Jackie will of course have different interpretations of who made the first move, since they are embedded in their own interests and values. There is no neutral perspective showing what really happened, since they cannot step outside of their assumptions, interests, and perspectives. Rather, Hyde's friends are likely to side with Hyde's account, while Jackie's friends are likely to side with Jackie, since they are likely to adopt the perspective that they hear from their friend. If they need a counsellor, the counsellor may remind them to listen to and respect the other side as well, given that each perspective is equally felt.

Objection 1: Self-Refuting

Relativism appears to be self-refuting. A statement is **self-refuting** if its being true would prove that it is false. For example, 'This statement is false' is a self-refuting statement. That is, if it is true that 'This statement is false,' then the statement must actually be false. Relativism faces the same problem. Relativism states "there is no truth." But if it is true that there is no truth, then relativism itself cannot be true. Since there is no truth, relativism is not true either, so it is not true that truth is relative to a culture or person. And, since there are no falsehoods, the correspondence model of truth is not false, so relativists should be tolerant of those who endorse the correspondence model. But relativists sometimes insist that relativism is the actual truth, which, ironically, leads to intolerance of those who claim to know an objective truth.

Objection 2: Reality Exists

A primary motivation for relativism is the difficulty humans have in accessing a mind-independent reality. Our experiences are mediated by our senses, which are further shaped by our theories and concepts, so it is difficult to access a mind-independent reality. But these issues do not change the fact that we live within a shared reality that is not of our own making. Jotham, playing a game of chicken, stands in front of an oncoming train. As the train approaches, he tells himself, "The perception of a train is just a construct of my senses, the idea of a *train* is just a construct of my English language, it isn't really there." One of two things will happen to Jotham. First, he may change his mind: he comes to believe that the train is really there, regardless of the fact that he doesn't want this to be true, and so he jumps off the tracks and saves himself. In this case, he is not a relativist anymore, since he grants there exists a mind-independent reality. Secondly, he may remain firm in his relativism, insisting the train is not real because he doesn't believe it is real. Unfortunately for Jotham, he will still be struck by the train. In this case, he is not a relativist anymore either, since he is dead. What is impossible is that reality bends to Jotham's will. Imagine the case: Jotham says the train doesn't really exist, so it magically disappears, obeying his beliefs, since a mind-independent reality never existed anyway, and he constructs reality! This just does not happen, which is proof that there exists a mind-independent reality, whether we like it or not.

Objection 3: Care for Truth

As discussed in Chapter 1, rejecting the view that humans can know a mind-independent truth can lead to a lack of concern for truth. If the miasma theory of disease (which says disease is caused by inhaling polluted air) and the germ theory of disease (which says disease is caused by microorganisms such as viruses or bacteria) are both equally accurate models of disease, and humans cannot know that the miasma theory is actually false, then what is the purpose of searching for the truth on this matter? Why do microbiology? Without the microbiology, there would be no discovery or classification of germs, and no science of vaccinations or value on hygiene. People would just get sick, and no one would be able to track why, and we wouldn't avoid the sickness. Here is another example: if the theist and atheist are equally correct about whether God exists, relative to their backgrounds and interests, what is the purpose of having an honest discussion about whether God exists? Moreover, how could an honest conversation even unfold, given that argumentation itself is relative to the conflicted interests of the disputants? Perhaps the theist deploys an invalid form of reasoning, while the atheist simply makes up a fact as part of his proof. When they try to challenge each other's error, they both wave their hands with incredulity, continuing to insist they are right. The discussion is liable to devolve into a shouting match—whoever yells the loudest is right—since appeal to truth and good reasoning is not possible. The realm of discourse turns into a battle over who can yell the loudest, or who can trick each other into doing what they want most effectively. Here is an excerpt from the contemporary philosopher **Susan Haack**, who finds that many ailments of our present society are in fact caused by the lack of concern for truth rooted in abandoning our ability to know objective truth:

"Post 'Post-Truth'" (Susan Haack, 2019)[10]

No doubt about it: Outright lies, half-truths, economy with the truth, massaged data, simple carelessness with the facts, and the like, are undeniably and alarmingly commonplace today, especially in political discourse, in advertising, public relations, in universities' publicity material, and indeed in just about every area of public life ... Nor is disillusionment with the whole idea of truth a new phenomenon. Here is Peirce, writing in 1896: 'When society is broken into bands now warring, now allied, now for a time subordinated one to another, man loses his conception of truth and of reason.... [he will] choose his side and

The question of truth is at present an important cultural issue. The 2016 Oxford Dictionary Word of the Year was post-truth, which they define as expressing circumstances where objective facts are less influential than emotional appeals. In 2017 the Collins Dictionary Word of the Year was fake news, which they define as occurring when the media reports something false. In 2018 the dictionary.com Word of the Year was misinformation, which is false information that is spread, knowingly or unknowingly.

10 Susan Haack, "Post 'Post-Truth': Are We There Yet?" *Theoria* 85, no. 4 (2019): 258–75.

set to work ... to silence his adversaries.' And again, the same year, writing of what happens when sham reasoning—where the conclusion determines what argument is given, rather than the other way round—becomes commonplace: 'men come to look upon reasoning as mainly decorative ... The result of this state of things is, of course, a rapid degeneration of intellectual vigor, very perceptible from one generation to the next. This is just what is taking place among us before our eyes.' And, I would add, this is just what is taking place among us, before our eyes, too.

It's not just politicians, and not just outright lies, we have to worry about. As I was beginning to think about this paper, for example, I received an e-mail from somewhere in the labyrinthine bureaucracy of my university headed 'Building a Learning Community.' This subject-heading turned out to be a grotesquely misleading euphemism for a curt instruction from the Powers that Be that the recipient was to complete a mandatory online "sexual-harassment training" program—now. And while I was writing the paper, I read of: (1) Pharmaceutical companies' marketing departments' having recruited ghost-writers to put their names on scientific (or 'scientific') studies of their drugs; (2) Affluent parents paying large sums of money to falsify their children's academic records or sporting achievements to ensure that these young people would be admitted to 'elite' universities and colleges; ... (5) A feature article in a major newspaper the headline of which announced 'Machines that Will Read your Mind,' but the text of which said only over and over again, that such machines might possibly, maybe, sometime in the unspecified future, be possible—perhaps, or perhaps not. And I haven't yet even mentioned the political lies, half-truths, quarter-truths, evasions, fudges, deliberate vagueness, etc., that we hear and read every day ...

Now it's time—no, it's past time!—to move on, to ask what we can do to reverse the disturbing trend toward unconcern about, and even despair of, truth, and the appalling idea that truth simply doesn't matter ... And then, I think of John Stuart Mill's observation 'bad men need nothing more to compass their ends, than that good men should look on and do nothing.' (Women, too, of course.) So I will add that each of us can contribute something beyond this: when I'm told, 'only 2% of claims of sexual harassment are false,' for example, I can speak up, and ask, 'How, exactly, do we know this? How could anyone possibly know?' More generally, when I hear large claims made without evidence, I can ask what the evidence is, and whether there is contrary evidence not mentioned. Sometimes— though not, of course, always—I can look into the basis of such claims myself; and I must find the courage to speak up if I conclude that the claim is not well-founded. Why courage? Because, in the monoculture of political correctness that pervades U.S. universities today, even raising such a question may get you in trouble.

That's too bad. But still and all, we must do what we can, reminding ourselves that the way to resist the tide of misinformation, exaggeration, etc., is—emphatically not to allow such outfits as Facebook and Pinterest to filter our information for us—but to renew our commitment to free speech and to a free marketplace of ideas; and our commitment not just to allowing, but to encouraging, and participating in, this marketplace, always conscious of our own, as well as others' fallibility. The best—the only—antidote to bad information is good information; the best—the only—antidote to flimsy and inadequate evidence is more and better evidence, the best—the only—antidote to misleading claims is to disambiguate the ambiguities and spell out the vague terms that are leading us astray; and the best—the only—antidote to lies is truth.

In this passage,

1. *Haack points out how popular the relativism that leads to bull-crap currently is.*
2. *Haack argues that the best way to overcome relativistic bull-crap is to dedicate ourselves to thinking fairly and well, encouraging all sides to share their views, speaking accurately, and believing things based on evidence rather than being fooled by other people's tricks and lies.*

What might Haack say about the case of Hyde and Jackie? She would say that they are both being deceptive—they are deceiving themselves and their friends into thinking they are more desirable than they actually are. Their friends should listen to both sides, as the personal biases become more evident when they are compared with other views and with more facts. Hyde and Jackie should tell their friends the truth—they were bored, so they decided to start making out—instead of trying to convince their friends of lies.

Summary

Chapter 1 outlined the difference between the philosopher, who cares for the truth, and the sophist, who does not care for the truth. This leads to the question: does truth even exist, and if it does, what is the nature of truth? There are three leading theories about truth: the correspondence theory, the coherence theory, and the pragmatic theory. While these models have different understandings of truth, they all have a model of truth. Relativism, on the other hand, says that humans cannot know truth, but this can lead to various unphilosophical attitudes. On the assumption that truth exists, and humans should care to know the truth, philosophers begin to wonder: what then is the truth about reality? In the next four chapters we will consider several important disputes about the nature of reality. In Chapter 3 we ask: what is reality like? Is it material or ideal, or both? Once we have these options under our belts, in Chapters 4 to 6 (and again in Chapter 11), we ask whether certain specific features of reality exist or not, and, if they exist, whether they are material or ideal, or both.

Key Terms in Chapter 2: Truth and Relativism		
Correspondence Theory	Comparison Problem	Anti-Realism
Corresponds	Coherence Theory	Relativism
Belief	Coherent	Local Relativism
Truth-Bearer	Law of	Global Relativism
Reality	Non-Contradiction	Subjective Relativism
Mind-Independent	Brand Blanshard	Cultural Relativism
Objective Truth	Materialism	View From Nowhere
Realism	Idealism	Tolerance
Fact	Pragmatic	Richard Rorty
Truth-Maker	Pragmatic Theory of	Self-Refuting
Truth-Value	Truth	Susan Haack
Bertrand Russell	William James	

Philosophy on Television: Truth and Relativism

Rashomon (1950)

Rashomon (1950) is a classic Japanese film where different characters interpret the same situation differently. The husband claims the bandit raped his wife so the husband killed himself. The bandit claims the wife fell in love with him and he then killed the husband in a duel. The wife claims she was raped by the bandit and when she woke from passing out the husband was dead. This film highlights the fact that different people have different versions of the truth, and it is difficult to sort out what actually happened. Other examples of multiple versions of the same story occur in *Star Wars: The Last Jedi* (2017), *Inside Man* (2006), and *Hero* (2002).

The Social Dilemma (2020)

The Social Dilemma (2020) is a documentary that shows how social media companies manipulate their users into spending more and more time on their platform. Some of their strategies render it difficult for their viewers to uncover the truth. For example, these companies recommend articles or videos that are similar to the content already viewed, which makes the viewer only see one side of a story. They also promote sensationalistic content that may involve conspiracy theories or misinformation, since that content will keep the user watching. In other words, social media companies often peddle in bull-crap rather than truth, as their goal is increased user interaction, not conveying the truth. In recent years, social media companies have begun censoring or tagging content that it considers misleading. While this shows these companies are showing concern for truth and accuracy, some worry that their fact-checking efforts are biased as well.

Fox News, CNN

These are two popular 24/7 news channels in the United States. They interpret daily events through drastically different perspectives, with Fox News presenting a right-wing perspective and CNN presenting a left-wing perspective. Thus, the same speech can be touted as historic and inspiring on one channel but dark and dangerous on the other channel. Each channel emphasizes certain story lines and ignores others in a manner that shapes their narrative. Each channel frequently has guests on their station that support their narrative, and often do not invite guests that question that narrative. These channels are often criticized for not presenting all the facts, or not reporting honestly. They are real-life examples of drastically different perspectives of the truth. Other news sources, such as AP or Reuters, aim at presenting just the facts, with as little bias as possible. Some news-aggregating sites, such as allsides.com, aggregate different perspectives of the same event together, so the viewer can get a more complete picture of the event.

Additional Resources

Visit this book's companion resources for additional materials, including video content and an automated tool for planning argumentative essays.

sites.broadviewpress.com/knowing/chapter-2

Chapter 3
Substances: Change and Sameness

THOUGHT EXPERIMENT 3.1
The Ship of Theseus

The puzzle of the Ship of Theseus is described by Plutarch: "The thirty-oared galley in which Theseus sailed with the youths and returned safely was preserved by the Athenians down to the time of Demetrius of Phalerum. At intervals they removed the old timbers and replaced them with sound ones, so that the ship became a classic illustration for the philosophers of the disputed question of growth and change, some of them arguing that it remained the same, and others that it had become a different vessel."[1] Here is another way to imagine the puzzle: Theseus sets sail on a long journey upon his wooden ship carrying a cargo of lumber. On the first day of the voyage, he notices one of the planks in his ship is rotten, so he replaces it with a fresh plank from the lumber in his cargo hold. On the second day, he notices another rotten plank, so he replaces it as well. He replaces another rotten plank on the third day. Every day, for the next thousand days, he replaces one rotten plank on his ship, until every plank on his ship has been replaced. Given that there is not one molecule of wood in the ship that remains the same, is the ship on day one the same ship as the ship on day 1,000?

The Ship of Theseus is just one example of a **substance**. While the term 'substance' may sound odd, a substance is actually just any ordinary object: a garbage can, a worm, a tree, a star, a rock, an amoeba, a pizza, a boat, a stuffed animal, a computer, a person, and so on. We are going to ask two questions about substances. First, what are substances made of? The basic answers: substances are material; substances are ideal; or substances are both material and ideal. The second question: do substances stay the same despite undergoing change, and if so, what makes the changed thing the same substance? The basic answers: yes, substances stay the same through change; no, substances do not stay the same through change; and both yes and no. These differing answers are given by differing theories we will look at, and these theories can be roughly depicted on the following spectrum:

---

1 Plutarch, *The Parallel Lives: Volume 1: The Life of Theseus*, trans. Bernadotte Perrin (Cambridge: Loeb Classical Library, 1914), 23.

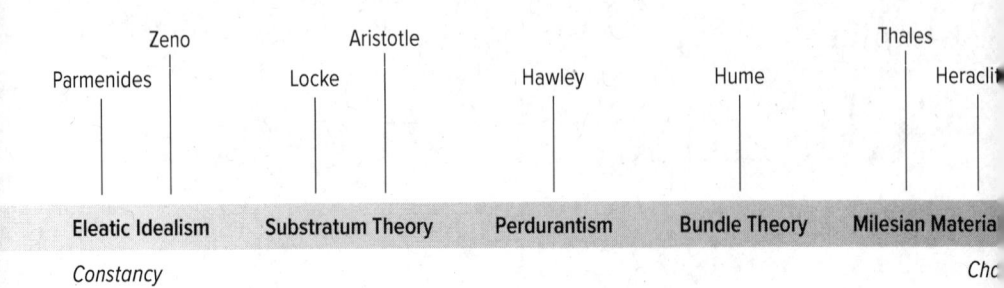

| Zeno | | Aristotle | | | | Thales | |
| Parmenides | | Locke | | Hawley | Hume | | Heracli* |

| Eleatic Idealism | Substratum Theory | Perdurantism | Bundle Theory | Milesian Materia* |

Constancy   *Cho*

Spectrum 3: Substance Identity

3.1 Milesian Materialism

Close your eyes. Now try to forget everything you know of the world. Pretend you have no idea what reality is like. When you open your eyes, you will see reality for the first time. Now open your eyes. What is your first impression of reality? This thought experiment is similar to the experience that the earliest philosophers had. As discussed in Chapter 1, they carried with them the fresh view that the world is understandable, so they set about the task of observing the world with new eyes, to see what reality is really like. One group of these ancient philosophers was known as **Milesian Materialists** (they were from near the town of Miletus, in present day western Turkey). They theorized that what was the same about everything was that it was all made of **matter**, and that these material objects were in an endless state of **change**. Seasons come and go. Days turn into nights. Objects, both living and crafted, come and go. People rush by. The leaves blow around. Rivers rush to the sea, where waves churn endlessly. So, on the question of what are substances made of, the answer is matter. On the question of whether substances stay the same through change, the answer is that substances just change.

One of these Milesian Materialists was **Thales**, who we bumped into in Chapter 1.2. In Thales' time, there were thought to be four material elements: earth, air, water, and fire. Of these elements, Thales takes **water** to be *the* fundamental element of reality—everything is made out of water. He noticed the tendency of water to change. Water, as a liquid, can turn into ice, then back into water, then into clouds and vapour, then back into rain falling down. He also noticed the role that water plays in the process of things changing: the seeds of living things are moist, vegetative life begins and grows when water is present, and babies are born surrounded by water. As Thales is reported to have said, "For moist natural substance, since it is easily formed into each different thing, is accustomed to undergo very various changes."[2] Water as the fundamental material element undergoes change and is the source of change and growth.

---

2   Heraclitus Homericus, "Homeric Questions," in *Philosophic Classics: Ancient Philosophy, Volume I*, ed. Forrest Baird (London: Routledge, 2019), 10.

Heraclitus (535–475 BCE) is another Milesian Materialist who follows Thales in thinking the fundamental nature of reality is material, and material is always changing, though he thinks **fire** is the fundamental element. Fire never stands still; it is constantly dancing about. Fire is at the root of the changes to water: heat up water, it becomes vapour; take away heat, it becomes solid. Fire represents destructive change, as wood is destroyed when touched by fire. Fire also represents biological change, as the great ball of fire called the sun is the source of growth for all living things. As Heraclitus says: "the cosmos ... was always and is and shall be: an ever-living fire being kindled in measures and being extinguished in measures" (Fragment B30). Not only is the fundamental element of nature, fire, constantly changing, but it is also a material element, so again reality is material and changing. Heraclitus' ideas are preserved in fragments, such as the following:

"Fragments" (Heraclitus, 490 BCE)[3]

B12: Upon those who step into the same rivers, different and again different waters flow.

B91: It is not possible to step twice into the same river ... It scatters and again comes together, and approaches and recedes.

B49: We step into and we do not step into the same rivers. We are and we are not.

B76: Fire lives in the death of earth and air lives in the death of fire, water lives in the death of air, earth that of water.

B52: For souls to becomes water is to die; for water to become earth is to die; but from earth, water comes to be; from water, soul.

B84: Changing it rests.

B126: Cold things grow hot, a hot thing cold, a moist thing withers, a parched thing is moistened.

B88: The same thing is both living and dead, and the waking and the sleeping, and young and old; for these things transformed are those, and those transformed back again are these.

---

3 Heraclitus, "Fragments," in *Readings in Ancient Greek Philosophy*, 30–40.

B30: The cosmos ... was always and is and shall be: an ever-living fire being kindled in measures and being extinguished in measures.

B90: All things are an exchange for fire, and fire for all things, as goods for gold and gold for goods.

B20: When they are born, they are willing to live and to have their destinies, and they leave children behind to become their destinies.

B6: The sun is new each day.

In these fragments,
1. *Heraclitus says that fire is the fundamental element, and fire is the source of constant change.*
2. *Heraclitus says the process of change is drastic. The sun is new each day, which means that the sun from yesterday is destroyed, and replaced by this new sun today. One cannot step into the same river twice, because when we return to the river there are new waters flowing and the old waters are gone. Heraclitus pushes this idea further: what prevents someone from stepping into the same river twice is also the fact that the person who returns to the river at a later time is a different person, since we are, and then we are not.*

Why would Heraclitus think that yesterday's sun is destroyed and replaced by a new sun during the process of transformation? It is difficult to interpret Heraclitus (and other early philosophers such as Parmenides and Zeno below), since his teachings only exist as fragments quoted in the writings of later philosophers. But several fragments show that Heraclitus may imagine the process of transformation in this way: the transformation of an object into a new object involves the extinction of the old object, and the coming into existence of the new object. Why would he think this? An object that changes is, by definition, different than it was, and a thing that is different than it was cannot be the same thing as it was. So, the old thing is gone, replaced by the new thing. Where did the new thing come from? It did not exist prior to the change, since the new thing is different from the old thing, so the old thing was not there. So, the new thing starts to exist at the moment of change. Imagine that June has blond hair. Now June dyes her hair blue. June has changed. But notice that June-with-blond-hair no longer exists. There is no such thing as June-with-blond-hair anymore. June-with-blond-hair is destroyed! But notice also: June-with-blue-hair suddenly sprang into existence! Yesterday, there was no June-with-blue-hair—after all, June had blond hair. June-with-blue-hair was born new today!

What would Heraclitus say about the Ship of Theseus? The ship on day one of the voyage is not the same as the ship on day one thousand of the voyage. But more radically: the ship on day one of the voyage is not the same as the ship on day two of the voyage. Any change in characteristics or makeup destroys the old object and replaces it with a new one. After all, the ship changed from having planks ABC on day one to having planks ABD on day two. Since the ship changed, the ship is different than it was. Since the ship is different than it was, the ship is not the same as it was.

Objection 1: Sameness and Change Exist

Heraclitus is correct that objects that change are different in certain respects. The ship with planks ABC is different from the ship with planks ABD, specifically because the ship lost plank C and gained plank D. But objects that change remain the same in other respects as well. The ship with planks ABC is the same as the ship with planks ABD, specifically because they both have planks AB in common. Even at the end of the voyage, the ship with planks ABC still has something in common with the ship with planks XYZ, namely, they are both still ships. Not only does Heraclitus suggest that sameness does not exist, but his model implies that change does not exist either. As Aristotle will argue below, change occurs when the same object undergoes modification: June had blond hair, and now June has blue hair, so June changes. If there is no object that stays the same through the process of change, then there is no change; rather, there are only two different objects. One object, June-with-blond-hair, stops existing then is replaced by a new object, June-with-blue-hair. These are different objects, not the same object that changes. But it seems like objects change. Consider two trees, one a maple, the other an oak. These trees are just different, the one does not change into the other. Now consider the leafless winter maple and the leafy summer maple. These trees are not totally different trees; rather, the same maple tree changes to its leafless state in the winter.

Objection 2: Knowledge Fails

Plato, who we encountered in Chapter 1.2, raises the following objection to Heraclitus' doctrine of unending change. Plato says that humans cannot have knowledge of objects that are constantly changing. The sun is bright; according to Heraclitus, by tomorrow that bright sun (call it sun$_1$) will pass out of existence, and will have been replaced by a new sun, call it sun$_2$. It will no longer be true that the sun is bright, because the sun—sun$_1$—we are speaking about no longer exists, so it cannot be bright. Perhaps we can change our claim to: 'the sun$_2$ is bright.' But by the time we are finished speaking, the sun$_2$

What happens if a band of pirates collects all the old planks from the old ship, and reconstitutes the old ship. Which is the real Ship of Theseus? What happens if, instead of one changed plank per day, a total repair of all the planks at the same time is completed. Is it still Theseus' Ship?

has changed as well, so the sun₂ no longer exists either, and our words are false again. Plato explains: "But if it is always passing away, can we correctly say of it first that it is this, and then that it is such and such? Or, at the very instant we are speaking, isn't it inevitably and immediately becoming a different thing and altering and no longer being as it was ... at the very instant the knower-to-be approaches, what he is approaching is becoming a different thing, or a different character, so that he can't yet come to know either what sort of thing it is or what it is like—surely, no kind of knowledge is knowledge of what isn't in any way."[4] As soon as we claim to know 'the sun is bright,' the sun is destroyed and is no longer bright, so it is false to say the sun is bright, and we do not know that the sun is bright.

3.2 Eleatic Idealism

At the other end of the spectrum stands a group of Idealists from the town of Elea in southern Italy. Where ancient materialists emphasize material elements such as earth, air, water, and fire as the fundamental feature of reality, ancient **idealists** emphasize ideal elements such as patterns, definitions, structures, and/or numbers as the fundamental feature of reality. Where material objects are always changing, ideas remain **constant**. Seasons come and go, yes, but the pattern remains the same: winter, spring, summer, fall, repeat. Days turn into nights, yes, but the pattern remains constant: day then night then day then night then day then night, forevermore. Objects come and go, yes: Dash the dog is born, grows old, then dies, proceeded by her offspring Benji, who is born, grows old, then dies, as the materialists notice. But, the definition of being a dog, the idea of being a domesticated carnivore of the family Canidae, remains constant. Dash remains a dog through the entire transition from her birth to her death, and Benji is a dog as well, confirming the constant law of nature that dogs beget dogs. Fire is a blaze of motion, yes, but it remains the same as well: fire is always hot, fire is always bright. The waters running through the river change, indeed, but the river defined as a steady flowing watercourse remains the same. So, on the question of what a substance is: the answer is an idea. And on the question of whether a substance stays the same through change, the answer is that substances are always constant.

    Zeno (495–430 BCE) is an **Eleatic Idealist** who labors to show that the possibility of change is false and illusory. His strategy is to introduce numerous paradoxes of motion and change. A **paradox** is a statement that expresses a possible truth that seems self-contradictory. For example, Socrates, in an excerpt provided in Chapter 1.2, arrives at the following paradox: I know one thing, that I know nothing. Later we will explore another paradox: God is powerful

---

4   Plato, *Cratylus* 439d–439e, in *Plato: Complete Works*, ed. John M. Cooper (Indianapolis: Hackett, 1997), 155.

enough to create a stone so big that God cannot lift it, but God is powerful enough to lift anything. Zeno proposes a **paradox of motion**. Imagine that you start walking to McDonald's to get some lunch. As you walk, you first have to get half way to McDonald's before you get to McDonald's. Once you pass the halfway point you now have to get halfway from where you currently stand to McDonald's. You keep walking to that point, but you now need to come to a new halfway point before you can reach McDonald's. Zeno asserts that

Zeno also presents this paradox of motion: an arrow (or an airplane in the photo above) flying through the air is stationary at every fraction of an instant, as captured by an extremely precise still-frame photograph. But the arrow or plane flying through the air seems to be moving swiftly at the same time.

this process must go on indefinitely, resulting in our inability to ever actually get to McDonald's. The result: motion leads to a contradiction. We can never arrive at McDonald's, yet we do arrive at McDonald's. Since motion is contradictory, the best thing is to reject the possibility of motion—motion must be an illusion.

Parmenides (540–470 BCE) is an Eleatic Idealist as well, and was Zeno's teacher. He argues that the fundamental element of reality is ideal, and ideas remain constant. While he writes in the form of a poem, which has given rise to various interpretations, he seems to start out by agreeing with Heraclitus' definition of change: a thing that changes is, by definition, different than it was, and hence not the same thing as it was. Thus, he agrees that if change occurs, the old thing must be destroyed and the new thing must be newly created. When June dyes her blond hair blue, June-with-blond-hair ceases to exist and June-with-blue-hair starts to exist. Contrary to Heraclitus, however, Parmenides shows that it is impossible for *real* objects that exist to stop existing, and for objects to come into being out of non-existence, so change is impossible. Here are some excerpts from his writings:

The Proem (Parmenides, 480 BCE)[5]

(B7) For in no way may this prevail, that things that are not are; but you, hold your thought back from this route of inquiry and do not let habit, rich in experience, compel you along this route to direct an aimless eye and an echoing ear and tongue, but judge by reasoning the much contested examination spoken by me.

(B8) ... Just one story of a route is still left: that it is. On this route there are signs very many, that what-is is ungenerated and imperishable, a whole of a single kind, unshaken, and complete. Nor was it ever, nor will it be, since it is

---

5   Parmenides, *The Proem*, B7–B8, in *Readings in Ancient Greek Philosophy*, 43–45.

now, all together one, holding together: For what birth will you seek out for it? How and from what did it grow? From what-is-not I will allow you neither to say nor to think: for it is not to be said or thought that it is not. What need would have roused it, later or earlier, having begun from nothing, to grow? In this way it is right either fully to be or not. Nor will the force of true conviction ever permit anything to come to be beside it from what-is-not. For this reason neither coming to be nor perishing did Justice allow....

Nor is it divisible, since it is all alike, and not at all more in any way, which would keep it from holding together, or at all less, but it is all full of what-is. Therefore it is all holding together; for what-is draws near to what-is. What is for thinking is the same as that on account of which there is thought. For not without what-is, on which it depends, having been solemnly pronounced, will you find thinking.

In this passage,

1. *Parmenides argues that objects cannot come into being out of non-existence based on the ancient principle of **ex nihilo, nihil fit**, which is Latin for 'out of nothing, nothing comes.' We shall see this principle at play in Chapters 6.1, 10.4, and 11.1 as well, so it is worth dwelling on. Imagine if I told you that a walrus suddenly popped into existence, out of nothing, in the middle of your room this morning and is currently eating your homework. Poof, it just appeared! You would think I am crazy; only children believe that magicians can wave their wands and make walruses pop into existence. Parmenides agrees by stating that he will not allow us to think that what exists began to grow from nothing. Since June-with-blue-hair did not exist before the hair dying incident, and it is impossible for things to pop into existence out of non-existence, it is impossible for June-with-blue-hair to start existing.*
2. *Parmenides argues that objects cannot fall out of existence, based on the logical impossibility of a thing which exists being a thing which does not exist. The old object, June-with-blond-hair, exists. In order for June to change her hair colour, June-with-blond-hair would have to not exist. But June-with-blond-hair does exist, and it is impossible for a thing that exists to be a thing which doesn't exist, so June-with-blond-hair cannot go out of existence.*
3. *Parmenides argues that since 'perishing' and 'coming to be' are impossible, and change requires perishing and coming to be, change is impossible. Any visible appearance of change, such as trees growing leaves or rocks falling, must be illusory. The material world of change is an illusion, so we should break the habit of trusting the experiences of our mistaken eyes.*
4. *Parmenides argues that the real world is apprehended by the mind, as it thinks about unchanging truths and ideas. The dancing fire seems to be constantly changing, but that is impossible, so the moving fire is an illusion. But the **idea** of fire, or, what the word 'fire' means, that fire is always hot,*

that fire is always bright, this remains constant, so is real. Dash the dog seems to run around, grow old and die, but that involves change, which is impossible, so the moving dog is an illusion. But the idea of a dog—that dogs are domesticated carnivores, that they chase sticks and have fur and four legs—this has always been true, so is real. The idea of dogs connects with the idea of carnivores—which are meat-eating animals—which remains constant as well. The idea of carnivores connects with the idea of animals—living beings that are able to move around—which has always been true and constant as well. What is real is the entire interconnected web of unchanging truths and ideas, which is apprehended by the thinking mind. The idealists' interconnected web of ideas bares certain similarities with Blanshard's coherence theory of truth discussed in Chapter 2.2.

What would Parmenides say about the Ship of Theseus? The ship-with-planks-ABC appears to stop existing, as the ship on day one thousand is the ship-with-planks-XYZ. And, the ship-with-planks-XYZ appears to pop into existence out of non-being, as the ship-with-planks-XYZ did not exist on day one. But, passing out of existence and popping into existence is impossible, so this appearance of change is an illusion. The material ship that changes is an illusion. The real ship, the idea of a ship as a sea-faring vessel, remains the same over the course of the journey. The Ship of Theseus, as defined as the idea or definition of being a ship, remains the same over the course of the voyage.

Objection 1: Change Exists

Parmenides' claim that the material world of change is an illusion is difficult to accept. While we shall encounter the possibility that the visible material world is an illusion in Chapters 5.1, 7.2, and 8.4 as well, we shall also encounter objections to these views. The ancient Greek philosopher Colotes raises the problem with Parmenides. Colotes claims that Parmenides has "taken away fire ... water ... rocks and precipices ... cities which are built and inhabited as well in Europe as in Asia ... in one word takes away the existence of all things by supposing that which is to be one."[6] Parmenides thinks that fire, water, precipices and cities do not exist, since they all involve change. But this is absurd. We live in bustling cities; how can we doubt they are real? If we thought precipices were not real, we would happily walk over them, but we do not do that, proving we think they are real. If we thought fire was not real, we could jump into fire without fear, but we do not do that either. More generally, Parmenides takes away the existence of every material object that changes, including the bodies of parents, children, and ourselves—the very things we care about most! Colotes adds that "by saying that the All (or the universe) is one, [Parmenides] hinders or obstructs our

---

6   Plutarch, *Plutarch's Morals: Volume 5*, ed. W. Goodwin (Boston: Little Brown and Company, 1878), 352–54.

living." Parmenides' view that the material world of change is illusory is unlivable. How can we safely cross the road if we believe that cars are illusions? How can we put food in our bodies if we believe the food approaching our mouths is illusory, and our mouths are illusory as well? Colotes' concerns can be framed as a **reductio ad absurdum** against Parmenides. Recall from Chapter 1.5.4 that a reductio ad absurdum takes the form of: if P is true then some consequent Q is true as well, but Q cannot possibly be true, so P cannot be true. Here is the reductio ad absurdum against Parmenides: if Parmenides is correct that motion is illusory then cities and fires and moving cars do not exist, but it is absurd to think cities and fires and cars do not exist, so Parmenides is incorrect.

Objection 2: Problems with Ex Nihilo

Parmenides relies on the ancient principle of *ex nihilo, nihil fit*. As mentioned, we will encounter advocates of this principle in later chapters as well. But we will also encounter those who disagree with this principle in various ways. Parmenides uses this principle to state that change can only occur when the new thing comes into existence out of nothing. But, as Aristotle will emphasize below, change may occur when the new thing is simply an alteration to an old thing that already exists. For example, Justin becomes musical, since he takes piano lessons. Justin-the-musical does not come into existence out of nothing, but rather is simply an alteration of Justin from Justin-the-not-musical to Justin-the-musical. The ship-with-new-planks does not come into existence out of nothing, but rather the ship comes into existence out of the pile of lumber.

THOUGHT EXPERIMENT 3.2
The *Mona Lisa* Forgery

A gang of thieves wants to steal the *Mona Lisa* without getting caught. In preparation, they make an exact copy of the *Mona Lisa*. They acquire the same oil paints, and have a machine paint an exact duplicate, such that every colour, every blend, and every shade is exactly the same. They paint the duplicate on the same kind of poplar panel that the original *Mona Lisa* is painted on. They even gently spray their painting with the same preservative chemicals the original *Mona Lisa* has been exposed to over time, and then slightly scratch and crack the painting in all the ways the original *Mona Lisa* has been. They then break into the Louvre, steal the original, and replace it with the exact duplicate. They escape, and no one notices the crime. Is the replica they left behind the same painting of *Mona Lisa*?

Where the Ship of Theseus asks us to imagine whether one object remains the same object despite having different parts, the *Mona Lisa* Forgery asks us to imagine whether two objects are different despite having exactly the same parts. It is worth introducing this puzzle here, as the next two models will answer the problem differently. Most people want to say that the forged *Mona Lisa* is not the same painting as the original, but finding an argument for this view is difficult. The two paintings have all the same properties, so that does not distinguish them. Some say that the paintings are distinguished because they exist in different spatial locations. But changing locations does not change the identity of something—the original *Mona Lisa* does not change into something else every time it is moved. Others say the paintings are distinguished by having different origins, as one was painted by da Vinci, the other by a machine. But how something comes to be may not be part of the nature of the thing—Mossan's new car seems to be what it is, no matter if it was manufactured in Michigan or California. Others distinguish the painting by the different meanings the paintings have for people, the original is a meaningful work of art and history for the world, while the other is a machine copy.

3.3 Substratum Theory

In Chapter 1.2 we saw that Socrates was the teacher of Plato. **Plato** makes an important contribution to the discussion on substances. Plato agrees with the Eleatic Idealist view that substances have an ideal essence described by its definition: the ship really has an essence, or nature, or idea, or definition, which is to be a seafaring vessel capable of carrying people and cargo. But Plato also agrees that the material world of change must exist: the ship really has changing material planks, the changing ship is not an illusion. Thus, the ship has an ideal part (i.e., it is defined as a ship) and material parts (i.e., the wooden planks). The material planks of the ship change, but the essence of the ship, the idea of being a ship, remains the same.

Aristotle (above center-right) was an impressive student. There is an apocryphal story of Plato (above center-left) lecturing at school but suddenly noticing that Aristotle is absent. Plato asks aloud 'Where is Aristotle?' Another student replies that Aristotle is sick. Upon hearing these words, Plato cancels the class, not wanting to waste time teaching minds that cannot understand.

Not only were Plato's views influential in its own right, but Plato also paved the way for the views of Plato's most famous student **Aristotle** (384–322 BCE). Aristotle also proposes a middle ground between the Milesian Materialists and the Eleatic Idealists. Where the Milesian Materialists claim that objects are constantly changing and the Eleatic Idealists claim that objects

Douglas Adams reports visiting the Golden Pavilion Temple in Kyoto, Japan, and being surprised how well it had stood up over the six centuries since it was built. He was told that it hadn't stood up well at all—in fact, it had burned down twice during the twentieth century. When asked if it was the same building anymore, his Japanese guide insisted it was the same: "But yes, of course it is."[7] To be overly concerned with the original materials, which are merely sentimental souvenirs of the past, is to fail to see the living building itself.

are unchangingly constant, Aristotle argues that objects can remain the same while undergoing change. The key is to state that the object has an unchanging **substratum** or base in which changing occurs. Imagine Fernanda has a full plate of tacos, and then eats them until there is an empty plate, then fills the plate again with apple pie. Change occurs: the tacos once existed, and then they are gone, replaced by apple pie. But constancy occurs as well: the plate that was full of tacos is the same as the plate that is emptied and filled with apple pie. Here the substratum, or the base, is the plate that contains the tacos and apple pie. Similarly, Fernanda was hungry but now she is full. Change occurs: Fernanda transitioned from being hungry to being full. But constancy occurs as well: the girl who was hungry is the same as the girl who is full. Here the substratum is the girl named Fernanda, as she stays the same through changes. Here is a passage from Aristotle where he explains this model, and how it differs from both those who say everything is changing and those who say everything is constant.

Physics I.7–I.8 (Aristotle, c. 350 BCE)[8]

When we say that something comes to be one thing from being another and different thing, we are speaking about either simple or compound things. What I mean is this: It is possible that a man comes to be musical, that the not-musical thing comes to be musical, and that the not-musical man comes to be a musical man....

When something comes to be F, in some cases it remains when it comes to be F, and in other cases it does not remain. The man, for instance, remains a man and is still a man when he comes to be musical, whereas the not-musical or unmusical thing, either simple or compound, does not remain. Now that we have made these distinctions, here is something we

---

7 Douglas Adams and Mark Carwardine, *Last Chance to See* (London: Pan Books, 1991), 141.

8 Aristotle, *Physics Book 1: 7–8*, in *Readings in Ancient Greek Philosophy*, 734–38.

can grasp from every case of coming to be, if we look at them all in the way described. In every case there must be some subject that comes to be something; even if it is one in number, it is not one in form, since being a man is not the same as being an unmusical thing. One thing that comes to be remains, and one does not remain. The thing that is not opposite remains, since the man remains; but the not-musical thing, or the unmusical thing, does not remain....

It is evident that there must be some subject that comes to be something; for in fact, when something comes to be of some quantity or quality; or relative to another, or somewhere, something is the subject underlying the change, because a substance is the only thing that is never said of any other subject, whereas everything else is said of a substance....

This is also the only solution to the puzzle raised by the earlier philosophers, as we shall now explain. Those who were the first to search for the truth philosophically and for the nature of beings were diverted and, so to speak, pushed off the track by inexperience. They say that nothing that is either comes to be or perishes. For, they say, what comes to be must come to be either from what is or from what is not, and coming to be is impossible in both cases; for what is cannot come to be (since it already is), while nothing can come to be from what is not (since there must be some subject). And then, having reached this result, they make things worse by going on to say that there is no plurality, but only being itself. They accepted this belief for the reason mentioned.

We reply as follows: the claim that something comes to be from what is or from what is not, or that what is or what is not acts on something or is acted on or comes to be anything whatever, is in one way no different from the claim that, for instance, a doctor acts on something or is acted on, or is or comes to be something from being a doctor. We say this about a doctor in two ways; and so, clearly, we also speak in two ways when we say that something is or comes to be something from what is, and that what is is acting on something or being acted on. Now a doctor builds a house, not insofar as he is a doctor, but insofar as he is a housebuilder; and he becomes pale, not insofar as he is a doctor, but insofar as he is dark. But he practices medicine, or loses his medical knowledge, insofar as he is a doctor. We speak in the fullest sense of a doctor acting on something or being acted on, or coming to be something, from being a doctor, if it is insofar as he is a doctor that he is acted on in this way or produces these things or comes to be these things. So it is also clear that coming to be from what is not signifies this: coming to be from it insofar as it is not.

The early philosophers failed to draw this distinction and gave up the question. This ignorance led them into more serious ignorance—so serious that they thought nothing else besides what already is either is or comes to be, and so they did away with all coming to be. We agree with them in saying that nothing comes to be without qualification from what is not, but we say that things come to be in a way from what is not.

In this passage,

1. *Aristotle argues that change involves a constant subject that changes from having one quality to having a different quality. For example, an unmusical man changes into a musical man, where the man as the subject remains constant while the man's qualities change from being unmusical to being musical. Since the subject that undergoes change remains the same while it undergoes change, it is possible for the subject to remain constant and to change, so the substratum theory provides both constancy and change.*

2. *Aristotle argues that Parmenides is incorrect in thinking that change is impossible. While Aristotle agrees with Parmenides that the musical man cannot come into being out of nothing, Aristotle thinks that the musical man can come into being out of the unmusical man, which is something.*

3. *Aristotle hints at the **subject-predicate language** argument for the substratum theory. Aristotle notes that people normally speak in terms of substances and the attributes that substances have. Language takes subject-predicate form: the sky is blue, the dog is barking, John is crying. In these sentences there is the name of a subject and a descriptive predicate about each subject: the subject 'sky' is said to be 'blue'; the subject 'dog' is said to be 'barking.' This common subject-predicate sentence structure lends credence to the view that nature consists of objects that have **properties**: we say 'the sky is blue' and we refer to an object, the sky, and assert that it has the property of being blue. The object here is the substratum, which is what underlies any change or any attribution of qualities. Objects have properties, which are attributes or qualities that correspond to the descriptions attributed to the object. When we say "the man is musical," we are saying the object, a man, has the property of being musical. The prevalence of subject-predicate language seems to indicate that nature contains objects with properties, which aligns with the substratum theory.*

The question arises: what is the nature of the substratum itself? To understand Aristotle's answer, remember that he stands in the middle between those philosophers endorsing constant ideas and changing matter. Not only does this mean that Aristotle thinks substances change and remain the same, but this also means that Aristotle thinks substances are both material and ideal. In fact, he invents a word, **hylomorphism**, to describe his model, which means that substances are part matter (Greek: *hule*) and part **form** or structure (Greek: *morphe*). Imagine that Michelangelo wants to sculpt the statue of *David*. He has the structure of the statue in his mind, but he has not carved it yet, so the actual substance, the statue of *David*, does not exist yet. Now imagine a slab of marble is waiting for Michelangelo, but he has not carved it up yet, so the actual substance, the statue of *David*, does not exist yet. The statue of *David* is a compound of both the marble material and the *David*-like structure, it is structured matter, or structure that has materialized. Both matter and structure are needed for the substance that is the statue of *David*. So, on the question of what is a substance, Aristotle answers that substances are structured matter. On the question of whether substances remain the same through change, Aristotle answers that the underlying substratum of the substance stays the same while change occurs.

What might Aristotle say about Theseus' ship? The ship is different as the material planks are different, but the ship remains the same as well, since the ship-like structure remains constant. What would Aristotle say about the *Mona Lisa* forgery? While the forgery has the same structure as the original (i.e., they are both shaped like *Mona Lisa*), they are different

Imagine if the exact same planks of the original Ship of Theseus were re-arranged to form a Trojan horse. Would it still be the Ship of Theseus? Probably not, indicating that the ship is defined by its structure, not just its matter.

form-matter compounds, they have different substrata—the original *Mona Lisa* is this *Mona Lisa*-shaped matter here, while the forged *Mona Lisa* is that other *Mona Lisa*-shaped matter there, so they are different substances.

Some later substratum theorists grew dissatisfied with Aristotle's hylomorphic substratum theory. They said that if the substratum is the object while its properties are predicated on the object, then we should take away all the properties that are predicated of the thing, and whatever is left over must be the substratum. Imagine a typical object with properties, say a sweet, ripe, red, juicy apple. We predicate the ripeness of the apple when we say 'the apple is ripe,' so take away the ripeness of the apple as a property of the apple and not as the substratum itself, and we are left with a sweet, red, juicy apple. Now, take away the redness and juiciness of the apple, and we are left with a sweet apple. Now take away the sweetness of the apple, and we are left with just an apple. But we are still describing the object as an apple when we say "this is an apple," so *being an apple* is a property describing the object, so we must take away the appleness of the apple, and we are left with just *this*. We are left with a substratum that has no properties, and cannot be described! The is called the **bare substratum** view, according to which the substratum is just a 'this,' an indescribable empty container ready to hold properties, a something that is nothing. John Locke (1632–1704) explains the bare substratum view as follows:

> So that if anyone will examine himself concerning his notion of pure substance in general, he will find he has no other idea of it at all, but only a supposition of he knows not what support of such qualities, ... The idea then we have, to which we give the general name substance, being nothing but the

supposed, but unknown support of those qualities we find existing, which we imagine cannot subsist, without something to support them, we call that support *substantia*; which, according to the true import of the word, is in plain English, *standing under*.[9]

While the substratum is bare in the sense in which it has no properties and it cannot be described, the substratum does play the essential role of being a particular container for properties. The substratum is like a mirror, or a blank TV screen. The mirror is able to reflect, which is a genuine capability that many things cannot do, but without someone standing in front of the mirror, the mirror itself is blank. A TV has the special ability to play movies but without a movie playing on it, it is just a blank screen. Likewise, the substratum lacks any nature other than being a particular container for properties.

How might the bare substratum theory handle the Ship of Theseus? The ship is different as the properties and parts of the ship are all different, but the ship remains the same as well, since the ship also has a constant bare substratum, which ensures that it remains this same thing. What might the bare substratum theory say about the *Mona Lisa* forgery? Even though the original *Mona Lisa* and the forged *Mona Lisa* have the exact same properties, they are still different. After all, there is more to a substance than just its many properties: there is the bare substratum as well. The original *Mona Lisa* and the forged *Mona Lisa* have different substrates, so the original *Mona Lisa* is 'this *Mona Lisa* here,' while the forged *Mona Lisa* is 'that *Mona Lisa* there.'

Objection 1: Incomprehensible

At best, the bare substratum is a mysterious thing, lying hidden beyond the reach of human intellect and observation. At worst, the bare substratum would be incomprehensible, which renders it unlikely that the bare substratum exists. The bare substratum seems incomprehensible because it is something that cannot be spoken about. As soon as one speaks about it, one predicates something about it, which would not be the substratum anymore, but would rather be a property of the substratum. Even saying "the substratum exists" is to ascribe the property of existing to the substratum, but the substratum cannot have properties, since it is instead the bearer of properties. The British philosopher Elizabeth Anscombe (1919–2001) raises this concern when she says this "notion of substance surely commits us ... to an unintelligible bare particular which underlies the appearances and is the subject of predication but just for that reason can't in itself be characterized by any predicates ... the picture of substance is too unacceptable."[10]

9 John Locke, *An Essay Concerning Human Understanding* (London: Routledge and Sons, 1894), Book II, Chapter xxiii.
10 E. Anscombe and J. Körner, "Substance," *Aristotelian Society Supplementary Volume* 38, no. 1 (1964): 69–70.

Objection 2: Unobservable

Anscombe also argues that the bare substratum is unobservable. This is because humans observe the properties of things, not the bare substratum itself. Consider the sweet, juicy, red apple again. We can taste the apple to notice that the apple is sweet and juicy, but the juiciness is a property of the apple, not the bare substratum, so we do not taste the substratum. We can see the apple to notice it is red and round, but these are properties of the apple, not the bare substratum, so we do not see the bare substratum. We can touch the apple to notice that it is hard and heavy, but these are properties of the apple, so we do not feel the substratum itself. We do not observe the substratum in any way, which leads many to doubt the existence of the substratum. One philosopher who argues that the bare substratum theory fails because it posits the existence of something unobservable is David Hume, whom we will spend some time on now.

3.4 Bundle Theory

Where the substratum theory of substances says that a substance is a group of properties inhering in a substratum, the **bundle theory** of substances simply removes the substratum, leaving a substance as a group of properties. The juicy, red, sweet apple amounts to the properties of being juicy, being red, being sweet, and being an apple, all collected together in one place and time. The bundle theory avoids the problems facing the substratum model by simply rejecting the existence of a substratum, thus avoiding the problems associated with positing an unintelligible and unobservable substratum. The bundle theory only posits the existence of the bundle of properties, all of which are comprehensible and observable, so the object is comprehensible and observable.

One leading bundle theorist of substances is the Scottish philosopher **David Hume** (1711–76). We shall encounter David Hume on several occasions including Chapter 4.2, where we apply this bundle theory of substances to persons, and Chapter 7.3, where we discuss how his empiricism motivates his bundle theory. As you can tell from the passage below, Hume is led to the bundle theory for precisely the concerns already raised against the substratum theory:

A Treatise of Human Nature (David Hume, 1739)[11]

1.1.6: I would fain ask those philosophers, who found so much of their reasonings on the distinction of substance and accident, and imagine we

---

11 David Hume, *A Treatise of Human Nature* (1739) (Oxford: Clarendon Press, 1888), Book 1.1.6, and Book 1.4.6.

have clear ideas of each, whether the idea of substance be derived from the impressions of sensation or of reflection? If it be conveyed to us by our senses, I ask, which of them; and after what manner? If it be perceived by the eyes, it must be a colour; if by the ears, a sound; if by the palate, a taste; and so of the other senses. But I believe none will assert, that substance is either a colour, or sound, or a taste. The idea of substance must therefore be derived from an impression of reflection, if it really exist. But the impressions of reflection resolve themselves into our passions and emotions: none of which can possibly represent a substance. We have therefore no idea of substance, distinct from that of a collection of particular qualities, nor have we any other meaning when we either talk or reason concerning it....

The idea of a substance ... is nothing but a collection of simple ideas, that are united by the imagination, and have a particular name assigned them, by which we are able to recall, either to ourselves or others, that collection. But the difference betwixt these ideas consists in this, that the particular qualities, which form a substance, are commonly referred to an unknown something, in which they are supposed to inhere; or granting this fiction should not take place, are at least supposed to be closely and inseparably connected by the relations of contiguity and causation....

2.4.6: Our last resource is to yield to it, and boldly assert that these different related objects are in effect the same, however interrupted and variable. In order to justify to ourselves this absurdity, we often feign some new and unintelligible principle, that connects the objects together, and prevents their interruption or variation. Thus we feign the continued existence of the perceptions of our senses, to remove the interruption: and run into the notion of a soul, and self, and substance, to disguise the variation. But we may farther observe, that where we do not give rise to such a fiction, our propension to confound identity with relation is so great, that we are apt to imagine something unknown and mysterious, connecting the parts, beside their relation; and this I take to be the case with regard to the identity we ascribe to plants and vegetables....

Our chief business, then, must be to prove, that all objects, to which we ascribe identity, without observing their invariableness and uninterruptedness, are such as consist of a succession of related objects. In order to [do] this, suppose any mass of matter, of which the parts are contiguous and connected, to be placed before us; it is plain we must attribute a perfect identity to this mass, provided all the parts continue uninterruptedly and invariably the same, whatever motion or change of place we may observe either in the whole or in any of the parts. But supposing some very small or inconsiderable part to be added to the mass, or subtracted from it; though this absolutely destroys the identity of the whole, strictly speaking; yet as we seldom think so accurately, we scruple not to pronounce a mass of matter the same, where we find so trivial an alteration. The passage of the thought from the object before the change to the object after it, is so smooth and easy, that we scarce perceive the transition, and are apt to imagine, that it is nothing but a continued survey of the same object....

But whatever precaution we may use in introducing the changes gradually, and making them proportionable to the whole, it is certain, that where the changes are at last observed to become considerable, we make a scruple of ascribing identity to such different objects. There is, however, another artifice, by which we may induce the imagination to advance a step farther; and that is, by producing a reference of the parts to each other, and a combination to some common end or purpose. A ship, of which a considerable part has been changed by frequent reparations, is still considered as the same; nor does the difference of the materials hinder us from ascribing an identity to it. The common end, in which the parts conspire, is the same under all their variations, and affords an easy transition of the imagination from one situation of the body to another.

In this passage,

1. *Hume rejects the bare substratum view of substances. He argues that when we observe substances, we observe the properties of the substance such as the colour and taste of the apple, we do not observe a substratum. It is our imagination that posits an unobservable, unknown substratum to connect these properties together. But this substratum is a fiction that is absurd to posit.*
2. *Hume endorses the bundle theory of substance. He says that the substance is a collection of qualities: an apple is a tasty, red, juicy, apple, so the substance is the bundled properties of being tasty, being red, being juicy, and being an apple. There is no further substratum to the apple.*
3. *Hume argues that we tend to posit a substratum to the substance rather than just the bundle of properties because we imagine that objects stay the same despite changes to their properties. In truth, objects do not stay the same once they change properties. But why do we sometimes think two objects are the same, while at other times we do not think that two different objects are the same? For example, we tend to think that two objects—say the tree in the winter and the tree in the spring—are the same when they are not. But we do not tend to think that two objects—say the tree in winter and the rock down the street—are the same since they are clearly not. Hume says the tree in the winter is so similar to the tree in the spring that we tend to think they are the same. For example, the winter tree exists so closely in time to the spring tree: one day the winter tree without buds is here, the next day the spring tree with buds is here. The winter tree also*

exists so closely in space to the spring tree: the winter tree exists in the back corner of Prince's yard, while the spring tree exists in the same back corner of Prince's yard. The winter tree also looks so much like the spring tree: the winter tree is twenty feet tall and has fifty-six branches but no buds while the spring tree is also twenty feet tall and also has fifty-six branches in the exact same formation but has buds. The winter tree also has the same purpose as the spring tree: the winter tree strives to grow and produce leaves while the spring tree also strives to grow and produce leaves. Hume uses the example of a ship on this point: the old ship has the purpose of transporting people on water, while the new ship has the same purpose, so our imagination artificially connects these objects, though in reality they are similar but different objects.

The Toronto Raptors started playing NBA basketball in 1995, and continue playing today. Is it still the Toronto Raptors that plays today? If so, what makes them the same team? All the original players and coaches are gone, so that isn't it. Perhaps the fact that they play in the same city? But while they are on the road, they do not play in Toronto. Perhaps the fact that one game happens right after another? But they stop playing for the off-season, and then start up again. Perhaps it is the fact that they have the same name? But sometimes they play under a different name, the Toronto Huskies.

How would Hume's bundle theory handle the Ship of Theseus? Hume says that objects, such as the ship, are a bundle of properties, and do not have a constant substratum underlying the properties. So, the Ship of Theseus on day one is the rotten-wooded, ship-like, heavy, floating thing with planks ABC, and the Ship of Theseus on day two is the rotten-wooded, ship-like, heavy, floating thing with planks ABD. These two bundles are not the same. As Hume mentions, if the second bundle had not occurred immediately after the first, it would be obvious to us that the rotten-planks-ABC ship is not the same as the rotten-planks-ABD ship; they are quite obviously different when considered apart from each other. But, because the second ship quickly proceeds after the first, our imagination makes us think they are the same. Hume says this is a fiction, that they aren't really the same. Hume's bundle theory ultimately leads to a similar result as Heraclitus' view: since bundle ABC is literally different from bundle ABD, bundle ABC is not the same as bundle ABD, so any change results in a different object. However, Hume adds that the reason we consider these objects the same is they are so similar and they appear so closely together in time and space.

Objection 1: No Constancy

The result that substances do not stay the same despite miniscule changes is unsatisfying. Consider the ship: as soon as the ship changes even one property, say one atom is swept away by the wind, the ship is not the same anymore. After all, the ship-with-one-zillion-and-one-atoms is not the same bundle as the ship-with-one-zillion-atoms. It seems like the ship remains constant through these small changes, as the ship remains constant in many ways. One zillion of the atoms of the ship remain the same through this change, the ship remains a ship through this change, the ship retains the properties of wood-enness and floatability through this change. Imagine you took your car in for repairs. The mechanic changes a tire. When you go in to pick up your car, the mechanic refuses to give you the car. He is versed in Hume, so he says even though this fixed car looks like your old car in many ways, this is not really your car anymore, since the car you brought in had a flat tire, and this car has a brand-new tire. You would be understandably upset at the mechanic for his line of reasoning.

Objection 2: Identity of Indiscernibles

How would Hume's bundle theory handle the forged *Mona Lisa*? For Hume, the original *Mona Lisa* is the oily-painted, softly blended, smiling lady portrait, and the forged *Mona Lisa* has all of these exact properties as well. Since the painting just is a bundle of properties ABC, and the forgery has all the same properties ABC as the original, the forgery is the same painting as the original. This results from a principle called the **identity of indiscernibles**: when one thing resembles another thing in every way, it is best to conclude that there is only one thing. Imagine you've lost your dog—a brown, happy old lab with a hobble—so you put up a poster offering a reward. A stranger calls you up and says she's found your dog—the dog is brown, old, happy, and a lab that hobbles. You grow excited, your dog is found! You are assuming that this dog, who perfectly matches the description of your lost dog, is your lost dog because of the exact resemblance.

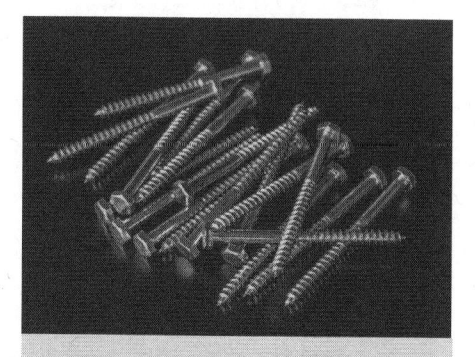

Two screws are molded out of the exact same material and into exactly the same shape. Are they different? What makes them different?

While the identity of indiscernibles initially makes sense, the principle falls apart on closer inspection. Imagine a factory that produces screws. Millions of screws come off the assembly line per day, each with the exact same colour, weight, size, and material constitution. Just because every screw is exactly the same doesn't mean that only one screw is made per day; rather, it means that millions of different screws, each of which have the same properties, are made. Likewise, the *Mona Lisa* forgery seems different than the original *Mona Lisa*, despite the fact that it exactly resembles the original in every way, so the identity of indiscernibles is not correct. The problem for the bundle theory is that it cannot explain how each screw is different, or how the *Mona Lisa*s are different. The bundle theorist says each screw just is its bundle of properties, and each screw has the same bundle of properties ABC, so these would be all the same screw—but they are not! The bundle theory is committed to the identity of indiscernibles, but the identity of indiscernibles is false, so the bundle theory is false. This is another example of a reductio ad absurdum, as discussed in 1.5.4.

3.5 Perdurantism

Despite the differences among all of the models discussed so far, they agree on two things. They agree that change occurs when a substance is in some way different from one moment to the next—the ship is changed because the ship transitioned from having planks ABC at one moment to having planks ABD at the next moment. The disagreement is only about whether the substance remains the same after it becomes different in the next moment. They also agree that a substance completely exists right now—the ship on day one is completely present on day one; all of the parts of the ship exist in that moment. The disagreement is only about whether the same substance continues to exist after change.

In the past fifty years, a new model of substances, and their ability to change while remaining constant, has questioned both of these assumptions. This is the **perdurantist** model of substances, according to which substances consist of all the properties they presently have, but also all of the properties they ever had and will ever have. This makes substances **four-dimensional objects** spanning all of their present three dimensions of space, and all of their life spans over time as well. Imagine, for example, a worm that is spread out over three dimensions. At every two-dimensional slice of the worm, it looks like a flat circle, but it has no length. Is this flat circle all there is to the worm? No, as we must mention its third dimension as well, its length, where two-dimensional flat circles stack beside each other to form the complete three-dimensional worm. In the same way, perdurantists say that objects are like four-dimensional worms spread through space and time. At every three-dimensional instant the worm is cylindrical and long, but is has no past or future. Is this all there is to the worm? No, as we must mention its fourth dimension, its duration, where the instants of its life stack beside each other to form the complete four-dimensional worm.

On this view, subjects remain the same because they always have all of the properties they will ever have. The leafy-at-times-leafless-at-times tree is the same tree in the winter and in the summer because it is still a leafy-at-times-leafless-at-times tree in both seasons. Substances change because they have different properties during different parts of their existences. The tree that is leafy in the summer and leafless in the winter changes over time because there are times when it is leafy and others when it is leafless. On the question of whether a substance remains the same through change, perdurantists say that it remains the same four-dimensional object, though at different times it has different properties. For perdurantists, change does not involve one substance that completely exists in the present moment becoming different in the next moment, but change involves one substance that partly exists in many different moments, but having different properties during those different moments of its existence.

Perdurantists often use an **analogy** between space and time to explain the view. Objects are spread out across multiple points in space. The same tree is under the ground in its roots, while also being twenty feet in the air with its leaves. Similarly, objects also are spread across multiple points in time. The same tree is a seedling twenty years ago, and a mature tree today, and a stump in one hundred years. Objects also have different properties in those different spatial locations. The tree is brown in its roots, but red in its leaves; soft in its leaves but firm in its bark. Similarly, objects can also have different properties in the different times of its existence. The tree is dormant and leafless in the winter, but flourishing and leafy in the summer—the same tree is leafy and leafless, though at different times. Here is how the British philosopher **Katherine Hawley** (1971–2021) explains the view:

How Things Persist (Katherine Hawley, 2002)[12]

We can say that persistence occurs when something exists at more than one time—you existed a few minutes ago, and still exist right now. The same is true of the book you hold and the rock on the shoreline, and thus you have all persisted. So far, so good. We can go on to ask whether things persist through time in anything like the way in which they spread out through space....

You occupy space by having parts down there in your shoes and parts up here under your hat; do you persist through time by having parts back then in bed and parts right now sitting in the chair? ... your little toe is merely a spatial part of you, and the whole you is not down there in your shoe. Similarly, say some, your current "phase" or "stage" is merely a "temporal part" of you, and the whole you is not present right now ...

You exist yesterday, today, and tomorrow by having a temporal part yesterday, a temporal part today, and a temporal part tomorrow. You are a single object which exists at different times by having different parts at

---

12 Katherine Hawley, *How Things Persist* (Oxford: Clarendon Press, 2002), 9–12.

different times, just as a road exists at different places by having different spatial parts at those different places....

Bananas ripen, your heart pumps, the book acquires a coffee stain. According to perdurance theorists, the way things change over time is very like the way they vary across space. The skin of the banana changes colour over time, from green to yellow, and the banana varies across its spatial extent right now. The banana is both tasty and bitter, because its flesh is tasty and its skin is bitter—its different spatial parts have different properties. And, according to perdurance theorists, the banana is first green all over then yellow all over because its earlier parts are green all over and its later parts are yellow all over—its different temporal parts have different properties, which means that the banana changes through time. On this picture, change over time is the possession of different properties by different temporal parts of an object....

The bad but tempting objection is that perdurance theory cannot account for change, because according to perdurance theory nothing really changes. According to perdurance theory, things 'change' by having a succession of different temporal parts with different properties. The objection is that, by definition, change consists in one and the same object having different properties at different times, not a succession of different things with different properties. As it stands, the objection is a bad one because it begs the question against perdurance theory. Any theory of persistence must account for ripening bananas, decaying books, and ageing people. But we cannot simply make the theoretical assumption that what we see around us are enduring objects with different properties at different times, rather than perduring objects, whose different temporal parts have different properties at different times.

In this passage,

1. *Hawley explains perdurantism as the view that an object is a single object that has different properties at different times or **stages** of its existence. An object changes just by having these different properties— the tree being leafless in the winter and leafy in the summer just is the tree's change.*
2. *Hawley uses the spatial analogy to explain perdurantism. As the road spread across space is the same road, despite being two-laned in some places and four-laned in other places, so a tree spread across time is the same tree, despite being leafy in the summer and leafless in the winter.*
3. *Hawley raises, and replies to, a common objection to perdurantism. The objection is that change does not exist on perdurantism. She thinks that this objection is **question begging**, which was a fallacy discussed in Chapter 1.5.4. We will look at this objection in some detail below.*

What might perdurantists say about the Ship of Theseus? The Ship of Theseus is seen as the four-dimensional object that has planks ABC during day one of its existence and planks ABD during another stage of its existence. The ship is the same ship on these two days because what we see on each day is merely two stages of the same four-dimensional object, with differing properties at these stages.

Objection 1: No Change

Perdurantism is introduced in order to answer how substances can remain constant through change, so it would be problematic if change does not exist on perdurantism. There are two ways that perdurantism fails to establish that change occurs. First, the substance is defined as a four-dimensional object that always has all of the properties it will ever have. So, the substance never really changes from one moment to the next. The tree in the winter is a leafy-at-times-leafless-at-times tree, and the tree in the summer is still a leafy-at-times-leafless-at-times tree as well, so it is always the same tree. Secondly, the differences with the substance actually remain constant in the different times of the substance's existence, so the same thing never transitions from being one way to being a different way. Rather, one moment where the substance's stage is one way is replaced by another moment where a different stage of the substance is another way, which is not change, but just difference. The winter tree is leafless, which is then replaced by the summer tree that is leafy, so it is never the case that the tree changes from being leafless to being leafy. On perdurantism change is like a painting that is white in one spot but red in another spot, but the same unaltered painting over all. It seems like real change only occurs if the artist paints over a white spot with a red spot; real change does not occur when we notice that one spot of the painting is red while another spot of the painting is white.

Objection 2: Presently Existing Objects

Perdurantism says that objects are never fully present at a time, but rather the same object is spread out across time. Both of these views lead to odd results. Consider the issue that an object is never fully present at a time. Consider the leafless tree in the winter. István points at it and asks: that tree in the backyard, does it have leaves? The answer should be: no, it doesn't have leaves, it is bare. But on perdurantism, the correct answer is: sometimes, since it is the tree that is leafy in the spring. Or again: Micah and Sareh are trying to have a baby, so Micah asks Sareh if she is ovulating. Sareh answers: sometimes. We care about the properties the object presently has, not the way the object is at different times. At the same time, for perdurantists an object that exists presently is also spread out over time. Imagine that twelve-year-old Rodney, who is a pleasant young boy, will commit a murder when he is 39. Is the twelve-year-old a morally blameworthy murderer? Intuitively, we think not. But on perdurantism, the twelve-year-old Rodney is, in part, a murderer. Or again: the eighteen-year-old Fatima falls in love with Mohammed, but they have a bad break up, and by age twenty she is madly in love with Ahmed. But there is, literally, still a part of her that loves Mohammed. Though she sincerely loves Ahmed, another part of Fatima is kissing Mohammed—a result that Ahmed will not be too happy with.

Summary

Substances are all around—the tree, the ship, the dog, the computer, the pen, the star, the amoeba, etc. ... So, it is important to understand the nature of substances, and whether they remain the same through changes. Numerous models answer these questions differently. The Milesian materialist says substances are changing matter, the Eleatic Idealist says substances are constant ideas, while Aristotle says substances are form-matter compounds that stay the same through change. Substratum theorists say substances are a bundle of properties in a substratum where the properties change but the substratum remains the same, where bundle theorists say substances are just bundles of properties that continuously change, but are combined in our minds into continuing objects. All of these views say that substances are three-dimensional objects that fully exist in the present moment, but perdurantists say that substances are four dimensional objects that retain the same bundle of past, present, and future properties at all times while having different properties during different moments. These models are not only helpful in understanding substances in general, but will also be helpful in understanding the nature of one particular substance we are all especially interested in understanding, namely, persons. This is the subject matter of the next chapter. In addition, the discussion between materialism and idealism will constantly re-emerge, as debates about the nature of persons, the mind, free will, and the existence of the universe, all boast of having models ranging from materialist to idealist, to both.

Key Terms in Chapter 3: Substances: Change and Sameness		
Ship of Theseus	Constancy	Hylomorphism
Substance	Zeno	Bare Substratum
Milesian Materialism	Paradox	David Hume
Material Matter	Paradox of Motion	Bundle Theory
Change	Parmenides	Identity of
Heraclitus	Ex Nihilo, Nihil Fit	Indiscernibles
Water	Form	Perdurantism
Fire	Reductio ad Absurdum	Four-Dimensional
Thales	Substratum	Object
Plato	Aristotle	Analogy
Eleatic Idealism	Subject-Predicate	Question Begging
Idealism	Language	Katherine Hawley
Idea	Properties	Stage

Philosophy on Television: Substances: Change and Sameness

McDonald's Commercial: Is It Still a Big Mac (2017)
In the McDonald's commercial where McDonald's introduces the new Big Mac with bacon on it, two actors argue over whether the new Bacon Big Mac is actually a Big Mac anymore. One actor says that the Bacon Big Mac is an "imposter," as it is not a Big Mac anymore. The other actor argues that it is still a Big Mac, since they only added bacon to it.

Only Fools and Horses: **Season 8, Episode 1: "Heroes and Villains" (1996)**
In this episode of the British comedy series *Only Fools and Horses*, Trigg, who is a street sweeper, explains that his broom has lasted twenty years. When quizzed about his broom, Trigg explains that he has replaced the handle fourteen times, and the head seventeen times. Trigg's friends tell him it cannot be the same broom anymore. Trigg disagrees.

Wall-E (2008)
In the animated movie *Wall-E*, a robot named Wall-E has replaced every one of its parts except its motherboard, though he still seems like the same robot. Toward the end of the movie, the motherboard of Wall-E is replaced as well, which resets his memory and personality, making it seem like he is not the same robot once all his parts are replaced. Finally, Wall-E receives a kiss from another robot, and he returns back to normal, suggesting it is possible for a robot to remain the same through change.

Ocean's 8 (2018)
In this heist movie, eight women plot to steal a priceless diamond necklace by replacing the necklace with an exact replica, so no one will know the original is gone. This is one of many heist movies, including *Ocean's 12* (2004) and *Octopussy* (1983), where thieves steal an object by replacing the original object with an exact copy.

Additional Resources

Visit this book's companion resources for additional materials, including video content and an automated tool for planning argumentative essays.

sites.broadviewpress.com/knowing/chapter-3

Chapter 4

Personal Identity

Teleportation

Stephon lives in Boston, but he wants to have lunch in Paris. Fortunately, since the year is 2300, he hops into the local teleporter in Boston and teleports to Paris to have lunch. This is how the teleportation machine works. Stephon steps into the teleporter in Boston, and a machine scans every particle in his body. When the teleporter operator presses 'Send,' every particle in Stephon's body in Boston is destroyed and an exact copy of Stephon's body materializes in Paris. Stephon steps out of the teleporter in Paris and carries on with his day. It is not the case that the original Stephon who lives in Boston is quickly beamed through space to Paris. Rather, the original Stephon is destroyed in Boston, and an exact copy is reconstituted in Paris. Is the Stephon who walks into the teleporter in Boston the same Stephon who walks out of the teleporter in Paris?

I s teleportation really possible? Yes, it is—but not of people (yet). In 2012, scientists in the Canary Islands teleported a single photon (i.e., one particle of light) over 100 kilometers.[1] How does this work? Scientists entangle two photons together, which means that the state of one photon A is connected to the state of another photon B such that whatever happens to A has an immediate effect on B. They then separate A from B as far away as they wish. A third photon C interacts with A in one location, and once this interaction occurs A is destroyed, but at the same time B takes on the nature of C in the distant location. This is similar to scanning a picture in one location, then printing out an exact copy of the picture in a different location.

Human teleportation would take the same form. Instead of one photon interacting with an entangled state such that the photon is destroyed in one location but reconstituted in a distant location, the billions of particles in a

---

1   Xiao-Song Ma et al., "Quantum Teleportation Over 143 Kilometres Using Active Feed-Forward," *Nature*, no. 489 (2012): 269–73.

human would have to be scanned, then interact with an extremely complex entangled state such that every particle in the human body would be simultaneously destroyed in one location while an exact copy would be reconstituted in a distant location. Needless to say, this type of technology is very far off, if it is even achievable at all. But the possibility raises difficult questions about personal identity. If Stephon teleports from Boston to Paris, which means that Stephon's body dissolves in Boston while an exact copy of Stephon materializes in Paris, is Stephon still the same person after teleporting? To answer this question, it is important to know what persons are made of, and whether persons can stay the same through change. We are going to ask these two questions in this chapter.

The question about whether the same person can last through change is often put in the technical terms of whether we are numerically the same despite being qualitatively different. A person has **numerical sameness** with themselves over time if they remain one and the same person over time. For example, Fred at age 3 may be numerically the same (i.e., one and the same person) as Fred at age 33, despite being older and taller and balder at age 33. Fred-at-3 does not have **qualitative sameness** with Fred-at-33, since he has different qualities or properties at these different times, namely, at 33 Fred is older, taller, and balder than he was at 3.

It is possible for two persons to be numerically distinct and qualitatively distinct: this young boy from Africa named Kwame is neither the same person as, nor resembles in any way, that old woman from Russia named Anna. It is possible for one person to be both numerically the same and qualitatively the same: Kwame at one moment is the same person, and has all the same properties as Kwame in the next immediate moment. It is possible for two persons to be numerically distinct but qualitatively (almost) the same: two newborn identical twins are different persons but have exactly the same properties. But our question is about whether it is possible for one person to be numerically the same but qualitatively different: can Anna as a young blonde cheerful girl be the same as Anna as an old grey bitter woman?

There are many different theories of personal identity, each of which answers the questions about 'what is a person?' and 'can the same person still persist through changes?' differently. These theories can be roughly depicted on the following visual spectrum:

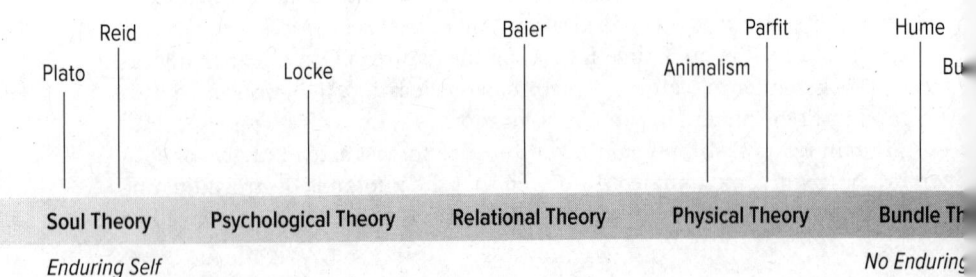

Spectrum 4: Personal Identity

4.1 Soul Theory

To understand the soul theory, first remember the puzzle of the Ship of Theseus: a ship has all of its planks replaced during a long journey, leaving us wondering whether the ship at the end of the journey is the same as the ship at the beginning of the journey. **Plato** responded to the problem by saying the ship has an ideal part (i.e., its essence or definition) and material parts (i.e., the wooden planks). The material planks of the ship change, but the essence of the ship, the idea of being a ship, remains the same. Plato has a similar view about persons. Our bodies are always changing. When we are babies we are ten pounds and tiny, but when we are twenty we are more than five feet tall and weigh over a hundred pounds. Our hair grows out, then we cut it, then it grows again. We grow fatter, or balder, or more wrinkled over time as well, sadly. The body replaces almost all of its cells—brain cells remain the same, while other cells replace themselves—every seven to ten years, so even if we don't look different, we still have largely different physical bodies.

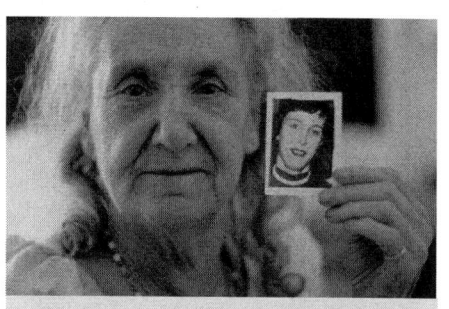

In the poem *For Anne Gregory*, William Butler Yeats writes: "Never shall a young man, thrown into despair, by those great honey-coloured ramparts at your ear, love you for yourself alone, and not your yellow hair."[2] The man falls for Anna's positive traits such as her golden hair and sense of humour. But people change: golden hair turns grey, so should the man no longer love Anne? Anne seems to want the man to love her for herself alone, rather than these passing traits. But this raises the question: does Anne have a 'self' that is independent of her physical and personality traits, so that she can be loved for herself alone? The soul theory of the person says yes.

But Plato says we also have an unchanging essence, a **soul**, which is not material and so does not change. What is the soul? When we speak of the "I," or "myself," or "me," we are talking about the soul. Or, when we refer to others using their name, we refer to their soul. Imagine that Juan says "I remember when Annette was a baby, but she's all grown up now!" Juan is noting that Annette's body changes from being small to big, but that "Annette" as her self or soul remains the same throughout her life. Here is how Plato describes it: "The soul is most like the divine, deathless, intelligible, uniform, indissoluble, always the same as itself, whereas the body is most like that which is human, mortal, multiform, unintelligible, soluble, and never consistently the same."[3] Where the body is always changing, the soul is something that remains constant throughout life. For Plato, the soul is most essentially the rational nature of humans, but also includes the emotional nature of humans. As we will see, a

---

2 William Butler Yeats, *The Collected Poems of W. B. Yeats*, ed. Richard J. Finneran (New York: MacMillan, 1991), 245.
3 Plato, *Phaedo* 80b, in *Readings in Ancient Greek Philosophy*, 288.

related definition of the soul as "**thinking being**," or "mind," where this points to the fact that humans think, feel, and have conscious experience more generally, will be expanded on later in history.

Diotima of Mantinea, a prophetess in ancient Greece, raises an objection to Plato's theory of an unchanging soul. She agrees with Plato that the body changes, but she adds that the soul changes as well:

> Though he is called the same, but he is always being renewed and in other respects passing away, in his hair and flesh and bones and blood and his entire body. And it's not just in his body, but in his soul, too, for none of his manners, customs, opinions, desires, pleasures, pains, or fears ever remains the same, but some are coming to be in him while others are passing away.[4]

When Faheema was five, she believed in Santa Claus, but as a twenty-year-old she no longer believes in Santa Claus. When she was four, she wanted to play with dolls and didn't want to play with boys, but now she has no interest in dolls but lots of interest in boys. When she was six her guiding ambition was to learn how to read, but now her ambition is to be a doctor. These are "soulish" changes. Her beliefs are different, her desires are different, her moral character is different, where beliefs, desires and character seem more likely to belong to the soul than the body. So, where Plato says the body changes but the soul stays the same, Diotima notices that the body changes and the soul changes as well, so the soul does not stay the same over time.

The soul theory is developed and refined by a number of philosophers, including René Descartes (1596–1650) and **Thomas Reid** (1710–96). We will consider Descartes' model of the soul as a thinking substance with conscious experience in Chapter 5.1, while focusing on Reid's model here. Reid provides a response to Diotima's objection. Reid agrees with Diotima that psychological or "soulish" traits such as our beliefs and desires change over time. But our beliefs and desires are not the soul itself; rather, beliefs and desires are *had* by the soul. Consider Faheema, who believed in Santa at age five, and does not believe in Santa at age twenty. Faheema's beliefs change from "believing in Santa" to "not believing in Santa." But the believer of those beliefs, Faheema herself, does not change, as the same Faheema is described as the subject of both beliefs. This is similar to the substratum theory of substances discussed in Chapter 3.3, where an underlying object remains the same throughout a process where the object gains or loses properties. In this case, the underlying subject is the soul, which is the thinker of thoughts, the believer of beliefs, and the feeler of feelings, or, more generally, the conscious observer that is observing all of these conscious states.

What reason is there to believe in an unchanging soul as a thinking being? Consider the eye. How do we know that we have eyes? We cannot see our own eyes (at least not without a mirror), but we know we have eyes because we can

---

4   Plato, *Symposium* 207e, in *Readings in Ancient Greek Philosophy*, 353–54.

see other things—if we did not have eyes, we could not see trees, but we can see trees, so we must have eyes. Similarly, how do we know that we are thinking beings? We do not observe ourselves as pure thinking substances, but we know we are thinking beings because we have thoughts and beliefs and feelings—if we were not thinkers we would not have thoughts, but we do have thoughts, so there is something that is thinking. Here is a sample of Thomas Reid's writings on personal identity:

Essays on the Intellectual Powers of Man (Thomas Reid, 1785)[5]

I see evidently that identity supposes an uninterrupted continuance of existence. That which has ceased to exist cannot be the same with that which afterwards begins to exist; for this would be to suppose a being to exist after it ceased to exist, and to have had existence before it was produced, which are manifest contradiction. Continued uninterrupted existence is therefore necessarily implied in identity. Hence we may infer, that identity cannot, in its proper sense, be applied to our pains, our pleasures, our thoughts, or any operation of our minds. The pain felt this day is not the same individual pain which I felt yesterday, though they may be similar in kind and degree, and have the same cause. The same can be said of every feeling, and of every operation of mind....

My personal identity, therefore, implies the continued existence of that indivisible thing which I call myself. Whatever this self may be, it is something which thinks, and deliberates, and resolves, and acts and suffers. I am not thought, I am not action, I am not feeling; I am something that thinks, and acts, and suffers. My thoughts, and actions, and feelings, change every moment; they have no continued, but a successive, existence; but that self, or I, to which they belong, is permanent, and has the same relation to all the succeeding thoughts, actions, and feelings which I call mine.

Such are the notions that I have of my personal identity. But perhaps it may be said, this may all be fancy without reality. How do you know, what evidence have you, that there is such a permanent self which has a claim to all the thoughts, actions, and feelings which you call yours? To this I answer, that the proper evidence I have of all this is remembrance. I remember that twenty years ago I conversed with such a person; I remember several things that passed in that conversation: my memory testifies, not only that this was done, but that it was done by me who now remember it. If it was

---

5   Thomas Reid, *Essays on the Intellectual Powers of Man* (1788), ed. J. Walker (Boston: Phillips, Sampson and Company: 1857), 3.3.1–2: 242–46.

done by me, I must have existed at that time, and continued to exist from that time to the present.

The identity of a person is a perfect identity: wherever it is real, it admits of no degrees; and it is impossible that a person should be in part the same, and in part different ... It may likewise be observed that the identity of objects of sense is never perfect. All bodies, as they consist of innumerable parts that may be disjoined from them by a great variety of causes, are subject to continual changes of their substance, increasing, diminishing, changing insensibly. When such alterations are gradual, because language could not afford a different name for every different state of such a changeable being, it retains the same name, and is considered as the same thing. Thus we say of an old regiment, that it did such a thing a century ago, though there now is not a man alive who then belonged to it. We say a tree is the same in the seed-bed and in the forest. A ship of war, which has successively changed her anchors, her tackle, her sail, her masts, her planks, and her timbers, while she keeps the same name, is the same.

The identity, therefore, which we ascribe to bodies, whether natural or artificial, is not perfect identity; it is rather something which, for the convenience of speech, we call identity.... questions about the identity of a body are very often questions about words. But identity, when applied to persons, has no ambiguity, and admits not of degrees, or of more and less. It is the foundation of all rights and obligations, and of all accountableness.

In this passage,

1. *Reid argues that while the beliefs and desires of a thinking being change over time, the thinking being itself does not change.*

2. *Reid says that memory attests to the unchanging nature of ourselves as thinking beings, as our memory reports that what happened many years ago happened to the same self that exists today, not some other, long gone self.*

3. *Reid introduces a distinction between **perfect identity** and **imperfect identity**. The person has perfect identity, which means that we call a person by the same name over time, and they really are the same thing over time. Every other object, including the body and ships and trees and stars, has imperfect identity, which means that we call these things the same name over time for the convenience of speech, but the objects themselves are not really the same thing since they have changed, and have no unchanging feature to them. For example, consider a podcast. A podcast is a digital broadcast downloaded to an iPod. As the iPod was replaced by smartphones, people started to download podcasts to their smartphones. Technically, these broadcasts are not podcasts anymore, since they are not listened to on an iPod, but we still call them podcasts since the name stuck. Likewise, the Ship of Theseus is*

> *called the same ship, since it would be cumbersome to rename the ship every time the ship changed a plank, but it is not really the same ship once a plank is removed. On this point Reid disagrees with Plato. Plato says many things—ships, trees, mice—really have an unchanging ideal essence, but Reid thinks these things do not really have an unchanging ideal essence, since they do not have souls. Rather, Reid says that only humans really have unchanging thinking souls.*

What might the soul theory say about teleportation? The teleporter scans all the particles in our bodies, and transmits this information to the new location and reconstitutes the exact same body. But the soul is not physical, since the material world changes but the soul does not. So, the teleporter would not be able to scan the soul, and would not be able to teleport the soul into the new body. The new body that walks out of the scanner in Paris would be a zombie. As we will discuss in Chapter 5.1, a zombie is an exact physical duplicate, but lacks consciousness. Since the zombie would not have a soul, and the person is defined as the soul, the zombie would not be a person, so would not be the same person.

Objection 1: Soul Switching

There are many movies where the soul of one person switches into the body of another person, and vice versa. Usually the personality traits and beliefs come with the soul. For example, in *The Change Up* (2011), the souls of two friends switch bodies. One friend, Dave, is a married man with a gentle disposition; the other friend, Mitch, is a sexually active bachelor who is more aggressive. When the soul of Mitch switches into Dave's body, Mitch brings his beliefs and aggression with him: he tells the children to fight back against bullies, and he pursues an aggressive business strategy. This movie supports the intuition that our "soul" includes our belief system, desires, and personality traits. But this intuition conflicts with the soul theory. On the soul theory, our beliefs, desires, and personality traits cannot be identical with our soul; after all, our beliefs, desires, and traits change but our soul does not.

This issue can be flipped around as well. Instead of imagining the case where the soul transfers into another body and the personality should come with it, imagine the case where the personality stays but the souls are switched. Imagine that Hien is an intelligent but quiet man with soul A, who goes to bed thinking about how to market fridges. While Hien is sleeping, God swaps his soul for soul B, but leaves all Hien's old memories, personality traits, and beliefs in place. Hien wakes up with the same quiet demeanour and continues to think about how to market fridges. But since his soul is different, and the person is defined as their soul, Hien is not the same person anymore. He goes to work and his colleagues all interact with him as normal, never knowing he is not the same person. Nobody, not even Hien, would have the slightest reason to think that he has been replaced.

Objection 2: Unobservable

Have you ever Googled yourself? Try it. Type your name into Google and see if you can find yourself. Most people have tried this. We are naturally curious about self-discovery, and Googling ourselves is just one recent method for doing so. A more traditional method of self-discovery is **introspection**, which amounts to searching within ourselves to come to a knowledge of ourselves (we will consider the process of introspection in greater depth in Chapter 9.1). According to the soul theory, every person is a soul, which is a thinking substance, a thinker of thoughts, a feeler of feelings, a doubter of doubts. If everyone is a soul, it should be possible for all of us to look inside ourselves and find it. Try it for yourself. Can you find your soul? After self-reflection, you may stumble upon an overt or buried emotion of anger, or a long-lost memory of a difficult time, or realize that you believe differently about your friend than you thought you did. But, do you find your soul? Do you find pure self-consciousness, just a bare "I," lurking behind all of these memories, beliefs, and emotions? As we saw earlier, something that *has* characteristics but which itself is without any characteristics may not be sensed—even by an internal sense.

4.2 Bundle Theory

David Hume famously takes up the challenge of introspecting himself, in hopes of coming into contact with this unchanging thinking self. He reports back that he is unable to find an unchanging thinking self. Whenever Hume enters into himself, he only finds percepts of hot or cold, memories that are happy or sad, beliefs that are old or surprising, but he never finds the bare 'I,' the unchanging thinking self. Hume concludes: "When I enter most intimately into what I call myself, I always stumble on some particular perception or other ... I never can catch myself at any time without a perception, and never can observe anything but the perception."[6] He concludes that the unchanging thinking self cannot be observed, so we have no justification for thinking it exists.

But if the unchanging thinking self does not exist, what is left of the self? Does the self even exist? It is helpful to remember Hume's bundle theory of substance. Hume rejects the view that objects have an unobservable substratum, and instead concludes that objects *are* their bundle of properties. Similarly, while the self does not have an unchanging thinking substance underlying all of its memories, perceptions, and beliefs, the self *is* a **bundle of perceptions**, including memories, beliefs, and experiences. You, as yourself, are the sum of all your experiences, past and present. When you introspect in an attempt to find yourself, and you find a hidden memory or repressed feeling, or become aware of your beating heart, that is you, you are the hidden memory, you are the

---

6   David Hume, *A Treatise of Human Nature*, Book 1.4.6.

repressed feeling, you are the perception of your beating heart. For Hume, the self does exist, the self just is not an unchanging thinking being, but rather the self is a bundle of perceptions which come and go—and change.

To understand Hume's bundle theory of the self, it is helpful to introduce some terms. First, **reduction** of some thing A occurs when A is actually some simpler or more basic thing B. When Thales said the four material elements (earth, air, water, fire) are ultimately all just water, he was reducing the four material elements to one simpler and more basic entity, namely, water. There are two types of reductionism. First, **conservative reductionism** is the view that a thing A gets reduced to a thing B, which means that A is B, or A turns out to be B, but which still accepts that A exists. Some examples: water is H_2O means that water reduces to H_2O, but water still exists as H_2O, so the existence of water is conserved in the reduction. Lightning is conservatively reduced to an electrical discharge. Does lightning still exist? Yes, so the existence of lightning is conserved in the reduction. But lightning is redefined as just electrical discharge; there is nothing more to lightning than electrical discharge.

Ludwig Wittgenstein says, "the strength of the thread does not reside in the fact that some one fibre runs through its whole length, but in the overlapping of many fibres."[7] For Hume, the self is like a rope which does not have one continuous thread running through it, but is an overlapping of many beliefs and experiences. The rope still exists, it just is a bundle of strands closely tied together. Likewise, the self still exists, it just is the bundle of perceptions closely tied together.

Sometimes conservative reduction fails to work. For example, recall Faheema, the five-year old girl who believes in Santa Claus. Every year she waits with excitement for Santa to sled to her house. But when she turns six, she hears a nasty rumour that Santa may not be real! She investigates the situation and discovers that her mother and father actually place presents under the tree. She is heartbroken for a moment, but then she gets an idea. Maybe she can conservatively reduce Santa to her parents. Santa just *is* her parents, Santa's sled just *is* her parents' minivan, and the North Pole just *is* the toy store. Santa Claus exists after all! Faheema is clever, but wrong. It is not possible to conservatively reduce Santa to her parents, since Santa is too different in nature from her parents, so it is not possible for Santa to be identical with her parents.

This leads to the second type of reductionism, **eliminative reductionism**, which is the view that a thing A gets reduced to a thing B, which means that A is really B, but A does not still exist, only B exists. A is eliminated rather than

---

7 Ludwig Wittgenstein, *Philosophical Investigations*, trans. G.E.M. Anscombe (Oxford: Basil Blackwell, 1958), 67.

conserved. Santa Claus is eliminatively reduced to Faheema's parents: Santa doesn't exist, and never did exist, only Faheema's parents exist. The witch's magical potion is eliminatively reduced to a sloppy soup of strange natural ingredients, there is no magical potion, there is just a sloppy soup consisting of muddy water, frog legs, and fur from a baby fox.

Sometimes neither conservative reductionism nor eliminative reductionism works. For example, most scientists endorse anthropogenic climate change, or the view that humans make a contribution to the changing climate of the planet. Some attempt to eliminatively reduce *anthropogenic* climate change: there is no human-made climate change, they say, the phenomenon does not exist. Others attempt to conservatively reduce anthropogenic climate change: climate change exists, but it just is the naturally occurring climate processes of the Earth, there is no distinct human-made contribution to climate change. Most scientists disagree with these claims. They say that there are two distinct phenomena: naturally occurring changes to the climate, and also a human-made contribution to climate change, and the one cannot be reduced to the other.

Even though Hume means different things by 'the self' at different times, he avoids committing the **fallacy of equivocation** discussed in Chapter 1.5.4. When Hume says 'the self doesn't exist,' he means the self as a simple, unchanging thinker doesn't exist. When Hume says 'the self exists,' he has first re-defined the self as a bundle of perceptions, and this bundle of perceptions does exist.

This leads to the third term, **non-reductionism**, which is the view that A exists as a distinct thing from B, both A and B exist, but A is not identical with B: there are two things. Anthropogenic climate change is non-reducible to naturally occurring climate change, as there are two distinct phenomena, both naturally occurring climate change and the human-made contribution to climate change. Gold is not reducible to pyrite (i.e., fool's gold); there are two different phenomena, though some get confused into thinking that fool's gold is gold. Other examples of eliminative reductionism, conservative reductionism, and non-reductionism will be discussed in Chapter 5.2 and 5.4, and Chapter 7.5.

These three terms are helpful in contrasting Hume's view of the self with Reid's view of the self. Reid is a non-reductionist about the self: the self exists as an unchanging thinking substance, as distinct from the memories, beliefs and emotions of the self. Hume is a conservative reductionist about the self: the self still exists, but the self just is a bundle of memories, beliefs, and emotions. Here is a passage where David Hume presents the bundle theory of the self:

A Treatise of Human Nature (David Hume, 1739)[8]

There are some philosophers who imagine we are every moment intimately conscious of what we call our Self; that we feel its existence and its continuance in existence; and are certain, beyond the evidence of a demonstration, both of its perfect identity and simplicity ... For from what impression could this idea be derived? This question it is impossible to answer without a manifest contradiction and absurdity; and yet it is a question, which must necessarily be answered, if we would have the idea of self pass for clear and intelligible, it must be some one impression, that gives rise to every real idea. But self or person is not any one impression, but that to which our several impressions and ideas are supposed to have a reference. If any impression gives rise to the idea of self, that impression must continue invariably the same, through the whole course of our lives; since self is supposed to exist after that manner. But there is no impression constant and invariable. Pain and pleasure, grief and joy, passions and sensations succeed each other, and never all exist at the same time. It cannot, therefore, be from any of these impressions, or from any other, that the idea of self is derived; and consequently there is no such idea.

But farther, what must become of all our particular perceptions upon this hypothesis? All these are different, and distinguishable, and separable from each other, and may be separately considered, and may exist separately, and have no deed of tiny thing to support their existence. After what manner, therefore, do they belong to self; and how are they connected with it? For my part, when I enter most intimately into what I call myself, I always stumble on some particular perception or other, of heat or cold, light or shade, love or hatred, pain or pleasure. I never can catch myself at any time without a perception, and never can observe anything but the perception. When my perceptions are removed for any time, as by sound sleep; so long am I insensible of myself, and may truly be said not to exist. And were all my perceptions removed by death, and could I neither think, nor feel, nor see, nor love, nor hate after the dissolution of my body, I should be entirely annihilated, nor do I conceive what is farther requisite to make me a perfect non-entity. If anyone, upon serious and unprejudiced reflection thinks he has a different notion of himself, I must confess I call reason no longer with him. All I can allow him is, that he may be in the right as well as I, and that we are essentially different in this particular. He may, perhaps, perceive something simple and continued, which he calls himself; though I am certain there is no such principle in me.

But setting aside some metaphysicians of this kind, I may venture to affirm of the rest of mankind, that they are nothing but a bundle or collection of different perceptions, which succeed each other with an

---

8 David Hume, *A Treatise of Human Nature*, Book 1.4.6 (London: John Noon, 1739).

inconceivable rapidity, and are in a perpetual flux and movement. Our eyes cannot turn in their sockets without varying our perceptions. Our thought is still more variable than our sight; and all our other senses and faculties contribute to this change; nor is there any single power of the soul, which remains unalterably the same, perhaps for one moment. The mind is a kind of theatre, where several perceptions successively make their appearance; pass, re-pass, glide away, and mingle in an infinite variety of postures and situations. There is properly no simplicity in it at one time, nor identity in different; whatever natural propension we may have to imagine that simplicity and identity. The comparison of the theatre must not mislead us. They are the successive perceptions only, that constitute the mind; nor have we the most distant notion of the place, where these scenes are represented, or of the materials, of which it is composed....

We now proceed to explain the nature of personal identity, which has become so great a question in philosophy, especially of late years in England, where all the abstruser sciences are studied with a peculiar ardour and application. And here it is evident, the same method of reasoning must be continued which has so successfully explained the identity of plants, and animals, and ships, and houses, and of all the compounded and changeable productions either of art or nature. The identity, which we ascribe to the mind of man, is only a fictitious one, and of a like kind with that which we ascribe to vegetables and animal bodies. It cannot, therefore, have a different origin, but must proceed from a like operation of the imagination upon like objects.

In this passage,

1. *Hume argues that an unchanging thinking substance is not observed upon introspection, so we have no justification for believing in an unchanging thinking substance.*
2. *Hume argues that when we look for an unchanging "self" all we find is a bundle of perceptions. Since these perceptions rapidly pass by, and each perception seems to cause the next perception to arise, we imagine a constant identity to the self, but such a constant identity is a fiction of the imagination. Hume connects this bundle theory of the self with his bundle theory of substances in general: as we imagine an unchanging Ship of Theseus, although there is no unchanging Ship of Theseus, so we imagine an unchanging self, but there is no unchanging self.*
3. *Hume argues that the self still exists, but he just defines the self as the bundle of perceptions, not as an unchanging thinking substance.*

What might Hume say about teleportation? For Hume, the self is a bundle of perceptions, memories, beliefs, and feelings. Stephon, at the moment of materializing in Paris, will have all of these same memories, beliefs, and perceptions, continuing those left off before his dissolution by Stephon in Boston; so Stephon remains the same person. There is no soul serving as a substratum to distinguish the self who goes into the teleporter with the self who comes out of the teleporter. As soon as Stephon looks around at the scenery in Paris or tastes lunch, new perceptions are added to Stephon's bundle of perceptions, making him mostly, but not exactly, the same person he was prior to teleportation.

Hume's bundle theory of the self has some similarities with the Buddhist doctrine of **anatman**, or not-self. According to Buddhist teaching, humans tend to crave and cling to impermanent or changing things, but these impermanent things cannot satisfy us, as they are impermanent. If we stop craving impermanent things, we will achieve peace. For example, we crave the summer day, but it passes away into winter, leaving us unsatisfied until we no longer crave that which cannot last. We crave health, but it passes away into sickness, leaving us unsatisfied until we accept that health and life pass away. We crave a shiny new car, but it rusts away, leaving us unsatisfied until we let go of our desire for shiny cars. We also crave a permanent self or soul, but the self is also impermanent. Our momentary perceptions come and go; a happy moment enjoying supper passes by and turns into frustration at having to clean the dishes. Clinging to the hope that we are an unchanging soul, or clinging to experiences that pass away, leave us unsatisfied as well. If we stop clinging to the idea that an unchanging self exists, or stop clinging to passing experiences as if they were our own, we will achieve peace. This is the doctrine of anatman, which suggests not only that we do not have a constant self, but that we should stop identifying the stream of passing mental experiences that occur with our selves. Here is how the **Buddha** explains this doctrine to a monk:

Majjhima Nikaya 109: The Greater Discourse on the Full-moon Night (attributed to Buddha, 3rd Century BCE)[9]

Bhikkhu: "But, venerable sir, how does personality view not come to be?"

Buddha: "Here, bhikkhu, a well-taught noble disciple, who has regard for noble ones and is skilled and disciplined in their Dhamma, who has regard for true men and is skilled and disciplined in their Dhamma, does not regard material form as self, or self as possessed of material form, or material form as in self, or self as in material form. He does not regard feeling as self ... perception as self ... formations as self ... consciousness as self, or self as possessed of consciousness, or consciousness as in self, or self as in consciousness. That is how personality view does not come to be."

---

9   http://www.suttas.com/mn-109-mahapunnama-sutta-the-greater-discourse-on-the-full-moon-night.html.

Bhikkhu: "What, venerable sir, is the gratification, what is the danger, and what is the escape in the case of material form? What is the gratification, what is the danger, and what is the escape in the case of feeling ... in the case of perception ... in the case of formations ... in the case of consciousness?"

Buddha: "The pleasure and joy, bhikkhu, that arise in dependence on material form—this is the gratification in the case of material form. Material form is impermanent, suffering, and subject to change—this is the danger in the case of material form. The removal of desire and lust, the abandonment of desire and lust for material form—this is the escape in the case of material form. The pleasure and joy that arise in dependence on feeling ... in dependence on perception ... in dependence on formations ... in dependence on consciousness—this is the gratification in the case of consciousness. Consciousness is impermanent, suffering, and subject to change—this is the danger in the case of consciousness. The removal of desire and lust, the abandonment of desire and lust for consciousness—this is the escape in the case of consciousness."

Bhikkhu: "Venerable sir, how does one know, how does one see, so that in regard to this body with its consciousness and all external signs, there is no I-making, mine-making, and underlying tendency to conceit?"

Buddha: "Bhikkhu, any land of material form whatever, whether past or present, internal or external, gross or subtle, inferior or superior, far or near—one sees all material form as it actually is with proper wisdom thus: 'This is not mine, this I am not, this is not my self.' Any kind of feeling whatever ... Any land of perception whatever ... Any kind of formations whatever ... Any kind of consciousness whatever ... one sees all consciousness as it actually is with proper wisdom thus: 'This is not mine, this I am not, this is not my self.' It is when one knows and sees thus that in regard to this body with its consciousness and all external signs there is no I-making, mine-making, or underlying tendency to conceit."

Then, in the mind of a certain bhikkhu this thought arose: "So, it seems, material form is not self, feeling is not self, perception is not self, formations are not self, consciousness is not self. What self, then, will actions done by the non-self affect?"

In this passage,
1. *The Buddha argues that what we normally call the "self" is composed of several parts, including material body, feeling, perceiving, and consciousness, each of which is impermanent. So, the self is impermanent.*

2. *The Buddha argues that we normally claim that these passing feelings or perceptions are our selves, but these passing feelings and perceptions are not ourselves. The Buddha is close to an eliminative reductionist about the self. Not only does the self not exist as an unchanging soul, but there is some suggestion that the passing perceptions are not the self either. Hence, while the Buddha's teachings are similar to Hume's bundle theory in the sense that an unchanging self does not exist, the Buddha is closer to the far-right side of the spectrum, indicating that he is closer to rejecting the existence of the self entirely.*

Objection 1: Personal, United Perceptions

For Hume, the self is a bundle of perceptions that come and go: a blue experience occurs, a grey experience occurs, a belief that it will rain occurs, an anger at the thought of rain occurs, a decision to fetch an umbrella occurs, etc. These perceptions are all distinct and separate perceptions that occur immediately after each other on the bundle theory. But perceptions are experienced as personal. It is not just free-floating anger that occurs, it is not Prabjyot or Rageesh that is angry, it is *me* that is angry—I feel it, they don't, so this is my anger percept. This suggests there is not only an anger that occurs, but a person or subject that the anger happens to. Percepts appear to be united together as well. It is not just a blue experience and a grey experience, but the mind blends these experiences together with pre-established concepts such as clouds, sky, and rain, into one united visual experience of a sky with rain clouds in it.

Immanuel Kant (1724–1804) appeals to these two kinds of unification when he famously raises this objection to David Hume: "If a multiplicity of representations are to form a single representation, they must be contained in the absolute unity of the thinking subject."[10] Kant uses the example of a single thought, say, my anger at the prospect that it might rain. If there is no united self, then each word in this thought is separate, and there is no complete thought. But there is a single complete thought: my anger is of the prospect that it may rain, the prospect that it may rain contains the concept of rain within it, which was learned years ago, and also depends on the visual experience of grey clouds in the sky, which integrates the grey and blue perceptions together to form the complex perceptual experience of a cloudy sky.

Objection 2: Personal Responsibility

On the bundle theory, we may not be the same person over the course of our lives. Five years ago, Frida was bundle of perceptions ABC, but now she is bundle of perceptions AFG. Since bundle ABC is not the same as bundle AFG, Frida from

---

10 Immanuel Kant, *The Critique of Pure Reason* (1787), trans. N. Smith (Hampshire, UK: Palgrave Macmillan: 2007), A352.

five years ago may not be the same person as Frida today. This is an unsatisfying result, since we typically think our memories are of our own selves from ten years ago, or the vows we made ten years ago still apply to the self that exists today, or the retirement savings we bank up today will be enjoyed by ourselves in thirty years. This issue becomes especially problematic when considering the nature of personal **responsibility**. As we will discuss in Chapters 5.1 and 6.1, a person is not normally considered responsible for things they do not do. Rubin murders an eight-year-old boy, but Damien is charged and imprisoned. This is unjust: Rubin committed the murder, so he should be held responsible, while Damien did not commit the murder, so he should not be held responsible. But now imagine that Rubin murders an eight-year-old boy, but he isn't caught. Twenty years later new DNA evidence proves that Rubin committed the murder. When the police come to arrest him, Rubin protests: "I'm a different man now, do not punish me for something that someone else did twenty years ago!" Our moral and legal intuitions lead us to putting Rubin in jail twenty years later, but if he is literally not the same person anymore, we should not put him in jail.

4.3 Psychological Theory

The problem with the soul theory is that the person is an unobservable soul that can be substituted out while switching the old memories and psychological states into the new soul. The problem with the bundle theory is that there may be no unchanging person that persists across time and is responsible for prior actions. Perhaps these problems are solved by endorsing the **psychological theory**, according to which persons persist across time by maintaining the same psychological traits. But, which traits? Can you think of any beliefs or desires that have remained the same throughout your entire life? Perhaps you have always desired to survive, or perhaps you have always believed your parents love you, or that you have a nose. But even if these desires and beliefs remain constant, is this really the essence of your personal identity? The belief that we have a nose, or our survival instinct, does not seem to form the core of our selfhood. Perhaps our moral values, which seem more central to our self-identity, must remain constant over time in order to remain the same person. Viktor has always been a faithful husband and father, but in a midlife crisis he abandons his family. His change is so drastic and central to his identity that his wife will justifiably ask, "Who are you anymore?" But our moral values were not with us as children, and people do convert into different ways of life while retaining the same sense of self-hood, so continuation of our moral values does not seem to be the essential psychological trait to establishing sameness of self.

Many psychological theorists believe that **memory** is the key psychological trait. If Jennie today remembers some thing Jennie did ten years ago, then the Jennie of today is the same person as the Jennie from ten years ago. After all, no one else has this memory of what Jennie did ten years ago, so why would Jennie have this memory if it wasn't her that was there? This memory criterion for personal identity solves the problems with the soul theory. Memory is observable—we can recall what happened in earlier stages of life, and no one doubts we have memories. It also handles the issue of soul switching. Recall the situation that occurs in the movie *The Change Up*. Dave the gentle married man goes to bed at night and wakes up in the body of his bachelor friend Mitch. All of Dave's memories come with him—he remembers going to bed in the bed of Dave, he remembers kissing the wife of Dave goodnight, but now he wakes up in the body of Mitch. Is it Dave or Mitch that is in the body of Mitch? Most agree that the person in the body of Mitch is Dave, because Dave continues to remember Dave's old life. The memory criterion of personal identity also solves the problems facing the bundle theory. On the memory view, even though Faheema changes her beliefs about Santa and feelings about boys over many years, she still remembers when she believed in Santa, so she is the same person. Since she is the same person, she is still presently responsible for keeping the promise she remembers making to her mother about finishing university. Here is an excerpt from the most famous proponent of this memory view of personal identity, the English philosopher **John Locke** (1632–1704).

An Essay Concerning Human Understanding (John Locke, 1689)[11]

4. ... if two or more atoms be joined together into the same mass, every one of those atoms will be the same, by the foregoing rule: and whilst they exist united together, the mass, consisting of the same atoms, must be the same mass, or the same body, let the parts be ever so differently jumbled. But if one of these atoms be taken away, or one new one added, it is no longer the same mass or the same body. In the state of living creatures, their identity depends not on a mass of the same particles, but on something else. For in them the variation of great parcels of matters alters not the identity: an oak growing from a plant to a great tree, and then lopped, is still the same oak; and a colt grown up to a horse, sometimes fat, sometimes lean, is all the while the same horse ...

7. This also shows wherein the identity of the same man consists; viz. in nothing but a participation of the same continued life, by constantly fleeting particles of matter, in succession vitally united to the same organized body. He that shall place the identity of man in anything else, but, like that of other animals, in one fitly organized body, taken in any one instant, and from thence continued, under one organization of life, in several successively fleeting particles of matter united to it, will find it hard to make an embryo, one of years, mad and sober, the same man, by any

---

11   John Locke, *An Essay Concerning Human Understanding*, 2.27.

supposition, that will not make it possible for Seth, Ismael, Socrates, Pilate, St. Austin, and Caesar Borgia, to be the same man ...

8. It is not therefore unity of substance that comprehends all sorts of identity, or will determine it in every case; but to conceive and judge of it aright, we must consider what idea the word it is applied to stands for: it being one thing to be the same substance, another the same man, and a third the same person, if person, man, and substance, are three names standing for three different ideas;—for such as is the idea belonging to that name, such must be the identity; which, if it had been a little more carefully attended to, would possibly have prevented a great deal of that confusion which often occurs about this matter, with no small seeming difficulties, especially concerning personal identity, which therefore we shall in the next place a little consider ...

11. This being premised, to find wherein personal identity consists, we must consider what person stands for;—which, I think, is a thinking intelligent being, that has reason and reflection, and can consider itself as itself, the same thinking thing, in different times and places; which it does only by that consciousness which is inseparable from thinking, and, as it seems to me, essential to it: it being impossible for any one to perceive without perceiving that he does perceive. When we see, hear, smell, taste, feel, meditate, or will anything, we know that we do so. Thus it is always as to our present sensations and perceptions: and by this every one is to himself that which he calls self:—it not being considered, in this case, whether the same self be continued in the same or diverse substances. For, since consciousness always accompanies thinking, and it is that which makes every one to be what he calls self, and thereby distinguishes himself from all other thinking things, in this alone consists personal identity, i.e., the sameness of a rational being: and as far as this consciousness can be extended backwards to any past action or thought, so far reaches the identity of that person; it is the same self now it was then; and it is by the same self with this present one that now reflects on it, that that action was done.

12. ... For as far as any intelligent being can repeat the idea of any past action with the same consciousness it had of it at first, and with the same consciousness it has of any present action; so far it is the same personal self. For it is by the consciousness it has of its present thoughts and actions, that it is self to itself now, and so will be the same self, as far as the same consciousness can extend to actions past or to come; and would be by distance of time, or change of substance, no more two persons, than a man be two men by wearing other clothes to-day than he did yesterday, with a long or a short sleep between: the same consciousness uniting those distant actions into the same person, whatever substances contributed to their production....

In this passage,

1. *Locke distinguishes between four different parts of someone. First, the body, where someone has the same body only if every particle remains the same. As soon as I pluck one hair from my body, my body is different. This is true of all physical objects: remove one particle from a rock, and it is not the same rock. Second, the humanity, where someone is the same biological human animal if they participate in the same organized life while it grows and changes. This is true of every living thing: a tree is the same tree if it continues to participate in the same life while it grows and changes. Third, the substance, where someone may be the same thinking substance (i.e., soul or substratum) over time, but this is not the person. Remember Locke thinks a bare substratum exists, so while the thinking substance exists, it has no qualities or personhood. Lastly, the person, which includes present consciousness and stretches back via memory to any earlier conscious experience. Persons alone, according to Locke, have consciousness.*
2. *Locke says that* personal *identity is related to the personhood of someone. Hence, as long as I am conscious, I am a person, and as much as I can remember, so far the same person extends. Having the same life does not amount to being the same person, nor does having the same substance amount to being the same person.*

What would Locke say about teleportation? Assuming that Stephon who materializes in Paris remembers getting into the teleporter in Boston, and remembers doing so because he wants lunch in Paris, then Stephon remains the same person through the teleportation process, even though he now inhabits a different body with a different life.

Objection 1: Forgetfulness

We forget things all the time. As one extreme example, in the movie *The Hangover* (2009), four friends are drugged and have a wild night of partying. The next morning, they remember nothing that happened. They slowly realize they did a lot of crazy things—one gets married to a stripper, they steal a police cruiser, they take a tiger from a boxer, and kidnap a gangster, among other things.

What is the largest organism on Earth? No, it's not a whale. It's a mushroom in Michigan. The main body of a mushroom is its very thin filaments which spread out underground (and occasionally produce the above-ground umbrella-shaped fruiting bodies we're familiar with). This giant mushroom, it's suspected, has spread its tendrils over much of Michigan. The catch is, however, that if a part of that network of filaments is detached from the main body, it still grows and is genetically identical to the rest. Do you think these detached filaments should be considered the same organism as the main body of the mushroom?

A peculiarity of the law is that if a person committed a crime, but later had genuine amnesia, so that the person later inhabiting that body genuinely remembers nothing of the crime, then that later person is not guilty. Does this sound right to you?

They don't remember anything, so they are constantly surprised at what they supposedly did: "I wouldn't do this! I didn't do this! It wasn't me!" Less outrageously, we cannot remember anything from when we were three years old, and we cannot remember uneventful moments from last month anymore either. On Locke's view, the same personhood only extends back to moments we remember. But memory does not extend back to those forgotten moments, so we are not the same person who lived those moments.

During his wild night of partying in *The Hangover*, Stu marries a stripper. When he wakes up, he doesn't remember doing this, so according to Locke he is not the person who married the stripper. Since we are only responsible for things we do, and Stu is not the person who married the stripper, he is not obligated to fulfill his wedding vows. Does this sound right? Locke imagines the case of a sleepwalking Socrates who stabs someone while sleepwalking, but he doesn't remember doing this, so it was not him that did it—should we hold him responsible?

Objection: The Brave Officer

Thomas Reid argues that Locke's memory criterion violates the **transitivity of identity**. The transitivity of identity says: if A is B, and B is C, then A is C. Detroit is the largest city in Michigan; The largest city in Michigan is the home of the Tigers baseball team; so Detroit is the home of the Tigers baseball team. This is logically valid deductive reasoning, so any theory that violates the view that identity relations are transitive is problematic. Now Reid asks us to imagine a **brave officer** that was flogged as a schoolboy and took a battle flag from the enemy as a soldier and was promoted to general late in life. When promoted to general, he remembers taking the battle flag as a soldier. At the time he took the battle flag, he remembered being flogged as a child. But, when promoted to general, he no longer remembers being flogged as a child. On Locke's view, the general is not the same person as the flogged boy, since the general does not remember being flogged. But, according to the transitivity of identity, the general is the same person as the flogged boy, since the general is the same as the soldier, and the soldier is the same as the flogged boy. Reid explains the problem: "the general is, and at the same time is not the same person as him who was flogged at school."[12]

---

12 Thomas Reid, *Essays on the Intellectual Powers of Man*, 249.

4.4 Brute Physical Theory

Locke's writings reveal two other possible models of personal identity, both of which are considered **brute physical theories** of personal identity. Though he does not endorse them as conditions of personal identity, numerous philosophers do. Brute physical theories locate personal identity, and the persistence of our personal identity, in bodily states. The first brute physical theory is based on Locke's condition for remaining the same *human* over time. Locke uses the term 'human' as a biological term that deals with our living human animality. We remain the same human if we participate in the same life over time. The doctrine of **animalism** takes this biological condition on humanity and applies it to personhood: we are the same person over time if we have the same life over time.

The second brute physical theory is more closely aligned with Locke's bodily criterion of identity. For Locke, we are the same body over time if we possess all the same atoms over time. Some brute physical theories of personal identity emphasize a **bodily theory** of personal identity, where we are the same person at different times if we have the same body. Others emphasize the **brain theory** of personal identity, where we are the same person at different times if we have the same brain.

Consider the following thought experiment. Imagine that Sylvia is near death from a brain disease, and Enrico's brain, the only part of his body that's not diseased, is transplanted into Sylvia's body. Is it Sylvia or Enrico that wakes up from the surgery? The brain theorist will say that it is Enrico, since personal identity is connected to the brain. This makes some sense, as the memories and personality traits will still be from Enrico. The bodily theorist will say that it is Sylvia, since personal identity is connected to the body. This also makes some sense, as the gymnastic ability will still be from Sylvia, and she will look exactly the same as she always has looked.

Derek Parfit (1942–2017) provides another thought experiment that helps to sort out the bodily theory from the brain theory. Here is the **brain fission** thought experiment: imagine you undergo a surgery where your brain is carefully split into two, and the surgeon places one half of your brain in some other body A and another half of your brain in another body B. Body A and body B are wakened, and they each have some of your memories and some of your personality. Parfit asks "What happens to me?" before answering, "There seem only three possibilities: (1) I do not survive; (2) I survive as one of the two people; (3) I survive as both."[13] Parfit says that (2) fails, because if the person in body A has a claim to be me, and the same thing happened with body B, namely, half of my brain was put in it, then the person in body B has an equal claim to be me as well. Perhaps (3) is true, I survive as both persons. But before the surgery I was one person, now I am two persons. One person cannot be two persons, so

---

13 Derek Parfit, "Personal Identity," *The Philosophical Review* 80, no. 1 (1971): 3–27, 5.

(3) fails. (1) fails in some way, as body A and body B are clearly alive and have some of my personality and memories, so it seems I survive. But at the same time (1) is true in some way, as body A and body B are disconnected from each other in a way I wasn't before, and there are two of them when there was one of me, and my old body is lying dead in the laboratory, so I do not survive. The result: my personal identity does not persist into these two bodies, but I have an extremely intimate relation with these two bodies that survive me. They are my descendants, they are my later selves, since they retain some memories and personality but are not identical to me.

Returning to the teleporter, imagine there is a teleporter malfunction, and Stephon is reconstituted in Paris, but not destroyed back in Boston, so now there are two people named Stephon. Which is the real Stephon? Can we say both? If not, which one is Stephon?

Brute physical theories, either as animalism or as the body/brain theory, solve several of the problems facing Locke's memory theory. First, the memory theory does not satisfy our intuition that we are the same person as the infant who learned how to walk many years ago. While we do not remember learning to walk, we have the same life, the same body, and/or the same brain as the walking infant, so we are the same person on brute physical theories. The forgetful criminal problem finds a new solution as well. While Yennsy does not remember getting into a fight last night while drunk, he is still the same life, he still has the same body, and/or he still has the same brain as when he brawled last night, so he is the same person, so he is responsible for his unruly behaviour.

Objection 1: Body Switching

In *The Change Up*, the personality, memories, and consciousness of Mitch enter into the body of Dave, while Mitch's body is left behind—his whole body, brain included—which now begin to exhibit Dave's personality, memories, and consciousness. Where is Mitch the person now? Seemingly, Mitch the person is with his personality, memories, and consciousness in Dave's body, and these psychological traits are central to Dave the person. But brute physical theories say that Mitch the person is still with the body of Mitch. The same issue arises in the case of teleportation. Stephon leaves his body behind in Boston; his original body, brain, and the organic life of his original body are destroyed in the teleportation. Although his personality, memory, and consciousness carry on in the new body that materializes in Paris, this is not Stephon, since Stephon is technically dead. Since Stephon persists for so long as his body, life, or brain persists, and all of these are destroyed in the teleportation event, Stephon is destroyed.

Objection 2: Changing Bodies

Brute physical theories assume that our bodies or brains remain the same over time. You look roughly the same as you did one year ago, so you possess the same body. Your body has not been disassembled lately, nor does it suddenly look like some other body, so you seem to be the same body over time. But our bodies are constantly changing. For Locke, as soon as we pluck one hair out, we are not the same body anymore. Most of our cells replace themselves every seven to ten years, we grow taller and older. If our personal identity persists for as long as our bodies persist, but our bodies are prone to change, then we may not be the same person as when we were young. When we were two years old, our bodies were pudgy and short and thirty pounds—is this really the same body that we currently possess? If not, then brute physical theories may not be able to establish persistence over time.

4.5 The Relational Self

While there are substantial disagreements between all of the theories advanced thus far, they all agree on one thing. Namely, they agree that some component internal to the person is the source of personhood and is what establishes persistence over time. The soul theory thinks each person has their own soul that remains the same over time. Psychological theories think each person has their own memories or personality or beliefs that remain the same over time. Bundle theorists think each person has their own bundle of perceptions that defines the person. Bodily theories think each person has their own life or body or brain, which remains the same over time. But there is also a relational component to each person, which means that each person is shaped, defined by, and persists in relation to others as well; this is the relational self.

Consider the Ship of Theseus once again: does it remain the same ship despite its changing planks? Here is a possibility we did not consider. Perhaps the ship is the same because it has the same crew during the voyage? Perhaps the ship is the same because it still belongs to Theseus for the entire journey? Perhaps the ship is the same because everyone agrees to call it the same ship, and everyone still agrees to use the word 'ship' to describe the object? These answers point to the relationship that the ship has to others. While the crew is not technically part of the ship—the crew could jump overboard while the ship remains the same—the ship bears an important relationship to

The word 'person' derives from the Latin word *persona*, which is a masked character in a play. We still say in English that one's persona is their outward social appearance.

the crew, and this relationship seems to be connected with the nature and persistence of the ship.

The relational connections between objects lead philosophers to distinguish between extrinsic properties and intrinsic properties of an object. **Intrinsic properties** of an object are traits that the object has independently of its surroundings. If we remove everything but the ship itself—remove from consideration its relation to the crew and Theseus—the ship is still wooden, so the woodenness of the ship is an intrinsic property of the ship. **Extrinsic properties** of an object are traits that the object has dependent on its surroundings. If we keep Theseus at the helm, this is still Theseus' ship; but if we remove Theseus, this is not Theseus' ship anymore, so the ship's being Theseus' ship is an extrinsic property of the object.

This distinction between intrinsic properties and extrinsic properties is relevant to the forged *Mona Lisa* problem as well. The original *Mona Lisa* and the forged *Mona Lisa* have exactly the same intrinsic properties—they have the same oil paint colours on the same poplar panel. But they have different extrinsic properties—one painted by da Vinci, the other by a robot arm; one was once briefly possessed by Napoleon, the other was not. Perhaps these extrinsic or relational differences are key to saying that the paintings are different. Imagine a child loses their favourite stuffed bear, so her parents buy her a brand new one just like it. The child cries: "No, this isn't *my* bear, I want *my* bear." The child has a point: the replacement bear does not have the same history with the child; this new bear did not comfort the child during the storm last month, and this makes a difference.

The relational theory of the person emphasizes the extrinsic properties constituting the person. This includes the relations to others that construct the person. Sammi's beliefs are influenced by her parents, teachers, and peers. Sammi's personality is shaped by how her parents and peers molded her, encouraged her, or discouraged her. Sammi's memories relate her to other things and people. This also includes the relations to others that presently define the person. Sammi is a mother, which is important to her identity, but her being a mother relates her to her child. Sammi is a daughter and sister, which is important to her identity, but her being so depends upon the continued existence of her parents and siblings. Sammi is a woman, which relates her to other women. Sammi is American, which relates her to others living within the same country and a set of values that she grew up with, such as embracing democracy. Sammi's personal identity is in many ways a relational or extrinsic identity.

While the relational view says that relational characteristics are very important parts of persons, the changing of these relational characteristics may or may not change the continuity of the same self. On the other hand, some relational properties are so important to an individual that the person may think her self-identity is altered once the relational properties are altered. Sammi is a mother, but her child dies, which devastates her self-identity immeasurably. Sammi gets fired from her dream job, which causes her to spiral into depression and alters her self-image. On the other hand, changing relational characteristics do not seem to make the person literally a different self. Sammi is a daughter, but after her parents die, though she is no longer a daughter anymore she still exists as Sammi. Sammi is American, but after she immigrates to Canada she is no longer American anymore, but she still exists as Sammi.

How can persons remain the same through changes to their relational properties? The relational model can endorse one of the earlier models of personal identity to secure the persistence of the same person. While Sammi's important relational properties are different after her child dies, she still remembers her days raising her child, or she still has the same beliefs and emotions about her child, or the same soul or body as when she had a child, which keeps her the same. The relational model can also secure the persistence of the same person through a relational analysis. While Sammi is no longer a mother, she is still a daughter. As long as these other relational properties remain the same over time, there is a sense in which she is the same person. Here is how the New Zealand born philosopher **Annette Baier** (1929–2012) articulates the relational theory of the person:

"Cartesian Persons" (Annette Baier, 1981)[14]

A person, perhaps, is best seen as one who was long enough dependent upon other persons to acquire the essential arts of personhood. Persons essentially are second persons, who grow up with other persons.... The fact that a person has a life history, and that a people collectively have a history, depends upon the humbler fact that each person has a childhood in which a cultural heritage is transmitted, ready for adolescent rejection and adult discriminating selection and contribution. Persons come after and before other persons.

Childhood is the period in which are acquired not only those skills essential for persons, but also the experience which generates those ambitions and goals typical of persons. Responses to dependency, and to changing degrees of it, to change of person on whom to depend, define our emotional life, form and display personality. Persons are beings who have some sort of personality, and although one may think of a personality in abstraction from its formation, even suppose it to be eternal, or to have come into being fully formed, like Athena's, all our understanding of personality relates it to its genesis, and, for us, that is in the conditions of biological life, in which one generation nurtures its successor generation, preparing it to take its place. Persons are essentially successors, heirs to other persons who formed and cared for them, and their personality is revealed both in their relations to others and in their response to their own recognized genesis....

---

14 Annette Baier, "Cartesian Persons," *Philosophia* 10, nos. 3–4 (1981): 169–88, 180–81, 186–87.

I have also emphasized the second personal pronoun. Persons are self conscious, know themselves to be persons among persons. Knowledge of this shows in the grasp of all the pronouns, none of which has sense except in relation to the others, but there are several ways in which the second person is the key person. My first concept of myself is as the referent of 'you,' spoken by someone whom I will address as 'you.' If never addressed, if excluded from the circle of speakers, a child becomes autistic, incapable of using any pronouns or indeed any words at all....

The standards by which our actions are judged are, like the standards by which thought is judged, interpersonal, and learned from others. The capacity for responsible action grows as we learn to receive and give reproaches such as 'But you said you would do it!' By being held responsible, we come to take responsibility for our actions.... I have linked this emphasis on the second person with the fact that, in learning from other persons, we acquire a sense of our place in a series of persons, to some of whom we have special responsibilities. We acquire a sense of ourselves as occupying a place in an historical and social order of persons, each of whom has a personal history interwoven with the history of a community.

In this passage,

1. *Baier argues that persons are second persons, or, that persons first know themselves as the 'you' that someone else (i.e., parents and caregivers) first speaks of them as. This roots personal identity in relations with others.*
2. *Baier argues that in the absence of interpersonal relations, the self will grow up autistic and incapable of speech. Thus, relations with others are needed for the formation of a person.*

What would the relational theory say about teleportation? Stephon continues to occupy the same relations before and after teleporting, and everyone else continues to relate to Stephon in the same way—his co-workers continue to reply to his emails, and his girlfriend continues to hug him—so he continues on as the same person with the same social relations.

Objection 1: Intrinsic Personhood

Many philosophers think that the extrinsic properties of an object are not essential to the nature of the object itself. For example, this guava has the extrinsic property of *having been picked by Juan* and the intrinsic property of *being a fruit*. The guava would still be that guava if it had been picked by Sofia instead. Being a fruit, however, is essential for being a guava—it can't be a guava unless it is a fruit. So, while the extrinsic, relational properties of the guava are important, they are not essential to the nature of the object. Consider another example that pertains to personhood: Amina is an eight-year-old girl. All of her classmates bully her and tell her she is terrible, her family yells at her all the time and does not treat her like a valuable person at all, her culture disrespects children, there is no one who thinks she has value. If Amina's extrinsic or relational properties are essential to her being a person with value, then she is not a person with value, since no one values her as a person. But this is wrong. Amina is still a person with value just because she is a human person, regardless of what others say about her. The social circumstances that Amina grows up in are surely important in shaping her (for better or worse), but these social relations are not essential to her nature as a person with intrinsic value.

Imagine that Federico's severe alcoholism results in his alienation from everyone he knew and loved. He loses his job and his house, and is now homeless, begging on the street. "He's not the guy we used to know; it's not Federico," his former friends say. But is that literally true?

Objection 2: The Imposter

Many movies revolve around one person impersonating another for extended periods of time. For example, in *Face/Off* (1997) an FBI agent named Sean undergoes a facial transplant in order to imitate Troy, the mastermind of a terror plot. Sean, with the face of Troy, then visits Troy's brother in jail, and carries on the brotherly relationship, eventually getting his brother to reveal the terror plot. Similarly, imagine someone takes over your life. They undergo surgery to look like you. They lock you in jail, then carry on your life with all of its relations intact. They kiss your partner like you normally would, they visit your parents, they go to your work, they play golf with your friends, and no one knows you are missing. The imposter maintains all your relations perfectly, so your relational elements remain perfectly intact. But is the imposter you? No, you are locked in jail! Your personhood goes with you to jail, perhaps as your bundle of perceptions, or your soul, or your memories, or your body.

Summary

In Chapter 3 we saw many different theories about the nature of substances: perhaps substances are ideal, perhaps they are material, perhaps they include a substratum, perhaps they are just a bundle of properties. In this chapter we focused on one particularly important type of substance, namely, the person. We saw many different theories about the nature of persons as well: perhaps persons are thinking souls or psychological beings with memories and personalities, perhaps they are living bodies or brains, perhaps they include a thinking substance as a substratum, perhaps they are just a bundle of perceptions. The question about the nature of personhood frequently overlapped with issues related to the mind and body, and their relations. If a person is a soul or thinking substance, what is that thinking substance and what evidence is there for the existence of a thinking substance? If a person is a living body or brain, what is that brain and what evidence is there for the dependence of the person on brains? If a person seems to have both a mind and a brain, how do we understand the relationship between the mind and the brain? These questions will concern us in the next chapter.

Key Terms in Chapter 4: Personal Identity		
Teleportation	Bundle of Perceptions	Transitivity of Identity
Numerical Sameness	Reduction	Brave Officer
Qualitative Sameness	Conservative	Brute Physical Theory
Plato	Reductionism	Animalism
Soul Theory	Eliminative	Bodily Theory
Soul	Reductionism	Brain Theory
Thinking Being	Non-Reductionism	Brain Fission
Diotima of Mantinea	Buddha	Derek Parfit
Thomas Reid	Anatman	Relational Self
Perfect Identity	Immanuel Kant	Persona
Imperfect Identity	Responsibility	Annette Baier
Introspection	Psychological Theory	Intrinsic Properties
Fallacy of Equivocation	John Locke	Extrinsic Properties
David Hume	Memory	

Philosophy on Television: Personal Identity

***Star Trek: The Next Generation*: Season 6, Episode 24: "Second Chances"**
Star Trek is set in the 2300s when starships are able to teleport people from ships to the surface of planets. During the episode "Second Chances," a teleporter malfunction accidentally reconstitutes Commander Riker both on the planet surface and back on the ship where he tried to teleport from, creating a second Riker. Questions arise: who is the real Riker? (One or the other? Neither? Both?)

***The Change Up* (2011)**
In *The Change Up* (2011) (discussed above) two friends, Mitch and Dave, swap bodies with each other and live the other person's life for a while. Mitch brings his aggressive, sexual personality into Dave's calm married life. Normally, when movies involve body swapping, the personality, beliefs, and memories of the character come into the new body as well, indicating that the person includes their personality and memories and beliefs. Other movies where characters exchange bodies include *Shrek the Third* (2007) and *It's a Boy Girl Thing* (2006).

The Hangover (2009)

In *The Hangover* (2009) four friends are drugged and forget the wild night they had in Las Vegas. This movie raises the question: if we do not remember doing something, are we the person that did that thing, and are we responsible for doing what we do not remember doing? Similarly, in *The Bourne Identity* (2002), Jason Bourne forgets his past in an accident. After the accident he is a normal, quiet man, and is upset to slowly learn he used to be an assassin. In *Eternal Sunshine of the Spotless Mind* (2004), Joel and Clementine end a bad relationship by erasing their memories of each other, thereby erasing any love they ever had for each other.

Blade Runner (1982)

In *Blade Runner* (1982) and the more recent sequel *Blade Runner: 2049* (2017), false memories are implanted in the minds of replicants, leading them to believe they are something different than they actually are. This theme recurs in *Frozen* (2013), where a girl named Anna has a traumatic childhood memory related to her sister altered, which leads her to become a fun-loving adult who loves her sister. These issues raise questions about the centrality of memory to personal identity.

Face/Off (1997)

In *Face/Off* (1997) an FBI agent named Sean undergoes a facial transplant in order imitate Troy, the mastermind of a terror plot. Sean then visits Troy's brother in jail, and carries on the brotherly relationship, getting his brother to reveal the terror plot. Similarly, in *X-Men* (2000) a character named Mystique transforms into the appearance of others and carries on their lives. In *Identity Thief* (2013), Diana steals the identity of Sandy, and racks up immense debts. Sandy claims that it was not he who bought these items. These scenarios raise questions about whether an identity thief who masquerades as you while maintaining all your social relations is actually you.

Additional Resources

Visit this book's companion resources for additional materials, including video content and an automated tool for planning argumentative essays.

sites.broadviewpress.com/knowing/chapter-4

Chapter 5
Mind and Brain

THOUGHT EXPERIMENT 5.1

Mind Uploading

In the movie *Transcendence* (2014), Johnny Depp plays a scientist named Will who only has a month to live. Will's friends scan the neural connections and structures of Will's brain, then copy this information into computer code and upload the code onto a computer. When Will dies, they turn on the computer and Will starts to live again on the computer. Do you think it is possible to upload your mind onto a computer? If so, would this be the real "you"? Is this a way to achieve immortality?

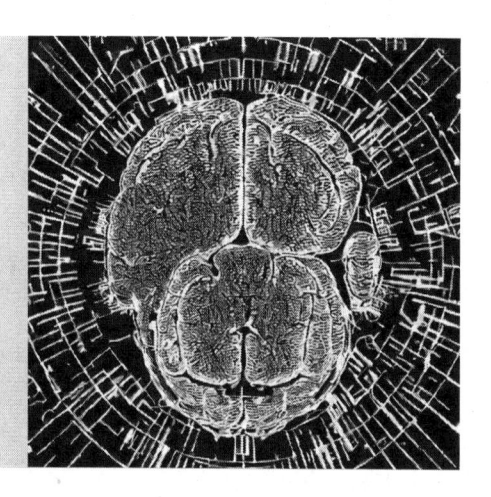

There comes a time in all of our lives when we are confronted with the reality of our own mortality. Leo Tolstoy describes the realization of our approaching death with the aid of the following Eastern fable: a traveler falls into a dried up well with a dragon waiting to devour him at the bottom. To stop his fall, he grabs a branch, but two mice start gnawing on the branch. Fortunately, there is some honey on the leaves of the branch, which the traveller licks up while he waits for the branch to break. Tolstoy summarizes: "So I too clung to the twig of life, knowing that the dragon of death was inevitably awaiting me, ready to tear me to pieces ... this is not a fable, but the real unanswerable truth intelligible to all."[1]

While everyone agrees that we face bodily death, philosophers have long wondered whether it may be possible for some part of us, a soul or mind, to survive bodily death and live forever. Some say that the answer is no. They say that the mind is identical with the brain, so when the brain dies, so do we. Others say that the answer is yes. They say that the mind is distinct from the brain, so when brain death occurs, the mind can detach from the brain and live on in an afterlife. More recently, others maintain that the answer is yes, but only because

---

1 Leo Tolstoy, *Confessions*, trans. Aylmer Maude (Mineola: Dover Publications, 2005), 18.

the mind is a functional system, and these functions can be copied into information and then uploaded onto a computer.

Underlying all of these views is a set of assumptions about what the mind is, and how the mind is related to the body—we explore both of those questions in this chapter. The views discussed can be plotted on the following spectrum, where those on the left emphasize the existence of the mind and its separability from the body, and those on the right emphasize the material nature of the mind and hence its inseparability from the body. Those in the middle emphasize the functional nature of the mind, hence the ability to theoretically copy its functions and replicate it in another physical system.

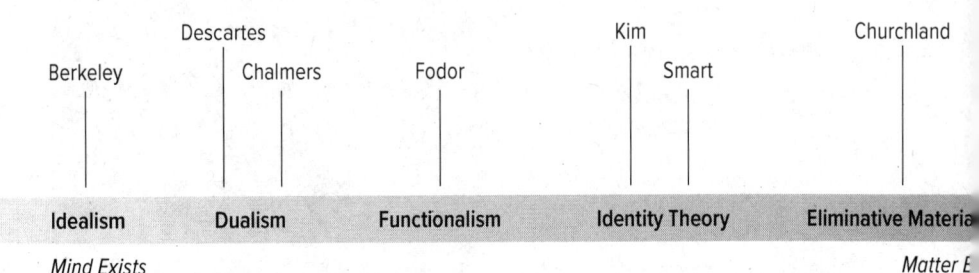

Spectrum 5: Mind-Brain

5.1 Dualism

The word duo or dual means two—say, a dynamic duo like Batman and Robin or having dual monitors for a computer. So, **mind-brain dualism** is the view that there are two things, a mind and a brain. Hence, the dualist appears on the center-left side of the spectrum, indicating that while both the mind and matter exist, the dualist emphasizes the distinct existence of the mind. But what is the mind? Dualists define the mind as thinking substance or conscious experience. How is the mind related to the body? Dualists think the mind is tightly connected to the body, but distinct from it. Dualists, therefore, endorse the non-reductionism discussed in Chapter 4.2 about the mind. With respect to the question of immortality, they think the mind is distinct from the brain, so brain death does not necessarily mean that the mind dies, so the mind may enjoy immortal life after the death of the brain.

Mind-body dualists have two common strategies for demonstrating that the mind is distinct from the body. First the **conceivability argument**, according to which it is possible to imagine the mind existing separately from the body, and it is possible to imagine the body existing separately from the mind, so the mind is not the same thing as the body. There are a variety of ways of imagining the mind existing without the body. Most strikingly, many people imagine the scenario where, upon brain death, the soul floats away toward an afterlife. This is not to suggest that there actually exists a soul, or that it actually departs toward an afterlife at death. Rather, the suggestion is only that it is possible to imagine this scenario. There are also a variety of ways of imagining that the brain exists without the mind. Many people imagine the possibility of **zombies**, which are hypothetical physical duplicates of us but they lack conscious experience. Recall the teleportation experiment in Chapter 4. Your body and brain are scanned, and an exact replica of you is produced. This replica is a physical duplicate of you, but does it have consciousness? Possibly yes, but possibly no. If we grant that it is possible our zombie duplicate lacks consciousness, then we grant the conceivability of zombies. If zombies are hypothetically possible—again, dualists do not say that zombies are real, just conceivable—we grant that it is theoretically possible to have a brain without a mind. If we can imagine separating the mind from the brain (and vice versa), we are assuming that they are two different things, for it is not possible to imagine one thing being separated from itself.

Brad Pitt and Angelina Jolie were a famous couple that came to be called 'Brangelina.' Imagine that a superfan claims: 'Brangelina is one person, not two people! Whenever Brad is on the red carpet, Angelina is on the red carpet; whenever Angelina is in Africa, Brad is in Africa! Brad is beautiful, so is Angelina; Brad is famous, so is Angelina!' How would we convince the superfan of her error? We could point out times where one of them appeared without the other: Brad was in the movie *Ocean's Eleven*, while Angelina was not. We might also point out some traits that differ between the two: Brad has facial hair, Angelina does not. These are the same strategies the mind-body dualist deploys.

Dualists also say the mind is separate from the brain because minds have properties that brains lack (and vice versa), so minds cannot be brains. This argument begins with a principle developed by the German philosopher Gottfried Leibniz (1646–1716) called the **indiscernibility of identicals**, which states that object A is identical with object B only if A has all the same properties as B, and B has all the same properties as A. Chloe lost her black-haired poodle, and offers a reward of $1000 for whoever finds it. Sharon claims she found the dog, bringing Chloe a brown-haired collie. Chloe shakes her head—the collie doesn't have the same properties as her dog, so the collie is not the same dog as her dog. It is worth noting that the indiscernibility of identicals is a slightly different principle from the identity of indiscernibles discussed in Chapter 3.4. The indiscernibility of identicals states that identical objects must have the same properties, where the identity of indiscernibles states objects with the same properties must be the same object.

Dualists point to various features that the mind has but the body lacks, and vice versa. In the passages below, the French mathematician and philosopher

René Descartes argues that the mind is indivisible but the body is divisible, while the contemporary Australian philosopher **David Chalmers** (1966–) argues that the mind is conscious which is different from the physical processing of the brain. Others take the mind to have intentionality, rationality, and goals, while material particles have gravitational force or electrochemical force. In Chapter 6, we will discuss the possibility that the mind has free will even though bodies behave deterministically. Likewise, bodies appear to be extended in space, but the mind cannot be found in space. Bodies have mass and height, but we do not literally have three square yards of love for our children, or a pound and a half of anger at our ex. Since minds have properties that bodies lack (and vice versa), and objects with different properties cannot be the same, the mind cannot be the same as the brain. Here is a passage from René Descartes, who is perhaps the most famous mind-brain dualist.

Meditations on First Philosophy, Meditation VI (René Descartes, 1641)[2]

First, since I know that all those things I understand clearly and distinctly could have been created by God in a way that matches my conception of them, the fact that I can clearly and distinctly understand one thing, distinguishing it from something else, is sufficient to convince me that the two of them are different, because they can be separated from each other, at least by God. The power by which this [separation] takes place is irrelevant to my judgment that they are distinct. And therefore, given the mere fact that I know I exist and that, at the moment, I look upon my nature or essence as absolutely nothing other than that I am a thinking thing, I reasonably conclude that my essence consists of this single fact: I am a thinking thing. And although I may well possess (or rather, as I will state later, although I certainly do possess) a body which is very closely joined to me, nonetheless, because, on the one hand, I have a clear and distinct idea of myself, insofar as I am merely a thinking thing, without extension, and, on the other hand, [I have] a distinct idea of body, insofar as it is merely an extended thing which does not think, it is certain that my mind is completely distinct from my body and can exist without it....

At this point, then, my initial observation is that there is a great difference between the mind and the body, given that the body is, by its very nature, always divisible, whereas the mind is completely indivisible. For, in fact, when I think of [my mind], that is, when I think of myself as purely a thinking thing, I cannot distinguish any parts within me. Instead, I understand that I am something completely individual and unified.

2 René Descartes, *Meditations on First Philosophy*, trans. Ian Johnston, ed. Andrew Bailey (Peterborough: Broadview Press, 2013), 82, 87.

And although my entire mind seems to be united with my entire body, nonetheless, I know that if a foot or arm or any other part of the body is sliced off, that loss will not take anything from my mind. And I cannot call the faculties of willing, feeling, understanding, and so on parts of the mind because it is the same single mind that wishes, feels, and understands. By contrast, I cannot think of any corporeal or extended substance that my thought is not capable of dividing easily into parts. From this very fact, I understand that the substance is divisible. (This point alone would be enough to teach me that the mind is completely different from the body, if I did not already know that well enough from other sources.)

In this passage,

1. *Descartes argues that the essence of the mind is just to think, so the body is not necessarily part of the essence of the mind, so he can apprehend the possibility of his mind existing without the body. He grants that his mind is intimately conjoined with his body, so the mind is not separated from the body in reality, but it is imaginable that the mind is separated from the body. Thus, Descartes provides a conceivability argument for mind-body dualism.*
2. *Descartes argues that the mind is a thinking thing and is not extended in space while the body does not think and is extended in space. He also argues that the mind is indivisible, as the "I" does not have parts. Descartes here employs the indiscernibility of identicals argument for mind-body dualism.*

While Descartes' dualism is historically the most influential version of dualism, the most prominent contemporary dualist is David Chalmers.

The Conscious Mind (David Chalmers, 1996)[3]

At the global level, we can consider the logical possibility of a zombie world: a world physically identical to ours, but in which there are no conscious experiences at all. In such a world, everybody is a zombie. So let us consider my zombie twin. This creature is molecule for molecule identical to me, and identical in all the low-level properties postulated by a completed physics, but he lacks conscious experience entirely. (Some might prefer to call a zombie "it," but I use the personal pronoun; I have grown quite fond of my zombie twin.) To fix ideas, we can imagine that right now I am gazing out the window, experiencing some nice green sensations from seeing the trees outside, having pleasant taste experiences through

---

3 David Chalmers, *The Conscious Mind* (Oxford: Oxford University Press, 1996), 94–103.

munching on a chocolate bar, and feeling a dull aching sensation in my right shoulder. What is going on in my zombie twin? He is physically identical to me, and we may as well suppose that he is embedded in an identical environment. He will certainly be identical to me functionally: he will be processing the same sort of information, reacting in a similar way to inputs, with his internal configurations being modified appropriately and with indistinguishable behavior resulting.... It is just that none of this functioning will be accompanied by any real conscious experience. There will be no phenomenal feel. There is nothing it is like to be a zombie.

The idea of zombies as I have described them is a strange one. For a start, it is unlikely that zombies are naturally possible. In the real world, it is likely that any replica of me would be conscious ... But the question is not whether it is plausible that zombies could exist in our world, or even whether the idea of a zombie replica is a natural one; the question is whether the notion of a zombie is conceptually coherent ... We can make a similar point by considering my silicon isomorph, who is organized like me but who has silicon chips where I have neurons. Whether such an isomorph would in fact be conscious is controversial, but it seems to most people that those who deny this are expressing a coherent possibility. From these cases it follows that the existence of my conscious experience is not logically entailed by the facts about my functional organization. But given that it is conceptually coherent that the group-mind set-up or my silicon isomorph could lack conscious experience, it follows that my zombie twin is an equally coherent possibility....

The most vivid argument against the logical supervenience of consciousness is suggested by Jackson (1982), following related arguments by Nagel (1974) and others. Imagine that we are living in an age of a completed neuroscience, where we know everything there is to know about the physical processes within our brain responsible for the generation of our behavior. Mary has been brought up in a black-and-white room and has never seen any colors except for black, white, and shades of gray. She is nevertheless one of the world's leading neuroscientists, specializing in the neurophysiology of color vision. She knows everything there is to know about the neural processes involved in visual information processing, about the physics of optical processes, and about the physical makeup of objects in the environment. But she does not know what it is like to see red. No amount of reasoning from the physical facts alone will give her this knowledge. It follows that the facts about the subjective experience of color vision are not entailed by the physical facts.

In this passage,

1. Chalmers uses the possibility of zombies—physical duplicates lacking consciousness—to show that the body could, hypothetically, exist separately from the mind. This is another conceivability argument for mind-body dualism.

2. *Chalmers uses the knowledge argument to show that the physical body could be present without the conscious experiences associated with it. According to the **knowledge argument**, a future all-knowing neuroscientist named Mary is raised in a black and white room, so never sees the colour red. She knows everything about the wavelengths associated with red, and all the objects that elicit the experience of red, and every detail of the neural processing that occurs when red objects are presented to people, but she doesn't know what red looks like. Lastly, someone brings her a blooming rose, and she learns something new about red, namely, what red looks like. In this case, Mary knew all the physical facts about red, but did not know the further fact about what red looked like, so conscious experience is distinct from the physical facts.*

While dualists agree that the mind is in some sense distinct from the body, there are nevertheless numerous versions of dualism. Here are two of the more popular versions.

(1) Interactionist Dualism

Descartes was an **interactionist dualist**, which combines the dualist view that the mind is distinct from the body with the view that the mind and body interact. Mind-body interactionism has two parts. First, acceptance of **mental causation**, according to which the mind causes the body to move in various ways. Jennie desires a peach, which causes her body to eat a peach. Devin believes his pet gecko just died, which causes him to cry. Second, the body also causes the mind to feel or think things. Ivan steps on a tack, causing a mental pain sensation. Although interactionism is the most common form of dualism, it suffers from the following objections.

Objection 1: Contact Problem

In 2012, the pop music star Kesha appeared on Conan O'Brien's talk show, and calmly explained how she had sexual relations with a ghost. Conan was baffled by the possibility, and asked for details about how it was possible. Kesha explained their interaction—"he [the ghost] started caressing me"—before ultimately conceding, "it was a sexy time, it wasn't sex." Most of us react, as Conan did, with questions such as "How is this possible? A ghost lacks a body, how does one touch it, and how does it touch you?" The difficulty in imagining how an immaterial spirit can interact with a body also applies to Descartes' interactionist dualism. Since the mind is distinct from the body, and lacks extension in space, how can the mind come in contact with the body? Princess Elisabeth of Bohemia (1618–80) frames this **contact objection** against Descartes' interactionist dualism in this way: "Tell me how the soul of a human being can determine the bodily spirits in order to bring about voluntary actions. For it

seems that all determination of movement happens through the impulsion of the thing moved, by the manner in which it is pushed by that which moves it ... [physical contact] appears to me incompatible with an immaterial thing."[4] Since interactionist dualism posits a non-spatial mind interacting with a spatially constrained body, it is natural to wonder how they can possibly come in contact with each other?

Descartes responds to the contact objection by using an **argument from analogy**, as discussed in Chapter 1.5.3: as the moon causes the tides to shift without contact, so the soul causes the body to move without contact. Unfortunately, this is a **false analogy** (see 1.5.4): the moon and the tides are both physical, and gravitation is a physical phenomenon, so this does not make sense of mental-to-physical interaction.

Objection 2: Physical Causal Completeness

According to Isaac Newton's (1642–1727) laws of motion, the total momentum of any set of interacting bodies (in an isolated system) remains constant throughout the interaction. A billiard ball with a weight of one kilogram and a velocity of 10 metres per second has a momentum of 10 kilogram metres per second (1 kg times 10 m/s). A stationary two-kilogram ball has a total momentum of 0 kilogram metres per second (2 kg times 0 m/s). The total momentum of the two balls before the interaction is 10 kilogram metres per second. The first ball strikes the second ball, causing the second ball to start moving, but slowing the speed of the first ball. After this interaction, the first ball may have a momentum of 3.33 kilogram metres per second, while the second ball may have a momentum of 6.67 kilogram metres per second, for a total of 10 kilogram metres per second. The total momentum is conserved, or remains constant across this interaction. Not only is momentum conserved across interactions, but force and energy are also conserved across interactions. These are called the **conservation laws** of physics, and they indicate that the total momentum, force, and/or energy in an isolated system is the same prior to an interaction and after an interaction.

There are two results of these conservation laws. First, the principle of **physical causal completeness**, according to which every physical event has a sufficient (or, complete) physical cause. Since the physical universe is an isolated system, every effect that occurs will have a complete physical cause. The total effect of our interaction was 10 kilogram metres per second of momentum spread over the two physical objects, so the total cause must be 10 kilogram metres per second of momentum from the physical billiard ball, so the physical cause has all the

---

4   Princess Elisabeth, Elisabeth to Descartes, 6 May 1643, in *The Correspondence between Princess Elisabeth of Bohemia and René Descartes*, ed. and trans. by L. Shapiro (University of Chicago Press: Chicago, 2007), 62.

causation needed to bring about the effect. Secondly, energy cannot be taken away from or added to the closed system. The second ball will not suddenly fly off at bullet speeds, as though an extra source of momentum from outside the closed system had been added to the system. Rather, the second ball will possess only the momentum calculable from the momentum of the billiard ball. This poses the following problem for interactionist dualism. On interactionist dualism, the mind is distinct from physical bodies, and the mind interacts with physical bodies. But, since the mind is distinct from physical bodies, this interaction amounts to adding surplus momentum into the closed physical system of the universe. Samir reaches for a peach, which is completely caused by various muscle contractions, which themselves are completely caused by various neural processes in the brain. Samir's distinct desire for a peach cannot break into this closed physical system to make her body reach for the peach. The mind is incapable of interacting with the body, so interactionist dualism fails.

(2) Epiphenomenalism

Since interactionist dualism runs into difficulties in showing how the mind can interact with the body, perhaps the best solution is to say that the mind does not interact with the body. This is the epiphenomenalist view. **Epiphenomenalism** says that dualism is true, as the conceivability argument and the indiscernibility of identicals argument are taken to show. At the same time, physical causal completeness is true as well, as physical conservation principles are taken to show. The result is that the brain causes all our behaviour, while a distinct mind comes along for the ride, but does not cause any behaviour. Samir's neural processing gives rise to her desire for a peach, but her desire for the peach does not cause her to bite the peach; rather, her neural processing causes her to bite the peach. Epiphenomenalism imagines the mind to be like a shadow cast by June's punch, where June's punch causes Vikki's jaw to break, but the shadow comes along as well, but does not cause any harm. Or, the gunshot causes the hole in the wall, but the gunshot brings a loud bang sound along with it, though the bang sound does not cause the hole in the wall.

Objection: Mental Causation

While epiphenomenalism benefits from endorsing both dualism and physical causal completeness, epiphenomenalism fails to establish that mental causation is true. But most people think mental causation must be true, for two reasons. First, the common-sense argument: most people experience themselves trying to make their bodies move in various ways, and their bodies commonly obey, which leads many to consider it obvious that the mind causes the body to move. Samir desires the peach, and so she tries to eat a peach. Her mind seems to be pushing her body toward a peach. Suddenly, her body moves toward the peach. It seems as though her desire for the peach is what pushed her body toward the peach. Second, the argument from personal **responsibility**. We are only responsible for doing things that we can actually do. Imagine that I am paralyzed, so my body doesn't do what my mind tells it to. If you yell for help, but I do not get up to help you, I cannot be blamed—precisely because my mind cannot cause the bodily reactions necessary for me to help. Similarly, what I want to do cannot be accomplished if I am in a room locked from outside. If we are only responsible for actions we can actually do, then we must be able to bring about actions in the first place. In order to be able to bring about actions in the first place, we must have mental causation, as mental causation just is the view that the mind can cause actions.

5.2 Mind-Brain Identity Theory

Where mind-body dualism posits the mind as distinct from the brain, **mind-brain identity theory** holds that the mind is identical with the brain. Where dualists take the mind to be thinking substance or conscious experience, identity theorists take the mind to be physical substance or neural processes. Imagine that Kwan loves the sunset, so every night he sits with his mother and watches the sun go down. Kwan bumps into an astronomer, who explains that the sunset is actually the Earth rotating away from the stationary sun. Kwan is incredulous. No, the setting sun must be different than the Earth rotating, since the sun is moving and going down during sunsets, unlike the situation proposed by the astronomer. Kwan becomes a sunset-rotation dualist, insisting they cannot possibly be the same thing. Our intuitions lie with the astronomer in this case: the sunset is our perspective of the same phenomenon, which is the Earth rotating away from the sun's light. We are sunset-rotation identity theorists. The mind-brain identity theorist takes the situation to be roughly the same for the mind and brain. While it may look as though the mind is distinct from the brain, in actual fact the mind is the brain. Identity theorists, therefore, are usually what we called conservative reductionists in Chapter 4.2. The mind exists (i.e., it is conserved), but the mind just is the brain. So, with respect to the question of immortality, they say that when the brain dies, the mind dies, so there is no immortality—at least not without an accompanying resurrection of the body.

Identity theorists commonly deploy two arguments in support of their view. First, the **simplicity argument**. Most people agree that what happens to the brain influences what happens to our mental lives—give someone hallucinogens, alcohol, or even sugar, and they suddenly perceive things differently or are in different moods. Neuroscience increasingly identifies specific brain regions associated with specific cognitive tasks such as perception, memory, executive function, and emotion. At present, neuroscientists can introduce electrodes into specific areas of the brain and report altering mood based on electrically stimulating specific brain regions. Most neuroscientists take these examples to show that mental states are correlated with brain states. Two things are correlated whenever the appearance of one thing accompanies the occurrence of the other thing. Fire and light are correlated, as increased temperatures are correlated with increased ice cream sales. **Mind-brain correlation** occurs if, whenever a mental state occurs, say a fear, there is some correlated brain state occurring, say neural activity in the amygdala.

In some cases, the proper analysis of correlated objects is to state that two objects exist, though they are constantly conjoined—the increase in temperature is correlated with, but is still distinct from, increasing ice cream sales. But these cases of correlation involve two objects, and then some explanation of why the two are connected. A simpler analysis of correlated objects in many cases is to state that there is only one object, and of course the self-same object will always occur whenever that object occurs. For example, Barack Obama's activities are correlated with the activities of the 44th president of the United States. Whenever Barack Obama tweets, the 44th president of the US tweets. Barack Obama kissed his wife Michelle yesterday, but the 44th president of the US also kissed Michelle yesterday! The 44th president of the US flew to France today, while Barack Obama also flew to France today. What is the best explanation for these amazing coincidences? The simplest explanation of the correlation is to say that Barack Obama is the 44th president, so of course whatever Barack Obama does, so will the 44th president do. Likewise, while dualists agree that mind-brain correlations exist, the identity theorist says the simplest explanation of the mind-brain correlations is that the mind is identical with the brain.

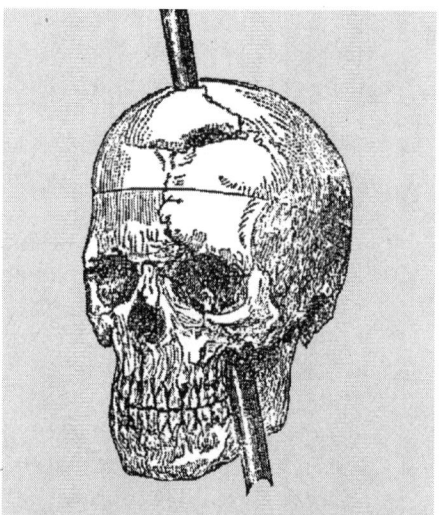

In 1848 a railroad worker named **Phineas Gage** was blasting a rock when an explosion caused a rod to shoot through his head. Gage survived, but his personality shifted. Before the accident he was a quiet, hard-working man, while after the accident he was "gross, profane, coarse and vulgar, to such a degree that his society was intolerable to decent people." Gage's personality shift following his brain injury was one of the first cases directly linking personality with brain physiology.[5]

Identity theorists argue that their simpler model should be preferred because of Ockham's Razor. **Ockham's Razor** is a principle, introduced by William of Ockham (1287–1347), whereby entities should not be multiplied beyond necessity, or, all things being equal, the simplest explanation should be preferred. Imagine you return home to discover that your garage door is wide open. What is the best explanation of this? Perhaps your forgetful housemate just left it open again, and perhaps a thief broke in and stole some things. What is more likely?

---

5   John M. Harlow, "Recovery from the Passage of an Iron Bar through the Head," *Publications of the Massachusetts Medical Society* 2, no. 3 (1868): 327–47.

Ockham's razor says the first explanation is probably true, since it only posits the usual routines of your housemate's forgetfulness rather than the unusual and additional occurrence of a thief breaking into the house. Similarly, the identity theory has a simpler explanation of mind-brain correlations, since it only posits one thing, the mind, which is the brain. The dualist must posit two things, the mind and the brain, and explain why they are constantly correlated.

Second, the **causal argument**, which starts by asking which of the following three principles is most likely false: physical causal completeness, dualism, or mental causation? They cannot all be true, for if behaviour is completely caused by physical processes, the behaviour cannot also have a distinct mental cause. The interactionist dualist says mental causation and dualism are true, so physical causal completeness fails. The epiphenomenalist says dualism and physical causal completeness are true, so mental causation fails. The identity theorist says physical causal completeness and mental causation are true, so dualism fails. Identity theorists take physical causal completeness to be a well-grounded scientific theory, while agreeing that mental causation must be true as well. The only way to secure these two principles is to abandon dualism: if behaviours only have sufficient physical causes, the only way for mental causes to influence behaviours is for mental causes to be identical with those sufficient physical causes—that is, for them to *be* physical.

Here's an analogy for this sort of reasoning. Imagine that Genevieve is hosting a Halloween party and everyone wants to go. But, she insists, no one will get in without wearing a costume. She places bouncers at the door to enforce her rule. Sareh desperately wants to go to the party, but she hates dressing up. Sareh has two choices: dress up, or don't go to the party; there is no way for her to go to the party without her costume. She decides it is more important to go to the party, so she dresses up and is let in without any trouble. Similarly, identity theorists argue that only physical causes can bring about human behaviour. So, mental causes can either not affect behaviour (i.e., epiphenomenalism) or be identical with physical causes. It is important for mental causation to occur, so mental causes must be physical causes.

One of the more famous proponents of mind-brain identity theory is the Australian philosopher **J.J.C. Smart** (1920–2012). In the following passages he describes the identity theory and responds to criticisms.

"Sensations and Brain Processes" (J.J.C. Smart, 1959)[6]

Suppose that I report that I have at this moment a roundish, blurry-edged after-image which is yellowish towards its edge and is orange towards its center. What is it that I am reporting? ... The suggestion I wish to resist is ...

---

6   J.J.C. Smart, "Sensations and Brain Processes," *The Philosophical Review* 68, no. 2 (1959): 141–43, 146, 150.

that to say "I have a yellowish-orange after-image" is to report something irreducibly psychical. Why do I wish to resist this suggestion? Mainly because of Occam's razor. It seems to me that science is increasingly giving us a viewpoint whereby organisms are able to be seen as physico-chemical mechanisms: it seems that even the behavior of man himself will one day be explicable in mechanistic terms. There does seem to be, so far as science is concerned, nothing in the world but increasingly complex arrangements of physical constituents. All except for one place: in consciousness. That is, for a full description of what is going on in a man you would have to mention not only the physical processes in his tissues, glands, nervous system, and so forth, but also his states of consciousness: his visual, auditory, and tactual sensations, his aches and pains. That these should be *correlated* with brain processes does not help, for to say that they are *correlated* is to say that they are something "over and above." You cannot correlate something with itself. You correlate footprints with burglars, but not Bill Sikes the burglar with Bill Sikes the burglar. So sensations, states of consciousness, do seem to be the one sort of thing left outside the physicalist picture, and for various reasons I just cannot believe that this can be so. That everything should be explicable in terms of physics (together of course with descriptions of the ways in which the parts are put together—roughly, biology is to physics as radio-engineering is to electromagnetism) except the occurrence of sensations seems to me to be frankly unbelievable ...

Objection 1. Any illiterate peasant can talk perfectly well about his after-images, or how things look or feel to him, or about his aches and pains, and yet he may know nothing whatever about neurophysiology. A man may, like Aristotle, believe that the brain is an organ for cooling the body without any impairment of his ability to make true statements about his sensations. Hence the things we are talking about when we describe our sensations cannot be processes in the brain.

Reply. You might as well say that a nation of slugabeds, who never saw the Morning Star or knew of its existence, or who had never thought of the expression "the Morning Star," but who used the expression "the Evening Star" perfectly well, could not use this expression to refer to the same entity as we refer to (and describe as) "the Morning Star." You may object that the Morning

'The Morning Star' and 'the Evening Star' are old-fashioned names for the bright planet Venus as it appears in the morning or evening sky, respectively. The very early Greeks did not realize that they were the same object; Pythagoras or Parmenides was supposed to have demonstrated that they were both Venus.

Star is in a sense not the very same thing as the Evening Star, but only something spatiotemporally continuous with it. That is, you may say that the Morning Star is not the Evening Star in the strict sense of "identity" that I distinguished earlier. There is, however, a more plausible example. Consider lightning. Modern physical science tells us that lightning is a certain kind of electrical discharge due to ionization of clouds of water vapor in the atmosphere. This, it is now believed, is what the true nature of lightning is. Note that there are not two things: a flash of lightning and an electrical discharge. There is one thing, a flash of lightning, which is described scientifically as an electrical discharge to the earth from a cloud of ionized water molecules.

Objection 4. The after-image is not in physical space. The brain-process is. So the after-image is not a brain-process. *Reply.* This is an *ignoratio elenchi.* I am not arguing that the after-image is a brain-process, but that the experience of having an after-image is a brain-process. It is the experience which is reported in the introspective report. Similarly, if it is objected that the after-image is yellowy-orange, my reply is that it is the experience of seeing yellowy-orange that is being described, and this experience is not a yellowy-orange something. So to say that a brain-process cannot be yellowy-orange is not to say that a brain-process cannot in fact be the experience of having a yellowy-orange after-image.

In this passage,
1. *Smart uses the simplicity argument to support mind-brain identity.*
2. *Smart says dualists commit an **intensional fallacy** (in Objection 1). This means that dualists mistakenly assume that two inequivalent descriptions cannot be true of the same thing. Clark Kent is described as a nerdy, quiet newspaper reporter, while Superman is described as an athletic, bold superhero. These two descriptions are clearly different, so Lana Lang imagines they cannot be the same person. We know better, however: Clark Kent is Superman.*
3. *Smart says dualists commit a **phenomenological fallacy** (in Objection 4). This means that dualists mistakenly assume that the same thing cannot be known or experienced in two different ways. The fourteen-year-old Jennie has learned all about what a kiss is like from her friends and from magazines. But when she finally has her first kiss, she comes to know the same thing, kissing, in a different way, by personal experience. Likewise, it is possible to know about our neural processes by observing our brains in a MRI machine or by directly experiencing what those neural processes feel like. This distinction between knowing about an object and knowing the object by acquaintance will re-appear in Chapter 7.1.*

The mind-brain identity theory was the dominant model from the middle of the twentieth century until the 1970s. Here is an excerpt from the Korean philosopher **Jaegwon Kim** (1934–2019), a contemporary mind-brain identity theorist:

Physicalism or Something Near Enough (Jaegwon Kim, 2005)[7]

Any positive argument for type physicalism must come up with reasons for moving from psychoneural correlations to psychoneural identities—that is, from, say, 'pain occurs if and only if C-Fiber stimulation occurs' to 'pain is identical with C-Fiber stimulation.' The thesis that there are pervasive psychoneural correlations is widely accepted. But the existence of such correlations is consistent with many dualist theories, like epiphenomenalism, ... and even substance dualism; in fact, it is entailed by some of them. The critical question, therefore, is what grounds there are that make it compelling, or at least reasonable, to upgrade the correlations to identities.

As I see it, there are three types of arguments that could be, and have been, advanced on behalf of psychoneural type identities. The first, originally promoted by Smart without much elaboration, is the simplicity argument, to the effect that identifying mental states, including states of consciousness, with neural/physical states of the brain, helps us attain the simplest, most parsimonious worldview....

The last is the causal argument, and it is the one I believe works best if anything does. The canonical form of the argument is very simple and goes like this: mentality has causal effects in the physical world; however, the physical world is causally closed; therefore, mentality must be part of the physical world, and, specifically, mental states are identical with brain states. David Papineau's argument in his recent book is a good example of this form of causal argument.... Of the three arguments in support of type physicalism, I believe the causal argument is the only one that goes some real distance, although not far enough ...

As for the simplicity argument, I believe it is difficult to formulate it in a non-questions-begging way, though it can provide reassurances to those who are already committed physicalists. What a physicalist may seize upon as the most parsimonious and elegant ontology would be apt to strike the dualist as a hopelessly inadequate scheme which discards, or ignores, the entities that are needed to save the phenomenon.

In this passage,

1. Kim says that the simplicity argument for mind-brain identity is **question begging**. In Chapter 1.5.4 we saw that question begging occurs when

7 Jaegwon Kim, *Physicalism or Something Near Enough* (Princeton: Princeton University Press, 2005), 124–25.

one assumes the conclusion in one of the premises that support the conclusion. In this case, the identity theorist assumes the truth of the identity theory in the premise stating that identity is the simplest explanation of mind-brain correlations. Of course, it would be simpler if the mind were identical with the brain, but the question is whether the mind is identical with the brain, so one cannot assume a stance on the very issue that is up for discussion.

2. *Kim argues that the causal argument is the most powerful argument for mind-brain identity.*

Objection 1: Indiscernibility of Identicals

Identity theorists say it is simpler if the mind is the brain, as we need not posit distinct mental processes any more, and we can easily secure mental causation. But dualists respond that the mind clearly has traits that the brain does not have. To return to the previous analogy, imagine that Genevieve is hosting a Halloween party, and everyone wants to go. But, she insists, only people with brown eyes can get in. She places bouncers at the door to enforce her rule. Sareh desperately wants to go to the party, but she has blue eyes. Sareh decides to lie by putting on coloured contacts and saying that she does have brown eyes. The bouncers, however, are clever, and they find out that she doesn't really have brown eyes, even though she says she does. Just because Sareh says she has brown eyes does not mean she actually has brown eyes. Likewise, just because the identity theorist says the mind is the brain does not mean the mind actually is the brain, so long as the mind seems to have different traits than the brain.

Identity theorists compare the mind-brain relation to other examples of conservative reduction, such as water is H_2O. Dualists compare the mind-brain relation to other examples of non-reductionism, such as the non-identity of the lost city of Atlantis to Venice. Which one is correct? Is the mind so similar to the brain that it can be reduced, or so distinct from the brain that it cannot be reduced?

Objection 2: Multiple Realizability

Dualists also use the conceivability argument to support dualism: it is possible for the mind to be present where the brain is not, so the mind cannot be identical with the brain. While Descartes imagines the strong case where the mind is completely disembodied, dualists also make the weaker claim that mental states can be present where a particular brain state is not, so long as another brain state takes the place of the original brain state. This is the doctrine of **multiple realizability**, according to which the same mental state, say, the hunger for fish, can be present though this mental state can have a variety of different physical correlates. As a child, Juan has a hunger for fish, where this hunger has some neural basis X in Juan's brain. Twenty years later, Juan once again gets a hunger for fish, but Juan's brain has developed over time, so his hunger now has neural basis Y. Maria is also hungry for fish, but she has a slightly different neural architecture (a few more neurons, different neural connections) than Juan, so her hunger for fish has neural basis Z. Some shark is also hungry for fish, but the shark has a radically different neural structure than Juan or Maria. Hypothetically, if we encountered an alien, it may also feel hungry for fish—and why wouldn't it?— though it would have an entirely different brain structure as well. This principle of multiple realizability has already been discussed in prior chapters, where the same ship seemed able to persist through changes to its planks (Chapter 3.3), and the same person seemed able to persist through changes to her physiology (Chapter 4.1). If this is true, however, then it is once again possible for mental state X to be present where brain state X is not, and a thing cannot be present where it is not present, so mental states are not identical with brain states.

5.3 Functionalism

The multiple realizability objection caused many to abandon mind-brain identity theory in the 1970s, in favour of a theory that could handle multiple realizability. Functionalism was introduced in the 1970s by the American philosophers Hilary Putnam (1926–2016) and Jerry Fodor (1935–2017) as a theory not only capable of handling multiple realizability, but also avoiding objections to dualism.

Where dualists say the mind is distinct from the brain, and identity theorists say the mind is the brain, functionalists say the mind is distinct from the brain, but requires a brain. Thus, functionalism appears in the middle of the mind-body spectrum. In this way, functionalism is similar to Aristotle's understanding of substances discussed in Chapter 3.3, where substances are distinct from matter, but need matter at the same time. Where dualists take the mind to be essentially thinking stuff such as conscious reasoning and feeling, and identity theorists take the mind to be essentially physical stuff such as neural processing, **functionalism** takes the mind to be essentially functional stuff. But what is functional stuff?

To understand functionalism, it is helpful to understand the term 'function.' The **function** of a thing is its job, or role, in a system. Mario plans to open a restaurant, but before he does so, he plots out his ideal organizational structure. He needs a host whose job is to take patrons to their seats. He needs a server whose job is to take this patron's orders. He needs a cook who makes the food. He needs an expeditor who takes the food to the table. He needs a dishwasher to clean the dishes. He hasn't hired anyone yet, but he knows he must fill these five jobs or functions, and knows what they all need to do at his restaurant. But Mario needs to hire some person to perform the job—the job description alone, without anyone performing the job, will not produce any entrées! So, Mario hires Katarina and Inga to perform the job of the cook, and

Since functionalists define mental states by their job, they do not specify that a physical system must implement that job description. They are theoretically open to the mental state being realized by a ghostly substance. But all functionalists these days assume that mental states are implemented by physical systems.

they fulfill the functions specified in the job description. Notice that Mario could have hired anyone as a cook—Katarina or Luigi or Louise could have all done the job well. And Katarina works some shifts while Inga works other shifts. Thus, the job of being Mario's cook is multiply realizable, since numerous people perform that function. Since being Mario's cook can be done by numerous people, it is false that being Mario's cook is identical to Katarina, as there are other people who have the job of being Mario's cook as well.

Mental states also perform jobs or functions in minds. Consider Annie's fear of dogs. The dualist defines this fear as the gripping feeling Annie experiences, while the identity theorist defines this fear as the neural processing in the amygdala. But the functionalist defines this fear by its "job"— by what it makes Annie do. Annie's fear of dogs causes her to run away when she sees dogs. Sophie, who loves dogs, hugs dogs whenever she sees dogs. So, Annie's fear of dogs makes her behave in certain specific ways whenever dogs are around. This is the functional analysis of Annie's fear of dogs. In the same way as Mario needs to hire someone to perform the cooking job, so Annie's behavioural profile about dogs needs to be implemented by some neural process, thus some brain state is essential for realizing the fear behaviour. But, in the same way that Mario can hire someone else to do the same job, Annie's behavioural profile can be implemented by different neural structures in her over time, so long as those neural structures still make her run away when dogs appear. Tigger the cat is also afraid of dogs, as she also runs away when dogs appear, but Tigger has a slightly different neural structure implementing this fear of dogs than Annie does. Thus, fear of dogs behaviour is multiply realizable, since cat brains and human brains can implement the same fear of dog behaviour. Since the fear of dogs can be present where Annie's neural state X is not present, the fear of dogs cannot be identical with Annie's neural state X. And, to return to our thought experiment, if a person's mind is defined as a set of behavioural patterns, and these behavioural patterns can be perfectly copied and uploaded to a computer, their mind can exist immortally on a computer. Here is how one leading proponent of functionalism, **Jerry Fodor**, makes the case for functionalism, over and against dualism and mind-brain identity theory.

"The Mind-Body Problem" (Jerry Fodor, 1981)[8]

The chief drawback of dualism is its failure to account adequately for mental causation. If the mind is nonphysical, it has no position in physical space. How, then, can a mental cause give rise to a behavioral effect that has a position in space? To put it another way, how can the nonphysical give rise to the physical without violating the laws of the conservation of mass, of energy and of momentum? ...

The problem with type physicalism is that the psychological constitution of a system seems to depend not on its hardware, or physical composition, but on its software, or program. Why should the philosopher dismiss the possibility that silicon-based Martians have pains, assuming that the silicon is properly organized? And why should the philosopher rule out the possibility of machines having beliefs, assuming that the machines are correctly programmed? If it is logically possible that Martians and machines could have mental properties, then mental properties and neurophysiological processes cannot be identical, however much they may prove to be coextensive.

What it all comes down to is that there seems to be a level of abstraction at which the generalizations of psychology are most naturally pitched. This level of abstraction cuts across differences in the physical composition of the systems to which psychological generalizations apply. In the cognitive sciences, at least, the natural domain for psychological theorizing seems to be all systems that process information. The problem with type physicalism is that there are possible information-processing systems with the same psychological constitution as human beings but not the same physical organization. In principle all kinds of physically different things could have human software.

This situation calls for a relational account of mental properties that abstracts them from the physical structure of their bearers. In spite of the objections to logical behaviorism that I presented above, logical behaviorism was at least on the right track in offering a relational interpretation of mental properties: to have a headache is to be disposed to exhibit a certain pattern of relations between the stimuli one encounters and the responses one exhibits. If that is what having a headache is, however, there is no reason in principle why only heads that are physically similar to ours can ache. Indeed, according to logical behaviorism, it is a necessary truth that any system that has our stimulus-response contingencies also has our headaches....

The intuition underlying functionalism is that what determines the psychological type to which a mental particular belongs is the causal role of the particular in the mental life of the organism. Functional individuation

---

8   Jerry Fodor, "The Mind-Body Problem," *Scientific American* 244, no. 1 (1981): 114, 117–19.

is differentiation with respect to causal role. A headache, for example, is identified with the type of mental state that among other things causes a disposition for taking aspirin in people who believe aspirin relieves a headache, causes a desire to rid oneself of the pain one is feeling, often causes someone who speaks English to say such things as "I have a headache" and is brought on by overwork, eyestrain and tension. This list is presumably not complete. More will be known about the nature of a headache as psychological and physiological research discovers more about its causal role. Functionalism construes the concept role in such a way that a mental state can be defined by its causal relations to other mental states ...

Since functionalism recognizes that mental particulars may be physical, it is compatible with the idea that mental causation is a species of physical causation. In other words, functionalism tolerates the materialist solution to the mind-body problem provided by the central state identity theory. It is possible for the functionalist to assert both that mental properties are typically defined in terms of their relations and that interactions of mind and body are typically causal in however robust a notion of causality is required by psychological explanations. The logical behaviorist can endorse only the first assertion and the type physicalist only the second. As a result functionalism seems to capture the best features of the materialist alternatives to dualism. It is no wonder that functionalism has become increasingly popular ...

In this passage,

1. *Fodor rejects dualism because of the mental causation problem. Since distinct minds are not located in space, they cannot contact the body, and, even if they could, they could not exert surplus causal power into the closed physical universe.*

2. *Fodor rejects a version of the identity theory called the **type identity theory** because of the multiple realizability problem. A **type** is a general category, whereas a **token** is one particular instance. For example, Johan has two types of soda in his fridge, Coke and Sprite. But Johan has seven tokens of soda in his fridge, three cans of Coke and four cans of Sprite. The type identity theorist takes the mental type fear to be identical with a specific type of brain states in humans, say brain state X. Thus, any other animal or human without brain state X cannot be in fear. But multiple realizability shows that other animals, humans or machines could still behave in fearful ways, so they still have fears, even though they do not have brain state X.*

3. *Fodor endorses a **token-identity theory**, which says that even though fear in general is not identical to one specific type of brain state X, a particular fear that someone has can be identical to the particular brain state that realizes their pain. While not all soda is Coke (since Sprite is soda too), this particular soda may be a Coke.*

4. *Fodor uses a **computer metaphor** to explain functionalism. As a line of code is defined by what it does in the program rather than its hardware implementation, so mental states are defined by the influence they have on the behaviour of people who have them, not on their physical correlates. As the same program can be run on different devices— the same Angry Birds game can be implemented in an iPhone or an Android phone—so different brains can have the same mental state.*

There is one type of fruit in this picture: apples. But there are eight tokens of fruit in this picture, namely, the eight apples.

This computer metaphor for functionalism is quite common, and quite helpful, so it is worth dwelling on the following thought experiment.

THOUGHT EXPERIMENT 5.2
Artificial Intelligence

In 1953, the computing pioneer Alan Turing posed this question: "Can machines think?" He proposed an Imitation Game in response to this question. In the **Imitation Game** (now known as the **Turing Test**), a human judge has five minutes to ask the hidden interviewee by text any series of questions they want. After five minutes they must guess whether they are interacting with a machine or a human. If the judge guesses correctly, the judge wins. If a machine is able to fool 30% of the human judges, the machine wins the game, or, passes the Turing Test. If you were the judge, what series of questions would you ask to determine whether you are speaking with a human or a machine? Try the game yourself. Ask a friend to text you their answer to a question, then get them to ask ChatGPT the same question, and text the bot's answer back as well. Try to figure out which answer your friend gave, and which answer ChatGPT gave.

The first machine to ever pass the Turing Test was a 2014 program called Eugene Goostman, which scored a fooling rate of 33%. Goostman imitated a poorly educated Ukrainian boy, so judges thought they must be talking to a human. These days, virtual assistants such as ChatGPT, Siri, Alexa, and Google Assistant are increasingly capable of carrying on text and audio conversations with people. It seems possible that someday we will seamlessly interact with machines, as imagined in *Her* (2013), *Ex Machina* (2014), *Westworld* (2018), *Black Mirror: Be Right Back* (2013), and *Black Mirror: Rachel, Jack and Ashley Too* (2019). If machines get to the point of perfectly carrying on conversations with humans, would you say that machines are thinking? Turing says yes. He reasons as follows: humans are thinking when they properly respond to questions, and this machine can perfectly imitate human responses to questions, so this machine is thinking too. Turing is a proponent of what is called **strong artificial intelligence**: if a machine responds to questions in a manner that is indistinguishable from human responses, the machine is thinking.

Functionalists tend to agree with Turing. For Turing, *thinking* is defined behaviourally. A set of questions is inputted into the system, and a series of responses are emitted from the system. No one knows what is inside the system, perhaps it is a machine, perhaps a human—but that's irrelevant. Thinking is entirely defined by how the system responds to the questions. For functionalists, *thinking* is also defined behaviourally. A set of questions, or any stimulus such as seeing a dog, is inputted into our minds. The key question is: how do these inputs influence our behaviour? You see a dog across the street, which causes you to turn around and walk the other way. Your desire to avoid contact with the dog is you engaging in dog-fearing behaviour. Hence, a cat who also avoids contact with the dog is also engaging in dog-fearing behaviour—all there is to dog fearing is engaging in dog-fearing behaviour when stimulated by perceiving dogs.

In 1980, the American philosopher **John Searle** (1932–) introduced the **Chinese Room** objection to strong artificial intelligence. Searle imagines that you are an English speaker locked in a room with Chinese symbols and

Does this mean that functionalists think *fish* can have mentality too? Functionalists owe us, and often try to give us, an account of what makes something with input/output functions *mental*.

a book of instructions for manipulating the symbols. A Chinese judge outside the room sends you questions in Chinese, to which you send back the series of Chinese symbols that the instruction book tells you to send back. The Chinese judge marvels at your excellent answers, and concludes you are a native Chinese speaker, but you do not understand a word of the Chinese questions. You have inputs and outputs that are indistinguishable from those of the native Chinese speaker, but Searle insists you "understand nothing."[9] As the English speaker responds properly to Chinese symbols without understanding Chinese, so machines may respond properly to questions without understanding

---

9 John Searle, "Minds, Brains, and Programs," *The Behavioral and Brain Sciences* 3, no. 3 (1980): 418.

the questions, or thinking through the answers. Searle concludes that passing the Turing test does not indicate mentality. Those following Searle endorse **Weak Artificial Intelligence**, according to which it's possible to program machines to respond to questions as humans do; but they would only be imitating thinking, not actually thinking.

It is worth considering what dualists and identity theorists would say about artificial intelligence. Dualists may reject the possibility of machines thinking as humans do. Dualists say that thinking is a non-physical activity involving consciousness, and machines are completely physical, so machines cannot think as humans do. Identity theorists may endorse artificial intelligence, as they agree that thinking is physical, so thinking is derivable from the physical substance that computers are made of. On the other hand, identity theorists think minds are identical to brains, which are carbon-based biological organs. Machines do not have carbon-based biological brains, so they may not be capable of thinking.

Objection 1: Consciousness

Functionalism suffers from a similar objection that Searle levels against Strong AI. It is this: functionalists, like Strong AI advocates, define mental states by their causes and behavioural results. But in so doing, as Strong AI advocates miss the importance of *understanding*, so functionalists miss the crucial element of consciousness in mental states. Jani touches a hot stove, causing her hand to violently withdraw from the heating element. This is the functional analysis of Jani's pain. But, if this is all there is to pain, pain doesn't seem so bad at all. Withdrawing one's hand when touching hot stoves is a rather non-strenuous muscle movement, and what is so bad about muscle movements? We intuitively want to answer: it is the painfulness of pain that is so bad, it is the raw, unbearable searing feeling that is so bad! But the painfulness of pain is not part of the functional definition of pain. The functionalist seems to leave out the core ingredient to mental states entirely, namely, what they feel like. In so doing, they offer an incomplete description of mental states. For example, imagine you and your zombie twin. They are behaviourally the same: zombies also quickly withdraw their hands from a hot stove. So functionalists say your zombie twin has the same mental states as you do. But you are conscious while the zombie is not: you *feel the pain*, they do not. They seem to be missing the mental state of pain, so it is not right to say their pain equals yours.

Objection 2: Mental Causation

Dualists faced the problem of mental causation: behaviour is fully caused by prior physical causes, which leaves no room for distinct mental causes to bring about behaviour. Functionalists face a similar problem of mental causation. Namely, mental states are defined as functional states that are distinct from the physical states implementing those functions. But, according to physical causal completeness, those physical states bring about behaviour all by themselves, which calls into question the ability for distinct mental/functional states to have any new causal power. To return to the restaurant example, imagine that Katarina is hired to fill the job of being Mario's cook. It is Katarina that does all the work: she barbeques the steak, she tosses the salad, etc. What work is the job description of 'being Mario's cook' doing? Nothing, as the implementer of this job, Katarina, does all this work. Or, to use another example, let us say that we want to provoke a bull, so we want to find something that will fulfill this provoking role. We consider a poking stick, a red blanket, and a clanging cymbal. We decide upon the red blanket, and we wave the blanket at the bull, angering the bull. What causes the bull to get angry? Was it the provocative function we wanted to fill, or the red blanket itself? Seemingly, the waving red blanket causes the bull to get angry, as the bull does not know or care about what function we were using the blanket for. Likewise, Annie's fear is defined by whatever makes her run when she sees a dog, but some neural process is what causes her to run whenever she sees a dog, leaving the functional definition with no work to do.

5.4 Eliminative Materialism

In Chapter 4.2 the distinction between conservative reduction and eliminative reduction was drawn. On conservative reduction, the entity being reduced is conserved, or, continues to exist, as the base entity. Water is conservatively reduced to H_2O, but water still exists as H_2O. Mind-brain identity theory embraces conservative reduction, where the mind still exists as the brain. On eliminative reduction, the entity being reduced is eliminated, or no longer exists, but only the base entity exists. Santa is eliminatively reduced, as Santa doesn't exist; rather, it is the parents of children who place the presents under the tree and eat the milk and cookies. **Eliminative materialism** embraces eliminative reduction about the mind; where the mind doesn't exist, only the brain exists. As such, eliminative materialism is located on the far right of the spectrum, indicating that mind does not exist, only the material world exists.

Eliminative materialism was popularized in the 1980s by **Patricia Churchland** (1943-) and **Paul Churchland** (1942-). They begin their defence of eliminative materialism by defining **folk psychology** as the traditional manner in which humans explain other people's behaviour. People behave in various ways: sometimes they smile, sometimes they cry, sometimes they scream. Why do people behave in these ways? For centuries humans were raised with a ready-made model for explaining human behaviour called folk psychology, according to which we explain behaviour by ascribing beliefs and desires to humans. Patel is running away, he must believe he is in danger, and desires to avoid danger; Simone is smiling, she must believe she got the job, and desired the job.

Folk theories are sometimes useful, but they ultimately make way for advanced scientific theories. Aristotle's folk physics suggested that the four elements (earth, air, water, fire) have a natural resting place that they tend toward, so rain falls down because its natural resting place is below air, and rocks sink in water because earth's natural resting place is below water. This model occasionally works, but it ultimately made way for advanced scientific explanations such as gravitational force. Similarly, while folk psychology is sometimes useful, it fails at times as well. Paul Churchland provides the example of sleep: "we do not know what sleep is, or why we have to have it, despite spending a full third of our lives in that condition. (The answer 'for rest' is mistaken.)"[10] Neuroscientists are learning that sleep is essential for memory consolidation and neural pathway formation, while folk psychology mistakenly suggests we only sleep for rest. Churchland also provides the example of mental illness: "we do not know what mental illness is, nor how to cure it." Folk psychology suggests that changing one's outlook in life can resolve depression, but neuroscientists find that medication and even electrically stimulating certain brain regions can also help with depression. These are just two examples of how the folk psychological theory of attributing beliefs and desires to humans to make sense of their behaviour should ultimately make way for an advanced neuroscience that accurately explains human behaviour.

Objection 1: Success of Folk Psychology

Eliminative materialism has few adherents. Some object that, contrary to Churchland's claim, folk psychological explanations, or, common-sense psychological explanations, of human behaviour are surprisingly accurate. Imagine that Raj buys a ticket to see his favourite band play at a concert two months from now. Raj's friend Alice, upon hearing this news, can accurately predict where Raj will be two months from now. She just needs to assume that Raj desires to go to the concert that he has tickets for, and she can accurately predict where Raj will be two months into the future. This is actually quite an impressive feat. It involves knowing how Raj's body will weave through space and time over the next sixty days, and being able to predict exactly where Raj's body will end up at a certain time. It would be difficult to make such a prediction based on an analysis of physical forces alone. It turns out that ordinary common-sense psychological explanations explain human behaviour quite well.

Objection 2: Self-Refuting

Eliminative materialism seems to be **self-refuting**. Recall from Chapter 2.4 that a self-refuting statement is a statement that, if it were true, it would prove itself false. Eliminative materialism is the belief that there are no beliefs. So, if eliminative materialism is true, then there are no beliefs, so eliminative materialism cannot be a belief one holds. Similarly, eliminative materialists argue in support of their conclusions by reasoning from premises. They say: folk psychology

---

10 Paul Churchland, *Matter and Consciousness* (Cambridge, MA: MIT Press, 1984), 45–46.

explains human behaviour, but it is a bad theory of human behaviour, and bad theories should be rejected, so folk psychology should be rejected as a theory explaining human behaviour. But, if eliminative materialism is true, people do not believe conclusions based on the reasoning from premises to conclusions, so the premises do not serve as reasons for believing eliminative materialism is true.

5.5 Idealism

While eliminative materialism occupies the furthest right of the spectrum, on the furthest left of the spectrum stands **idealism**, which is the doctrine that only the mind exists: there is no material world. One form of idealism was discussed in Chapter 3.2: Parmenides is an idealist who says that only ideas exist. With Descartes, the nature of mind shifts to emphasizing the mind as involving consciousness, and later idealists, such as **George Berkeley**, emphasize ideas as including conscious perceiving. Berkeley, an eighteenth-century British philosopher, claims that our world is in fact composed of ideas or perceptions. Consider Ivan, who is eating a pineapple. It seems as if Ivan is interacting with an ordinary material object—the pineapple. But, as Ivan takes a taste, the sweet taste of the pineapple exists as a perception in his mind, delivered to him by his own taste buds. If he did not have taste buds, there would have been no sweet flavour. While he first thought the pineapple was a material object because it exists outside of himself, he realizes that the colour and shape and perception of the distance of the pineapple from his body exists as perceptions of his mind as well, delivered to him by his own visual system. If he were colour blind, or if he were another type of animal, he would not experience the same colours and shapes. Berkeley thinks every ordinary object can be likewise analyzed as being ideas or perceptions: "It is indeed an opinion strangely prevailing amongst men that houses, mountains, rivers, and in a word all sensible objects, have an existence, natural or real, distinct from their being perceived by the under-standing.... what are the forementioned objects but the things we perceive by sense? And what do we perceive besides our own ideas or sensations?"[11] Thus, when we first think a tree is a material object, it turns out that we perceive our own sense experience, which is an idea of the mind. Everything we think and perceive is ideal: there is no mind-independent material world.

Like Eliminative Materialism on the opposite far end of the spectrum, Idealism also has few adherents. In Chapter 8.4 we will spend more time unpacking Berkeley's argument for idealism, and various objections levelled against it. It suffices here to note the general contours of the position that occupies the furthest left of the spectrum, to see the view that only mind exists, and the material world does not exist.

---

11 George Berkeley, *A Treatise Concerning the Principles of Human Knowledge*, 193.

Summary

Dualists say the mind is conscious stuff such as experience and thinking, which is distinct from the brain. They tend to agree with those who focus on ideal or mental elements to reality, as those occupying the soul and psychological model of personal identity do as well. Mind-brain identity theorists say the mind is physical stuff such as the neural processing in the brain. They tend to focus on the material elements of reality, as those occupying the brute physical models of personal identity do as well. At the extreme of the materialist camp stands the eliminative materialist who says the mind does not even exist, while at the extreme of the idealist camp stands Berkeley's idealism which says the material world does not even exist. In the middle of the idealist-materialist spectrum stand the functionalists who say that the mind is functional stuff such as behavioural tendencies. They say that while the mind is distinct from the brain, the mind nevertheless must be realized in brains. In the next chapter we zero in on one particular aspect of the mind, namely, the ability of the mind to freely choose. We shall see, once again, that some models emphasize the agent's autonomy from physical processing while other models emphasize the agent's dependence upon physical processing.

Key Terms in Chapter 5: Mind and Brain

Mind-Body Dualism	Mind-Brain Identity	Computer Metaphor
Conceivability	Theory	Imitation Game
Argument	J.J.C. Smart	Strong Artificial
Zombies	Jaegwon Kim	Intelligence
David Chalmers	Mind-Brain Correlation	Turing Test
Indiscernibility of	Begging the Question	Weak Artificial
Identicals	Ockham's Razor	Intelligence
René Descartes	Simplicity Argument	Phineas Gage
Knowledge Argument	Causal Argument	Chinese Room
Interactionist Dualism	Intensional Fallacy	John Searle
Mental Causation	Phenomenological	Eliminative
Responsibility	Fallacy	Materialism
Argument from	Multiple Realizability	Folk Psychology
Analogy	Type	Self-Refuting
Contact Objection	Token	George Berkeley
False Analogy	Type Identity Theory	Idealism
Physical Causal	Token-Identity Theory	Patricia and Paul
Completeness	Functionalism	Churchland
Conservation Laws	Function	
Epiphenomenalism	Jerry Fodor	

Philosophy on Television: Mind and Brain

Ghost (1990)

This film is one in a long line of films about people who experience bodily death, but whose souls live on in ghostly form. Other films in this genre include *The Sixth Sense* (1999), *Coco* (2017), and *Soul* (2020). These films focus on the possibility, raised by Descartes' model of dualism, of the mind being separable from the body. They also frequently gesture at the contact objection by introducing difficulties with the ghosts interacting with the physical world. In *Ghost*, the ghost Sam cannot speak with his former wife Molly—although he can walk on floors without falling through. In *Soul*, it is possible to slap souls, though they don't have bodies, without them feeling pain. In addition, souls cannot taste anything, as taste is a bodily sensation.

Transcendence (2014)

In the movie *Transcendence* (2014), a scientist named Will has a month left to live, so his friends scan the neural connections and structures of Will's brain, then copy this information into computer code, and upload the code onto a computer. When Will dies, they turn on the computer and Will starts to live online. The theme of uploading minds to computers occurs in other shows as well, such as *Black Mirror: San Junipero* (2016), *Black Mirror: USS Callister* (2017), and the *Westworld* and *Upload* series.

Ex Machina (2014)

In the movie *Ex Machina* (2014), a machine is programmed so well that it is able to fool people into treating it as human. The Turing Test is raised in this movie, and considers the Artificial Intelligence question about whether a machine will someday be able to perfectly mimic typical human responses to questions, and if such a machine is genuinely thinking or not. Other shows with similar themes include *Black Mirror: Be Right Back* (2013) and *Black Mirror: Rachel, Jack and Ashley Too* (2019).

Divergent (2014)

In the movie *Divergent* (2014), the leaders of a dystopian city inject chemicals into the brains of its citizens in order to control their minds. At one point, the leader remarks: "everything we think of what makes up a person, thoughts, emotions, history, all wiped away by chemistry." This aligns with the mind-brain identity theory, according to which thoughts and emotions are complex chemical processes in the brain.

Additional Resources

Visit this book's companion resources for additional materials, including video content and an automated tool for planning argumentative essays.

sites.broadviewpress.com/knowing/chapter-5

Chapter 6
Free Will and Determinism

THOUGHT EXPERIMENT 6
Buridan's Donkey

A donkey is placed midway between two equally appealing bales of hay. The hay on the right exactly resembles in size, nutrition, and taste the hay on the left, so neither bale is more tempting to the donkey. The donkey is exactly ten feet from each bale, so neither bale is easier to reach for the donkey. The donkey has no limp in his legs to favour him going in one direction over another, and there is no wind wafting the smell from one bale rather than another. His preferences are exactly equal in every way. As the donkey gets increasingly hungry, it realizes it must make a choice. But which bale of hay will the donkey select, and why will it choose that bale over the other one? Or, will the donkey simply sit and wait until it finally dies of starvation?

This thought experiment, known as the puzzle of **Buridan's Donkey**, is named after the fourteenth-century moral philosopher Jean Buridan (1301–59), who argued that humans must will to do whatever presents itself as the greatest good. Buridan's critics satirically imagined a donkey caught between two equally compelling goods, leaving the will incapable of acting. This puzzle is historically preceded by the medieval philosopher al-Ghazali (1058–1111), who imagined a camel starving between two groves of date trees. And, prior to both of them, Aristotle imagined the case involving "A man who, though exceedingly hungry and thirsty, and both equally, yet being equidistant from food and drink, is therefore bound to stay where he is."[1]

---

1   Aristotle, *On the Heavens* 295b30, in *Complete Works of Aristotle: Volume 1*, trans. J. Barnes (Princeton: Princeton University Press, 2014).

This puzzle serves as an example of the longstanding clash between intuitions supporting free will and intuitions supporting determinism. If donkeys behave deterministically, then Buridan's donkey will go to whichever bale of hay it is compelled to go to. But it is not compelled to go to any one bale of hay over the other, so the donkey will simply wait until it dies—a counterintuitive result. However, if donkeys have free will, it would simply select one course of action at random, where this course of action, since it is not based on preferences or deliberation, would be arbitrary and based on chance—another counterintuitive result.

These unpalatable options highlight the dispute between those endorsing free will and those endorsing determinism. If **determinism** is true then, given the same starting conditions—say standing in your kitchen while contemplating which restaurant to go to tonight—only one possible outcome can occur—say choosing McDonald's. If **free will** is true, then the same starting conditions can lead to various outcomes—you could go to McDonald's or Burger King. Which one is true? Or, is it possible for both free will and determinism to be true? Many have weighed in on this issue, resulting in a variety of possible positions. A thousand years ago, the Persian poet Jalaluddin Rumi (1207–73) summarized as follows: "There is a disputation, (which will continue) till mankind are raised from the dead, between the Necessitarians and the partisans of (absolute) Free-will."[2] The various positions can be roughly placed on the following spectrum:

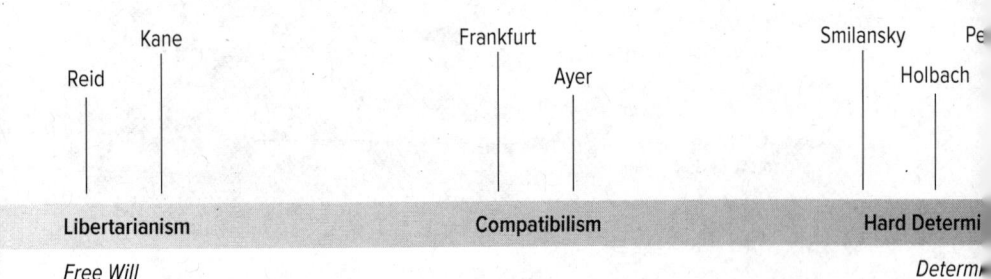

Spectrum 6: Free Will and Determinism

On the left side of the spectrum stand the libertarians who argue that since free will is true, determinism is false. On the right stand the hard determinists, who argue that since determinism is true, free will is false. Occupying the middle ground are the compatibilists who assert that both free will and determinism are true. Let us begin with hard determinism.

---

2   Jalalu'ddin Rumi, *Masnawi Book 5*, ed. Reza Nazari and Somayeh Nazari, trans. Reynald A. Nicholson, www.learnpersianonline.com.

6.1 Hard Determinism

Two things are incompatible when they are so opposed that they cannot exist together. For example, two people in a relationship are incompatible when they cannot co-exist together—Dominic and Dalia tried to date for a while, but they started fighting all the time and ended in a bitter break up. They were not compatible with each other. Likewise, it is possible for two principles to be incompatible. We saw in Chapter 5.2 that the principles of mental causation, dualism, and physical causal completeness are incompatible—we can't have all three of them. The hard determinist endorses **incompatibilism** about free will and determinism, which is to say that the hard determinist thinks that free will and determinism are so opposed that we cannot think they are both true. Since free will and determinism are incompatible, we can only select one of the two principles, and the other must be false. The **hard determinist** is persuaded by the argumentation supporting determinism, so they take determinism to be true, and free will to be false. But what is determinism, and what is the argumentation supporting determinism?

There are several versions of determinism, but they all share a common theme. On determinism, a set of conditions that obtains at a given time determines, or makes happen, only one specific outcome at a later time. The **theological determinist** says God is omnipotent (i.e., all powerful), so God has absolute power over human action and ultimately determines all our actions. Or, God is omniscient (i.e., all knowing), so God knows how you will act tomorrow and you must act how God knows you will. **Biological determinism** says that biological factors, such as our genetic predispositions and instincts, not only determine our height but completely determine how we act. **Cultural determinism** says that sociological factors, such as public institutions, family values, peer-influence, and social media, completely determine how we act. **Psychological determinists** say that unconscious and/or uncontrollable psychological or neurological factors, such as anxiety disorders, obsessive-compulsive disorders, suppressed memories, and addictions, completely determine how we act. Lastly, according to **microphysical causal determinism**, the arrangement of particles in the remote past, combined with the laws of physics, completely determines, via a chain of cause-effect relations between then and now, how we presently act. Thus, the manner in which events unfolded during the initial big bang moment of the universe, combined with the laws of nature, necessitated every proceeding event until ultimately it was inevitable that you would exist today and be reading this sentence right now.

There are several arguments supporting determinism. First, the principle of sufficient reason supports determinism. As you recall from Chapter 3.2, Parmenides argued that *ex nihilo, nihil fit*, or, out of nothing, nothing comes. Gottfried Leibniz expresses a similar view, which he calls the **Principle of Sufficient Reason**, according to which every event, including every human action, can be completely explained, or, has a sufficient cause or reason for its existence. Imagine, for example, that Neil Armstrong lands on the surface of the

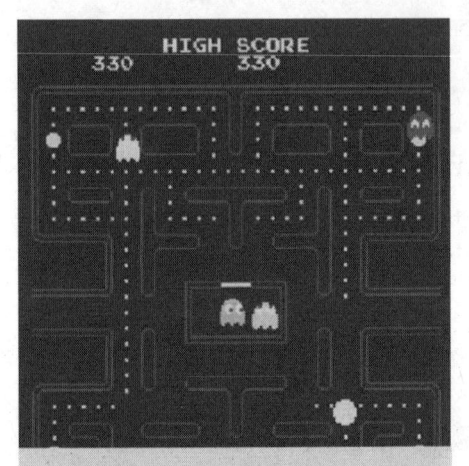

A joke is told about a Nintendo spokesperson named Kristian Wilson who was asked whether computer games negatively affect kids. Her reply: "computer games don't affect kids; I mean, if Pac-Man affected us as kids, we'd all be running around in darkened rooms, munching magic pills and listening to repetitive electronic music." This joke highlights how cultural and unconscious forces may control our behaviour.

moon for the first time but finds a spacecraft is already there! Armstrong, and the rest of the world, would be astonished and would call for an investigation into the origins of this other spacecraft. Did another country secretly land on the moon first? Is it an alien vessel? Imagine instead that NASA responds by saying, "There is no explanation for this strange spacecraft we found on the moon; we do not need a cause or reason for this spacecraft: it is just there, that is all." Few would be satisfied. This is because humans typically assume that events have a complete explanation for their occurrence: they do not just occur without a complete cause or reason. The same is true for everyday events. If you saw leaves rustling on a tree, but there was no wind, no birds hidden in the leaves, no earthquake, etc., you would believe that there is a cause you didn't know about. You wouldn't believe that this was a causeless event. If the Principle of Sufficient Reason is true, then our actions require some completely determining cause.

Another argument for determinism comes from the principle of physical causal completeness, according to which every effect, including each human action, has a sufficient physical cause. This principle is perhaps best applied to the free will debate through a series of experiments performed by **Benjamin Libet** and others. In the 1980s, Libet developed an experiment whereby participants had electrodes placed upon their scalps to measure neural activity in their brains. Participants were instructed to press a button on a keyboard at a random time of their choosing while noting the exact time at which they felt the desire to press the button. Libet discovered that electrical buildup in the motor region of the brain began first, then 300 milliseconds later the conscious urge to press the button occurred, then 200 milliseconds later the button was actually pressed. Libet concluded that "the initiation of the voluntary act appears to be an unconscious cerebral process. Clearly free will or free choice of whether to act now could not be the initiating agent."[3] If Libet is correct, then our brains are already in the process of determining when and how we act before we are even aware of what is going to happen.

---

3 Benjamin Libet, "The Neural Time-Factor in Perception, Volition, and Free Will," *Revue de Métaphysique et de Morale* 97, no. 2 (1992): 269.

One of the most famous historical defences of hard determinism comes from the eighteenth-century philosopher **Baron Henry d'Holbach** (1723–89). Here is an excerpt:

The System of Nature (Baron Henry d'Holbach, 1770)[4]

Thus man is a being purely physical; in whatever manner he is considered, he is connected to universal Nature: submitted to the necessary, to the immutable laws that she imposes on all the beings she contains, according to their peculiar essences; conformable to the respective properties with which, without consulting them, she endows each particular species. Man's life is a line that Nature commands him to describe upon the surface of the earth: without his ever being able to swerve from it even for an instant. He is born without his own consent; his organization does in no wise depend upon himself; his ideas come to him involuntarily; his habits are in the power of those who cause him to contract them; he is unceasingly modified by causes, whether visible or concealed, over which he has no control; give the hue to his way of thinking, and determine his manner of acting. He is good or bad—happy or miserable—wise or foolish—reasonable or irrational, without his will going for anything in these various states ...

This example will serve to explain the whole phenomena of the human will. This will, or rather the brain, finds itself in the same situation as a ball, which although it has received an impulse that drives it forward in a straight line, is deranged in its course, whenever a force, superior to the first, obliges it to change its direction. The man who drinks the poisoned water, appears a madman; but the actions of fools are as necessary as those of the most prudent individuals.... But it will be insisted, the debauchee may be prevailed on to change his conduct; this does not imply that he is a free agent; but that motives may be found sufficiently powerful to annihilate the effect of those that previously acted upon him; then these new motives determine his will to the new mode of conduct he may adopt, as necessarily as the former did to the old mode....

When the soul is assailed by two motives that act alternately upon it, or modify it successively, it deliberates; the brain is in a sort of equilibrium, accompanied with perpetual oscillations, sometimes towards one object, sometimes towards the other, until the most forcible carries the point, and thereby extricates it, from this state of suspense, in which consists the indecision of his will. But when the brain is simultaneously assailed by causes equally strong, that move it in opposite directions; agreeable to the general law of all bodies, when they are struck equally by contrary powers,

---

4   Baron d'Holbach, "Of the System of Man's Free Agency," *The System of Nature* (1770), trans. H. Robinson (Kitchener: Batoche Books, 2001), LXI.

it stops; it is neither capable to will nor to act; it waits until one of the two causes has obtained sufficient force to overpower the other, to determine its will, to attract it in such a manner that it may prevail over the efforts of the other cause.

... because he cannot perceive the chain of operations in his soul, or the motive-principle that acts within him, he supposes himself a free agent; which, literally translated, signifies that he moves himself by himself; that he determines himself without cause; when he rather ought to say, he is ignorant how or for why he acts in the manner he does.

In this passage,

1. *d'Holbach embraces determinism by saying that our behaviour is ultimately determined by natural causes beyond our control. We mistakenly think we are free because we are actually unaware of the natural forces that determine our behaviour.*
2. *d'Holbach argues that action contrary to our regular patterns of behaviour is not proof of free will, but is proof that some new countervailing idea or motive is acting upon us. Indecisiveness occurs when contrasting motives are simultaneously at work in us. We remain indecisive until some further motive causes us to move in a certain direction. Thus, d'Holbach articulates the typical hard determinist reply to the puzzle of Buridan's Donkey: the donkey stands still in the middle of the bales of hay until some new motive enters its mind, leading it toward one of the bales of hay.*

Objection 1: Responsibility

Recall the **responsibility** argument for mental causation from Chapter 5.1. It states that humans are responsible for their actions, but they can only be responsible for their actions if they control whether they commit the action or not, so mental causation must be true. There is a similar argument against hard determinism. Namely, if humans are determined to behave as they do by physical forces they have no control over, then humans are not responsible for their actions. But it is absurd to think humans are not responsible for their actions, so hard determinism cannot be true. This is a **reductio ad absurdum** argument against hard determinism. Recall from Chapter 1.5.4, a reductio ad absurdum argument states that a belief leads to an absurd conclusion, so the belief is false. In this case, the belief in hard determinism leads to the absurd conclusion that we are not responsible for our actions, so hard determinism is false. As an example of how absurd it would be to deny personal responsibility because of the truth of determinism, consider the case of Nathan Leopold and Richard Loeb, two wealthy teenagers who committed a heinous murder in the 1920s—they dismembered a teenager in their search for thrills. Clarence Darrow, a famous criminal lawyer, defended them. Part of his defence consisted in the fact that **Leopold and Loeb** were determined to commit the murder, so they cannot be blamed: "Nature is strong and she is pitiless. She works in her own mysterious way, and we are her victims ... What had this boy to do with it? He was not his own father, he was not his own mother; he was not his own grandparents. All of this was handed to him ... this terrible crime was inherent in his organism, and it came from some ancestor ... he did not surround himself with governesses and wealth. He did not make himself ... if he had been trained as he should have been it would not have happened."[5] In other words, Leopold and Loeb were biologically and culturally determined to commit this murder, so they should not be blamed. But this sounds absurd; of course they are responsible for their crime.

Objection 2: Reactive Attitudes

Not only does putting criminals in jail assume humans are responsible for their actions, but a host of other attitudes we regularly hold, called **reactive attitudes**, also assumes responsibility. We blame and condemn others when they do wrong, but this attitude of blame assumes people have control over their behaviour. Genevieve cheats on Gustave, and Gustave thinks she is a bad person for it, but this assumes Genevieve can control how she behaves. We praise and admire others when they are virtuous, but this attitude also assumes their behaviour is up to them. Harmony gives her money to charity, and we admire her for it, but this assumes her donation was up to her. We feel pride in ourselves or our children for certain accomplishments, but pride also assumes that we had something to do with making these accomplishments happen. We feel guilty when we do bad things, but this also assumes that we could have done something else instead. If hard determinism is true, then we are not in control of ourselves, and these natural reactive attitudes make little sense anymore. Why would we blame others when they couldn't have done otherwise? Why would we be proud of our children for making the soccer team when natural forces in the remote past determined they would be born, be athletic, and work hard at soccer? This is another reductio ad absurdum argument against hard determinism: the belief in hard determinism leads to the absurd conclusion that our reactive attitudes make no sense anymore, so hard determinism is false.

Recall from Chapter 1.5.4 that a reductio ad absurdum is only good reasoning if the absurd consequences do indeed follow from the belief. **Derk Pereboom** (1957–) is a contemporary proponent of a position similar to hard determinism. He responds to some of these objections by saying that these consequences are not absurd after all. Here is an excerpt from his writings:

---

5   Clarence Darrow, *The Plea of Clarence Darrow* (Chicago: Ralph Fletcher Seymour, 1924), 70–71.

Living Without Free Will (Derk Pereboom, 2004)[6]

A much more resilient theory for justifying policies for protecting society from criminals, and one that is not threatened by hard incompatibilism, proceeds precisely by an analogy with the right to quarantine. Ferdinand Schoeman has argued that if in order to protect society, we have the right to quarantine people who are carriers of severe communicable diseases, then we also have the right to isolate the criminally dangerous to protect society. For the carriers, it is morally acceptable to restrict their activities and even keep them isolated from anyone else in order to protect society. If the danger to society is great enough, it is acceptable to deprive carriers of their liberty to the degree that the safety of society requires. This is true irrespective of the carriers' moral responsibility for the disease. If a child is a carrier of the Ebola virus by its being passed on to her at birth from her parent, quarantine is nevertheless intuitively legitimate. Suppose a person poses a danger to society by a sufficiently strong tendency to commit murder. Even if he is not in general a morally responsible agent, society would nevertheless seem to have as much right to detain him as it does to quarantine a carrier of a deadly communicable disease who is not responsible for being a carrier....

Schoeman's article explores the acceptability of preventative detention for those who have not yet committed crimes, reflection on which occasions the following objection to the quarantine view. If justification of detention by this analogy is tenable, must it not then be legitimate to detain those who have not committed a violent crime, if by some means it has been ascertained that they are quite likely to do so? ...

Gratitude might well require the supposition that the person to whom one is grateful is morally responsible for an other-regarding act, and therefore hard incompatibilism might well undermine gratitude. However, certain aspects of this attitude would be left untouched, aspects that can play the role gratitude commonly has in interpersonal relationships. First, gratitude includes an element of thankfulness toward those who have benefited us. Sometimes, being thankful involves the belief that the object of one's attitude is praiseworthy for some action. But one can also be thankful to a pet or a small child for some favor, even if one does not believe that he is morally responsible. Perhaps one can even be thankful for the sun or the rain even if one does not believe that these elements are backed by morally responsible agency. In general, if one believed hard incompatibilism, one's thankfulness might lack features that it would have if one did not, but nevertheless, this aspect of gratitude can survive....

If we indeed desire freely willed love, then we desire a kind of love whose possibility hard incompatibilism denies. Still, the possibilities for

---

6   Derk Pereboom, *Living Without Free Will* (Oxford: Oxford University Press, 2004), 174–211.

love that remain are surely sufficient for good interpersonal relationships. If we can aspire to the sort of love parents typically have toward children, or the kind romantic lovers ideally have toward one another, or the type shared by friends who are immediately attracted to one another, and whose relationship is deepened by their interactions, then the possibility of fulfillment in interpersonal relationships is far from undermined....

Destructive anger in relationships is nourished by the belief that the other is blameworthy for having done wrong. The anger that fuels many ethnic conflicts results partly from the belief that a group of people deserves blame for some large-scale evil. Hard incompatibilism advocates retracting such beliefs because they are false, and as a result the associated anger could be diminished, and its expressions curtailed.

If imprisonment is based on public safety, can we imprison someone who is planning to commit a crime in the future? Can we let someone walk freely because their crime was a one-time crime of passion that would not be repeated?

In this passage,

1. *Pereboom agrees that hard determinism implies the loss of personal responsibility for our behaviour, but the loss of responsibility is not absurd. As patients with infectious diseases are quarantined for public safety though they are not blamed for their illness, so criminals can be detained for the sake of public safety though they are not blamed for their crimes.*

2. *Pereboom says that other features of humanity that seem to fail if determinism is true do not actually fail. We can still be grateful for things that were not freely given, as we are grateful for sunsets. We can still enjoy deterministic forms of love, such as occurs when parents are biologically disposed to love their offspring.*

3. *Pereboom argues that there are practical virtues of hard determinism. These include the alleviation of anger at others when we realize they are not to blame for their actions, the loss of guilt and pride in ourselves for blaming or praising ourselves, and the peacefulness that arises from accepting fated circumstances.*

If you knew a terrible truth that another person did not know (say, that Santa does not exist), would you keep the secret in order to protect their feelings, or would you tell them?

Objection: The Noble Lie

Some contemporary hard determinists, such as **Saul Smilansky**, agree that determinism is true and free will is false, but disagree with Pereboom's view that the loss of free will is no problem. They think that if the population at large knew that free will was false then people would despair at the meaninglessness of their lives and be more likely to engage in immoral behaviour. For example, Kathleen Vohs and Jonathan Schooler recently exposed participants in their study to a deterministic text and a neutral text, and then presented the possibility of secretly cheating on a test to them. Subjects were more likely to cheat after reading the deterministic text than they were after reading the neutral text.[7] They conclude that belief in determinism makes us more likely to cheat. Smilansky says, therefore, that hard determinists ought to hide the truth of determinism from the masses, in order to preserve the fabric of society: "People as a rule ought not to be fully aware of the ultimate inevitability of what they have done, for this will affect the way in which they hold themselves responsible ... we often want a person to blame himself, feel guilty ... such a person is not likely to do all this if he internalizes the ultimate hard determinist perspective."[8] Minimizing guilt and moral outrage would unshackle the only restraint preventing some people from harming others, while minimizing pride and praise would make people less likely to accomplish great things. So it is best to hide the truth of determinism and the falsity of free will away from the masses.

6.2 Libertarianism

Libertarianism is, like hard determinism, an incompatibilist view. **Libertarians** agree that free will and determinism are incompatible, so one of the two principles must be rejected. Libertarians, however, say that free will is true, so determinism must be false. But what is free will, and what reason is there to suppose free will is true? Libertarians often define free will in two ways. First, free will means that humans have **alternative possibilities**, or, when

---

7   Kathleen D. Vohs and Jonathan W. Schooler, "The Value of Believing in Free Will," *Psychological Science* 19, no. 1 (2008): 49–54.

8   Saul Smilansky, "Free Will, Fundamental Dualism and the Centrality of Illusion," in *The Oxford Handbook of Free Will*, ed. Robert H. Kane (Oxford: Oxford University Press, 2002), 498.

presented with multiple options, we can select whichever option we wish. Howard is standing in the food court, wondering whether to eat at Subway, New York Fries, or McDonald's. Howard can select whichever of these options he wishes. Second, free will means that humans have **ultimate sourcehood**, which means that we are the source of our own actions. It is up to us whether our actions occur or not: they are not caused by factors outside us and beyond our control. Imagine Howard once again, standing in the food court and wondering whether to eat at Subway, New York Fries, or McDonald's. Howard is the originating source of his choice of Subway. If Howard only selects Subway because his parents raised him to love Subway, and he was genetically predisposed to prefer the

The principle of alternative possibilities is captured well in Robert Frost's (1874–1963) famous poem "The Road Not Taken," where he writes "Two roads diverged in a wood, and I—I took the one less traveled by." Frost imagines someone coming to a fork in a road, and that person can select to either travel to the left or to the right.

tastes associated with Subway sandwiches, then the originating source of the action lies outside of Howard, and he is not the ultimate source of his action.

While the doctrine of free will suggests that it is up to us which outcome we select from a variety of possible outcomes, there are some reasonable limits placed on our free will. No one who endorses free will thinks we can do *anything* we want. Chopra has three options of ice cream he can buy, but the one he really wants is sold out. Does this mean he is not free? No, since he still has a few options he can choose from. Ronald has domineering parents who heavily influence him to become a fire fighter. Does this mean that Ronald is not free? No, since there is still a small chance for him to become a baker or lawyer. Having free will does not mean that we can always do whatever we want; rather, free will means that we sometimes (perhaps rarely) make decisions that are up to us, even if our options are limited and we are heavily influenced to select one of the options.

The arguments for free will mirror the arguments for mental causation discussed in Chapter 5.1. First, free will is a common-sense position. Most humans believe that they have free will. They believe this because they experience their own ability to consciously deliberate and select between alternative outcomes, and notice how their decisions push their bodies to act in accordance with those decisions. Howard notices himself deliberating between Subway, New York Fries, and McDonald's—he genuinely seems able to select any of those locales. He then selects Subway, and he moves toward Subway—this seems to be up to him. Given that humans report having this "free-will-like experience," it is reasonable to assume humans have free will.

Free will is also supported by the responsibility argument. Humans are responsible for their actions when they can control which action they perform

Shaun Nichols and Joshua Knobe conducted an experiment where participants were presented with two possible universes: Universe A: everything that happens is completely caused by whatever happened before it. This is true from the beginning of the universe, so what happened in the beginning of the universe caused what happened next, and so on right up until the present. Universe B: almost everything that happens is completely caused by whatever happened before it. The one exception is human decision making. Nichols and Knobe ask participants to select which universe most resembles our universe. Ninety per cent of participants choose the free will universe of Universe B, indicating that it is common-sensical to believe humans possess free will.

or do not perform. But free will just is the view that humans can control which actions they perform or do not perform, so we are only responsible for our actions if we have free will. In a 2007 study by Nichols and Knobe discussed in the side box, 86 per cent of people responded that, in Universe A, where free will fails, it is not possible for a person to be fully morally responsible for their actions.[9] Likewise, in a more recent study by Miklos Kurthy and others, participants were presented with the following puzzle:

Walter promised to pick up Brown from the airport. But on the day of Brown's flight, Walter is in a serious car accident. So, Walter is not physically able to pick up Brown at the airport. Which is true: (A) Walter is obligated to pick up Brown at the airport, even if Walter is not able to do so; (B) Walter is not obligated to pick up Brown at the airport, as Walter is not able to do so.[10]

When given this vignette, 88 per cent of participants report that (B), Walter is not obligated to pick up Brown, again indicating that our inability to control whether we perform an action or not means that we are not responsible for that action. Thomas Reid, who we encountered in Chapter 4.1, uses both of these arguments to argue for the truth of libertarian free will.

Essays on the Active Powers of Man (Thomas Reid, 1788)[11]

By the liberty of a moral agent I mean an agent's power over the determinations of his own will. Consider someone who has the power to will to unlock a door and the power not to will that: if he then voluntarily unlocks

---

9   Shaun Nichols and Joshua Knobe, "Moral Responsibility and Determinism," *Nous* 41, no. 4 (2007): 669.

10 Miklos Kurthy, Holly Lawford-Smith, and Paulo Sousa, "Does Ought Imply Can?" *PloS One* 12, no. 4 (2017): 7–9.

11 Thomas Reid, *Essays on the Active Powers of Man*, 1788, ed. Jonathan Bennett, Essay 4, https://www.earlymoderntexts.com/authors/reid.

the door, he is free with respect to that action. But if the determination of his will to unlock the door is the necessary consequence of something involuntary in the state of his mind, or of something in his external circumstances, he is not free with respect to that unlocking of the door ...

By 'necessity' I understand the lack of the moral liberty that I have defined above. Consider a man who is necessarily determined always to will and to do the best thing there is to do. This man who always does the best possible thing would surely be innocent and blameless. But as far as I can see he wouldn't be entitled to the admiration and moral approval of those who knew and believed that all his conduct was necessitated. We could apply to him what an ancient author said of Cato: 'He was good because he couldn't be any other way.' Understood literally and strictly, this statement is praise not for Cato but for his basic make-up, which was no more Cato's doing than his existence was ...

The modern advocates for the doctrine of necessity put the weight of their argument on the influence of motives. They say: 'every deliberate action must have a motive. When there is no motive on the other side, this motive must determine the agent; when there are contrary motives, the strongest must prevail.' ... I grant that all thinking beings are and ought to be influenced by motives.... So, motives can influence action, but they don't themselves act. They are comparable with advice or urging, which leaves a man still at liberty. For it is pointless to give advice to someone who doesn't have the power to do, and the power not to do, the recommended action ...

Our conviction that we act freely is a natural one. It is built into us.... This notion and this belief must have their origin in something in our constitution; and their being natural to man is supported by the following five observations. (1) We are conscious of many voluntary exertions—some easy, others harder, and some requiring a great effort. These are exercises of power. And though a man may be unconscious of his power when he doesn't exercise it, he must have both the conception of it and the belief in it when he knowingly and willingly exercises it intending to produce some effect. (2) Deliberating about whether or not to do something involves a conviction that doing it is in our power.... (3) You have concluded your deliberation and now resolve to do what has appeared to you to be the best thing to do: can you form such a resolution or purpose without thinking that you have the power to carry it out? No; it is impossible.... (4) When I pledge my word in a promise or contract, I must believe that I'll have the power to do what I promise. Otherwise the promise would be outright fraud....

In this passage,

1. *Reid defines free will, or 'moral liberty,' as the agent having the ability to choose between alternative possibilities. He contrasts free will with determinism or "necessity," which occurs if we lack alternative possibilities.*

2. *Reid uses the common-sense argument and the responsibility argument to show that humans have free will.*
3. *Reid responds to determinists such as d'Holbach who say that motives necessitate actions. He says that motives influence us to act, but do not necessitate our actions. Thus, he provides a libertarian response to the puzzle of Buridan's donkey. Namely, the donkey has motives influencing it to go in both directions, but the donkey can still choose one or the other.*

Objection 1: Arbitrary

Libertarians reject determinism, but determinism is supported by several arguments, so the libertarian must address those arguments. First, determinism is supported by the principle of sufficient reason. Reid responds that our choices themselves are the sufficient causes of our actions. This is not entirely satisfactory, as the complete explanation of why we choose one course of action over another appears to be that we simply choose it. This makes decision making appear **arbitrary** or based on luck and randomness. Since our motivations do not completely determine one course of action over another, the course of action we select is not determined by those motivations, and could have just as easily gone the other way given the same motivations. This arbitrariness problem has recently been expressed through the following **Rollback Argument**. Imagine that Fatima is in the process of deciding between perjuring herself on the stand, or telling a damning truth. She concludes that she does not want to face the penalty of getting caught lying on the stand, but she doesn't think she will get caught, so she ultimately decides to lie. She is morally blameworthy for lying. But, imagine that God rolls time back ten minutes and lets the process play out again. Fatima once again deliberates in the same way: she does not want to get caught lying, and she probably won't get caught, but this time she decides to tell the truth. We no longer blame her for lying, but why not? Her deliberations were the same. The only difference is that she chose not to lie this time. But her choice not to lie begins to look like a matter of chance—it seems random that she didn't lie this time, when the last time she had the same deliberations she chose to lie. Now, God rolls back the scenario one thousand times and finds that 499 times she lies, and 501 times she tells the truth. What will happen when it is rolled back one more time? What she will end up doing seems arbitrary. So, why hold her responsible for lying next time, when it is just bad luck that she ends up lying then?

Objection 2: Physical Causal Completeness

The second argument in support of determinism was the principle of physical causal completeness, according to which all actions have a sufficient physical cause that fully determines the action. Reid argues, however, that prior motivations, including physical causes and reasons, influence without necessitating our actions, leaving the will the chance to decide for itself. On this scenario prior physical causes do not completely necessitate our actions, so libertarian free will appears to violate physical causal completeness.

A leading contemporary libertarian, **Robert Kane** (1938–), develops a libertarian model that responds to both of these objections. Here is an excerpt:

A Contemporary Introduction to Free Will (Robert Kane, 2005)[12]

One might say that to have free will ... is to be the ultimate designer of at least some of one's own purposes. And to be such an ultimate designer, some actions in our life histories must be both will-setting and undetermined. We might call these undetermined will-setting actions "*self-forming actions*," or SFAs for short. For they would be the actions in our lives by which we *form* our character and motives (i.e., our wills) and make ourselves into the kinds of persons we are ...

We must grant, first of all, that if any libertarian theory of free will is to succeed there must be some genuine indeterminism in nature to make room for it. As the ancient Epicurean philosophers said, the atoms must sometimes "swerve" in undetermined ways if there is to be room in nature for free will. Moreover, it would be no use if the atoms swerved in outer space somewhere far from human affairs. They must swerve where it would matter for human choice and action, for example, in the brain.... This is the point, as we have seen, where some scientists want to bring modern quantum physics into the picture to help account for free will. Suppose there were quantum jumps or other undetermined quantum events occurring in the brain.... Some neuroscientists have suggested that quantum indeterminacies in the transmission of these chemical ions across the cell walls of neurons might make the exact timing of the firings of individual neurons uncertain, thus introducing indeterminism into the activity of the brain and making "room" for free will.

Not all acts done of our own free wills have to be undetermined, only those acts by which we made ourselves into the kinds of persons we are— namely, the "will-setting" or "self-forming actions" (SFAs) that are required for ultimate responsibility. Now I believe that these undetermined self-forming actions, or SFAs, occur at those difficult times of life when we are torn between competing visions of what we should do or become. Perhaps we are torn between doing the moral thing or acting from ambition, or between powerful present desires and long-term goals; or we may be faced with difficult tasks for which we have aversions. In all such cases

---

12 Robert Kane, *A Contemporary Introduction to Free Will* (Oxford: Oxford University Press 2002), 130–37.

of difficult self-forming choices in our lives, we are faced with competing motivations and have to make an effort to overcome the temptation to do something else we also strongly want. There is tension and uncertainty in our minds about what to do at such times, let us suppose, that is reflected in appropriate regions of our brains by movement away from thermodynamic equilibrium—in short, a kind of "stirring up of chaos" in the brain that makes it sensitive to micro-indeterminacies at the neuronal level. The uncertainty and inner tension we feel at such soul-searching moments of self-formation would thus be reflected in the indeterminacy of our neural processes themselves.

What we experience internally as uncertainty about what to do on such occasions would correspond physically to the opening of a window of opportunity that temporarily screens off complete determination by influences of the past.

When we do decide under such conditions of uncertainty the outcome is not determined, thanks to the indeterminacy that preceded it. Yet the outcome can be willed either way we choose, rationally and voluntarily, because in such self-formation, the agents' prior wills are divided by conflicting motives. Consider a businesswoman who faces a conflict of this kind. She is on her way to an important meeting when she observes an assault taking place in an alley. An inner struggle arises between her conscience on the one hand (to stop and call for help for the assault victim) and her career ambitions, on the other hand, which tell her she cannot miss this important business meeting. She has to make an effort of will to overcome the temptation to do the selfish thing and go on to the meeting. If she overcomes this temptation, it will be the result of her effort to do the moral thing; but if she fails, it will be because she did not allow her effort to succeed. For while she willed to overcome temptation, she also willed to fail. That is to say, she had strong reasons to will the moral thing, but she also had strong reasons, ambitious reasons, to make the selfish choice that were different from, and incommensurable with, her moral reasons. When we, like the woman, decide in such circumstances, and the indeterminate efforts we are making become determinate choices, we make one set of competing reasons or motives prevail over the others then and there by deciding. Thus the choice we eventually make, though undetermined, can still be rational (made for reasons) and voluntary (made in accordance with our wills), whichever way we choose.

In this passage,

1. *Kane argues that we choose freely when we are the ultimate source of our actions, and this occurs when we form our own characters through self-forming actions.* **Self-forming actions** *occur when we are torn between two competing motivations, both of which we have reason to do, and we choose one course of action over the other.*

2. *Kane responds to the deterministic challenge motivated by physical causal completeness. He says that **quantum physics** is showing us that microphysical states are ultimately indeterministic, so libertarianism is compatible with contemporary science.*
3. *Kane responds to the arbitrariness challenge to libertarianism. Rather than free choices being arbitrary and a matter of chance, Kane argues that indecisive moments occur when competing reasons are at play. Thus, no matter what the outcome of the deliberation, the choice will always be motivated by deliberation and reasons, so will not be arbitrary.*

Objection: Quantum Indeterminism

While quantum indeterminism is established science, there are difficulties with appealing to quantum indeterminism to secure free will. Some argue that quantum states only exist in isolated locales where there is little interference, and brains are busy locales with much potential for interference, so quantum processes may not occur in brains. Others worry that, even if quantum processes occur in the brain, these are sub-personal processes that the agent has no control over, such as whether an electron is present at a specific location in the brain or whether a neurotransmitter will be released or not. If these types of microphysical indeterminacies settle whether an agent acts in one way rather than the other, then the agent still seems to lack control over the outcome, so does not freely choose the outcome himself. Imagine that Logan is torn between stealing a car or not, so he has reasons for both outcomes. While he has reasons for both outcomes, it is unconscious quantum processing in Logan's brain that settles which of these outcomes actually occur. Is this really free will? Can we really hold Logan responsible for stealing the car when his action occurs because of how unconscious quantum processing in his brain played out?

6.3 Compatibilism

Hard determinists and libertarians agree on one thing: free will and determinism are incompatible, so only one of these principles can be true. **Compatibilists** disagree; they say that both free will and determinism can be true at the same time. The advantage of compatibilism is that it is supported by both the reasons for free will and the reasons for determinism. It is common-sensical that humans have free will, and free will is required for personal responsibility, so a position endorsing free will is desirable. At the same time, the principle of sufficient reason and the principle of physical causal completeness seem plausible, so a position endorsing determinism is desirable. Compatibilism endorses both free will and determinism, so it is doubly motivated.

The central task for the compatibilist is to show how free will and determinism can both be true. At first glance, this task seems daunting. Free will states that, given the same starting conditions, alternative possible futures can occur.

Determinism states that, given the same starting conditions, only one possible future can occur. Free will states that the ultimate source of action lies in us, not outside us. Determinism states that the ultimate source of action does not lie in us, but outside us. How can both of these principles be true? The compatibilist strategy is to understand free will in such a way as to avoid the clash with determinism. Free will does not involve the ability to choose one out of several different possible courses of action, or being the ultimate source of action. Rather, free will is the ability to do what we want. If there is, as Thomas Hobbes expresses it, "no stop, in doing what [we have] the will, desire, or inclination to do," then we are free.[13] Jasmin wants to join the soccer team, and as she is not forbidden by her parents from doing so, she freely joins the soccer team. On the other hand, we lack free will if we are unable to do what we want. Jasmin wants to join the soccer team, but her parents forbid her to do so, so she is not free to join the soccer team. Or, Jasmin does not want to join the soccer team, but her parents force her to, so she does not freely join the soccer team.

What counts as an impediment to doing what you want? There are typically two types of impediments: constraints and compulsions. We are **constrained** from doing what we want when we want to perform some act but cannot do it. There are physical constraints: Jens wants to walk in the sunshine, but he can't because he is imprisoned; Fiona wants to play soccer, but she can't because she is paralyzed. There are also psycho-social constraints: Sophie wants to retire to the Bahamas, but she can't because she doesn't have enough money; Marwin wants to fly, but his anxiety disorder is preventing him from getting on the plane.

While constraint occurs when we are blocked from doing what we want, **compulsion** occurs when we are forced to do something we do not want. There are physical compulsions. Liam doesn't want to pay the ransom, but he has to because he has a gun pointed at this head; Emma doesn't want to forget the names of her loved ones, but she does because dementia is setting in. There are also psycho-social compulsions: Damien doesn't want to work the fields, but he has to because he has been enslaved; Smith doesn't want to take heroin anymore, but his addiction compels him to keep taking it. In these cases of compulsion and constraint we are not free since we cannot act in line with how we want to act. In the following reading, **A.J. Ayer** (1910–89) articulates this compatibilist model of free will and shows how, he claims, it is consistent with determinism.

"Freedom and Necessity" (A.J. Ayer, 1954)[14]

Let it be granted, then, that when we speak of reconciling freedom with determinism we are using the word 'freedom' in an ordinary sense. It still

---

13 Thomas Hobbes, *Leviathan*, 1651, Part 2, Chapter 21, in *The Broadview Anthology of Social and Political Thought, Volume 1: From Plato to Nietzsche*, ed. Andrew Bailey et al. (Peterborough: Broadview Press, 2008), 454.

14 A.J. Ayer, "Freedom and Necessity," in *Philosophical Essays* (London: Macmillan, 1954), 271–84.

remains for us to make this usage clear: and perhaps the best way to make it clear is to show what it is that freedom, in this sense, is contrasted with. Now we began with the assumption that freedom is contrasted with causality: so that a man cannot be said to be acting freely if his action is causally determined. But this assumption has led us into difficulties and I now wish to suggest that it is mistaken. For it is not, I think, causality that freedom is to be contrasted with, but constraint. And while it is true that being constrained to do an action entails being caused to do it, I shall try to show that the converse does not hold. I shall try to show that from the fact that my action is causally determined it does not necessarily follow that I am constrained to do it: and this is equivalent to saying that it does not necessarily follow that I am not free.

If I am constrained, I do not act freely. But in what circumstances can I legitimately be said to be constrained? An obvious instance is the case in which I am compelled by another person to do what he wants. In a case of this sort the compulsion need not be such as to deprive one of the power of choice. It is not required that the other person should have hypnotized me, or that he should make it physically impossible for me to go against his will. It is enough that he should induce me to do what he wants by making it clear to me that, if I do not, he will bring about some situation that I regard as even more undesirable than the consequences of the action that he wishes me to do. Thus, if the man points a pistol at my head I may still choose to disobey him: but this does not prevent its being true that if I do fall in with his wishes he can legitimately be said to have compelled me. And if the circumstances are such that no reasonable person would be expected to choose the other alternative, then the action that I am made to do is not one for which I am held to be morally responsible....

But now it may be asked whether there is any essential difference between these cases and those in which the agent is commonly thought to be free. No doubt the ordinary thief does go through a process of deciding whether or not to steal, and no doubt it does affect his behaviour. If he resolved to refrain from stealing, he could carry his resolution out. But if it be allowed that his making or not making this resolution is causally determined, then how can he be any more free than the kleptomaniac? It may be true that unlike the kleptomaniac he could refrain from stealing if he chose: but if there is a cause, or set of causes, which necessitate his choosing as he does, how can he be said to have the power of choice? Again, it may be true that no one now compels me to get up and walk across the room: but if my doing so can be causally explained in terms of my history or my environment, or whatever it may be, then how am I any more free than if some other person had compelled me? I do not have the feeling of constraint that I have when a pistol is manifestly pointed at my head; but the chains of causation by which I am bound are no less effective for being invisible.

The answer to this is that the cases I have mentioned as examples of constraint do differ from the others: and they differ just in the ways that I have tried to bring out. If I suffered from a compulsion neurosis, so that I got up and walked across the room, whether I wanted to or not, or if I did so because somebody else compelled me, then I should not be acting freely. But if I do it now, I shall be acting freely, just because these conditions do not obtain; and the fact that my action may nevertheless have a cause is, from this point of view, irrelevant. For it is not when my action has any cause at all, but only when it has a special sort of cause, that it is reckoned not to be free.

In this passage,

1. *Ayer argues that free will, rather than being contrasted with necessary causation, is contrasted with constraint.*
2. *Ayer argues that the ability to do as we want is compatible with determinism. Constraint takes away free will, since we notice the constraining force blocking us from acting as we wish. Being determined by heredity and environment to act as we wish involves no force blocking us from acting as we wish. Jasmin wants to join the soccer team, and there is no block from her joining the soccer team, so she does join the soccer team, so she is free. But she was raised in a soccer-loving country by sporty parents who always put her in soccer lessons, all of which determined her to want to join the soccer team. So, while she is determined to want to play soccer, she is free because she can do what she is determined to want to do.*

Imagine you go skydiving, and your attitude shifts during the fall from enjoyment to terror, at one moment wanting to fall to the ground, at another moment wishing you could stop falling. Does your freedom flicker on and off as well, depending on whether you want to fall toward the ground or not? Or, does the fact that you are now determined to fall make you no longer free about falling toward the Earth?

Objection 1: Free Will Fails

Critics worry that the compatibilist definition of free will, which says we are free if we want to do what we are determined to do, is an unsatisfactory definition of free will. Consider Aldous Huxley's *Brave New World* (1932). In this novel, people are genetically engineered in artificial wombs to possess whatever degree of intelligence and labour capability determined useful to society. They are then indoctrinated throughout their youth via messages playing on sound systems day and night about how wonderful the specific role they have been bred to fill is. Lower-caste citizens such as the deltas and epsilons are given powerful drugs to sustain them every day.

These lower-caste citizens have been biologically and culturally engineered to be slaves to the higher-caste citizens—seemingly they are not free. However, they are engineered to *want* to do the work they do, and to *want* to be the low-caste citizens they are. So, on compatibilism, these lower-caste citizens, who are doing what they want, are free. This is a counterintuitive result. Being biologically and culturally manipulated so thoroughly that we are even conditioned to love our subservience does not seem to make us free. As Sam Harris summarizes, the compatibilist view asserts that "A puppet is free as long as he loves his strings."[15] But why would the puppet suddenly become free, just because it starts to like its strings?

Objection 2: Consequence Argument

Compatibilism also faces the following **Consequence Argument**: we can do nothing to change the arrangements of particles in the remote past (i.e., many years prior to our births), and we can do nothing to change the laws of nature. But, according to determinism, our present actions are determined by the arrangements of particles in the remote past combined with the laws of nature. So, we can do nothing to change our present actions, and we have no power to influence or alter how our futures will unfold. As **Peter van Inwagen** (1942–) summarizes: "If determinism is true, then our acts are the consequences of the laws of nature and events in the remote past. But it is not up to us what went on before we were born, and neither is it up to us what the laws of nature are. Therefore the consequences of these things (including our present acts) are not up to us."[16] The result is once again that compatibilism does not genuinely provide us with free will, since we have no power to influence which actions we take.

Harry Frankfurt (1929–), a leading contemporary compatibilist, attempts to solve these problems by introducing a novel form of compatibilism:

"Freedom of the Will and the Concept of a Person" (Harry Frankfurt, 1971)[17]

The distinction between a person and a wanton may be illustrated by the difference between two narcotics addicts. Let us suppose that the physiological condition accounting for the addiction is the same in both men, and that both succumb inevitably to their periodic desires for the drug to which they are addicted. One of the addicts hates his addiction and always struggles desperately, although to no avail, against its thrust. He tries everything that he thinks might enable him to overcome his desires

---

15 Sam Harris, *Free Will* (New York: Simon and Schuster, 2012), 20.
16 Peter van Inwagen, *An Essay on Free Will* (Oxford: Clarendon Press, 1983), 56.
17 Harry Frankfurt, "Freedom of the Will and the Concept of a Person," *The Journal of Philosophy* 68, no. 1 (1971): 12–20.

for the drug. But these desires are too powerful for him to withstand, and invariably, in the end, they conquer him. He is an unwilling addict, helplessly violated by his own desires.

The unwilling addict has conflicting first-order desires: he wants to take the drug, and he also wants to refrain from taking it. In addition to these first-order desires, however, he has a volition of the second order. He is not a neutral with regard to the conflict between his desire to take the drug and his desire to refrain from taking it. It is the latter desire, and not the former, that he wants to constitute his will; it is the latter desire, rather than the former, that he wants to be effective and to provide the purpose that he will seek to realize in what he actually does.

The other addict is a wanton. His actions reflect the economy of his first-order desires, without this being concerned whether the desires that move him to act are desires by which he wants to be moved to act. If he encounters problems in obtaining the drug or in administering it to himself, his responses to his urges to take it may involve deliberation. But it never occurs to him to consider whether he wants the relations among his desires to result in his having the will he has. The wanton addict may be an animal, and thus incapable of being concerned about his will. In any event he is, in respect of his wanton lack of concern, no different from an animal ...

Suppose that a person has done what he wanted to do, that he did it because he wanted to do it, and that the will by which he was moved when he did it was his will because it was the will he wanted. Then he did it freely and of his own free will. Moreover, since the will that moved him when he acted was his will because he wanted it to be, he cannot claim that his will was forced upon him or that he was a passive bystander to its constitution.... In illustration, consider a third kind of addict. Suppose that his addiction has the same physiological basis and the same irresistible thrust as the addictions of the unwilling and wanton addicts, but that he is altogether delighted with his condition. He is a willing addict, who would not have things any other way. If the grip of his addiction should somehow weaken, he would do whatever he could to reinstate it; if his desire for the drug should begin to fade, he would take steps to renew its intensity.... But when he takes the drug, he takes it freely and of his own free will.... This desire is his effective desire because he is physiologically addicted. But it is his effective desire also because he wants it to be. His will is outside his control, but, by his second-order desire that his desire for the drug should be effective, he has made this will his own. Given that it is therefore not only because of his addiction that his desire for the drug is effective, he may be morally responsible for taking the drug.

My conception of freedom of the will appears to be neutral with regard to the problem of determinism. It seems conceivable that it should be causally determined that a person is free to want what he wants to want. If this is conceivable, then it might be causally determined that a person enjoys a free will....

In these passages,

1. *Frankfurt provides a way for the compatibilist to deliver ultimate sourcehood as free will. According to classical compatibilism, we are free when we can do as we want, even though what we want to do is determined by factors beyond our control. This fails to provide ultimate sourcehood since what we want is determined by factors beyond our control, so is not up to us—someone manipulated by social forces into wanting to be a slave is not free. Frankfurt responds by introducing a distinction between first-order desires and second-order desires. First-order desires are desires about objects: Xavier desires a chocolate cake; Enrique desires to eat healthy and lose five pounds. Second-order desires are desires about our desires: Xavier desires to not have the desire for chocolate cake; Enrique desires to continue having the desire to eat healthy and lose five pounds. Given this distinction, Frankfurt imagines three cases. First, the **wanton**, who does not have any second-order desires, but only first-order desires. The wanton is controlled by her impulses, and does not deliberate about whether her impulses are good or bad. Frankfurt compares the wanton to animals, and goes so far as to say that wantons are not persons. Second, the **unwilling addict**, who has a first-order desire for drugs, but a second-order desire not to have the desire for drugs. She continues to act on her desire for drugs by taking drugs, despite her second-order desire to stop having that desire. The unwilling addict is not free, since she has identified her true self as not desiring drugs, but she can't overcome that desire. Third, the **willing addict**, who has a first-order desire for drugs, and a second-order desire to continue wanting drugs. As it turns out, the willing addict continues to take drugs, but she enjoys it, and desires to keep wanting to take the drugs. The willing addict is free, as her second-order desire comes to fruition—she enjoys the fact that she desires to take drugs and that she keeps taking drugs.*

In 1521, Martin Luther was given a chance to recant his criticism of the Catholic Church or face excommunication. Rather than recant, he stood firm in his convictions, saying 'Here I stand, I can do nothing else.' The puzzle is that Luther seems to freely choose to stand by his convictions, but he admits he can do nothing else, or, he does not have alternative possibilities. Does this mean he is not free in this moment? Frankfurt says Luther is wholeheartedly free in this moment, since he desires to do what he does. Kane says Luther is free since his will is set by prior self-forming actions.

2. *Frankfurt argues that this model of freedom, where we are free when we act on the second-order desires that we identify with, is compatible with determinism. We may be determined to affirm the first-order wants we have, but the fact that we affirm our desires that we act on suffices for free will. Xavier desires chocolate cake, but he desires that his desire for chocolate cake not lead him to an eating binge. If his desire for self-restraint prevails, then he has freed himself from his impulsive desire for chocolate cake.*

Objection: Willing Slaves

Frankfurt tries to provide a compatibilist model that delivers ultimate source-hood, but he may not actually succeed in providing ultimate sourcehood. Imagine again the case of the lower-caste deltas in *Brave New World*. They are genetically hardwired and culturally conditioned to not only perform slave labour, and not only enjoy performing slave labour, but also to identify themselves with the desire to continue desiring to perform slave labour—they love being deltas, and wouldn't want to be anything else. On Frankfurt's model, the deltas are free, as the will they want to have is the will they have. But the will they want to have is still not "up to them," as they are completely conditioned and modified as to want to continue desiring to perform the slave labour they perform. Seemingly, true free will involves the view that our beliefs, desires, and wants must, in some sense, be "up to us" in the sense that they are not completely determined by forces outside ourselves beyond our control.

Summary

Libertarian free will embraces free will and rejects determinism. It is similar to the dualist view that focuses on mental or ideal realities as distinct from physical realities. Hard determinism embraces determinism and rejects free will. In so doing it is similar to the eliminative reductionist view that focuses on physical realities and says there is no distinct mental reality. Compatibilism occupies a middle position, according to which both free will and determinism exist, which is similar to the mind-brain identity view that mental realities exist but they just are physical realities. Each of these models face significant criticism, but each of them has recent solutions that make some progress in overcoming those objections.

Key Terms in Chapter 6: Free Will and Determinism

Buridan's Donkey	Microphysical Causal	Rollback Argument
Alternative Possibilities	Determinism	Self-Forming Actions
Free Will	Benjamin Libet	Quantum Physics
Ultimate Sourcehood	Psychological	Compatibilism
Responsibility	Determinism	Consequence Argument
Biological Determinism	Principle of Sufficient	A.J. Ayer
Theological	Reason	Constrained
Determinism	Incompatibilism	Compulsion
Determinism	Hard Determinism	Harry Frankfurt
Cultural Determinism	Baron Henry d'Holbach	Peter van Inwagen
Leopold and Loeb	Derk Pereboom	Robert Kane
Reductio ad Absurdum	Quarantine Model	Wanton
Reactive Attitudes	Libertarianism	Unwilling Addict
Saul Smilansky	Arbitrary	Willing Addict

Philosophy on Television: Free Will and Determinism

Brave New World (1980)

In this film, a society genetically engineers and culturally conditions citizens, including low-caste citizens, to want to serve as slave labourers. According to **compatibilism**, we are free if we want to do what we are determined to do; thus these low-caste citizens would be free.

Minority Report (2002)

In this film, a futuristic society allows the police to pre-emptively apprehend citizens based on them foreknowing they will commit a crime. This film raises questions about whether Derk Pereboom's **quarantine model** of punishment is correct. If public safety is the basis of punishment, not blameworthiness, can police pre-emptively incarcerate a citizen?

Person of Interest (2003)

In this television series, a powerful artificial intelligence, based on social media usage, text and email analysis, and public audio/video footage, is able to predict when citizens will commit a crime, then pre-emptively apprehends these citizens.

Black Mirror: Bandersnatch (2018)

In this interactive film, viewers choose the outcome of Stephan, who is coding a computer game that allows players to choose their own outcomes. This episode captures the sense that free will involves alternative possibilities, though Stephan begins to feel he is being controlled by external forces.

***The Big Bang Theory*: Season 10, Episode 7 (2016)**
Sheldon mimics Buridan's Donkey. He is standing equidistant from two apartment doors, one of which is his friend Leonard's apartment and the other his girlfriend Amy's apartment. While contemplating which door to knock on, Amy comes up the stairs, and they engage in a discussion about the problem of Buridan's Donkey.

Additional Resources

Visit this book's companion resources for additional materials, including video content and an automated tool for planning argumentative essays.

sites.broadviewpress.com/knowing/chapter-6

Chapter 7

Knowledge

THOUGHT EXPERIMENT 7.1

The Impossible Wheel of Fortune Puzzle

In March of 2014, a contestant on Wheel of Fortune named Emil De Leon had to solve this three-word puzzle after receiving only these two letters as clues: '_ _ _   B A _ _   _ _ _ _ _.' Can you figure out the answer? The first thing he guessed was 'New Baby Buggy.' As he kept guessing at the puzzle, the lights suddenly started flashing and the answer revealed itself as actually being 'New Baby Buggy.' Emil was shocked, everyone was amazed. He won! But how did he solve such an impossible riddle? He later explained that 'New' was obvious, and he knew that words normally start with consonants, and 'B' is the first one to try. A common vowel

other than 'E' and 'O,' which were already ruled out, was 'A.' So, he thought 'BA,' which, combined with 'New,' could be 'Baby,' as babies are always new. Once he knew 'New Baby,' he just took a guess at the last word, and got it right. This raises the question: did Emil know the answer, or did he just get lucky?

Have you ever guessed on a multiple-choice question on an exam, but later found out you got it correct? Nice! In this situation, did you *know* the right answer? Here is a similar puzzle: in April of 1972, US President Richard Nixon toasted the infant child of Canadian Prime Minister Pierre Trudeau by saying, "I'd like to toast the future prime minister of Canada—to Justin Pierre Trudeau." In 2015 this infant child became the prime minister of Canada. Did Nixon *know* that Justin Trudeau would become prime minister? These puzzles make us ask: what do we mean by *know*? **Epistemology** is the branch of philosophy that studies the nature of knowledge. The central questions they ask include: what does it mean to know something, and what are the sources of knowledge (i.e., where do we get knowledge from). In this chapter we will focus on these two questions.

There are three different ways to know something. First, there is **know-how**. This is knowledge gained by doing. You *know* how to ride a bike. How did you come to know this? You did not read about it in a book, and suddenly just know. Rather, when you were five, you tried many times, and failed many times, until you figured out how to rotate the pedals at just the right speed, while you also figured out how to correctly balance through various tilts and veers, while you also figured out how to steer not too hard but not too little in response to the various tilts and veers. Now it is muscle memory. Now you climb on a bike and do not think about how to do these tricks, you just know it. Know-how occurs

Is it possible to get some kinds of "know-how" just by reading a book—i.e., other than by doing? Think about knowing how to solve a quadratic equation, restart your computer, make a martini, juggle.

whenever we learn a skill. Iman knows how to swim, but Tora does not, the difference is that Iman practised and tried until he figured it out.

A second way is knowledge by **acquaintance**. This is knowledge gained by having direct experience of the thing known. Avi has never kissed a boy. She wonders what it is like. She reads in the magazines that it is fluttery and wet, while her friends tell her it is a bit sloppy but it feels like lots of tiny bubbles popping. Does she now *know* what a kiss feels like? No. Avi finally meets someone who she wants to kiss, and when their lips touch, she suddenly knows what it is like to kiss someone. Another example: a colour-blind person is told what red and green look like, but he does not really know what red and green look like. When he puts on special colour-blindness glasses for the first time, he finally knows by acquaintance how different red looks from green. An eye-witness has knowledge by acquaintance of the crime, but the jury does not.

If we only have know-how and knowledge by acquaintance, we don't know very much at all. Consider this: have you ever been to the moon, or the Antarctic? No. So does that mean that you cannot know about the moon or the Antarctic? You never experienced anything prior to your birth twenty years ago, so does that mean you cannot know that Columbus sailed to the Americas, and that the Roman empire existed, and that Edison invented the light bulb? You have never been a bird, but does that mean you cannot figure out how they fly? We think we are able to know about many more things than what we directly experience and know how to do. But where does this extra knowledge come from?

7.1 Propositional Knowledge

The answer is found in the third way of knowing, called **propositional knowledge**, which is knowledge-that. To understand what propositional knowledge is, it is helpful to understand what a proposition is. A proposition involves an utterance (either in printed words, spoken words, or in our own minds in the form of beliefs) that is either true or false. There are all sorts of utterances that are not true or false. For example, childish gibberish ("goo-goo-ga-ga"), questions ("Can I watch TV?"), and exclamations ("Hooray!"). But some utterances are true or false. For example, "The sky is blue," and "Santa wears green," and "2 + 2 = 4," and "Kangaroos are native to Peru." Propositions involve these types of utterances that we can evaluate as being true or false. Some propositions are false; for example, 'Kangaroos are native to Peru' and 'Santa wears green.'

Propositional knowledge, since it involves true/false utterances, allows us to acquire and pass on knowledge through speaking, listening, and reading. Zahra, while she can't fly, and has never been a bird, studies the science textbook and comes to know that birds fly by angling their wings as they glide through air such that air is forced downwards, thus lifting them upwards. Vlad, while he has never been to the Antarctic listens to someone tell him he saw penguins in the Antarctic, so now Vlad knows that penguins live in the Antarctic. Maja, though she wasn't alive hundreds of years ago, reads in her history book that Columbus landed in the Americas in 1492. Propositional knowledge opens us up to the possibility of knowing almost any fact about the universe, even facts in distant regions of space and time.

If someone gets down on their knees and proposes marriage to you, it is not the correct time to tell them that they are actually not stating a proposition after all, since they are just asking a question.

Is simply believing a proposition enough for knowledge? Shirley believes that wearing a copper bracelet relieves arthritis, but does she know that? Charmides, who lived 2,500 years ago, believes that the Earth is flat, but does he know that? No, because the propositions they believe are false. We cannot know something that is false because there is nothing to know in this case, there is no fact that is known.

But is believing a true proposition enough for knowledge? Vlad believes "Penguins live in the Antarctic," and this is true. Does he now know penguins live in the Antarctic? No. Simply having a true belief is not enough, as true beliefs could be arrived at by luck. On a famous episode of the 1970s show *The Newlywed Game*, Gloria is asked how many decades Joe will say his mother has lived. Gloria, not knowing what a decade is, guesses "10 decades." Later, when Joe is asked how many decades his mother has lived, he says: "I don't know what a decade is ... 44th birthday, so at 4 years a decade, she'd be 10 decades." Gloria rejoices as she gleefully holds up the matching answer of 10, and they win! Did Gloria *know* Joe would say 10? No. She just got lucky. If Zelda spins around until dizzy, and falls to the ground pointing while saying "Montréal is that way," and happens to point in the right direction, she was lucky; Zelda did not *know* Montréal is that way.

How do we avoid arriving at true beliefs by luck? By having a justification for that true belief. A **justification** provides an account of why we should have a belief, it is the support or evidence for a belief. Alayah believes that her friend Pablo was born in a Spanish-speaking country, because of some of her other beliefs: that Pablo told her he was born in Ecuador, and Pablo would not have lied about this, and Ecuador is a Spanish-speaking country. That's good justification, and if Alayah's justified belief that Pablo was born in a Spanish-speaking country is right, then she knows it. Chao-xing believes that there is a hole in her sock, because of her experiential evidence: she is looking at her sock right now, and she can see the hole in her sock. That's good justification as well.

Justification for a belief is different from explanation for a belief. An **explanation** provides an account of how a belief was arrived at, but does not attempt to justify the belief. Matéo believes there is an elephant in his room. How does he come to believe this? He ingested some hallucinogens and had a vision of an elephant, so now he believes there is an elephant in his room. This explains Matéo's belief, but does not justify Matéo's belief. Bliss believes balloons are scary because one popped in her ear when she was three years old. This explains Bliss's belief that balloons are scary, but does not justify it.

Is having a **justified true belief** enough for having propositional knowledge? Many think so, though we shall encounter an objection to this view below. But for the moment, let us assume that it is. The question becomes: what counts as justification? What is the source of the evidence we need to turn our true beliefs into well-justified knowledge? We shall now explore some responses to this question, which can be placed on the following spectrum:

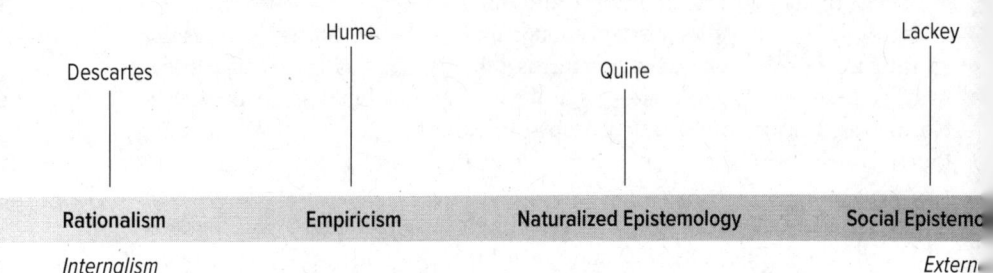

Spectrum 7: Justification Theories

While all of these philosophers agree that justification is required for knowledge, they disagree on what counts as the source of justification. The theories toward the left of the spectrum endorse **internalism**, which is the view that true beliefs are justified by something internal to the knower. The theories toward the right of the spectrum endorse **externalism**, which is the view that true beliefs are justified by something external to the knower. Let us begin by looking at the view on the furthest left of the spectrum, Descartes' rationalism.

THOUGHT EXPERIMENT 7.2
The Computer Simulation

In *The Matrix* (1999), humans are stored in pods of nutrients while a powerful AI system streams signals into the brains of the humans, giving rise to them having experiences of walking in the park and living normal life. Do you think you could be stuck in the Matrix right now? Could we be inside a computer-simulated video game right now? Some think the answer is: probably yes. Their reasoning: video games have progressed from simple Pac-Man to multiplayer photorealistic virtual reality. Assuming progress continues, video games will someday be indistinguishable from reality, with more and more players capable of playing together and more and more resemblance to reality. Assuming video games remain popular, there will be billions of people playing these games. So, we have billions of games that are indistinguishable from reality, and one reality. We cannot tell which one we are in by comparing how they look, because they look the same. But since there are billions of games and only one reality, it is more likely we are in a game. Do you agree?

7.2 Descartes' Rationalism

The question is: what is it that justifies true beliefs? We are already familiar with the following answer: other beliefs justify true beliefs. In Chapter 1.5.1 we looked at the structure of arguments: conclusions are supported by premises. All humans are mortal, and Socrates is a human, so Socrates is mortal. We can now reframe an argument as involving a true belief as the conclusion which is justified through the reasoning from other beliefs acting as premises, so the arguer knows their belief serving as the conclusion is true. Henry believes that Socrates is mortal, and this belief is true, and his belief is justified by his other beliefs, namely, that Socrates is a human, and all humans are mortal, so Henry knows that Socrates is mortal.

But there is a problem. Now we have to ask: how can we know that the premises themselves are true? How do we know that "All humans are mortal" is true in the first place? Here is one possibility: we know that "All humans are mortal" because this is itself the conclusion from earlier premises. All animals are mortal, and humans are animals, so humans are mortal. But how do we know that humans are animals? From still earlier premises? Humans are life forms that move, all life forms that move are animals, so humans are animals. But how do we know this? A **vicious regress** threatens, where we keep asking the same question of the new answer in a way that causes us to doubt our ability to ever solve the problem.

One way to solve this regress threat is to endorse **foundationalism**. Foundationalists say the regress comes to an end when a **self-justifying** belief, that is, a belief that proves itself true, serves as the foundation for all the later beliefs that follow from it. The 100th storey of a skyscraper is held up by the 99th floor, which is held up by the 98th level. And so on down to the lowest level, where the foundation of the building holds everything up, but is not itself held up by some lower level. Likewise, foundationalists say that one belief justifies another belief, which justifies another belief, but some one belief must serve as the foundation for all the other beliefs in order to hold the entire edifice up and prevent the vicious regress.

But what is this foundational belief, and how would it justify itself? Have you ever wondered: is there any belief you have that is absolutely certainly true? What is that belief? René Descartes is a famous foundationalist who provides one possible answer. We encountered Descartes in Chapter 5.1. There he endorsed interactionist dualism, according to which the mind is a distinct substance from the body. He defined the mind as a thinking substance. There were worries about defining the person or mind as a thinking substance. One concern came from David Hume in Chapter 4.2: we cannot experience the thinking substance itself, so we are not justified in believing that a simple unchanging thinking substance exists. Another concern came from mind-brain identity theorists: why define the mind as essentially a thinking substance that is distinct from matter? Both of these concerns find responses in Descartes' epistemology. Descartes' theory of knowledge is called **rationalism**, which means that reason and rationality provide the foundational belief, and justify the passage from there to other beliefs. Notice in the following excerpt how Descartes uses reason to arrive at a self-justifying belief, and then uses reason to infer the truth of other beliefs from this self-justifying belief.

Meditations on First Philosophy (René Descartes, 1641)[1]

It is now several years since I noticed how from the time of my early youth I had accepted many false claims as true, how everything I had later constructed on top of those [falsehoods] was doubtful, and thus how at some point in my life I needed to tear everything down completely and begin again from the most basic foundations, if I wished to establish something firm and lasting in the sciences. But this seemed an immense undertaking, and I kept waiting until I would be old enough and sufficiently mature to know that no later period of my life would come [in which I was] better equipped to undertake this disciplined enquiry. This reason made me delay for so long that I would now be at fault if, by [further] deliberation, I used up the time which still remains to carry out that project. And so today, when I have conveniently rid my mind of all worries and have managed to find myself secure leisure in solitary withdrawal, I will at

---

1   René Descartes, *Meditations on First Philosophy*, trans. Ian Johnston, ed. Andrew Bailey (Peterborough: Broadview Press, 2013), 41–44.

last find the time for an earnest and unfettered general demolition of my [former] opinions.

Now, for this task it will not be necessary to show that every opinion I hold is false, something which I might well be incapable of ever carrying out. But reason now convinces me that I should withhold my assent from opinions which are not entirely certain and indubitable, no less than from those which are plainly false; so if I uncover any reason for doubt in each of them, that will be enough to reject them all. For that I will not need to run through them separately, a task that would take forever, because once the foundations are destroyed, whatever is built above them will collapse on its own. Thus, I shall at once assault the very principles upon which all my earlier beliefs rested.

Up to this point, what I have accepted as true I have derived either from the senses or through the senses. However, sometimes I have discovered that these are mistaken, and it is prudent never to place one's entire trust in things which have deceived us even once.

However, although from time to time the senses deceive us about minuscule things or those further away, it could well be that there are still many other matters about which we cannot entertain the slightest doubt, even though we derive [our knowledge] of them from sense experience— for example, the fact that I am now here, seated by the fire, wearing a winter robe, holding this paper in my hands, and so on. And, in fact, how could I deny that these very hands and this whole body are mine, ... How often have I had an experience like this: while sleeping at night, I am convinced that I am here, dressed in a robe and seated by the fire, when, in fact, I am lying between the covers with my clothes off! At the moment, my eyes are certainly wide open and I am looking at this piece of paper, this head which I am moving is not asleep, and I am aware of this hand as I move it consciously and purposefully. None of what happens while I am asleep is so distinct. Yes, of course—but nevertheless I recall other times when I have been deceived by similar thoughts in my sleep. As I reflect on this matter carefully, it becomes completely clear to me that there are no certain indicators which ever enable us to differentiate between being awake and being asleep, and this is astounding; in my confusion I am almost convinced that I may be sleeping....

Therefore, I will assume that it is not God, who is supremely good and the fountain of truth, but some malicious demon, at once omnipotent and supremely cunning, who has been using all the energy he possesses to deceive me. I will suppose that sky, air, earth, colours, shapes, sounds, and all other external things are nothing but the illusions of my dreams, set by this spirit as traps for my credulity. I will think of myself as if I had no hands, no eyes, no flesh, no blood, nor any senses, and yet as if I still falsely believed I had all these things....

Therefore, I assume that everything I see is false. I believe that none of those things my lying memory represents has ever existed, that I have no senses at all, and that body, shape, extension, motion, and location are chimeras. What, then, will be true? Perhaps this one thing: there is nothing certain.

But how do I know that there exists nothing other than the items I just listed, about which one could not entertain the slightest momentary doubt? Is there not some God, by whatever name I call him, who places these very thoughts inside me? But why would I think this, since I myself could perhaps have produced them? ... So then, is it the case that I, too, do not exist? No, not at all: if I persuaded myself of something, then I certainly existed. But there is some kind of deceiver, supremely powerful and supremely cunning, who is constantly and intentionally deceiving me. But then, if he is deceiving me, there again is no doubt that I exist—for that very reason. Let him trick me as much as he can, he will never succeed in making me nothing, as long as I am aware that I am something. And so, after thinking all these things through in great detail, I must finally settle on this proposition: the statement I am, I exist is necessarily true every time I say it or conceive of it in my mind....

What about thinking? Here I discover something: thinking does exist. This is the only thing which cannot be detached from me. I am, I exist—that is certain. But for how long? Surely for as long as I am thinking. For it could perhaps be the case that, if I were to abandon thinking altogether, then in that moment I would completely cease to be. At this point I am not agreeing to anything except what is necessarily true. Therefore, strictly speaking, I am merely a thinking thing, that is, a mind or spirit, or understanding, or reason—words whose significance I did not realize before. However, I am something real, and I truly exist. But what kind of thing? As I have said, a thing that thinks.

In this passage,

1. *Descartes argues that knowledge requires a foundational self-justifying belief that proves itself true; then the rest of our beliefs can be built upon this foundational belief.*

2. *Descartes engages in a project of **methodological doubt** in order to find this foundational belief. That is, his strategy for finding the foundational belief is to doubt everything in order to find out what survives his criticisms and doubts. Imagine you want to find the strongest tree in the forest. You may think: let the wind blow stronger and stronger until all the trees but one blow over, and the remaining tree is the strongest tree. This is Descartes' strategy. Subject every thought and source of information to extreme criticism, to see what withstands the scrutiny. Whatever withstands the scrutiny is the foundational belief.*

3. Descartes concludes that sense experience fails the test of his doubting strategy. **Sense experiences** are perception of the five senses—sight, taste, touch, hearing, and smell. Descartes thinks that sense experience is unreliable. First, he notices that our senses deceive us: we experience the sun as a tiny circle that we could squish with our fingers, but in reality the sun is bigger than the Earth. Second, he provides a **dream argument**. Might we be dreaming right now? Surely not, we protest! But while dreaming we usually do not think we are dreaming either, so we may now be dreaming. Then Descartes introduces the **evil demon**. Perhaps there is a powerful but evil being that is continuously trying to deceive us by showing us perceptions and convincing us they are true. So, what might Descartes say about the possibility that we are stuck in the Matrix? Descartes says we could be stuck in the Matrix and not even know it, so sense experience is not the undoubtable foundation for justifying belief.

4. Descartes concludes that the only thing he cannot doubt is the fact that he is doubting, for as soon as he doubts that he is doubting, this doubt proves that doubting is occurring. But doubting is a form of thinking, so he cannot doubt that he is thinking either, since that thought proves that he is thinking. But the fact that thinking is occurring is proof that he as the thinker of those thoughts exists. In Latin, he says **cogito ergo sum**, which means I think, therefore I am. This is his self-justifying belief that serves as the foundation for other beliefs. "I exist as a thinking being" is undeniably true, as even doubting the truth of this statement proves that thinking exists, so there is no way for it to be false.

Descartes' rationalism provides the following responses to the worries about interactionist dualist views of the mind and person. First, about the concern that we cannot experience the thinking substance, Descartes replies: experience is not the ultimate source of knowledge; rather, the thinking substance is proven to exist by reasoning from the fact that thinking occurs to the implication that a thinker exists. Second, about the concern that the mind should not be defined as a thinking substance distinct from matter, Descartes replies: thinking is the very definition of the thinking substance and is known with certainty, where the brain is not part of the definition of thinking, but instead exists in the sense world that could be subject to mass deception.

Descartes is sitting in a bar. The bartender says, "Want another beer?" Descartes replies, "I think not," and POOF he disappears.

7.3 Hume's Empiricism

In previous chapters, we examined Hume's bundle theory of substances and persons, where substances are bundles of properties and persons are bundles of perceptions, and there exists no substratum in objects and no unchanging thinking self in persons. His epistemology, which we will look at now, is closely connected with those views.

Descartes responds to the regress problem by locating a self-justifying belief, namely that the thinking self exists. Hume offers up another possible solution: rather than grounding our chain of beliefs in the thinking self, we should ground our chain of beliefs in experience: the belief that someone's at the door is justified by the ringing of the doorbell, which is justified by hearing the doorbell with our own ears. Here the chain of beliefs comes to an end in sense evidence, where the experience of hearing the ringing sound provides the justification for the belief that someone is at the door. The view that true belief is justified by experience is called **empiricism**. Hume explains his empiricism in the following passage:

A Treatise of Human Nature (David Hume, 1739)[2]

All the perceptions of the human mind resolve themselves into two distinct kinds, which I shall call Impressions and Ideas. The difference betwixt these consists in the degrees of force and liveliness with which they strike upon the mind, and make their way into our thought or consciousness. Those perceptions, which enter with most force and violence, we may name impressions; and under this name I comprehend all our sensations, passions and emotions, as they make their first appearance in the soul. By ideas I mean the faint images of these in thinking and reasoning ...

There is another division of our perceptions, which it will be convenient to observe, and which extends itself both to our impressions and ideas. This division is into Simple and Complex. Simple perceptions or impressions and ideas are such as admit of no distinction nor separation. The complex are the contrary to these, and may be distinguished into parts. Tho' a particular colour, taste, and smell are qualities all united together in this apple, 'tis easy to perceive they are not the same, but are at least distinguishable from each other....

The first circumstance, that strikes my eye, is the great resemblance betwixt our impressions and ideas in every other particular, except their degree of force and vivacity. The one seem to be in a manner the reflexion of the other; so that all the perceptions of the mind are double, and appear both as impressions and ideas. When I shut my eyes and think of my chamber, the ideas I form are exact representations of the impressions

---

2   David Hume, *A Treatise of Human Nature*, Book 1.1.I.

I felt; nor is there any circumstance of the one, which is not to be found in the other. In running over my other perceptions, I find still the same resemblance and representation. Ideas and impressions appear always to correspond to each other. This circumstance seems to me remarkable, and engages my attention for a moment.

Upon a more accurate survey I find I have been carried away too far by the first appearance, and that I must make use of the distinction of perceptions into simple and complex, to limit this general decision, that all our ideas and impressions are resembling. I observe, that many of our complex ideas never had impressions, that corresponded to them, and that many of our complex impressions never are exactly copied in ideas. I can imagine to myself such a city as the New Jerusalem, whose pavement is gold and walls are rubies, tho' I never saw any such. I have seen Paris; but shall I affirm I can form such an idea of that city, as will perfectly represent all its streets and houses in their real and just proportions? ...

Suppose therefore a person to have enjoyed his sight for thirty years, and to have become perfectly well acquainted with colours of all kinds, excepting one particular shade of blue, for instance, which it never has been his fortune to meet with. Let all the different shades of that colour, except that single one, be plac'd before him, descending gradually from the deepest to the lightest; 'tis plain, that he will perceive a blank, where that shade is wanting, and will be sensible, that there is a greater distance in that place betwixt the contiguous colours, than in any other. Now I ask, whether 'tis possible for him, from his own imagination, to supply this deficiency, and raise up to himself the idea of that particular shade, tho' it had never been conveyed to him by his senses? ...

This then is the first principle I establish in the science of human nature; nor ought we to despise it because of the simplicity of its appearance. For 'tis remarkable, that the present question concerning the precedency of our impressions or ideas, is the same with what has made so much noise in other terms, when it has been disputed whether there be any innate ideas, or whether all ideas be derived from sensation and reflexion. We may observe, that in order to prove the ideas of extension and colour not to be innate, philosophers do nothing but shew, that they are conveyed by our senses. To prove the ideas of passion and desire not to be innate, they observe that we have a preceding experience of these emotions in ourselves.

In this passage,

1. Hume outlines his empiricism, according to which there are **impressions**, which are experiences that are forceful and lively. There are two types of impressions: **sensations** (which are experiences derived from the five senses, such as taste, touch, smell, sound, and sight) and **feelings** (which are derived from reflection, such as desires

*and emotions). Anish sees and hears an elephant charging, which is a sensation, and then feels afraid, which is a feeling. The sight and sound of the elephant and the feeling of fear are impressions, since those experiences impress or force themselves upon Anish. Hume thinks that our impressions lead us to form **ideas**, which are images or copies of the original impression: years later, Anish remembers the frightful moment of seeing and hearing an elephant charging, and believes he saw an elephant. These memories and beliefs are ideas.*

Some commit the **Straw Person** fallacy against either Hume or Descartes, as discussed in Chapter 1.5.4. Against Hume, they say that all ideas cannot come from sense experience, since we have ideas like 'unicorns' and 'God' that were not in sense experience. Hume's doctrine of complex ideas allows for this possibility. Against Descartes, they say we cannot have innate ideas because babies are not already smart at birth. Descartes' doctrine of innate ideas accepts this fact.

2. *Hume says that, since ideas are copies of impressions, every idea originates in an experience. Someone who has never had an experience will not have any ideas in their mind. A man born blind cannot have even the slightest imagination of what red looks like. Newborn babies, with no experiences, have no ideas in their minds at all. The mind of the baby at birth is a **tabula rasa**, or blank slate; it is like a blank piece of paper waiting for experience to inform it of what the world is like. This view contrasts with Descartes' view that the mind possesses **innate** [inborn] **ideas**, or that the structure of the mind makes a contribution to knowledge as well, above and beyond experience. We shall return to the debate between the tabula rasa and innate ideas in Chapter 10.4.*

3. *Hume argues that ideas are faint images of impressions. This means that ideas are less reliable than impressions. Memory can fail us: Anish may remember seeing an elephant, but he has forgotten many of the details, and misremembers some of the other parts of the experience. Beliefs can fail us as well. Anish believes he saw the elephant in the Jaipur Zoo, but he is mistaken: he actually saw the elephant in the wild. But impressions are forceful and cannot be mistaken. Anish, while feeling fear, cannot be incorrect about the fact that he is feeling afraid. A man tasting steak inside the Matrix cannot be mistaken about what the steak tastes like, though the cause of this taste—whether it be an*

actual steak or a computer simulation of a steak—cannot be known with certainty. Similarly, one cannot be mistaken about the presence of an audio, visual, or taste sensation, though one might be wrong about what caused it.

4. *Hume responds to an objection to the view that all ideas can be traced back to experience. Here is the objection: we have many ideas in our minds that we did not experience. For example, we have ideas of unicorns, cities with gold pavement and ruby walls, or goblins and ghosts, but we have never experienced these things. Hume solves this problem by introducing a distinction between **simple ideas** and **complex ideas**. Simple ideas are traced back to experience, but complex ideas are combinations of simple ideas. So, we experience white horses, and we experience horns, so we have the simple ideas of white horses and horns. But we then combine these simple ideas into the complex idea of the unicorn. When inventors invent, they combine previously existing ideas together: the smart phone isn't really brand new; it is just a phone combined with a computer, both of which already existed.*

Descartes and Hume disagree about a lot of things. Descartes says that sense experience is an unreliable foundation for justifying true beliefs, as we could be dreaming right now or stuck in the Matrix. So, it does not matter that the thinking self cannot be experienced, as experience does not prove whether things exist or not. Rather, the mind can use its own thinking power to figure out for itself that it exists, and then reason from this firm foundation. This shows that the mind is capable of generating knowledge independently of experience. Hume, on the contrary, says that ideas are an unreliable foundation for justifying true beliefs, as they are faint and often mistaken images of experiences. So, it does not matter that the thinking self has the idea that it exists, as we imagine many fanciful ideas of things that do not exist. Rather, what can be experienced is what we know exists, and the self experiences their bundle of perceptions, so that is what we know exists. This shows that every idea in our minds originates in experience. In Chapter 10.4 we will see how this controversy between Descartes' rationalism and Hume's empiricism sorts itself out in the work of Immanuel Kant.

What product would you like to invent? Maybe beersicles (popsicles made out of beer)? Maybe a shower that adds shampoo to the streaming water? Once you have your idea, ask yourself: is this invention just the combination of old products, or is your invention radically new and there is nothing else like it? If all of our ideas come from sense experience, then we can't have any new ideas that are not merely combinations of old ones. On the other hand, if Descartes is right, then the mind can make up brand new ideas.

Descartes and Hume agree on several things as well. First, they agree that we must solve the regress problem by appealing to something other than prior beliefs. Descartes proposes self-justifying beliefs, whereas Hume proposes experience. They are also both internalists, which means that the source of justification for true beliefs is *inside the mind*, so humans have access to the justification of true beliefs. Descartes thinks that mental reasoning provides the justification for true beliefs, whereas Hume thinks our experiences provide the justification. But our ideas and our experiences are both internal to our minds. Some form of internalism was the dominant model of justification until the 1960s. But here are several of the problems that internalism faces.

Objection 1: Problems with Reason and Experience

Descartes and Hume both point out a difficulty with the idea that experience is the source of justification: it is that our experiences may not correspond to the way the external world actually is. We shall consider additional difficulties with perception in Chapter 8.1, 8.2, and 8.4. Hume points out a difficulty with internal reasoning alone being the source of justification: it is that our memories and beliefs are prone to error and there are no ideas to reason about that do not start as experience. In Chapter 9.2 and 9.5, we will consider further problems with trusting our mind's ability to know itself. Perhaps the best solution is to abandon both experience and reason as the source of justification, since both have questions surrounding them.

While walking through a pasture, you see what looks like a sheep in the distance, though it is actually a rock. You form the belief 'there is a sheep in the pasture.' This belief is justified by your visual experience—the rock really looks very much like a sheep. Little do you know there was a sheep hiding behind the rock. So your belief that there is a sheep in the pasture turns out to be true. You have a justified true belief, but you did not know there was a sheep in the pasture.

Objection 2: Gettier Cases

Earlier the question was: what is propositional knowledge? The answer: true belief alone is not enough for propositional knowledge, since we can luckily stumble upon a true belief, so we need a justification for our true belief. But maybe justified true belief is not enough for propositional knowledge either, since we can luckily stumble upon a justification for true belief as well. In the 1960s, the American philosopher **Edmund Gettier** (1927–2021) introduced exactly this problem by providing several examples where luck is involved in the justified true belief, so knowledge fails.

Here is his **ten coins** example. Imagine that Smith and Jones apply for the same job. Smith hears from the CEO that Jones will get the job, so Smith believes "Jones will get the job," and his justification is good. While waiting for his interview, Smith sees Jones playing with ten coins, then putting them in his pocket, so Smith believes "Jones has ten coins in his pocket," another well-justified belief. Smith then concludes "The man who will get the job has ten coins in his pocket," another well-justified belief. As it turns out, the CEO decides to let the manager make the hiring decision, and the manager hires Smith. Now, just by coincidence, Smith has ten coins in his pocket too; so Smith's belief that "The man who will get the job has ten coins in his pocket" is true after all! Smith has a justified true belief, but most agree that he did not know this. These types of **Gettier cases** lead many to conclude that knowledge requires more than justified true belief.

Objection 3: The Chicken Sexer

A chicken sexer is a person with the unique skill of being able to accurately tell the difference between male and female newly-hatched chickens. This is no easy task: they look indistinguishable to the rest of us. When asked how they tell the difference, some cannot provide an answer. They just know how to do it.[3] The chicken sexer knows, for example, that a particular chick is female, but does not know her justification for that belief. Here is another example: as a child Simone learned that Abe Lincoln was the 16th president of the US. This is a true belief, and she was provided historical evidence (maybe by her reliable textbook, or her knowledgeable teacher) at the time, so she has justification for her propositional knowledge. As a sixty-year-old, she still believes correctly that Abe Lincoln was the 16th president of the US, but she can't remember how she learned it and she can't remember any support for her belief. She has knowledge without "having" the justification for her true belief, or at least, without having any idea of what that justification might be. These cases show that it seems possible to have knowledge without having awareness of our justification for the true belief, which calls into question the internalist view that propositional knowledge is justified true belief and we have access to the justification.

7.4 Naturalized Epistemology

After Gettier showed the difficulties that justification has with turning true belief into knowledge, new proposals sprouted up. In the next two sections, we will consider two of these new proposals, both of which reject internalism and instead support externalism. Externalists about justification believe that that knowledge does not involve true beliefs that are justified by factors

---

3   This turns out not to be a mysterious form of ESP. There's a very tiny difference between the visible anatomy of male and female chicks; it's hard to see, and chicken sexers need training to learn to do so. It could be, however, that they can't describe what they're looking for. For details of this example and discussion of its significance, see "The Art of Chicken Sexing" by Richard Horsey, *UCL Working Papers in Linguistics* 14 (2002).

within minds. Rather, knowledge depends in part upon conditions outside of the knower. What are these conditions? Numerous different models propose different conditions, but they fit broadly into two categories: naturalistic conditions and social conditions. This section is devoted to the proposal that naturalistic conditions influence whether someone has knowledge or not.

Naturalized epistemology takes knowledge to depend on factors external to the knower, where these factors are "naturalistic." That is, these factors exist within nature itself and are subject to the natural sciences. There are many different possible naturalistic factors. First, the naturalistic factor may be a true fact in the world that causes our experiences and beliefs. Thus, if a bear starts chasing you, which makes you believe that a bear is chasing you, what makes your belief knowledge is not something internal to you, but it is the fact that the bear is chasing you. The internal mental experience might be identical to one in which you are hallucinating or dreaming, but what makes the real case knowledge that a bear is chasing you is not something about the internal state. It's that you're seeing a real bear.

Second, the natural factor may be the way our brains are formed to process information and arrive at beliefs. We learn of how our brains are formed by studying the natural sciences such as psychology, neuroscience, and biology. Psychology studies the psychological causes of our beliefs. Hilary believes her husband is cheating on her. Why? Because she saw him texting while hiding his phone from her, and she had a terrible experience of an old boyfriend cheating on her ten years ago, which triggered her present fear that her husband is cheating. Neuroscience studies the unconscious neural causes of our beliefs. Hilary believes her husband is cheating because the painful experience ten years ago established deep neural connections from the perception of secretive behaviour to the amygdala, the fear center of the brain. Biology studies the biological causes of our beliefs, focused largely on the instinctive survival or reproductive value of our beliefs. Hilary believes her husband is cheating because she is biologically adapted to sense potential threats to her safety and pay attention to them. By studying the ways in which these natural sciences explain belief formation, we can discern whether our beliefs are likely to be true or not.

How can studying the brain help us discern whether our beliefs are likely to be true or not? Many naturalistic epistemologists answer this question by endorsing **reliabilism**, the view that our beliefs are likely to be true knowledge if our beliefs are formed by a reliable mechanism, and our beliefs are likely to be false if our beliefs are formed by an unreliable mechanism. A belief-formation mechanism is reliable when it produces true beliefs about the external world most of the time. Imagine a brand-new thermometer and a smashed-up thermometer. The new thermometer tracks the correct temperature ten days in a row, while the smashed thermometer is stuck at indicating it is 20° Celsius all the time. The new thermometer is a reliable or accurate temperature reader, so the thermometer's results can be said to be knowledge about the temperature. The smashed thermometer is not reliable, so it is not trusted to provide knowledge about the temperature. Similarly, if our beliefs are produced by an unreliable process, then our beliefs are not likely true. If we believe "There is a grey sky today" because we are hypnotized into believing it, or we pointed randomly at a colour chart to pick a colour, then our belief does not count as knowledge, even if the sky is really grey. After all, hypnosis and random pointing often yields incorrect results, so it is just lucky if they get it right once. But, if we believe "There is a grey sky today" because the grey sky reliably caused us to perceive a grey sky which reliably caused our brains to conclude that the sky is grey today, then we know the sky is grey today. Here is an excerpt from **W.V.O. Quine** (1908–2000), an important pioneer of naturalistic epistemology:

"Epistemology Naturalized" (W.V.O. Quine, 1969)[4]

The stimulation of his sensory receptors is all the evidence anybody has had to go on, ultimately, in arriving at his picture of the world. Why not just see how this construction really proceeds? Why not settle for psychology? ... If all we hope for is a reconstruction that links science to experience in explicit ways short of translation, then it would seem more sensible to settle for psychology. Better to discover how science is in fact developed and learned than to fabricate a fictitious structure to a similar effect....

Epistemology, or something like it, simply falls into place as a chapter of psychology and hence of natural science. It studies a natural phenomenon, viz., a physical human subject. This human subject is accorded a certain experimentally controlled input—certain patterns of irradiation in assorted frequencies, for instance—and in the fullness of time the subject delivers as output a description of the three-dimensional external world and its history. The relation between the meager input and the torrential output is a relation that we are prompted to study for somewhat the same reasons that always prompted epistemology: namely, in order to see how evidence relates to theory, and in what ways one's theory of nature transcends any available evidence ... But a conspicuous difference between old epistemology and the epistemological enterprise in this new psychological setting is that we can now make free use of empirical psychology....

One effect of seeing epistemology in a psychological setting is that it resolves a stubborn old enigma of epistemological priority. Our retinas are irradiated in two dimensions, yet we see things as three-dimensional without conscious inference. Which is to count as observation—the unconscious two-dimensional reception or the conscious three-dimensional apprehension? In the old epistemological context the conscious form had priority, for we were out to justify our knowledge of the external world by rational reconstruction, and that demands awareness. Awareness ceased

---

4   W.V.O. Quine, "Epistemology Naturalized," in *Ontological Relativity and Other Essays* (New York: Columbia University Press, 1969), 75, 78, 82–83, 90.

to be demanded when we gave up trying to justify our knowledge of the external world by rational reconstruction. What to count as observation now can be settled in terms of the stimulation of sensory receptors, let consciousness fall where it may.

Again there is the area that the psychologist Donald Campbell calls evolutionary epistemology ... some structural traits of color perception could have been predicted from survival value. And a more emphatically epistemological topic that evolution helps to clarify is induction, now that we are allowing epistemology the resources of natural science.

In this passage,

1. *Quine endorses the view that the causes of our perceptions figure into whether we have knowledge or not. This model presents an interesting response to the Matrix problem. Namely, in the Matrix, the perception of a cow in a field would not be caused by a real cow (since it would be caused by computer coding), so we would not know there is a cow in a field. Similarly, if we perceive in a dream that there is a dragon in a field, we would not know there is a dragon in a field because an actual dragon did not cause the perception. In the sheep example raised above, we do not know there's a sheep because a real sheep did not cause the perception.*

2. *Quine endorses the view that psychology tells us how our beliefs are actually formed, so it is important to study the actual psychological and neural mechanisms that form our beliefs.*

3. *Quine provides several examples of how the study of the natural science of biology will yield the result that the brain is a reliable belief-forming mechanism, so many of our beliefs are likely true knowledge. Specifically, he points to evolutionary epistemology for proof of the reliability of perception and inductive reasoning. Evolution is the view that our present traits evolved through the process of natural selection. Why do we have sharp teeth today? Sharp teeth bestowed an adaptive benefit on our biological ancestors, such as the ability to chew food or scare predators away, which explains why we have sharp teeth today. Likewise, **evolutionary epistemology** is the view that our knowledge-acquiring systems (i.e., our brains, our perceptual capabilities, and our reasoning capabilities) evolved through the process of natural selection. Why do we have visual perception today? Visual perception bestowed adaptive benefits on our biological ancestors, such as the ability to notice predators and find food, which explains why we have vision today, and why it works the way it does. Those born with perceptual systems or brains not suitable for finding out facts relevant to their survival would have died out before reproducing offspring. So, it is likely that those of us that are alive today have a largely reliable perceptual system.*

Objection 1: Explanation vs. Justification

Recall the earlier discussion on the difference between justification and explanation. An explanation provides an account of the cause of a belief, while a justification provides good reasons and evidence for the truth of the belief. Naturalized epistemology focuses on explanations for beliefs. Hilary believes her husband is cheating because her terrible experience hardwired a fear response into her whenever she sees secretive behaviour. This is the explanation for what causes her belief. But epistemologists want to know whether a belief is justified or not. Is Hilary's fearful belief true or not? If Hilary's husband is not actually cheating, and she has years of evidence that her husband is actually loving and faithful, she should believe he is faithful rather than adulterous. Many worry that naturalized epistemologists, by settling for explanations rather than insisting on justifications, abandon the project of epistemology entirely. As Jaegwon Kim worries, "[Quine] is asking us to set aside the entire framework of justification-centered epistemology.... Quine is asking us to put in its place a purely descriptive, causal-nomological science of human cognition [i.e., one that seeks causes and natural regularities] ... for epistemology to go out of the business of justification is for it to go out of business."[5] Kim is worried that losing justification and replacing it with a causal explanation of the origins of our beliefs is not satisfactory for analyzing knowledge. We know that Fatima believes in God because she grew up in a religious family, but we want to know if there are good reasons for believing in God.

Objection 2: Unreliable Brains

We saw in Chapter 1.4 and 1.5 that people are prone to make errors in reasoning. We are susceptible to cognitive biases, social biases, and fallacies of reasoning. In Chapter 8.1 and 8.2 we will investigate further ways in which our perceptions can be mistaken, while in Chapter 9.2 and 9.5 we shall investigate further ways in which our mind is prone to error and bias. In short, our brains are sometimes unreliable mechanisms for delivering true beliefs about ourselves, about the world, and about our place in the world. Some think this problem is worsened by the possibility that our brains evolved through natural selection, as our brains would then be structured for survival, not for truth acquisition. For example, take a look at these Mach bands.

Do you think that each band is the same shade throughout, or do you think that each band has darker shading near the edge of the lighter band beside it?

Mach bands

---

5   Jaegwon Kim, "What Is Naturalized Epistemology?" in *Philosophical Perspectives*, ed. James Tomberlin (Atascadero, CA: Ridgeview Publishing, 1988), 388, 391.

Each band is the same shade throughout, but our brains do not see this. Our brains exaggerate the contrast between the edges of different shades to facilitate edge detection. The ability to detect edges, whether it be the edge of a cliff or the edges separating berries from leaves, has survival value, so the brain is willing to sacrifice the truth. So, while naturalistic epistemologists point out how brains that produce true perceptions and beliefs are likely to help us survive, detractors note that brains frequently sacrifice true perceptions and beliefs for beliefs that contribute to survival. This issue was discussed in Chapter 1.2 and 1.3 when we considered the temptation to use our minds for practical gain rather than truth, and in Chapter 2.3 when we considered those who say that beliefs with practical benefits are true. We return to this issue again in Chapter 9.5 and 9.6.

7.5 Social Epistemology

Where naturalized epistemology locates the source of knowledge in factors outside the knower, some of those factors are still close to the knower, for example, in their brains or in their biological instincts. The naturalistic epistemologist suggests, however, that one source of knowledge could be far removed from the knower, namely, the true fact in nature that causes our perceptions and beliefs. In this section we consider another externalist view that locates the source of knowledge far away from the knower. Rather than locating the source of knowledge in the true fact of nature that causes our perceptions and beliefs, however, **social epistemology** locates the source of knowledge in the other people or in the institutions that we acquire evidence or beliefs from. Simone knows that Abe Lincoln was the 16th president of the US. How does she know this? She learned it when she was a child. How did she learn it? She read it in a book, and her teacher taught her, and her parents confirmed it when she asked. So, she learned about it from others, from the author of the book, from her teacher, and from her parents.

Social epistemologists focus on how our knowledge is sourced in the **testimony** of others, or the statements one hears from other people or reads. Notice that Simone was a child when she heard that Abe Lincoln was the 16th president. So, she did not do her own research to arrive at deductive evidence, and she did not herself see Abe Lincoln to arrive at empirical evidence, and she did not surmise based on her own reasoning and experience that this teacher was honest or lying, correct or incorrect. Rather, she just believed, based on trusting the testimony of the teacher, that Abe Lincoln was the 16th president.

Should we just believe everything everyone ever says? Imagine that Simone's teacher says that the Earth is flat. Should Simone just believe the teacher? No. The teacher could be lying or an unreliable source of information. But should we just doubt everything everyone ever says? Imagine that Simone's teacher says that Abe Lincoln was the 16th president, and Simone shakes her head and stomps out of the room yelling "Prove it! Why are you trying to lie to me?" Simone is making a mistake here. It is mean and unfounded to doubt everything everyone says. People usually speak honestly and make claims with some background knowledge on the issue. Social epistemologists propose middle ground views about trusting testimony, where a person is justified in accepting the truth of testimony until the speaker is proven unreliable, or once the speaker is proven reliable. Here is a passage from **Jennifer Lackey**, a contemporary proponent of social epistemology:

In the movie *Elf*, Buddy is a naïve elf from the North Pole who visits our civilization for the first time. He sees a sign in the window of a run-down New York coffee shop that advertises 'World's Best Cup of Coffee.' Naively believing the sign, Buddy goes into the store and shouts out: 'You did it! Congratulations! World's best cup of coffee. Great job, everybody!' Buddy is making a mistake here. It is naïve to blindly trust that everything everyone says is true. But we shouldn't just doubt everyone either. Where is the line?

"Testimony" (Jennifer Lackey, 2011)[6]

Virtually everything we know depends in some way or other on the testimony of others—what we eat, how things work, where we go, even who we are. We do not, after all, perceive firsthand the preparation of the ingredients in many of our meals, or the construction of the devices we use to get around the world, or the layout of our planet, or our own births and familial histories. These are all things we are told. Indeed, subtracting from our lives the information that we possess via testimony leaves them barely recognizable. Scientific discoveries, battles won and lost, geographical developments, customs and traditions of distant lands—all of these facts would be completely lost to us. It is, therefore, no surprise that the importance of testimony, both epistemological and practical, is nearly universally accepted ...

One of the central questions in the epistemology of testimony is how, exactly, hearers acquire justified beliefs from the testimony of speakers. Answers to this question have traditionally fallen into one of two camps: nonreductionism or reductionism. According to nonreductionists—whose historical roots are typically traced to the work of Thomas Reid—testimony is a basic source of justification, on an epistemic par with sense perception, memory, inference, and the like. Given this, nonreductionists maintain that, so long as there are no relevant undefeated defeaters, hearers can be justified in accepting what they are told merely on the basis of the testimony of speakers. So, for instance, Tyler Burge writes that "[a] person

6   Jennifer Lackey, "Testimony: Acquiring Knowledge from Others," in *Social Epistemology*, ed. Alvin Goldman and Dennis Whitcomb (Oxford: Oxford University Press, 2011), 71–75.

is entitled to accept as true something that is presented as true and that is intelligible to him, unless there are stronger reasons not to do so." Similarly, Matthew Weiner argues that "[w]e are justified in accepting anything that we are told unless there is positive evidence against doing so." ...

In contrast to nonreductionism, reductionists—whose historical roots are standardly traced to the work of David Hume—maintain that, in addition to the absence of undefeated defeaters, hearers must also possess *nontestimonally based positive reasons* in order to be justified in accepting the testimony of speakers. These reasons are typically the result of induction: for instance, hearers observe a general conformity between reports and the corresponding facts and, with the assistance of memory and reason, inductively infer that certain speakers, contexts, or types of reports are reliable sources of information. In this way, the justification of testimony is *reduced* to the justification for sense perception, memory, and inductive inference ...

The central problem raised against nonreductionism is that it is said to sanction gullibility, epistemic irrationality, and intellectual irresponsibility. For given that, on such a view, hearers can acquire testimonially justified beliefs in the complete absence of any relevant positive reasons, randomly selected speakers, arbitrarily chosen postings on the Internet, and unidentified telemarketers can be trusted, so long as there is no negative evidence against such sources. Yet surely, the opponent of nonreductionism urges, accepting testimony in these kinds of cases is a paradigm of gullibility, epistemic irrationality, and irresponsibility.

Against reductionism, it is frequently argued that young children clearly acquire a great deal of knowledge from their parents and teachers and yet it is said to be doubtful that they possess—or even could possess—nontestimonially based positive reasons for accepting much of what they are told. For instance, an eighteen-month-old baby may come to know that the stove is hot from the testimony of her mother, but it is unclear whether she has the cognitive sophistication to have reasons for believing her mother to be a reliable source of information, let alone for believing that testimony is generally reliable ...

In this passage,

1. *Lackey points to numerous ways in which our beliefs are justified based on the testimony of others.*
2. *Lackey discusses the distinction between **nonreductionism** and **reductionism** with respect to testimony. We defined reductionism and nonreductionism in Chapter 4.2, where A reduces to B if A is nothing but B, and A is not reducible to B if A exists as a distinct phenomenon from B. In this case, the question is whether testimony is a foundational form of justification itself, or whether testimony reduces to other forms of justification, such as the reliability of auditory perception and the*

> *inferring from past accurate comments of this speaker that the speaker can presently be trusted. The reductionist says testimony is reduced to other forms of justification, and we will consider that view below. The nonreductionist says testimony cannot be reduced to other forms of justification, rather trusting the testimony of others is a distinct pathway for justification of our beliefs.*

Social epistemologists also point to systems set up in society that yield good, bad, or neutral epistemic results. The judicial system is an example of a good epistemic system. The defence and the prosecution both have lawyers presenting their case, with the capacity for cross-examination, where a judge moderates the proceedings and a jury of impartial peers decides the case. The result of this epistemic system is, more times than not, a true and well justified verdict on the case. The scientific method is another example of a good epistemic system (we will consider this system in Chapter 10). There are also systems in society that yield bad epistemic results—some that are even designed to do this. The advertising industry is set up to maximize profits rather than accuracy, which leads them to deploy bull-crap and logical fallacies to persuade the listener to buy their product, as studied in Chapter 1. The political system is both a good and bad epistemic system. On the one hand, everyone gets to vote, which allows for everyone to weigh in on issues affecting them. But on the other hand, politicians use various forms of bull-crap to maximize votes cast for them, the press can engage in propaganda for one side over the other, and social media can censor or recommend information for political purposes.

Objection 1: Vulnerability Problem

Lackey hints at the **vulnerability problem** in the passage above. Whenever we trust the testimony of others, this renders us vulnerable to the competence and honesty of the speaker. In the extreme case of Buddy, the advertisement is lying, but Buddy believes what it says. No one wants to play the fool like Buddy does. Conditions are normally put in place to avoid the vulnerability problem. For example, some social epistemologists say the speaker can be trusted, provided there is no reason to suspect they are unreliable or untrustworthy. A speaker is **unreliable** when their testimony may be mistaken due to lack of knowledge: a child explains gravity, but her youth gives us reason to suspect she is unreliable. A speaker is **untrustworthy** when their testimony may be mistaken due to an attempt at deception: a car salesman tells you how great the car is, but the fact that he will profit from the sale gives us reason to suspect he is untrustworthy. The view that a speaker can be trusted until proven otherwise is usually associated with the nonreductive model of testimony, and is similar to the view presented in Chapter 12.3. Other social epistemologists say the speaker can only be trusted once they have been proven reliable and trustworthy—this model is usually associated with the reductive model of testimony.

Even with these additional conditions in place, there is still a vulnerability problem for testimony. In appealing to testimony, hearers place themselves in an epistemically weaker position than speakers. Demar asks his peer Dorian whether the price of gas is going to fall, and Dorian says it will, and Demar believes her. Demar is trusting in Dorian's knowledge ahead of his own knowledge. But if he is planning on trusting in testimony, why wouldn't he just trust his own testimony about what is going to happen? And why shouldn't Dorian defer to Demar's testimony instead? This problem may be avoided if one of them is an **expert** or authority on the issue. In this case, Demar should defer to the expert testimony of Dorian. But there are problems associated with trusting the testimony of seeming experts as well, as discussed in the fallacy of the **illicit appeal to authority** in Chapter 1.5.4.

Objection 2: Reductionism

In order to avoid the blind trust that leads to the vulnerability problem, speakers must be reliable and trustworthy. These added conditions, however, are a move away from grounding knowledge in testimony and back toward grounding knowledge in our own perceptions or reasoning skills. The reductionist accepts this slide away from focusing on trusting the testimony alone. On reductionism, grounding knowledge in testimony involves grounding knowledge in our own evaluation of their testimony, and our own evaluation of whether the speaker is reliable, and on our own evaluation of whether testimony in general has proven reliable in the past, and whether the speaker is trustworthy, and whether they are an expert in the field or not. The more that testimony reduces to other sources of knowledge, whether it be our own evaluation of the testimony, our own reasoning to confirm the testimony, or our own experiences that the testimony lines up with, the less we base knowledge on testimony.

Summary

There are three kinds of knowledge: know-how, knowledge by acquaintance, and propositional knowledge. Propositional knowledge involves true belief that has justification or evidence in support of it. The question arises: what counts as justification or evidence for true belief? The rationalist René Descartes argues that true belief is justified by self-evidently true beliefs and reasoning. The empiricist David Hume argues that true belief is justified by experience. These are both internalist views, as the source of justification is "inside" knowers—in their reasoning or their experiences—and knowers have access to the justification. The naturalistic epistemologist W.V.O. Quine argues that true belief is justified by the world causing our reliably functioning brains to cause correct beliefs to occur to us. The social epistemologist Jennifer Lackey argues that true belief is justified by the testimony we hear from others. These last two views are externalist, as the source of justification is outside the knower in the world or in others. It is common for philosophers to claim that one of these views is the true source of justification. But it is also possible that they are all legitimate sources of knowledge when properly used. In upcoming chapters, we will investigate several epistemological issues that arise out of the themes and positions discussed here. In Chapter 8 we investigate the accuracy of our perception of the world—a theme connected to empiricism. In Chapter 9 we investigate the accuracy of our mind's ability to know—a theme connected to rationalism. In Chapter 10 we investigate the scientific method—a theme connected to all of the positions discussed here. And in Chapter 12 we investigate religious experience and faith—a theme likewise connected to all of the positions discussed here.

Key Terms in Chapter 7: Knowledge		
Epistemology	Cogito Ergo Sum	Evolutionary
Know-How	Rationalism	Epistemology
Acquaintance	Empiricism	W.V.O. Quine
Propositional	Impression	Social Epistemology
Knowledge	Sensations	Testimony
Justification	Feelings	Nonreductionism
Justified True Belief	Ideas	Reductionism
Explanation	Tabula Rasa	Vulnerability Problem
Internalism	Innate Ideas	Jennifer Lackey
Externalism	Simple Ideas	Unreliable
Vicious Regress	Complex Ideas	Untrustworthy
Foundationalism	Edmund Gettier	Expert
Self-Justifying	Ten Coins	Straw Person Fallacy
Methodological Doubt	Gettier Cases	Illicit Appeal to
Sense Experience	Naturalized	Authority
Dream Argument	Epistemology	
Evil Demon	Reliabilism	

Philosophy on Television: Knowledge

The Matrix (1999)

This film is one of many where the characters are caught inside of an illusory reality. *The Matrix* begins with Neo living a normal life in a large American city, only for him to find out that he was living inside a computer simulation, while his actual body was suspended in a pod of nutrients. The Matrix resembles Descartes' suggestion that our experience of the world may be mistaken, as we may be dreaming or an evil demon may be tricking us. Other shows that take place inside an illusory reality include *Vanilla Sky* (2001), *Inception* (2010), and *Marvel's Agents of S.H.I.E.L.D.*: Season 4 (2017).

Shark Tank (2009–)

In the TV series *Shark Tank* and *Dragon's Den* (2005–), entrepreneurs introduce their inventions to potential investors. Some of their inventions are fairly simple, others very innovative. In both cases, questions are raised about whether their inventions are merely combinations of old ideas, as Hume supposes, or whether the mind can create genuinely new things.

Additional Resources

Visit this book's companion resources for additional materials, including video content and an automated tool for planning argumentative essays.

sites.broadviewpress.com/knowing/chapter-7

Chapter 8

Perception

THOUGHT EXPERIMENT 8.1

If a Tree Falls in a Forest ...

Perhaps the most famous philosophical puzzle is: "If a tree falls in a forest, and no one is around to hear it, does it make a sound?" Perhaps you think, "Yes, of course!" But, how would you know that? No one is there to hear the sound, so there is no proof that it makes a sound. Perhaps you think, "Let's leave a recording device turned on in the forest to see if there is a sound while we're gone!" But the recording device is like a perceiver, so this doesn't show that the tree makes a sound when there is no perceiver there. Perhaps you think, "No, it doesn't make a sound, there are only compression waves of air particles passing through space, but no ears nearby to translate these waves into sound." But aren't these compression waves just what sound is? How can there be no sound if these compression waves are present? And, how do we know the compression waves are present, given that no one is around to check that either?

Perception is our experience of things, as informed by the five senses: hearing, sight, touch, taste, and smell. We've encountered issues involving perception before. In Chapter 7.3 we considered empiricism, which is the view that knowledge is justified by experience, where experience is sense impressions delivered by the five senses, plus internal awareness (e.g., of pain or anger). A **sense impression** is a raw, unconceptualized experience such as seeing redness, seeing roundness, tasting sweetness, tasting juiciness, and smelling an apple-like smell. Perception occurs when the mind combines these sense impressions together to form a complete experience of a thing such as eating an apple. As another example, we feel heat in our throats, we taste bitterness and some sweetness, we smell coffee-like smells, we see a dark brown liquid. Our perception is this combined experience of drinking coffee.

There are three central aspects to perception, each of which leads to various controversies and various models of perception. Let us look at these three aspects before spending the remainder of the chapter considering the problems associated with them. First, perception involves *our **experience*** of things, which means that there is something it is like for us to encounter this thing. Consider Lian, who has two cans of beer. She pours one down her throat and the other down the sink. The sink experiences nothing as the beer flows through—there is nothing it feels like for the sink when beer flows through—so it is fair to say that the sink does not experience the beer flowing down. On the other hand, Lian experiences much as the beer flows down her throat—it feels cold and fizzy and there is a distinct beer-like taste that occurs to her—so it is fair to say that she experiences the beer flowing down. That we have experiences of the things we encounter sounds obvious, and it should be. Experience is probably the most frequent occurrence in our lives.

Second, perception involves our experience of *things*—that is, of objects in the **external world**, which is just the normal material world that exists outside, independently of, our mind. When we perceive the red balloon, we perceive the balloon that exists outside of ourselves in the world, and it is the balloon that is red and round. It is the pineapple that tastes sweet and juicy, it is not our own mind that tastes sweet and juicy. Since it is the balloon that is red, we can say that the balloon, and the redness of the balloon, are **mind-independent**. Imagine a meteor struck the Earth and killed all the humans and animals, so there were no more perceiving beings in the world. Would the balloon still be red? Would the sun still be yellow? Yes, because it is the balloon that is red, and it exists as a thing in the world on its own, independently of us.

When you take a selfie on your camera, the photo is a representation of you. In one way, it is you, since the person in the photo looks like you, but in another way, it is not you, since it is a screen sized two-dimensional picture that only exists on your phone.

Third, perception involves our experience *of* things. Our experience is a **representation** *of* the thing that exists in the external world, which means that the thing is re-presented in our experience. A representation is, in one way, the thing itself, and in another way, not the thing itself. The king's representative is, in one way, the king, since she speaks for the king and represents the king, but is, in another way, not the king, since the king isn't actually there. Similarly, our experience of things represents those things to us. Our experience of the red, sweet apple is a representation of the apple, it is the apple as characterized as red by our eyes, and characterized as sweet by our taste buds.

These three features of perception are embraced to different degrees by different theories. But, together, they lead to one of the central issues of perception. Namely, what is the relationship between our perception of things, and the things themselves? When the tree falls and we perceive the sound, is the sound really out in the external world, or does the sound depend on a perceiver? If we take the perceiver away, is there still a sound? If we hear a banging drum, and the banging drum is really there, then we are having a **veridical experience**, which means that our experience corresponds with reality. I perceive an apple in front of me, and there really is an apple in front of me! We feel like (and hope that) our perceptions are veridical experiences, but unfortunately things are not always as they seem. Before diving into the difficulties, let us plot the major positions on the following spectrum:

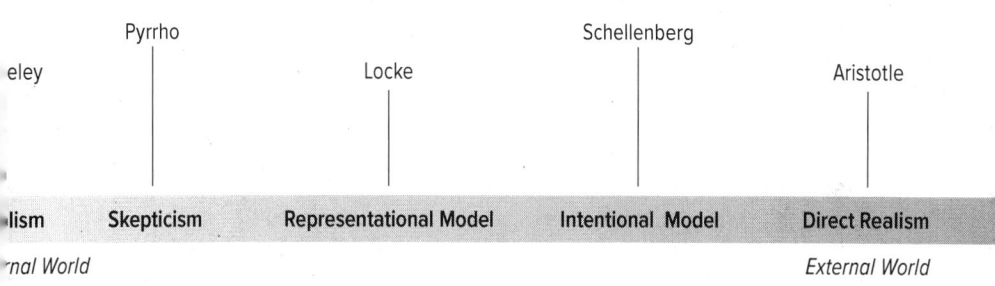

Spectrum 8: What We Perceive

On the right stand those who think we perceive the external material world, and that we are not perceiving our own experience that is internal to our minds. On the left stand those who think we do not perceive an external material world at all, but that we are instead merely having experiences internal to our minds. In the middle stand those who think our experiences are mental representations of the external material world, so that we partly perceive our own mental realm and partly perceive the external material world. Let us now consider each of the models, beginning with the one on the right side of the spectrum: direct realism.

8.1 Direct Realism

Direct realists say that our experience of things amounts to us looking straight at the things themselves—we perceive things directly, with nothing standing in between our perception and the thing itself. Direct realists are sometimes called **common sense realists**, as it just seems to be common sense that when we look at things, we are looking straight at the things themselves. When you perceive a hard, grey wall in front of you, that is you staring at the grey wall, and you touching the hard wall. On direct realism, there are two things involved in perception. There is the perceiver, namely you, and there is the thing itself, namely the wall, and perception involves the perceiver directly experiencing the wall. The thing perceived exists in the external material world, and exists independently of whether we are perceiving it or not. If we leave the room where the grey wall is, and we close the door to make sure no one sees the wall anymore, the wall is still grey when we are gone. The greyness of the wall is a property of the wall itself, and does not depend on someone perceiving it.

Most people start out as direct realists, as it seems to be the common-sense view. This is because perception presents objects as existing outside of ourselves, in an external world that is independent from us. This is called the **transparency** of perception, where in perception it seems as though we are looking straight through our own eyes, right at external objects themselves. Consider two cases. Maya is in her house looking outside at a horse in the field. She has two windows to look through. The first window is wide open, no glass panel and no screen, and through it she looks straight at the horse. The second window is dirty and has a crack in it and there is a screen in the window as well. When she looks through it, she sees the horse, but she also notices the dirt and distortions of the window. Our perception is more like the first window. Our eyes do not distort or blur the actual object, but instead our eyes (as it were) get out of the way, leaving us able to see the actual objects as they appear.

The **commonality of perception** also supports direct realism. This is the view that different people report having the same experience of things, which makes it likely that the thing exists as it is in a shared external world. Imagine that Rylan perceives a red balloon and she asks her friend Nuhan what she sees. Nuhan also says she sees a red balloon, not a green balloon, or a red apple. They talk to their friends Vedant and Anka, who both agree that there is a red balloon in front of them. It is quite normal for many people to agree on the look or smell of an object. Contrast this with, say, emotions. Rylan is feeling sad today, and she asks her friend if she feels sad too. Nuhan says no, she is feeling anxious at the moment. They call their other friends together, and it turns out that Vedant is feeling excited about the day, while Anka is feeling tired. They are not sharing in the same emotions, and this makes it likely that their emotions are internal to their own individual minds; they do not exist out in the world. But since they all agree that the balloon is red, it seems like they are not all having their own different visual experiences in their own minds, but rather they are all looking directly at the same thing, namely, the balloon that is itself red.

Another advantage of direct realism is that it places the perceiver in direct contact with the external world. When we perceive a horse in the field, we are looking directly at a horse in the field, and we are in visual contact with the external material world. Thus, the skeptical questions Descartes raised in Chapter 7.2, such as whether we may be dreaming or deceived by an evil demon, cannot even get off the ground. On direct realism, it is not possible for our experience of the horse in the field to not be a horse in the field, as we are already looking straight at the horse in the field. One of the earliest advocates of direct realism was **Aristotle**, and here is an excerpt from his writings:

Physics, Book 2.1, and *De Anima*, Books 2 and 3 (Aristotle, 350 BCE)[1]

To attempt to prove that there is such a thing as nature would be ridiculous; for it is evident that there are many things of the sort we have described. To prove what is evident from what is not evident betrays an inability to discriminate what is known because of itself from what is not ...

The perceiver is potentially what the perceptible object actually is already, as we have said. When it is being affected, then, it is unlike the object; but when it has been affected it has been made like the object and has acquired its quality ...

A general point to be grasped is that each sense receives the perceptible forms without the matter. Wax, for instance, receives the design on a signet-ring without the iron or gold; it acquires the design in the gold or bronze, but not insofar as the design is gold or bronze. Similarly, each sense is affected by the thing that has color or flavor or sound, but not insofar as it is said to be that thing, for instance, a horse, but insofar as it has a given quality, for instance, color, and in accordance with the form of the sense ...

Further, perceptions are always true, whereas most appearances are false. Again, whenever we are actually perceiving accurately, we do not say that this appears to us to be a man; we are more inclined to say that something appears to be so in cases where we do not see clearly whether something is true or false ... Perception of the objects of the special senses is true, or subject to the minimum of error. Next comes the perception that they are attributes: and at this point error may come in. As to the whiteness of an object sense is never mistaken, but it may be mistaken as to whether the white object is this thing or something else ...

Within the soul the faculties of knowledge and sensation are potentially these objects, the one what is knowable, the other what is sensible. They must be either the things themselves or their forms. The former alternative is of course impossible: it is not the stone which is present in the soul but its form. It follows that the soul is analogous to the hand; for as the hand is a tool of tools, so thought is the form of forms and sense the form of sensible things.

In this passage,

1. *Aristotle appeals to common sense to show that we directly experience ordinary natural objects. It is so obvious to Aristotle that we are perceiving natural objects that it needs no proof, for everything else is*

---

1   Aristotle, *Physics* 193a3–5 and *De Anima* 418a4–6; 424a17–24, 428a12–15, in *Readings in Ancient Greek Philosophy*, 741, 861–62, 864; *De Anima* 431b21–432a3, trans. J.A. Smith (1931), 3.8.

> *less likely than this fact, so looking for proof would only result in proving what is certain with evidence that is less than certain.*
> 2. *Aristotle argues that the sense impressions that we perceive are present in the objects themselves. We perceive the fire as hot, and the fire has heat in it, so our experience of the hot fire is veridical.*

What would the direct realist say about the tree falling in the forest with no one around? The sound that comes with the falling tree is a property of the falling tree; it exists in the mind-independent external world. So even if there is no one present to hear the sound, there is still a sound that occurs.

Objection 1: Hallucinations

Direct realism is sometimes called "**naïve realism**." This is because, while everyone starts out as a direct realist, once they are better informed about the issues, most abandon direct realism. Why abandon direct realism? On direct realism, what we perceive corresponds to what is actually there: we perceive the heat of the fire, and the fire is hot. But there are many cases where what we perceive does not correspond to what is actually there. A **hallucination** occurs when we seem to experience a thing, but the thing is not really there. Samir ingests hallucinogenic drugs and he experiences a pink elephant in his room, but the elephant is not there. Damian is driving down the road and he sees what looks like a puddle of water in the distance, but as his car arrives the puddle disappears. In Shakespeare's play, Macbeth sees a dagger in front of him, and wonders if it is real: "Is this a dagger which I see before me ... or art thou but a dagger of the mind, a false creation, proceeding from the heat-oppressed brain?" The dagger was a hallucination: it was never really there. Hallucinations introduce a divide between our perception of things, and the things themselves, which undermines the direct realist view that we are in direct contact with the things themselves.

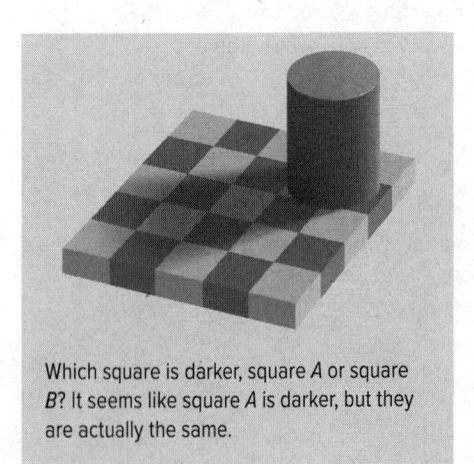

Which square is darker, square *A* or square *B*? It seems like square *A* is darker, but they are actually the same.

Objection 2: Illusions

Where hallucinations involve us experiencing things that are not there, **illusions** involve us experiencing things differently than they actually are. One famous example is the checkerboard illusion from Edward Adelson.

Do you think that square *A* and square *B* are the same shade of grey, or do you think *A* is darker than *B*? In reality, they are the same shade (which you can tell by covering over everything but those two squares), but they do not look the same.

It is quite easy to trick ourselves into thinking that two lines of the same length are not really the same length, or two of the same colours look like different colours. Illusions once again show us that our experience of things can be quite different than the things themselves, which calls into question the direct realist view that we directly experience the things that exist in the material world.

8.2 Skepticism

Whereas Aristotle was an ancient Greek philosopher who argued that our experience of things corresponds to the way things are, **Pyrrho** (360 BCE–270 BCE) was an ancient Greek philosopher who argued that our experience of things is likely not the way things actually are. He uses the **relativity of perception** to prove his case, according to which different animals, different humans, and even different sense organs within the same human provide vastly different perceptual experiences of exactly the same thing. We now know many more examples of this than Pyrrho knew. The mantis shrimp is able to perceive ultraviolet wavelengths of light, whereas humans cannot. Bats are able to echolocate (to perceive their surroundings by processing how sounds echo off of objects) while humans cannot. Some pigeons are able to perceive the direction of the magnetic north, while humans cannot. Dogs can hear higher sound frequencies than humans. Teenagers are able to hear higher frequencies than adults. Adults who need glasses see things as blurry while adults with perfect vision see the same things clearly. Broccoli tastes delicious to Jan, but broccoli tastes disgusting to Simone—and to every other reasonable person too! Simone's visual system reports coffee as being brown, while her sense of smell reports no colours but instead reports that coffee smells aromatic, while her sense of touch reports that coffee is hot but knows nothing of colour or aroma. In all these cases, different perceptual faculties report the thing as being vastly different from other perceptual reports, which leaves it unclear what the actual thing is really like.

The relativity of perception is contrasted with the commonality of perception—the commonality of perception suggests that different people experience the same thing in the same way, the relativity of perception suggests that different people experience the same thing in different ways. Whereas the commonality of perception leads toward direct realism, the relativity of perception leads away from direct realism. Since different people experience the same thing in different ways, our experiences of things are the products of different sense organs; hence we are not directly perceiving the way things actually are. Here is a passage from **Sextus Empiricus** about Pyrrho's skepticism, where he outlines the relativity of perception and describes how Pyrrhonian skepticism handles these issues:

Outlines of Pyrrhonism, Book I (Sextus Empiricus, late 2nd Century)[2]

IV. Scepticism is an ability, or mental attitude, which opposes appearances to judgements in any way whatsoever, with the result that, owing to the equipollence of the objects and reasons thus opposed, we are brought firstly to a state of mental suspense and next to a state of 'unperturbedness' or quietude ...

VII. When we say that the Sceptic refrains from dogmatizing we do not use the term 'dogma,' as some do, in the broader sense of 'approval of a thing' for the Sceptic gives assent to the feelings which are the necessary results of sense-impressions, and he would not, for example, say when feeling hot or cold 'I believe that I am not hot or cold'; but we say that 'he does not dogmatize' using 'dogma' in the sense, which some give it, of 'assent to one of the non-evident objects of scientific inquiry'; for the Pyrrhonean philosopher assents to nothing that is non-evident.... For whereas the dogmatizer posits the things about which he is said to be dogmatizing as really existent, the Sceptic does not posit these formulae in any absolute sense; for he conceives that, just as the formula 'All things are false' asserts the falsity of itself as well as of everything else, as does the formula 'Nothing is true,' ... If then, while the dogmatizer posits the matter of his dogma as substantial truth, the Sceptic enunciates his formulae so that they are virtually cancelled by themselves, he should not be said to dogmatize in his enunciation of them ...

X. Those who say that 'the Sceptics abolish appearances,' or phenomena, seem to me to be unacquainted with the statements of our School. For, as we said above, we do not overthrow the affective sense-impressions which induce our assent involuntarily; and these impressions are 'the appearances.' And when we question whether the underlying object is such as it appears, we grant the fact that it appears, and our doubt does not concern the appearance itself but the account given of that appearance—and that is a different thing from questioning the appearance itself. For example, honey appears to us to be sweet (and this we grant, for we perceive sweetness through the senses), but whether it is also sweet in its essence is for us a matter of doubt, since this is not an appearance but a judgement regarding the appearance ...

XIV. The First argument, as we said, is that which shows that the same impressions are not produced by the same objects owing to the differences

---

2 Sextus Empiricus, *Outlines of Pyrrhonism, Book I*, trans. R. Bury (Cambridge: Harvard University Press, 1933), 7–55.

in animals. This we infer both from the differences in their origins and from the variety of their bodily structures ... It is natural, then, that these dissimilar and variant modes of birth should produce much contrariety of sense affection, and that this is a source of its divergent, discordant, and conflicting character. Moreover, the differences found in the most important parts of the body, and especially in those of which the natural function is judging and perceiving, are capable of producing a vast deal of divergence in the sense-impressions owing to the variety in the animals. Thus, sufferers from jaundice declare that objects which seem to us white are yellow, while those whose eyes are bloodshot call them blood-red ...

This Third Mode is, we say, based on differences in the senses. That the senses differ from one another is obvious. Thus, to the eye paintings seem to have recesses and projections, but not so to the touch. Honey, too, seems to some pleasant to the tongue but unpleasant to the eyes; so that it is impossible to say whether it is absolutely pleasant or unpleasant. The same is true of sweet oil, for it pleases the sense of smell but displeases the taste.

In this passage,

1. *Sextus uses the relativity of perception to conclude that our experience of things does not guarantee that the things themselves are the way we perceive them to be.*

2. *Sextus endorses external world **skepticism**. We encountered skepticism in Chapter 1.3 where the sophists doubted our ability to know truth, and in Chapter 7.2 when Descartes doubted the accuracy of our sense experiences. To be a skeptic is to doubt our ability to know about something. Most people are **local skeptics** about some things, which means they doubt our knowledge of some particular thing. Archie is a local skeptic about aliens, which means he doubts that aliens exist. Sextus is a local skeptic about the external world, which means he doubts that the external world is as it appears. Some people are **global skeptics**, which means that they doubt our ability to know anything at all. The sophists were global skeptics.*

3. *Sextus contrasts three different attitudes one can take regarding our knowledge of the truth. First, there are dogmatists. **Dogmatists** are certain that they know truths, even when they do not in fact know the truth as clearly as they think they do. Saagar, the basketball fanatic from Cleveland, is absolutely certain that LeBron James is the best basketball player of all time, and will vigorously argue with anyone who thinks otherwise, even though there are legitimate reasons for people to think Michael Jordan is in fact the greatest basketball player of all time. **Academic skeptics** are negative dogmatists, which means they are absolutely certain that no one can ever know any truth, and they will argue vehemently against anyone who thinks humans can*

*possess truth. Sextus claims that academic skepticism is self-refuting, since, as we saw in Chapter 2.4, if the claim 'no one can know truth' is true, then this is a truth we know, which means that there is some truth we can know, which means 'no one can know truth' is false. Sextus endorses the third attitude, **Pyrrhonian skepticism**, according to which we are at peace with suspending judgement about our knowledge of things. We do not insist, as dogmatists do, that we have the truth on an issue, nor do we insist, as academic skeptics do, that no one can ever know the truth on an issue. Rather, we are at peace with not being certain about an issue, but we keep searching for the truth anyway. Socrates, as discussed in Chapter 1.2, has some similarities with the Pyrrhonian skeptic.*

What would skeptics say about the tree falling in the forest? They would not know if the falling tree makes a sound or not; they would not even know if there exists a tree or a forest. If someone were present to hear the falling tree, they would be confident that the sound was heard, but they would not know that the sound came from a real tree. We do not know what lies beyond our sense experience.

Objection 1: Phenomenal Conservatism

Phenomenal conservatism is the view that the way things appear to be should be accepted as the way things are, unless there is reason to doubt it. Joni sees a peach on the tree, and she should believe there really is a peach on the tree, unless she has reason to believe she is dreaming. The direct realist endorses phenomenal conservatism—they see a brown door in front of them, and this is reason to believe there really is a brown door in front of them. Skeptics reject phenomenal conservatism—there appears to be a brown door in front of them, but we should be skeptical of that: perhaps it is a hallucination. But why should we be skeptical of what appears to be the case? As discussed in Chapter 1.5.4, the **burden of proof** belongs to the person making the claim. So, if Joni says there is a peach in front of her, we ask her for proof. She answers that her proof is that she is having an experience of seeing a peach, so she has discharged her burden to provide evidence for her belief. The skeptic now has the burden to prove that her experience is not veridical. So, all things being equal, we should accept the way things appear to be since there is experiential evidence for the way things appear to be, until there is reason to doubt appearances. In fact, the skeptical view may be self-refuting. If we default to doubting rather than believing, then the skeptical attitude should lead us to doubting our own skepticism as well. Joni sees a peach, but if she doubts that it is really there since she may be dreaming, shouldn't she also doubt that she is really dreaming? This leads her back to just believing the peach is there in the first place, or it leads her to doubt everything, which is impractical.

Objection 2: Practical Problems

In Chapter 3.2 we saw some difficulties associated with doubting the external material world—Parmenides' view that the material world is illusory led to the problematic view that fires and bustling cities do not exist. Similarly, another ancient Greek philosopher named Diogenes suggests that skeptics have difficulty navigating the world. Pyrrho, for example, doubted the accuracy of his sense experiences, so his friends had to follow him closely to prevent him from being run over by passing carts.[3] How can we even move if we doubt that the ground beneath our feet is sturdy? Why would we eat the banana if we doubt that our bodies really exist, or that we doubt that the banana will nourish rather than kill us, or that humans need to eat food to live? Why would we move away from oncoming traffic if we aren't sure that cars really exist? The fact that we move away from oncoming traffic is proof that we do believe in the existence of the external material world.

8.3 Representational Model

Aristotle's direct realism presumes we are in closer contact with things than we may actually be, while skepticism assumes we are further away from things than we may actually be. A new model rose to prominence in the seventeenth century that serves as a middle ground between these two views. This is the **representational model** of perception, and it takes our experience of things to involve our experiences, which are the products of our particular sense organs, representing things in the material world to us. Unlike direct realism, where we directly perceive external things, the representational model says we perceive the sense experience itself, which is an internal mental state sometimes called a **percept** produced by our sense organs. With the representational model, the thing perceived by us is our internal percept. The percept that we perceive represents the external thing that caused it. The coffee causes Julio's eyes to produce the percept of brownness, which is what Julio sees. The coffee (i.e., the external thing) causes Julio's taste buds to produce a bitter taste (i.e., a percept), whereas Julio smells the bitter taste percept. The bitter percept represents the coffee to Julio as the coffee being bitter, rather than, say, representing the coffee to Julio as being sweet.

The representational model seems most plausible when considering distant objects. A star in a distant galaxy shoots out a ray of light, and it takes one hundred years to reach Earth, where a camper observes it while looking at the night sky. During this hundred-year interval, the star explodes and no longer exists. The camper is perceiving a star that no longer exists, so he cannot be

---

3 Diogenes Laertius, *Diogenes Laertius: Lives of Eminent Philosophers*, trans. R. Hicks (Cambridge: Harvard University Press, 1991), 9.62.

directly looking at the star; rather, he must be perceiving his white percept of the star. While this is an extreme case, there exists a momentary temporal gap between every object and our perception of it, as it takes fractions of a second for the light to travel from the object to the perceiver. In a way, our eyes are time machines, always observing things as they used to be, not as they presently are. The representational model is comfortable with this fact, as it takes our percepts to be representations of things, not the things themselves.

Another motivation for the representational model was the **scientific revolution**. During the 1600s, new scientific theories presented the world as being drastically different than the ancient scientists and philosophers such as Aristotle saw it. Isaac Newton presents his laws of motion, universal gravitation, and the refraction of light, while Gilbert and Boyle set forth laws of magnetism and chemistry, respectively. These new scientific theories analyze things mechanistically, according to which things operate according to the interactions of the parts making them up. The parts interact with each other through their electrical properties, chemical properties, or their masses and momenta coming in contact with each other in accordance with the physical laws of motion. While these laws explain the motions and make-up of things, they do not mention the familiar experiences humans have of those objects. They speak of wavelengths of light, not colours; they speak of vibrating air particles, not sounds; they speak of the kinetic energy of molecules, not hot and cold. A gap emerged between human perception of things and the way the sciences describe those things as actually being.

The representational model makes sense of this divide between the scientific picture of things as they actually are in the mind-independent physical world and the common-sense picture of things that appears to us in our perception. The representational model says that things in the external world possess scientific properties such as mass, charge, momentum, and wavelengths of light. But when material objects impinge upon our senses, they cause us to have sense impressions such as blue, heat, and sweetness, where these sense impressions exist in our own experiences but are not described in scientific vocabulary, so are not in the objects themselves. Here is an excerpt from

If a meteor destroyed all sentient life, would colours, tastes, and sounds still exist? Galileo says:

> I think that tastes, odors, colors, and so on are no more than mere names so far as the object in which we locate them are concerned, and that they reside in consciousness. Hence if the living creature were removed, all these qualities would be wiped away and annihilated.[4]

Do you agree?

---

4 Galileo Galilei, "The Assayer" in *Discoveries and Opinions of Galileo*, trans. S. Drake (Garden City: Doubleday, 1957), 274.

John Locke, one of the leading advocates of the representational model in the seventeenth century:

An Essay Concerning Human Understanding (John Locke, 1689)[5]

9. Qualities thus considered in bodies are, first, such as are utterly inseparable from the body, in what estate soever it be; ... Take a grain of wheat, divide it into two parts, each part has still solidity, extension, figure, and mobility; divide it again, and it retains still the same qualities; and so divide it on till the parts become insensible, they must retain still each of them all those qualities. For division can never take away either solidity, extension, figure, or mobility from any body, but only makes two or more distinct separate masses of matter, of that which was but one before: all which distinct masses, reckoned as so many distinct bodies, after division make a certain number. These I call original or primary qualities of body, which I think we may observe to produce simple ideas in us, viz. solidity, extension, figure, motion or rest, and number.

10. Secondly, such qualities which in truth are nothing in the objects themselves, but powers to produce various sensations in us by their primary qualities, i.e. by the bulk, figure, texture, and motion of their insensible parts, as colours, sounds, tastes, etc. these I call secondary qualities.... For the power in fire to produce a new colour, or consistency, in wax or clay, by its primary qualities, is as much a quality in fire, as the power it has to produce in me a new idea or sensation of warmth or burning, which I felt not before by the same primary qualities, viz. the bulk, texture, and motion of its insensible parts....

14. What I have said concerning colours and smells may be understood also of tastes and sounds, and other the like sensible qualities; which, whatever reality we by mistake attribute to them, are in truth nothing in the objects themselves, but powers to produce various sensations in us, and depend on those primary qualities, viz. bulk, figure, texture, and motion of parts; as I have said.

15. From whence I think it easy to draw this observation, that the ideas of primary qualities of bodies are resemblances of them, and their patterns do really exist in the bodies themselves; but the ideas, produced in us by these secondary qualities, have no resemblance of them at all. There is nothing like our ideas existing in the bodies themselves. They are in

---

5   John Locke, *An Essay Concerning Human Understanding*, Book II, Chapter VIII.

the bodies, we denominate from them, only a power to produce those sensations in us: and what is sweet, blue or warm in idea, is but the certain bulk, figure, and motion of the insensible parts in the bodies themselves, which we call so.

16. Flame is denominated hot and light; snow, white and cold; and manna, white and sweet, from the ideas they produce in us: which qualities are commonly thought to be the same in those bodies that those ideas are in us, the one the perfect resemblance of the other, as they are in a mirror; and it would by most men be judged very extravagant, if one should say otherwise. And yet he that will consider that the same fire, that at one distance produces in us the sensation of warmth, does at a nearer approach produce in us the far different sensation of pain, ought to bethink himself what reason he has to say, that his idea of warmth, which was produced in him by the fire, is actually in the fire; and his idea of pain, which the same fire produced in him the same way, is not in the fire.

In this passage,

1. *Locke introduces the distinction between primary qualities and secondary qualities.* **Primary qualities** *are the properties that objects have independently of someone perceiving them. If all the humans died, a cup of coffee would still have caffeine molecules, and would still have a certain molecular kinetic energy and weight. These primary qualities are the qualities described in scientific laws.* **Secondary qualities** *are the properties that objects cause our perceptual faculties to produce in us, and our percepts represent those objects to us. The coffee causes us to perceive heat and bitterness, and these percepts represent the coffee to us, but if all the humans died, the coffee would not still be hot or bitter.*

What would the representational model say about the tree falling in the forest? They might say that the compression waves of air particles would still travel through space. But sounds are percepts produced by ears, so without any ears present in the forest, there will be no sounds.

Objection 1: The Veil of Perception

The representational model was the dominant model of perception during the scientific revolution, and was one of the few things that Hume, Descartes, and Locke all agreed upon. Thomas Reid, who we encountered in Chapters 4.1 and 6.2, rejects the representational model. He thinks it leads either to skepticism about the external world, or idealism (which we will consider below), both of which are problematic. How does the representational model lead toward skepticism (or, idealism)? According to the representational model, we perceive our own percepts of things, but we do not perceive the things themselves. We taste the bitterness of coffee, which is our percept of coffee as produced by our taste buds, but we do not taste the coffee itself. This means we cannot see beyond our own perceptions of things and view the thing itself. We cannot step outside of our own eyesight to see what the coffee actually looks like, independently of our perception of it; rather, we are forever stuck seeing the coffee through the lens of our own eyes. This is the **veil of perception**, where our perception is like a veil placed over our eyes such that we only see the veil of our own percepts of things, and we are blocked off from seeing the things themselves. The result: we cannot know that things are as they seem, since we have never seen them. This is the skeptical result. We will consider the idealist result below, but suffice it to say that Reid thinks it is problematic as well.

Objection 2: Reductionism

A leading motivation for the representational model is the seeming distinction between the scientific descriptions of things and the different ways those things appear to us. In material reality, the molecular kinetic energy of water is increasing, but we perceive this as the water getting hotter, but there is nothing in the scientific description of water as 'getting hotter,' only as increasing in molecular

kinetic energy. In Chapter 4.2, however, we encountered the notion of **reductionism**, according to which A reduces to B, which means that A is B. It seems possible to reduce the perceptual experience of things to the scientific description of how things really are. On reductionism, increased heat just is identical with an increase in molecular kinetic energy, so the water is getting hotter. Redness just is a wavelength of light of approximately 700 nanometers, so the apple is red, as a wavelength of light of 700 nanometers reflects off of the apple. The crashing sound of the falling tree just is the compression waves of air particles, so sound exists when no one is present, since the compression waves of air particles exist, and that is sound. If perceptual experiences of things can be reduced to the scientific descriptions of things in themselves, then the gap between our sensations of things and the way things actually are gets closed, and a primary motivation for the representational model fails.

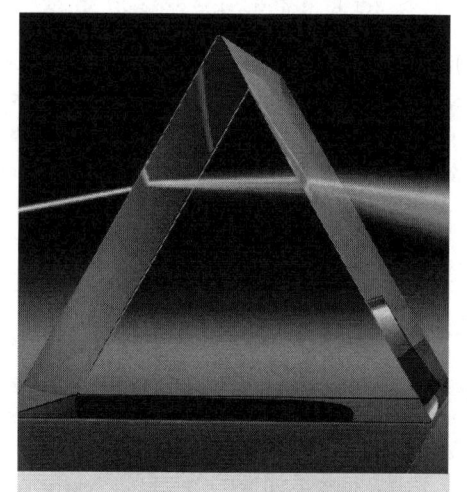

One the one hand, red seems identical to a 700-nanometer wavelength of light, since most people perceive red then. On the other hand, red is not identical to a specific wavelength of light, since some animals or colour-blind people don't perceive red then and a complex variety of different combinations of wavelengths can stimulate the perception of red.

8.4 Idealism

According to the representational model, the secondary qualities of taste, colour, and smell are percepts produced by minds, whereas the primary qualities of motion, shape, and mass are mind-independent and exist in external objects. But isn't it the case that we perceive motion with our eyes as well? Isn't it the case that we perceive the shapes of things with our eyes? Don't we feel the mass of things with our sense of touch? If the secondary qualities belong to the mind because they are the products of our sense organs, don't primary qualities belong to the mind as well since they are the products of our sense organs as well? The idealist thinks so. In Chapter 3.2 we encountered the idealists Parmenides and Zeno, but this meant that everything is an idea or a definition, such as the meaning of 'ship' or 'cow.' Now we focus on the slightly different version of **idealism** that was briefly discussed in Chapter 5.5, where everything is a percept, or a collection of them, or a mind that perceives those percepts.

Idealism is supported by the considerations raised above suggesting that everything humans think and experience is in some sense dependent on our minds. Humans are, after all, minds. There is no way to think or perceive anything without a mind. If we had no minds, could we still think? No. If we had no minds, could we still perceive? No. So, everything we perceive is produced by our minds, and are percepts of our minds. The representational model goes half way to this conclusion, as it holds that secondary qualities are percepts of our minds. But primary qualities such as extension, mass, and motion are also percepts of our minds. The mathematics in the laws of nature are produced by human minds as well, as it is human minds that calculate and reason to those conclusions. Everything is mind-dependent, which is the idealist view. The leading proponent of this type of idealism is **George Berkeley**, and here is an excerpt:

A Treatise Concerning the Principles of Human Knowledge (George Berkeley, 1710)[6]

3. That neither our thoughts, nor passions, nor ideas formed by the imagination, exist without the mind, is what everybody will allow. And to me it is no less evident that the various sensations or ideas imprinted on the sense, however blended or combined together (that is, whatever objects they compose), cannot exist otherwise than in a mind perceiving them ... their *esse* is *percipi*, nor is it possible they should have any existence out of the minds or things which perceive them.

4. It is indeed an opinion strangely prevailing amongst men that houses, mountains, rivers, and in a word all sensible objects, have an existence,

---

6   George Berkeley, *A Treatise Concerning the Principles of Human Knowledge*, 193–99.

natural or real, distinct from their being perceived by the understanding. But, with how great an assurance and acquiescence soever this principle may be entertained in the world, yet whoever shall find in his heart to call it in question may, if I mistake not, perceive it to involve a manifest contradiction. For, what are the forementioned objects but the things we perceive by sense? And what do we perceive besides our own ideas or sensations? And is it not plainly repugnant that any one of these, or any combination of them, should exist unperceived? ...

6. Some truths there are so near and obvious to the mind that a man need only open his eyes to see them. Such I take this important one to be, viz. that all the choir of heaven and furniture of the earth, in a word all those bodies which compose the mighty frame of the world, have not any subsistence without a mind, that their being is to be perceived or known; that consequently so long as they are not actually perceived by me, or do not exist in my mind or that of any other created spirit, they must either have no existence at all, or else subsist in the mind of some Eternal Spirit ...

9. Some there are who make a distinction betwixt primary and secondary qualities. By the former they mean extension, figure, motion, rest, solidity or impenetrability, and number; by the latter they denote all other sensible qualities, as colours, sounds, tastes, and so forth. The ideas we have of these they acknowledge not to be the resemblances of anything existing without the mind, or unperceived, but they will have our ideas of the primary qualities to be patterns or images of things which exist without the mind, in an unthinking substance which they call matter.... but it is evident, from what we have already shewn, that extension, figure, and motion are only ideas existing in the mind, and that an idea can be like nothing but another idea, and that consequently neither they nor their archetypes can exist in an unperceiving substance.

In this passage,

1. *Berkeley argues that the representational model must be augmented to include the fact that both primary and secondary qualities are mind-dependent, so are not features of the external material world, but are rather perceptions of minds.*
2. *Berkeley introduces the view that "**esse is percipi**," or, "to be is to be perceived." Things only exist when they are being perceived, so things that are not being perceived do not exist. To see his point, imagine a room in your house where no one is presently located. This room has a bed in it, or so you think. But does the bed still exist in the present moment when no one is there to perceive it? The obvious answer is: yes. But how do we prove that? You may say: we can just walk into the room to see the bed! But now the bed is being perceived, so of course*

> it exists now. The question was: does the bed exist when it was not being perceived? How would we prove that it does exist then? And for Berkeley the difficulty of the notion of the unperceived bed is not just that we can't prove it's there, it is also that the only thing we can think or talk about is mental perceptions, so it doesn't even make sense to ask questions about unperceived objects.

What would Berkeley say about the tree falling in the forest with no one around? If no perceiver is there, no person, no snake, no mosquito, then not only does the tree not make a sound, but the tree doesn't fall either, and this is because there is no tree that exists when no one is around, and there is no ground for the tree to fall on either.

Objection 1: Flickering Existence

Critics of Berkeley complain that his idealism leads to the flickering on and off of existence. Right now, you are looking at the bed, so it exists. Close your eyes, and the bed flickers out of existence since it is not being perceived. Open your eyes again, and the bed flickers back into existence. Surely the universe cannot flicker in and out of existence like this. One critic framed this objection to Berkeley in terms of the following limerick: "There was a young man who said God, must think it exceedingly odd, if he finds that the tree, continues to be, when no one's about in the Quad."[7] In other words, God would notice that no one is observing the tree, so God would notice the tree passing out of existence at that time, which is very odd.

Berkeley, a former bishop, replies to this concern by noting that God is always perceiving everything, so the universe does not flicker in and out of existence based on whether humans or mosquitos enter into the room or not; rather, the universe is sustained by God always perceiving it. One advocate of Berkeley framed this response in terms of the following limerick: "Dear Sir, your astonishment's odd, I am always about in the Quad, and that's why the tree, continues to be, since observed by, Yours faithfully, God." While Berkeley may solve this worry by appealing to the existence of God, those who reject the existence of God will not endorse Berkeley's response. Without a God continuously perceiving things, the tree continues to flicker in and out of existence depending on whether a perceiver looks at it, which continues to be a problematic result.

Objection 2: Inference to the Best Explanation

Bertrand Russell is a famous opponent of idealism. He grants Berkeley's point that all we directly encounter is our own percepts (he calls them "sense-data"),

---

7 This limerick was composed by Monsignor Ronald Knox in 1913 and has been quoted widely; e.g., in Noel Fleming, "The Tree in the Quad," *American Philosophical Quarterly* 22 (1985): 25–36, 22. The author of the "Dear Sir" reply is not known.

but he uses **inference to the best explanation** to reject idealism. Recall from Chapter 1.5.3 that an inference to the best explanation is a form of inductive reasoning whereby some phenomenon occurs and we posit one of several possible explanations as the most likely explanation. In this case, the phenomenon is our experience of things. Russell uses the following example of a cat as a typical thing:

> If the cat appears at one moment in one part of the room, and at another in another part, it is natural to suppose that it has moved from the one to the other, passing over a series of intermediate positions. But if it is merely a set of sense-data, it cannot have ever been in any place where I did not see it; thus we shall have to suppose that it did not exist at all while I was not looking, but suddenly sprang into being in a new place.[8]

Idealism suggests that the cat flickers in and out of existence and re-appears at exactly the right spot, while the view that an external world exists suggests that the cat just keeps walking. Both explanations are possible, but the second explanation is better, since it is simpler and more common-sensical.

8.5 Intentionalism

The representational model, since it says we perceive our own percepts of the external world, not the external world itself, leads to idealism or skepticism about the external world. Perhaps what is needed is a view that does not say that we perceive our own percepts, but rather that we are looking straight at the external world. This is the direct realist view, but this view could not account for the relativity of perception or illusions and hallucinations. Maybe what is needed is a representational model that does not endorse the view that we perceive our own percepts, but rather says we perceive the external world. In recent years this type of view, called the intentional model, has gained popularity. Whereas the representational model says we perceive a percept that represents the external world, the **intentional model** says that in perception the external world is represented to us as being one way rather than another, so we perceive the external world, not our own percepts.

The intentional model is rooted in the notion of **intentionality**, which is the feature of "aboutness" that mental states possess. Consider a weblink on the Internet. If you press on the weblink, you are directed to another webpage. The weblink is "about" the other webpage, or, the weblink has the webpage as its **content**, which means that the weblink is like an empty container that is filled with only the webpage as its content. The important thing about the weblink is that it directs people to another page. Similarly, a signpost on a road

---

8   Bertrand Russell, *The Problems of Philosophy*, 10.

that points ahead and says 'Boston' is about the city of Boston; it is pointed at Boston and the important thing about the sign is that it points to Boston. It would be a mistake to focus on the blue coloured words of the weblink instead of focusing on the fact that the weblink points to another page. It would be a mistake to focus on the wood the sign is made of rather than the fact that the sign points to Boston.

Mental states also have intentionality, or, mental states are also about the world. Quan believes "the sky is blue," which is his belief about the blue sky, or, the blue sky is the content of his belief. Theresa is afraid of bears, which is about bears. Henry desires chocolate cake, which is his desire about chocolate cake, or, the chocolate cake is the content of his desire. The intentional model of perception treats perception the same way. Lucille perceives a red apple—that is, she has a perception about the red apple. The important part about her perception of the red apple is what her perception is about: the red apple. It would be a mistake for Lucille to focus on her experience of redness rather than focusing on the fact that there is a red apple in front of her.

The intentional model has a response to several of the problems plaguing other models. As mentioned, it avoids skepticism and idealism by suggesting that we are looking at, and touching, the external world. It handles the problem of illusions and hallucinations by drawing a parallel between mistaken beliefs and mistaken perceptions. Clarke believes that Santa wears green, but this is just a mistaken belief, and mistaken beliefs are very common and do not pose any theoretical problems for beliefs, and do not suggest that there cannot be true beliefs as well. Similarly, Clarke is colour blind so she sees a green rose, but this is just a mistaken perception from the red rose mistakenly representing itself as being green to Clarke. But this does not prevent Samuel, who is not colour blind, from correctly perceiving the red rose. The relativity of perception is solved in a similar way. The rose represents itself as being red to Clarke, but the rose also represents itself as being soft and having a flowery smell to Clarke. There is no difficulty with the rose representing itself differently to different perceptual faculties, or to different animals.

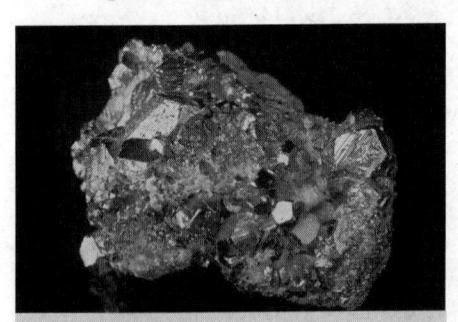

Doug holds a lump of gold in one hand, and a lump of fool's gold in the other hand. They look the same, so is Doug experiencing the same thing? No: they are very different objects.

The intentional model is also supported by the fact that two things that look the same are nevertheless different. Antoine sees a white cup, then closes his eyes for a minute while the white cup is replaced by an exact copy of the white cup. He opens his eyes and has exactly the same experience of seeing a white cup. Is Antoine perceiving the same thing? On the representational model, where we perceive our percepts of things, the answer is yes, since the percepts are the same, as they look the same. But the answer seems to be no. He was looking at cup *A*, now he is looking at cup *B*. This makes sense if Antoine is looking at the cup rather than his percept of the cup. The difference is not in what they look like, but the way the world is. **Susanna Schellenberg** makes this type of argument in the following excerpt:

"Externalism and the Gappy Content of Hallucination" (Susanna Schellenberg, 2013)[9]

When a subject perceives a white coffee cup on her desk, she is in a conscious mental state: it seems to her that there is a white coffee cup on her desk. When a subject hallucinates that there is a white coffee cup on her desk, her experience can be subjectively indistinguishable from a perception: it seems to her that there is a white coffee cup on her desk. If perceptions and hallucinations can be subjectively indistinguishable, what is the connection between the sensory character of experience and the subject's perceptual or causal relations to objects in the world? ...

One reason for holding that the content of experience is externally individuated is that only such a view of content gives a good account of the accuracy conditions of experience.... More precisely, the content C of experience E is accurate if and only if the world is the way it seems to the experiencing subject and C corresponds to the way the world seems to the experiencing subject. In all other cases, content C of experience E is inaccurate. When I have a perceptual experience of a white coffee cup on my desk, the content of my experience will, for instance, be "that is a white coffee cup." My experience is accurate only if the very white coffee cup that it seems to me is present is in fact the one to which I am perceptually related. So if the cup is replaced with a qualitatively indistinguishable coffee cup, then the accuracy conditions of my experience change—even if I cannot tell the two coffee cups apart ...

This approach contrasts with strong representationalist views according to which representational facts about experience are understood to be facts about the sensory character of experience. If content covaries with sensory character, as such views hold, then there naturally will be no difference between my experiences of distinct objects as long as my experiences are subjectively indistinguishable....

Consider the following case: Anna sees cup$_1$ at time t$_1$, but she closes her eyes briefly, and without her noticing, the cup is replaced with the numerically distinct but qualitatively indistinguishable cup$_2$. So when she reopens her eyes, she is causally related to a different cup. Although she cannot tell, her experience before the cup has been exchanged. If she

---

9 Susanna Schellenberg, "Externalism and the Gappy Content of Hallucination," *Hallucination*, ed. F.E. Macpherson and D. Platchias (Cambridge: MIT Press, 2013), 291–311.

perceives cup$_1$ at t$_1$ and then at t$_2$ perceives cup$_2$, her claim that the cup she sees at t$_2$ is the same as the cup she saw at t$_1$ does not have the status of knowledge, since the claim is false ... Perceptual experience can ground such knowledge only if the particular cup perceived makes a constitutive difference to the experience ...

Now, naïve realists give awareness relations to the environment so much explanatory weight that it is rendered mysterious how one could be having an experience with a certain sensory character if one is not related to the relevant mind-independent objects or property instances. By introducing perceptual capacities that ground our ability to single out external, mind-independent objects and property instances, the suggested view gives an account of hallucinations on which subjectively indistinguishable hallucinations and perceptions share a common factor that grounds the sensory character of these experiences ... In this sense, hallucinations are understood to exhibit a deficiency that can only be explained with reference to successful perceptual experiences.

In this passage,

1. *Schellenberg distinguishes her view from representational models. On representational models, we perceive percepts, so we perceive the same thing when we perceive a hallucination of a cup and an actual cup—a result that Schellenberg disagrees with.*
2. *Schellenberg distinguishes her view from naïve realist (i.e., direct realist) models. On naïve realist models, we directly perceive objects, which makes it difficult to imagine how hallucinations are possible—another result that Schellenberg disagrees with.*
3. *Schellenberg imagines a case where a white cup is replaced by a second exactly similar white cup while the perceiver is not looking. The representational model leads to the view that the perceiver is perceiving the same thing in both cases, as the percepts delivered by our sense organs are the same. But this is wrong, as the perceiver is perceiving cup$_1$ during the first moment and then is perceiving a different cup$_2$ in the next moment. Thus the content of the perception is the object that the perception is about, which aligns with the intentional model.*

What would the intentional model say about the tree falling in the forest? The falling tree does represent itself as making a loud noise, though no one is there to perceive this sound, so the sound goes unheard.

Objection: The Experience of Perception

The intentional model captures two of the three components to perception, namely, the representational component and the external world component to perception. The intentional model leaves out the experiential part of perception, or, what the perception looks or feels like to us. This leads to problems, since perception seems to have an experiential component to it. Philosophers such as **Christopher Peacocke** raise various examples to highlight these problems. Imagine driving down a road and seeing a series of telephone poles on the side of the road. The pole closest to you is represented as being twenty feet tall and wooden, while the distant pole is also represented to you as being twenty feet tall and wooden. They represent the same thing, wooden telephone poles, but the closer one looks a lot bigger and occupies a lot more of your visual field. The experience of the two poles is different, though they are both about telephone poles. Similar problems arise in the case of blurry vision. Imagine you take off and put on your glasses while

The same car looks blurry to some people and not blurry to others, showing us that the same object can be experienced in two different ways, falsifying the intentional theory. On the other hand, different coffee cups look the same to the same person, showing us that the same experience can have two different objects, supporting the intentional theory. Which thought experiment is more convincing?

staring at a distant car. The car is represented as being the same car the whole time, but the experience is different. At one moment, the car looks blurry, at the other moment the car looks clear. And, the difference is not a difference in the car itself—no one thinks the car itself is blurry; rather, we agree that we are blurrily seeing a non-blurry car.

Another example of this issue arises in the case of **inverted qualia**. 'Qualia' is another word for experiences, so 'inverted qualia' refers to cases of inverted experiences, where you experience something opposite to what another sees. Have you ever wondered if your red is someone else's blue? Maybel looks at ripe tomatoes and calls them "red" and what she is seeing is the colour red. But when Bella looks at ripe tomatoes, she calls them "red" but what she sees is the colour violet. This type of situation happens to colour-blind people before they realize they are colour blind. In this case, the tomato is represented to both Maybel and Bella as being a ripe tomato that is round and red, but what they experience is very different.

The same issue occurs with **absent qualia**, where there appears to be a difference between an object representing itself to us unconsciously and the same object representing itself to us in the same way, but also with consciousness. Open and close your eyes for a moment. Let us say you looked outside your window at the apartment building across the street. While your eyes were opened, you saw your entire visual field that was full of information, but you only consciously processed a small portion of it. You noticed two cars on the street, and the red light. But did you notice how many windows were open in the apartment building? No. But that information was present in your visual field. If you had a perfect memory of that building, you could go back and count the answer. This shows that it is possible for objects to represent themselves to us without our conscious awareness. For example, a subliminal advertisement has a goal of representing itself to us without our awareness of it. There is a difference between an object representing itself to us without us experiencing it, say in a subliminal advertisement, and that object representing itself in the same way, but with us experiencing it, say in a regular advertisement of the same product. The difference shows that there is more to perception than simply how the object presents itself to us; there is also the experiential aspect to perception.

Summary

Perception is an experience of things. There are three components to perception: our *experience*, the *things* in the external world, and our representation *of* the things. Different models of perception deal with these three components in different ways. The direct realist gives us perception of things in the external world, but fails to appreciate the different types of experiences different people and animals have of the external world. The representational model succeeds in capturing our unique experience, and how that experience is about things, but fails to ensure that we perceive things in the external world. Both skepticism and idealism focus on our experience without focusing on how our experience represents the external world. The intentional model gives us the external world, and how it represents itself to us in perception, but fails to account for the different experiences we all have of things.

Key Terms in Chapter 8: Perception		
Perception	Relativity of Perception	Phenomenal
Sense Impression	Sextus Empiricus	Conservatism
Experience	Skepticism	Idealism
External World	Local Skeptic	George Berkeley
Mind-Independent	Global Skeptic	*Esse* is *Percipi*
Representation	Dogmatism	Bertrand Russell
Veridical Experience	Academic Skepticism	Inference to the Best
Direct Realism	Percept	Explanation
Transparency	Pyrrhonian Skepticism	Intentional Model
Common Sense Realism	Representational Model	Intentionality
Commonality of	Scientific Revolution	Content
Perception	John Locke	Susanna Schellenberg
Aristotle	Primary Qualities	Inverted Qualia
Naïve Realism	Secondary Qualities	Absent Qualia
Hallucination	Veil of Perception	Christopher Peacocke
Illusion	Reductionism	
Pyrrho	Burden of Proof	

Philosophy on Television: Perception

The Matrix (1999)

This film is one of many films where the characters are caught inside of an illusory reality. *The Matrix* begins with Neo living a normal life in a large American city, only for him to find out that he was living inside a computer simulation, while his actual body was suspended in a pod of nutrients. The possibility of living in a Matrix suggests our experience of things may not be veridical, which is supported by external world skepticism. Other shows that take place inside an illusory reality include *Vanilla Sky* (2001), *Inception* (2010), and *Marvel's Agents of S.H.I.E.L.D.*: Season 4 (2017).

Brain Games (2011–20)

Brain Games (2011–20) is an eight-season popular science television series that explores how the brain works. Many of the episodes present surprising perceptual illusions, but several episodes focus entirely on how perception works (and doesn't work), including *Brain Games* 1.1: "Watch This," *Brain Games* 2.8: "Seeing Is Believing," and *Brain Games* 2.11: "Illusion Confusion." The fact that we frequently misperceive objects poses problems for the direct realist model of perception.

A Beautiful Mind (2001)

Based on a true story, *A Beautiful Mind* (2001) follows the life of John Nash, a brilliant but reclusive mathematician, as he becomes a renowned academic while also carrying on a secret life of cracking codes for the government. As the movie progresses, it turns out that John suffers from auditory hallucinations and delusions, and his secret life of cracking codes is illusory. This movie highlights the possibly large gaps between our perception of reality and reality itself. Hallucinations occurs in many other movies as well, including *Maze Runner: The Scorch Trials* (2015) and *The Hunger Games* (2012).

Additional Resources

Visit this book's companion resources for additional materials, including video content and an automated tool for planning argumentative essays.

sites.broadviewpress.com/knowing/chapter-8

Chapter 9
Self-Knowledge

THOUGHT EXPERIMENT 9.1
Who Knows Truman Better?

In *The Truman Show* (1998), Truman Burbank is a middle-aged man who thinks he has a normal life with a normal job and a normal wife in a normal town. Little does he know that he is the star of a reality TV show centred on his life, and that his wife and everyone else in town is a paid actor. As time goes by, Truman begins to behave erratically, and the producers, actors, and viewers try to figure out what he is thinking. This team of observers has witnessed every moment of his life, so they should know what he is thinking. On the other hand, Truman is the person doing the thinking, so he should know what he is thinking too. Who knows what

Truman is thinking better: Truman himself, or a team of observers that has followed his every move for his entire life?

In Chapter 7.2 we looked at the rationalist model of justification for knowledge. Rationalists justify knowledge through processes internal to our minds, such as apprehending the obviousness of self-justifying beliefs and through our reasoning processes. In this chapter we consider in greater detail the reliability of these internal processes. This will be done first by discussing self-knowledge, or our ability (or inability) to know our own selves, then by discussing our ability (or inability) to reason well.

A main philosophical question about **self-knowledge** is this one: how well do we know ourselves? Sometimes it seems like the answer is: quite well. Simone feels a rush of attraction when Lonzo walks into the room, and she knows very well the attraction that she feels for him. Maja feels a rush of anger when Lonzo walks into the room, and she knows very well the anger she has for him too. Lonzo tends to avoid Maja ever since "the incident," and he knows it is because he doesn't want to face the hurt that the incident caused Maja. Other times it seems like the answer to "how well do we know ourselves?" is: not very well at all. While Lonzo always hung around with Simone, he didn't notice he had feelings for Simone, until his friend called him out on it. Lonzo knew that something just wasn't clicking between him and Maja, but he couldn't figure out what was wrong. Now he knows that something is really clicking between him and Simone, but he isn't sure exactly why he fell for her, since she isn't anything like the type of woman he thought he would fall for.

There are several positions in the self-knowledge debate, each of which provide different answers on the question of how, and how well, we know ourselves.

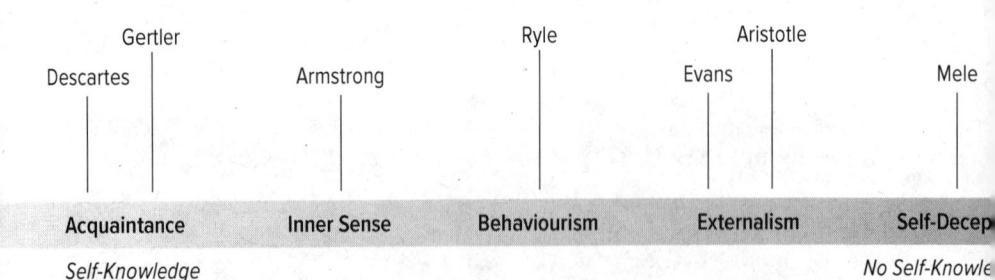

Spectrum 9: Self-Knowledge

On the left of this spectrum stand those who say we can know ourselves very well, while on the right of the spectrum stand those who point out how mistaken we often are about ourselves. Let us begin to the left of the spectrum, with the Inner Sense Model.

9.1 Inner Sense Model

We are already familiar with some of the background of the inner sense model of self-knowledge. In Chapter 8 we considered perception. In every model of perception, there is a perceiver and a thing being perceived. When we say Jenni perceives the tree, the perceiver is Jenni and the thing being perceived is the tree. The **inner sense model** takes self-knowledge to be similar to perception, though what is perceived is not an external object such as a tree, but an internal mental state such as our own beliefs, desires, or attitudes. Although the thing being perceived exists within the perceiver, there is also another part to the self that is the perceiver. Thus, in self-knowledge, one part of the self perceives another part of the self. Matthias notices his body is tense, so he wonders why. He looks within himself and notices that he is anxious. Then, he wonders why he is so anxious. He inspects deeper within and realizes that the words from his boss about layoffs are worrying him. Matthias is able to figure out what is going on with himself by inspecting his own mental states. The ability to inspect our own mental states is sometimes called **introspection**, which comes from the Latin roots *intro* (within) and *spect* (observe or look), so it means to look within.

Since the thing being perceived is an internal mental state, only the self has the ability to perceive these states, others cannot perceive our mental states. This means that we have **privileged access** to our own mental states: we are able to know ourselves in a way that other people cannot know us. Iman can know that he is feeling sad, and inspect his reasons for why he is sad, but others do not have access to Iman's mental states. Since Iman has privileged access to his mental states, Iman (it's often held) has **first-person authority** about his own mental states. Imagine that Iman says he is sad, while Sareh says Iman is just bored. Whom should we believe? We should believe Iman, as he is an authority on the subject, since he is able to inspect his own mental states. Sareh can only infer Iman's inner states by observing his behavioural cues, such as noticing that Iman's face is downcast.

The inner sense model takes self-knowledge to be similar to a virus scanner on a computer, or the thermostat of a heating system. In these cases, there is a process within a wider system, where the job of that process is to monitor the system. The virus scanner inspects the programs within the computer to see if it contains any viruses. The thermostat monitors the temperature that the heating system has produced. Likewise, we have an introspective process that is capable of monitoring what we are thinking and feeling. Here is an excerpt from **David Armstrong** (1926–2014), a proponent of the inner sense model of self-knowledge:

The Mind-Body Problem (David Armstrong, 1998)[1]

Besides the traditional "five senses" of sight, hearing, taste, smell, touch, there is also bodily perception. This is our awareness of current goings on in, and current states of, our own body, where this awareness is not derived from the five senses. Bodily perception breaks down into a number of systems. Kinaesthetic sensations advise us of the motion and position of our limbs; our sense of balance tells us how we are oriented to the earth ... without these systems we would be in a bad way.

Bodily perception is, for each of us, confined to our own body. Each of us has a series of systems that monitors our own body. These systems are not infallible, of course, and they are certainly not all-embracing, and they are of the utmost importance in our life ... the importance of proprioception and the other modes of bodily perception for us here is that they give us an unmysterious model for introspection. Introspection is a system, one that we still hardly understand in physiological terms, by which we monitor our own mind. In bodily perception, the mind monitors its own body. In introspection, the mind monitors itself....

The importance of access to our own minds goes well beyond this. In this animal kingdom, a particular evolutionary strategy has been followed, at least by human beings, and perhaps by some of the higher mammals, especially the apes. It is the policy of thinking, planning, before one acts ... How is the mind to get the needed feedback on its operations and recognize that these operations have reached a certain terminus, unless it,

---

1 David Armstrong, *The Mind-Body Problem: An Opinionated Introduction* (New York: Routledge, 2018), 116–18.

also, can know how the mental scene develops? Ordinary perception, even bodily perception, is no use here, because it is not directed within the mind. Had there not better be a substitute? The substitute, I suggest, is provided by "inner" perception, inner sense, introspective consciousness. That, I hypothesize is what introspective awareness is for....

I suggest that introspection exists because "inner sense" has a "watching brief" (as the lawyers say). At any time, something that demands thought and attention may transpire in our body and environment. Continuous but "reflex" introspective attention to our perceptions, in particular, is an alarm system that keeps us ready to bring thought and attention to bear if it is needed.

In this passage,

1. *Armstrong says that self-knowledge involves us sensing our mental states. He compares this process to bodily perception.*
2. *Armstrong argues that this internal monitoring system allows us to consider our beliefs and attitudes to see why we do certain things, and revise them if necessary. This ability comes with tremendous advantages. Imagine a computer program that gets stuck in an infinite loop so it is unable to proceed, or a computer that does not have a virus scanner so it is unable to delete harmful programming. Wouldn't it be better if the computer could monitor its own code, to spot corruptions and fix them? Humans can do this. Humans have this internal monitoring system, where they can monitor their own code (i.e., sense their own beliefs, motivations, and desires) as it runs, and modify any corrupted or mistaken parts.*
3. *Armstrong says that our introspective abilities, while largely reliable, can be mistaken. A virus scanner can mischaracterize certain lines of code, or it may not be able to spot certain viruses and programs. Similarly, we can make mistakes while we analyze our own mental states.*

What might the proponent of the inner sense model say about Truman? Truman, unlike his observers, has the ability to monitor his own mental states and notice what is going on with him. He notices that he is suspicious, and then he notices that his suspicion is rooted in several deceptive and unusual events that recently happened to him.

Objection 1: Self-Scanning Issues

The inner sense model suggests that self-knowledge occurs when a perceiving part of the self observes a second part of the self. This two-part process opens up several problems. First, it may lead to an infinite regress. If we know our feelings by a second part of the self that observes our feelings, then how do we know that we have that second perceiving part to the self, and that this second perceiving part works well? Presumably, a third part to the self must observe the second perceiving part. And how do we know there exists this well-functioning third part to the self? Presumably, there must be a fourth part that observes the third part. A regress ensues.

Others worry that it is impossible to be both the perceiver and the thing perceived at the same time. David Hume introduces the **theatre of the mind** analogy in support of this concern. In concerts, the actor is on the stage as the thing being observed. The things on the stage, namely the feelings and thoughts in our minds, are all that exist for Hume, there is no observer in the stands observing those feelings and thoughts. This makes some sense, as it is difficult to imagine the same self being both on the stage as the thing observed and in the audience as the observer at the same time.

Objection 2: Unaware of Self

We are often unaware of ourselves. We are unaware of our motives, unaware of our emotions, unaware of the reasons we do things. Rachel says she is not jealous when her boyfriend has a business lunch with another woman, but she clearly is. Tyson says his workout partner is just a friend, though his attraction to him is repressed, so he is not aware of it. Inga wonders why she is nervous around strangers; she can't quite remember when she developed these hesitancies, or whether they are well founded or not. When asked what he believes about capital punishment, Cortez answers that he is not sure what he believes about that issue. In all of these cases, we are unaware of our motivations, feelings, or beliefs, which shows that we may not be able to inspect ourselves very well at all—the spotlight is too dim to shine on all of our mental states, or there are areas where the spotlight cannot reach.

Objection 3: Mistakes of Self-Knowledge

Not only are we often unaware of ourselves, but we can also be mistaken about ourselves. In 1977, Nisbett and Wilson conducted a famous experiment where they asked participants to select the most appealing sock out of several socks sitting in front of them. When asked why they selected the specific sock, they often reported preferring the aesthetics of the chosen sock. As it turns out, they all came from the same unopened package of socks, so there were no aesthetic differences. However, participants routinely selected the nearest sock to them, though few reported selecting the sock because it was

In 1997, Robert Baron presented a study showing people tend to be more helpful when they are first presented with pleasant smells. Do you think that pleasant smells unconsciously influence you to be more helpful?

easiest to grab. Nisbett and Wilson conclude: "the accuracy of subject reports is so poor as to suggest that any introspective access that may exist is not sufficient to produce generally correct or reliable reports."[2] Social psychologists present various similar studies as evidence that humans act from unconscious motivations rather than from the motivations from which they think they are acting.

9.2 Behaviourism

Given the difficulties associated with our abilities to perceive our own mental states, it is worth considering the **behaviourist** model, which was prominent in philosophy and psychology from 1920 to 1960. For the behaviourist, the "mental" states we attribute to ourselves and to others are just publicly observable behaviour. **Behaviour** is observable bodily movements, facial expressions, posture changes, or utterances in response to some stimulus. Fatima sees a dog and she runs away, where her running away is her flight behaviour in response to seeing the dog. Fatima's fear of the dog is not her fearful feeling when she sees the dog; rather, it is her running-away behaviour when she sees the dog.

The scientists and philosophers attracted to this movement had the following troubles with the internal model of mental states: if only the subject can know they are there or identify them, then how can we know anything about anyone else's mind; and how can minds be studied by objective science? As **B.F. Skinner** (1904–90), an influential behaviourist psychologist, explains: "In this way we repair the major damage wrought by mentalism. When what a person does is attributed to what is going on inside him, investigation is brought to an end."[3] If mental states are defined by feelings or private attitudes and beliefs that only the person can introspect for herself, then scientific investigation of those mental states is impossible. But if mental states are defined as behavioural responses to stimuli, then friends and scientists can study those mental states as well. Fatima's fear of dogs is not some internal feeling that only she has access to. Rather, Fatima's fear of dogs is her tendency to run away when dogs approach, which is a public response to publicly observable stimuli. Fatima tells her friend Iman that she is feeling afraid of the approaching dog, and Iman replies, "I already knew that, I saw your worried facial expression."

How do we gain self-knowledge on the behaviourist model? We know our mental states in the same way that everyone else knows our mental states: by studying our behaviour. Faith-Anne knows she is thirsty, but this does not mean she perceives her parched feelings, rather she knows this because she notices her dry mouth and dark urine, and she knows this is the common result of decreased water consumption. Prince knows he doesn't like rock climbing, but he does not know this because he introspected his fears of rock climbing;

---

2   Richard E. Nisbett and Timothy DeCamp Wilson, "Telling More Than We Can Know: Verbal Reports on Mental Processes," *Psychological Review*, 84 (1977): 233.

3   B.F. Skinner, *About Behaviorism* (New York: Random House, 1976), 19–20.

rather, he knows this because his heart races and his palms sweat whenever he is asked about rock climbing.

One difficulty with behaviourism is that we have plenty of beliefs, desires, and emotions that are rarely accompanied by their defining behaviour. Faith-Anne is thirsty, but she is in the middle of an important meeting, so she continues to sit quietly. Michael is afraid of bears, even though he has never encountered a bear, so has never exhibited any bear-fearing behaviour. Mona wants to retire at 60, though she has never saved a penny in her life or told anyone about it. Gilbert Ryle solves this problem by adding that mental states are not only behavioural states, but also dispositional states. A **disposition** is a tendency to behave in a certain way, given the appropriate situation. A vase is fragile, which is a disposition or tendency to break when dropped. The vase is still fragile while it is sitting safely on the mantle,

Behaviourism is similar to, and in fact gave rise to, the functionalist model of mind we studied in Chapter 5.3. Both views understand mental states as dispositions to behave in a certain way given a certain stimulus. Fear of bears is not the feeling one has when seeing bears, but involves running away when seeing bears. Functionalism adds that mental states are not only defined by this stimulus and response, but also by how other states of the mind influence this stimulus-response pattern.

not just when it is smashing into pieces, because fragility is a disposition to break. Likewise, Faith-Anne is still thirsty, which means that she is disposed to engage in water-seeking behaviour when appropriate. Michael is still afraid of bears, which means he is disposed to run away if he sees a bear. Mona still wants to retire at 60, which means that she is disposed to stop working at 60, if given the chance. Here is a passage from **Gilbert Ryle** (1900–76), one of the leading behaviourist philosophers of the twentieth century:

The Concept of Mind (Gilbert Ryle, 1949)[4]

The questions 'What knowledge can a person get of the workings of his own mind?' and 'How does he get it?' by their very wording suggest absurd answers. They suggest that, for a person to know that he is lazy, or has done a sum carefully, he must have taken a peep into a windowless chamber, illuminated by a very peculiar sort of light, and one to which only he has access. And when the question is construed in this sort of way, the parallel questions, 'What knowledge can one person get of the workings of another mind?' and 'How does he get it?' by their very wording seem

---

4 Gilbert Ryle, *The Concept of Mind* (1949) (London: Routledge, 2009), 150–54.

to preclude any answer at all; for they suggest that one person could only know that another person was lazy, or had done a sum carefully, by peering into another secret chamber to which, *ex hypothesi*, he has no access.

In fact the problem is not one of this sort. It is simply the methodological question, how we establish, and how we apply, certain sorts of law-like propositions about the overt and the silent behaviour of persons. I come to appreciate the skill and tactics of a chess-player by watching him and others playing chess, and I learn that a certain pupil of mine is lazy, ambitious and witty by following his work, noticing his excuses, listening to his conversation and comparing his performances with those of others. Nor does it make any important difference if I happen myself to be that pupil. I can indeed then listen to more of his conversations, as I am the addressee of his unspoken soliloquies; I notice more of his excuses, as I am never absent, when they are made. On the other hand, my comparison of his performances with those of others is more difficult, since the examiner is himself taking the examination, which makes neutrality hard to preserve and precludes the demeanour of the candidate, when under interrogation, from being in good view ...

I discover my or your motives in much, though not quite the same way as I discover my or your abilities ... To discover how conceited or patriotic you are, I must still observe your conduct, remarks, demeanour and tones of voice, but I cannot subject you to examination-tests or experiments which you recognise as such. You would have a special motive for responding to such experiments in a particular way. From mere conceit, perhaps, you would try to behave self-effacingly, or from mere modesty you might try to behave conceitedly. None the less, ordinary day to day observation normally serves swiftly to settle such questions. To be conceited is to tend to boast of one's own excellences, to pity or ridicule the deficiencies of others, to daydream about imaginary triumphs, to reminisce about actual triumphs, to weary quickly of conversations which reflect unfavourably upon oneself, to lavish one's society upon distinguished persons and to economise in association with the undistinguished. The tests of whether a person is conceited are the actions he takes and the reactions he manifests in such circumstances. Not many anecdotes, sneers or sycophancies are required from the subject for the ordinary observer to make up his mind, unless the candidate and the examiner happen to be identical.

The ascertainment of a person's mental capacities and propensities is an inductive process, an induction to law-like propositions from observed actions and reactions. Having ascertained these long-term qualities, we explain a particular action or reaction by applying the result of such an induction to the new specimen, save where open avowals let us know the explanation without research ...

In this passage,

1. *Ryle rejects the inner sense model, saying that the requirement to "peep inside a windowless chamber" is not needed for self-knowledge.*
2. *Ryle argues that we gain self-knowledge in the same way that we gain knowledge of others. Namely, we observe our/their behaviour over a period of time, then judge the type of person that we/they are.*
3. *Ryle points out that we have a more difficult time properly assessing ourselves than others, since we are clouded by pride and other biases when observing ourselves.*

What would the behaviourist say about Truman? Truman can know himself by observing his behavioural patterns. He notices that he is not answering questions from his wife, which may fit into a pattern of being elusive and untrusting. But others can observe his behaviour as well, and come to the same conclusions about his sudden elusiveness. On the one hand Truman can know himself better than others, since he is constantly around himself, so he has more behavioural information than others. But on the other hand, Truman knows himself worse than others know him, since he can mistakenly interpret his behaviour due to his personal biases.

Objection 1: Stoics and Actors

One problem for behaviourism is that it is possible for people to behave in ways that they do not actually feel or think. Actors behave as though they are angry for the sake of the script, but they are not actually angry. The politician is behaving as though she cares about an issue, but she secretly does not care about the issue: she is just trying to win votes. It is also possible for people to actually think and feel things but show no behaviour indicating that they do. Vinny is feeling depressed, but he doesn't let it show because he doesn't want his friends to think he is struggling. Shanice has a good poker hand, but she is concealing her glee for the sake of bluffing her opponents. Since it is possible to manipulate our behaviour in a way that covers over the truth of what we are thinking or feeling, the behavioural model does not always effectively reveal who someone really is.

Objection 2: Introspection and Consciousness

Behaviourism says that people cannot know themselves by introspecting their own mental states. But it appears we do gain self-knowledge by introspecting our own mental states. Genevieve touches a hot stove and her hand recoils as she starts to scream. She does not look to her hand movements and screams in order to know that she is in pain. Rather, she has a more direct path to knowing she is in pain—she feels the pain for herself! In fact, this concern goes one step further. Behaviourism defines mental states by what they dispose us to do, rather than what they feel like. But it is problematic to say that Genevieve's

A behaviourist notices someone coming toward him. As they greet each other, the behaviourist says: 'You're fine. How am I?'

pain is defined as her hand recoiling from the stove, instead of defining pain by the searing feeling she is experiencing. If pain is just a recoil response, what is so bad about touching a hot stove? There is nothing really dreadful about moving one's hand away swiftly. This concern is similar to the objection the functionalists faced in Chapter 5.3. They also defined mental states by their behavioural profile, so they also neglected to include the important part about how those mental states feel.

Objection 3: The Black Box

One of the main reasons that behaviourism was replaced by functionalism was that functionalism solves a black box problem that behaviourism faces. Here is the problem: on behaviourism, what happens within the mind is a black box, which means that we cannot know what happens inside the mind, and it does not matter what happens inside the mind. By defining mental states as how people respond to stimuli, this dismisses as irrelevant or non-existent any internal mental states. In the last objection this was considered problematic because those internal mental states seem to exist. But there is an additional worry: internal mental states actually impact our behavioural responses to stimuli as well. If we present the same stimulus to Judy and Trudy, say they both see a strange dog, one will run away while the other will smile and pet the dog. The different response does not come from a different stimulus, but comes from having different internal mental states—Judy was bitten by a dog when she was young, but Trudy believes all dogs are friendly. Different behavioural responses to the same stimulus even happen within the same person: every time Charlize has ever been offered cake, she has reacted by eating it, but today, for the first time in her life, she says no. Overnight she decided she wanted to go on a diet, which broke her typical stimulus-response pattern. It seems like internal mental states are needed in order to account for these different responses to the same stimulus.

Behaviourism faces the opposite problem as well: it is possible for two people to have drastically different internal mental states, but the same stimulus-response pattern. Yuan believes that the liquid in the glass is healthy water that will keep her alive, and she desires to stay alive, so she drinks the water. Rutvik believes the liquid in the glass is poison that will kill him, but he wants to die, so he drinks the liquid. Do they have the same mental states? No. But on behaviourism they may, since they have the same response to the same stimulus. For these reasons, functionalism replaced behaviourism in the philosophy of mind, while cognitive models replaced behaviourism in psychology, as both of those replacements emphasize how internal cognitive states influence how we respond to stimuli.

9.3 Acquaintance Model

Given the difficulty with trusting that behaviour accurately reflects our mental states, and the fact that we do actually have internal mental states, let us consider a model that not only says we have internal mental states, but says we can have unmistakably true knowledge of those states. We already have some of the background for this type of view. In Chapter 5.1 to 5.3, the functionalist/behaviourist definition of mental states as behavioural responses was contrasted with Descartes' model of mental states as conscious occurrences. Pain is not the recoil of the hand from the stove; rather, pain is the searing feeling we experience when touching the hot stove. In Chapter 7.2, Descartes takes this emphasis on conscious experience as a foundation for arguing that the mind can be certain that it exists when it consciously apprehends itself. In other texts, Descartes says that we can likewise know with certainty every other conscious mental state that we are presently experiencing as well:

> 25. The perceptions that we relate only to the soul are those whose effects we feel as being in the soul itself, and for which we usually don't know any more immediate cause to which we can relate them. These include the feelings of joy, anger and the like, ...

> 26. But we can't be misled in that way with regard to the passions, because they are so close, so internal to our soul, that it can't possibly feel them unless they are truly as it feels them to be. Thus often when asleep, and sometimes even when awake, we imagine certain things so vividly that we think we see them before us or feel them in our body although they aren't there at all; but even when asleep and dreaming we can't feel sad or moved by any other passion unless the soul truly has this passion within it.[5]

In this passage Descartes argues that we can know, with no possibility of error, any mental state we consciously feel or experience. How? In the same way that we can be certain that conscious thinking exists whenever conscious thinking occurs, we can be certain that an angry feeling exists whenever we feel that angry feeling. We know our thoughts and desires and feelings by **acquaintance** with them. Recall from Chapter 7.1 that knowledge by acquaintance is a type of non-propositional knowledge where we know something by directly experiencing the thing. In the same way we know what a kiss feels like by having a

---

5   René Descartes, *Passions of the Soul* (1649), trans. Jonathan Bennett, https://www.earlymoderntexts.com/authors/descartes, I.25–26.

direct experience of being kissed, so we know what we desire, believe, or feel by having a direct experience of that desire, belief, or feeling.

When Iman says "I am feeling happy," Sareh does not say "that is an interesting theory about yourself, what arguments convinced you that you are feeling happy?" Rather, Iman is feeling the happiness he speaks of, which makes it undeniable that he is feeling the way he feels. The conscious feeling of happiness just is his knowledge of his own mental state of being happy.

The acquaintance model endorses introspective self-knowledge. We know ourselves by inspecting our own mental states. But introspection no longer involves one part of the self perceiving another part of the self—that inner sense model faced the regress and "theatre of the mind" problems. Rather, introspection now involves experiencing one's own mental states directly. Iman is able to know that he is happy by experiencing the happiness itself. On the acquaintance model, self-knowledge is immediate, or **direct**. This means that we are in direct contact with the thing known: there is nothing mediating, or in the middle of, the self and the thing known. Rather, the happy feeling that exists is the thing that is experienced and known. The behavioural model posited indirect or mediated self-knowledge: we know ourselves by studying our behaviour, which informs us of our mental states. The inner sense model also posited indirect or mediated self-knowledge: we know ourselves by a perceiving part of the self scanning the belief or feeling.

Since self-knowledge is direct, we can have **infallible** self-knowledge, which means that we cannot be mistaken about our knowledge of ourselves. Iman does not say, "I am feeling happiness right now, but I could be wrong about that, I may not be having any feelings right now, or maybe I am actually sad." Rather, Iman says, "I am feeling happiness right now, and I know that for certain, since I am feeling the feeling I am feeling right now, so I know it is happening." The inner sense model does not provide infallible self-knowledge, as it acknowledges that the perceiver could misperceive the self. The behavioural model does not provide infallible self-knowledge, as it acknowledges that the behaviour may be deceptive. But the acquaintance model provides infallible self-knowledge, as a feeling cannot feel other than it feels.

The acquaintance model is supported by the existence of consciousness. There are many things within our minds that we do not have conscious awareness of. For example, the brain stem is currently regulating our heart rate and blood pressure, but we are not conscious of these systems. There are many things within other minds that we do not have conscious awareness of as well. For example, we hear another person's stomach grumbling, but we do not feel the hunger they may be feeling; we only hear their grumbling stomachs. Contrast these cases with the many things within our minds that we do have conscious awareness of: we are hungry and this is not an unconscious bodily process, and we are not left with only hearing our stomach grumble, but we also have a conscious hunger feeling. Some of our mental states are consciously experienced, and this conscious awareness just is self-knowledge via acquaintance with those experiences. Mental states are **luminous**, which means they are brightly conscious rather than unconsciously dark, so whenever mental states occur to subjects, the subject is by definition consciously aware of that mental state, which is what self-knowledge means on the acquaintance model. Here is a passage from **Brie Gertler**, a contemporary proponent of the acquaintance model:

"Renewed Acquaintance" (Brie Gertler, 2012)[6]

Pinch yourself (gently). By focusing your attention on the phenomenal quality of the sensation that results, you can come to know something about your current experience. Philosophers generally agree on this much. Yet there is widespread and profound disagreement about what this kind of knowledge consists in, and how it is achieved.... I will elaborate and defend a set of metaphysical and epistemic claims that comprise what I call the *acquaintance approach* to introspective knowledge of the phenomenal qualities of experience. The hallmark of this approach is the thesis that, in some introspective judgments about experience, (phenomenal) reality intersects with the epistemic, that is, with the subject's grasp of that reality. This thesis—or something close to it—is implied by the claim that we sometimes grasp our experiences *directly*, by using an experience's defining phenomenal quality to form an epistemically substantive conception of the experience itself.

The acquaintance approach is inspired by [Bertrand] Russell's claim that we are acquainted with certain aspects of mentality. Here is Russell's characterization of acquaintance: "We shall say that we have acquaintance with anything of which we are directly aware, without the intermediary of any process of inference or any knowledge of truths" (Russell 1912, 73). To determine whether you are acquainted with an object, Russell says, you should consider whether you can doubt the object's existence. If you cannot, your awareness of the object is *direct*; you are therefore acquainted with the object. Russell does not provide an analysis of the acquaintance relation. Perhaps on his view this relation can be fully grasped only *through* acquaintance. But it seems clear that Russellian acquaintance has both an epistemic and a metaphysical dimension. When I am acquainted with an object, my awareness of that object is epistemically direct: it is non-inferential and does not epistemically depend on an awareness of anything else. My awareness is also metaphysically direct: there is no object, fact, event, or process that mediates my access to the object.

Russell's picture suggests that, if my access to the object were not metaphysically direct, I would be able to doubt the object's existence. For

---

6   Brie Gertler, "Renewed Acquaintance," in *Introspection and Consciousness*, ed. Declan Smithies and Daniel Stoljar (Oxford: Oxford University Press, 2012), 89–123.

instance, on Russell's view my awareness of the table I see before me is metaphysically indirect; it is mediated by a causal process (involving light reflecting off of the table, striking my retina, and causing a visual experience). The presence of this mediating factor enables me to doubt the existence of the table, since I can recognize that, for all I know, my visual experience has an aberrant cause. So while the criterion for acquaintance is indubitability—an epistemic and/or psychological phenomenon—the acquaintance relation itself is both epistemic and metaphysical ...

... Any judgment that is directly tied to its truthmaker will be true ... we cannot isolate the epistemic basis for knowledge by acquaintance by specifying how such knowledge differs from merely true belief, since on Russell's view knowledge by acquaintance does not consist in belief or, for that matter, anything that bears a truth value. The best way to identify Russell's epistemological position as regards knowledge by acquaintance is to ask what makes acquaintance with an object sufficient for *knowing* the object. That is, what makes this relation to an object truly *epistemic* rather than, say, a matter of brutely metaphysical *contact* with the object? Russell's answer seems to be that acquaintance with an object involves— or perhaps simply consists in—that object's being *immediately present to consciousness*, where such presence is an epistemic matter. This is not very illuminating as an analysis of acquaintance. But the salient point for our purposes is that Russellian knowledge by acquaintance is epistemically grounded exclusively in the presence of certain objects to consciousness.

In this passage,

1. *Gertler compares the acquaintance model of self-knowledge with knowledge by acquaintance as described by **Bertrand Russell**. As we know what kissing feels like by having a kiss, so we know we are happy by having a happy feeling.*
2. *Gertler argues that self-knowledge by acquaintance is direct and therefore infallible. She describes the situation as involving an overlap of epistemology with metaphysics. That is, the conscious experience of fear occurs (i.e., metaphysically exists), and the conscious experience is able to inform us that the conscious experience of fear occurred (i.e., we know it exists).*

What would the acquaintance model say about Truman? Truman is the only one capable of feeling his own feelings and hearing his own train of thoughts. Truman feels suspicious and hears himself doubting his friends and family, so he knows these things about himself. His observers can only make educated guesses about how he is feeling based on how he behaves. He is trying to hide his suspicions, so studying his behaviour will not be very effective.

Objection: Fallible Experience

The acquaintance model suffers from two of the problems plaguing the inner sense model. Namely, we seem to be unaware of ourselves at times and mistaken about ourselves at times, which calls into question our ability to know ourselves. This is especially problematic for the acquaintance model, as it supposes we can have infallible self-knowledge, so any mistakes in self-knowledge count against infallibility. But we have already seen ways in which we seem to misidentify inner states—e.g., by thinking that one is feeling dislike, when that feeling is really jealousy. The acquaintance theorist typically grants that there are some aspects of the self that we are unaware of, or that we are mistaken about, but they insist that we cannot be mistaken about what a conscious experience feels like. Critics reply that we are even subject to errors when it comes to feeling what our feelings feel like. Paul Churchland provides the following example: a captured spy is repeatedly tortured by having a hot iron pressed against his back. After twenty times, the spy grimaces as the torturer presses down again, but the torturer presses a block of ice against his back instead. The spy feels the burning, but it is not burning, it is freezing. The spy is wrong about what the feeling feels like.

Daniel Dennett (1942–) provides another example: Mr. Sanborne has the job of being a coffee-taster. When he started, he loved the flavour of the coffee; now he dislikes the flavour. He thinks his taste buds have changed, but in speaking with his colleague Mr. Chase, he realizes that his taste buds may not have changed; rather, his judgements about what tastes good have changed. He doesn't know his sense of flavour, so his ability to infallibly know his conscious states are called into question.

9.4 Externalist Models

The models of self-knowledge covered thus far roughly follow the same pattern of models for the justification of true belief in Chapter 7. Namely, the internalist models of rationalism and empiricism have echoes in some internalist models of self-knowledge, where knowledge of the self is acquired through some internal process, either of inner sense perception or direct acquaintance. The middle-ground model of justifying true belief through bodily or biological factors is echoed in the behaviourist model of self-knowledge where our bodily behaviour provides self-knowledge. There were also two externalist models for the justification of true belief, namely, appealing to true facts in the world or appealing to social factors such as testimony. In this section we look at two externalist models of self-knowledge, one based in facts in the world, the other based in social relations.

9.4.1 Natural Externalism of Self-Knowledge

Externalist models of self-knowledge replace introspective self-knowledge with what is sometimes called **extrospection**, or looking outward. Imagine this: the doorbell rings. Do you believe the doorbell just rang? Yes. How do you know you believe the doorbell just rang? The fact that you heard the doorbell places in your mind a corresponding belief that the doorbell just rang. So, the way to know whether you believe that the doorbell just rang or not is to check out whether the doorbell actually rang or not. Or try this: what time do you believe it is? You look at the clock, and the clock says 4:10 PM, and you believe it is 4:10 PM. You know what time you believe it is by looking at what time it is, then letting this fact inform your beliefs. In this way we know our beliefs by inspecting the factors external to ourselves that give rise to our specific beliefs.

This view gains support from the transparency of perception discussed in Chapter 8.1. Our perceptions seem to be transparent, which means that we look straight through our eyes at external objects. Likewise, beliefs appear to be transparent: in coming to know what we believe, we do not look at our beliefs, but we look at how the world is, which informs our beliefs. Enya believes it is raining, but she does not come to know this belief of hers by looking inward at her mental states, but by looking at the weather outside. While self-knowledge of beliefs is most easily imagined on this view, some think we can know our attitudes and emotions in the same way. To know what flavour of ice cream we desire, we need to look at all the flavours available to us at the store right now. To know what we are afraid of, we need to look at what is happening in the world that caused our fear.

While externalists replace introspection with extrospection, they are able to preserve first person authority and privileged access to our own mental states. How so? Normally, only the subject knows what they have been looking at, and only the subject knows what they have been wondering about, so only the subject knows what they believe. Dora knows that she believes it is snowing because she knows she was curious about the weather, and she knows she looked outside. Her mother does not know what Dora has been up to, so her mother does not know that Dora believes it is snowing. The externalist model rejects infallible self-knowledge, as there is a substantial gap between external facts and the subject's belief about the external fact. This gap opens up room for mistakes in perception, or mistakes in understanding what is perceived. Dora's baby sister also looks outside and sees the snow, but she has never seen snow before, so she doesn't believe it is snowing, rather she is just confused. Here is an excerpt from one of the main advocates of this externalist model, **Gareth Evans** (1946–80):

The Varieties of Reference (Gareth Evans, 1982)[7]

I shall concentrate upon the ways we have of knowing what we believe and what we experience, for I believe that if we get these right, we shall have a good model of self-knowledge (or introspection) to follow in other cases. In particular, I shall quite avoid the idea of this kind of self-knowledge as a form of perception-mysterious in being incapable of delivering inaccurate results.

Wittgenstein is reported to have said in an Oxford discussion:

> If a man says to me, *looking at the sky*, 'I think it is going to rain, therefore I exist,' I do not understand him.

The contribution is certainly gnomic; but I think Wittgenstein was trying to undermine the temptation to adopt a Cartesian position, by forcing us to look more closely at the nature of our knowledge of our own mental properties, and, in particular, by forcing us to abandon the idea that it always involves an inward glance at the states and doings of something to which only the person himself has access. The crucial point is the one I have italicized: in making a self-ascription of belief, one's eyes are, so to speak, or occasionally literally, directed outward—upon the world. If someone asks me 'Do you think there is going to be a third world war?,' I must attend, in answering him, to precisely the same outward phenomena as I would attend to if I were answering the question 'Will there be a third world war?' I get myself in a position to answer the question whether I believe that *p* by putting into operation whatever procedure I have for answering the question whether *p* ... If a judging subject applies this procedure, then necessarily he will gain knowledge of one of his own mental states: even the most determined sceptic cannot find here a gap in which to insert his knife.

We can encapsulate this procedure for answering questions about what one believes in the following simple rule: whenever you are in a position to assert that *p*, you are *ipso facto* in a position to assert 'I believe that *p*.'

In this passage,

1. *Evans says that self-knowledge does not arise by introspecting our own minds, and he rejects the proposed infallibility of self-knowledge that comes from introspective accounts.*
2. *Evans argues that we know our beliefs by attending to the world that causes us to have the beliefs we have. This view lends support to the behaviourist view that others can know our beliefs as well. After all, if our beliefs are known by attending to the world around us, and*

---

7   Gareth Evans, *The Varieties of Reference* (Oxford: Oxford University Press 1982), 224–26.

> *others can attend to this world as well, others can know our beliefs as well. Dora's mother asks Dora what she is thinking about, and Dora says 'I was just wondering if it was snowing outside.' Dora's mother, knowing the weather outside as well, now knows that Dora believes it is snowing outside.*

What would the externalist say about Truman? Truman knows that he is suspicious that his life is a big lie because he saw several suspicious events occur, such as when he saw several actors having a lunch break in a building that he doesn't normally go in. Others do not know for sure what Truman is trying to figure out, or what Truman is paying attention to, so they cannot be certain that Truman is suspicious that his life is a big lie.

Objection 1: Limited Self-Knowledge

Recall that acquaintance accounts provide more secure self-knowledge about conscious states than other mental states such as our motivations and beliefs. Similarly, externalist models provide more secure self-knowledge about our beliefs than about other mental states such as emotions, desires, and motivations. While we tend to have beliefs that correspond to the way the world is, our desires, motivations, and emotions do not always arise from the way the world is. In fact, desires are sometimes defined as flowing in the opposite direction. That is, we tend to have desires that do not correspond to the way the world is, rather, we want the world to correspond to the way our desires are. Even within the realm of beliefs, it is not clear that the world is solely responsible for our belief states. Indeed, a lot of background beliefs are required in order to correctly believe the world is the way it is. Dora's sister sees snow, but does not know what snow is, so the link from the snow to a belief about the snow is not formed. Seemingly, in order for the world to inform our beliefs, we need to already be familiar with our beliefs and interpretation of what is happening in the world.

Objection 2: No Self-Knowledge

In Chapter 8.2 and 8.3, we considered several views which lead to the conclusion that the external world lies beyond our immediate epistemic grasp, either because we can never access the external world (i.e., skepticism) or because the external world is grasped scientifically, not perceptually (i.e., representationalism). If this is true, and if self-knowledge can only arise by looking at the external world, then there is no way for us to have self-knowledge. Marshall finds yellow flakes in stones in a river, and he then believes he has found gold. But whether it is actually gold, or just worthless fool's gold, lies beyond his perceptual abilities, and can only be discerned by a scientific investigation. He does not know what he has found, so he does not really know what he believes.

9.4.2. Social Externalism of Self-Knowledge

As externalism about justification has both a naturalistic model and a social model, so externalism about self-knowledge has the prior naturalistic model and also a social model. The social externalist about self-knowledge thinks that interaction with other people contributes to our knowledge of ourselves. There are several ways this can occur. Most obviously, other people have minds as well, so seeing others think, feel and act informs us of how minds, including our own, work. When observing other people, we sometimes recognize traits in them that we realize we also possess. Or, on the other hand, when observing other people, we sometimes recognize traits in others that we realize we do not possess, which informs us of our own quirks, or which informs us of the type of person we desire to be or not to be. We also come to know ourselves better by observing how we interact with other people. While interacting with others, we

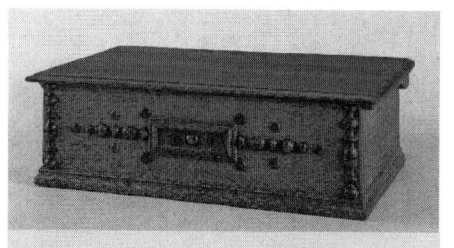

Ludwig Wittgenstein (1889–1951) imagines a community of people who all carry around a little box with a beetle in it, but no one can look into the box of others. When people talk about beetles in that community, "it could not be as the name of something—because it is entirely possible that each person had something completely different in their box, … the content of the box is irrelevant."[8] By analogy, it does not matter that we cannot experience another's subjective sensations, because whatever is going on there can't be what we're talking about when we talk about "pain" or "jealousy." These terms are public terms.

may become irritable or express compassion, which informs us of the type of person we are. People often discuss ideas with others in order to settle their own beliefs, or figure out their feelings. Charlie Brown interacts with a counsellor to figure out his motives and tendencies, Levin talks with his friends to help him figure out his belief system and to help him figure out what he wants to do with his life. In all of these cases, we acquire knowledge of ourselves by interacting with other people.

The social model rejects first-person authority and privileged access, as we cannot inspect our own mental states by ourselves, but rather come to understand ourselves through interactions with others. Where behaviourism places us on par with others when it comes to knowing ourselves, since we can all look at our behaviour, the social model places us in an epistemically weaker position than others when it comes to knowing ourselves, for others have a more objective view of us than we do.

One argument in support of acquiring self-knowledge from others comes from the outward-directed nature of perception. Our eyes can see other things, but they cannot see themselves (without the aid of a mirror). Our ears can hear

---

8   Ludwig Wittgenstein, *Philosophical Investigations*, §291.

other things, but they cannot hear themselves. It is also possible that our minds are able to understand other things, but they are not able to understand themselves. If our minds are outwardly directed, then the only way we can know ourselves is by placing ourselves in front of a "mirror for our minds," or something which the mind can interact with until it somehow reflects the mind back on itself, so it can comprehend itself. In the following passage, **Aristotle** argues that this "mirror for the mind" is other people, where we come to understand ourselves through discussing issues with other people:

Nicomachean Ethics 9.9 & 9.12 (Aristotle, 350 BCE)[9]

9.9 For we said at the outset that happiness is a certain exercise of our faculties; but the exercise of our faculties plainly comes to be in time, and is not like a piece of property acquired once for all. But if happiness consists in living and exercising our faculties ... but it is easier to contemplate others than ourselves, and others' acts than our own—then the acts of the good men who are his friends are pleasant to the good man. The happy or blessed man, therefore, will need such friends, since he desires to contemplate acts that are good and belong to him, and such are the acts of a good man who is his friend ...

Now, life is defined in the case of animals by the power of feeling, in the case of man by the power of feeling or thought: ... But he who sees feels that he sees, and he who hears feels that he hears, and he who walks feels that he walks; and similarly, whatever else we do, there is something that perceives that we are putting forth power, so that whether we feel or think, we must be conscious of feeling or thinking ... But the good man stands in the same relation to his friend as to himself, for his friend is another self: just as his own existence, then, is desirable to each, so, or nearly so, is his friend's existence desirable ... The good man, then, should be conscious of the existence of his friend also, and this consciousness will be given by living with him and by rational converse with him ...

9.12 In like manner, we may venture to say, do friends find living together more desirable than anything else; for friendship is essentially community, and a man stands to his friend in the same relation in which he stands to himself; but with regard to himself the consciousness of existence is desirable; therefore the same consciousness with regard to his friend is desirable; but it is in a common life that they attain this consciousness; therefore they naturally desire a life in common ... Thus the friendship of those who are not good comes to be positively bad; for, having no stability of character, they confirm each other in things that are not good, and thus become positively

9   Aristotle, *Nicomachean Ethics*, trans. F. Peters (London: Kegan Paul, 1893), 9.9, 9.12.

bad as they become more like one another. But the friendship of good men is good, and grows with their intercourse; and they seem to become better as they exercise their faculties and correct each other's deficiencies: for each moulds himself to the likeness of that which he approves in the other; whence the saying, 'From good men thou shalt learn good things.'

In this passage,

1. *Aristotle argues that thinking is similar to perception, where it is easier to perceive or contemplate others than perceive or contemplate ourselves. Thus, we know ourselves best by having rational discourse with other people, or more specifically, virtuous friends.*
2. *Aristotle argues that virtuous friends are like another self, so by discussing issues with them we come to understand ourselves, and by understanding what they believe we become aware of the similar beliefs that we have as well.*

What would the social externalist say about Truman? He's in no position even to tell what he thinks or feels, and that's the result of being so extraordinarily isolated from genuine relations with others. Could he sit down with an old friend to try to sort out the strange events of his life, he might be able to figure out what he is thinking, what he is feeling, and what he wants to do about these strange events. This friend may bring up old events, beliefs or promises that he knows about Truman in order to help Truman figure things out.

Objection 1: Mistaken Others

The supposition that others are better than ourselves at analyzing ourselves may be true in some cases. But there is also reason to suppose that we can understand ourselves better than, or at least as well as, others understand us. We can feel our feelings and hear our thoughts as they pass by, while others cannot. We have been around ourselves much longer than any friend has been around, so we know all our life experiences, everything that has shaped us, and how we react to everything. Friends only have glimpses of our lives while we experience all of it. There is reason to suspect that others are biased when it comes to evaluating us as well. For example, people have a variety of **attribution biases**, which are common mistakes of reasoning that occur when people attribute reasons to other people, and evaluate them. For example, we tend to give less credit to others than they deserve for their successes, but more blame than they deserve for their failures. We tend to interpret the behaviour of others negatively, especially outsiders. We commit these types of errors because it is in our self-interest to be more highly esteemed than others, and so we see others more negatively than they actually are. In addition, if we are unable to evaluate ourselves, then we would be subject to believing whatever anyone says about us, which is especially problematic if numerous people offer different interpretations of us, or if people start assessing us negatively.

9.5 Self-Deception

On the far right of the spectrum stands the problem of self-deception, representing the possibility that we are mistaken in knowing ourselves. We already discussed the fact that we make certain errors or mistakes in reasoning about ourselves that prevent us from knowing ourselves correctly—for example, we often think we are better drivers than we are (Chapter 1.4) or we mistakenly assess why we select a pair of socks (Chapter 9.1). Self-deception goes one step further. In **self-deception**, we not only err in assessing ourselves, but we have cognitive systems set up to intentionally trick ourselves into believing these assessments.

Deception occurs when a deceiver intentionally tricks others into thinking some fact is true while the deceiver knows it is false. Miguel deceives his parents when he tells the lie that he did not break the vase, all the while knowing that he did. Self-deception then is intentionally tricking ourselves into thinking something is true while we know it is false. This definition immediately leads to the **paradox of self-deception**: self-deceivers know the truth of the case, and that they are intentionally trying to trick themselves, and yet they believe the lie anyway! Rachel is jealous that her boyfriend had lunch with a stripper, but she tries to tell herself that she is not jealous, and she believes herself! How can she believe herself when she must know what she is up to? In the following passage, American philosopher **Alfred Mele** (1951–) provides several examples, as well as his interpretation of how self-deception occurs:

Self-Deception Unmasked (Alfred Mele, 2001)[10]

"A survey of university professors found that 94% thought they were better at their jobs than their average colleague." Are university professors exceptionally adept at self-deception? Perhaps not. "A survey of one million high school seniors found that ... all students thought they were above average" in their "ability to get along with others ... and 25% thought they were in the top 1%." One might suspect that the respondents to these surveys were not being entirely sincere in their answers. Then again, how many university professors do you know who do not think that they are better at what they do than their average colleague? ...

On the one hand, it is hard to imagine how one person can deceive another into believing that *p* if the latter person knows exactly what the former is up to, and it is difficult to see how the trick can be any easier when the intending deceiver and the intended victim are the same person ...

---

10 Alfred R. Mele, *Self-Deception Unmasked* (Princeton: Princeton University Press, 2001), 1, 10.

Thomas Gilovich reports: "A survey of one million high school seniors found that 70% thought they were above average in leadership ability, and only 2% thought they were below average. In terms of ability to get along with others, all students thought they were above average, 60% thought they were in the top 10%, and 25% thought they were in the top 1%!" ... If we assume the sincerity of the people surveyed, a likely hypothesis is that motivation had a hand in producing many of the beliefs reported. The aggregated self-assessments are radically out of line with the facts (e.g., only 1 percent can be in the top 1 percent), and the qualities asked about are desirable ones. We may have a tendency to believe propositions that we want to be true even when an impartial investigation of readily available data would indicate that they are probably false. A plausible hypothesis about that tendency is that our desiring something to be true sometimes exerts a biasing influence on what we believe. And there is evidence that our beliefs about our own traits "become more biased when the trait is highly desirable or undesirable" (Brown and Dutton 1995, p. 1290).

Ziva Kunda ably defends the view that motivation can influence "the generation and evaluation of hypotheses, of inference rules, and of evidence," and that motivationally "biased memory search will result in the formation of additional biased beliefs and theories" that cohere with "desired conclusions" (1990, p. 483).

In this passage,

1. *Mele provides several examples of self-deception.*
2. *Mele argues that self-deception occurs when our desires or emotions bias us to believe some statement p about ourselves, but p is false. We are **biased** about some statement p when we are motivated to, and hence likely to, believe p is true, though the average impartial observer with the same amount of information would be likely to believe p is false. Esteban desires to be a nice guy, which causes him to want to believe he is not bitter toward his ex-girlfriend. But if an impartial observer conducted an investigation of all the things Esteban said about his ex-girlfriend in the past month, this observer would reasonably conclude that Esteban is bitter toward his ex-girlfriend. Estaban is self-deceived, since his desire to believe he is not bitter clouds his judgement, and prevents him from seeing that he is bitter. Self-deceiving motivations are themselves rooted in more fundamental processes, such as our own self-interests. Most high school students think they are above average at socialization because they want to be better than average at socialization. They want to be better than average at socialization because they are **self-interested**, or, they care more about their own interests than they care about (the interests of) others.*

People and teams often speak positive words such as 'we can do this; we will do this!' to themselves before a big game. These are sometimes called self-fulfilling beliefs—if we believe we can do it, we will probably do it; if we believe we cannot do it, we will probably not do it. Are self-fulfilling beliefs cases of self-deception, since we believe something that is not yet true?

What may those endorsing self-deception say about Truman? Truman, for his whole life, was deceived into thinking his wife and friends cared for him, partly because he wanted that to be true. And, while he was deceived into thinking he was not the star of a TV show, it is more common for us to be self-deceived into thinking we should be the star of a TV show. We think our singing voice is a great undiscovered talent, or our sports abilities are good enough to make it to the big leagues, or we are one of the more popular kids at school. In these cases, what we (and Truman) want to be true about ourselves clouds our judgement into thinking it is true.

Objection: Overcoming Self-Deception

Self-deception is like any other case of deception—it is possible to be foolish enough to succumb to it, but also possible to avoid, and ought to be avoided. The Wall Street investor deceives Clara out of her life savings, but Edna does not fall for the fraud. And, everyone agrees that this investor's lie is both epistemically wrong (since what he said is false) and morally wrong (since his deception harmed Clara). Likewise, we can successfully deceive ourselves, for example, by letting our pride convince us we are far better than average, or by letting our insecurity convince us we are far worse than average. But we do not have to believe these self-deceptions. In fact, in Chapter 1.4 we saw how philosophy gives us some tools to overcome self-deception. Philosophy, which aims to know the truth about things, encourages self-awareness as a means to knowing the truth about ourselves. This includes knowing who we truly are and who we truly are not, and also includes being aware of our tendency to believe things we want to be true. Philosophy, in its aim for truth, is also a bull-crap detector, which includes sniffing out the bull-crap we tell ourselves about ourselves.

Not only is it possible to avoid self-deception in these ways, but we ought to avoid self-deception as well. Why? Self-deceived beliefs are false, and that is reason in itself to not believe them. Belief in Santa Claus is just false, and that is reason to not believe in Santa Claus. The same is true for false beliefs about ourselves too. There are also practical reasons for avoiding self-deception, as false opinions about ourselves can be damaging. Thinking we are better than we are in some way can bother others and embarrass ourselves and cause us to take on tasks we cannot succeed at. Thinking we are worse than we actually are in some way can prevent us from acting on things we should act on. If we are self-deceived into thinking we have few faults, then we miss the chance to grow and improve ourselves, which can harm ourselves in the long run. Hank tends to be lazy but he is self-deceived about this character fault. He is let go from one job after the other, always blaming his boss rather than perceiving his own character flaws. If he were reflective enough to notice his own laziness, he could work on improving this flaw and avoid losing future jobs.

9.6 Rationality and Irrationality

The previous sections introduced a number of factors suggesting that we have difficulty knowing ourselves, or we make errors in evaluating ourselves, or we are self-deceived about who we truly are. This raises the question: perhaps our minds are so error-prone that they should not be trusted to evaluate anything, either ourselves or the strength of reasons given in support of a claim. Maybe we are epistemically defective, unequipped to know anything at all? If this is so, then not only is the possibility of self-knowledge endangered, but so is the possibility for justifying true beliefs based on reasons.

To see whether this is true or not, we must assess whether we are mostly rational beings that usually grasp the truth, or mostly irrational beings that often fail to know the truth. To answer this question, we must know what it means to be rational and irrational. Two models of rationality are evident throughout this text. First, we are **epistemically rational** when we successfully use reason to acquire the truth. The early philosophers in Chapter 1.2 were epistemically rational since they used their minds to figure out the truth. Adherents of the correspondence theories and coherence theories in Chapter 2.1 and 2.2 were epistemically rational as they aimed at having beliefs that were true. Rationalists and empiricists alike were epistemically rational in Chapter 7.2 and 7.3 when they aimed to arrive at conclusions based on reasons and experiential evidence. In Chapter 10 a group of philosophers of science will deploy the scientific method in order to find truth, for the sake of truth alone, about the natural world. In all these cases, the reasoning, beliefs and truths we endorse are all aimed at understanding the truth about reality. An intrepid reporter follows the facts wherever they lead, with the goal of arriving at the truth, no matter if the truth is ugly or good. Chevon studies hard at university for the purpose of learning and understanding how the universe works, not for the sake of getting a job at the end of it. We are **epistemically irrational** if we fail in the task of acquiring the truth. Aarti tries to figure out whether a certain disease is dangerous or not, but he depends upon unreliable sources, is led by his fears, and bases his conclusions on only one experience he heard from a family member, so he comes to a false conclusion about the disease.

We are **instrumentally rational** when we successfully use reason as an instrument to achieve our own goals. The sophists in Chapter 1.3 were instrumentally rational since they used their minds to get what they wanted. The pragmatists in Chapter 2.3 proposed that beliefs are true if they work well for us. In Chapter 6.1, Saul Smilansky proposed hiding the truth of determinism from the masses in order to avoid cultural collapse, once again using reason for the sake of human security and well-being rather than the truth. In Chapter 10.7, we shall meet some philosophers of science who think that scientific theorizing should not solely be aimed at truth, but should also be based on human interests. In Chapter 12.6.2, we shall encounter the view that we should believe in God not solely based on whether we believe God exists or not, but in order to secure heavenly rewards. In these cases, the reasoning, beliefs, and truths we endorse are aimed at achieving our goals, where these goals are usually connected to our well-being and interests. A lawyer brings in a character witness in support of his client in order to reach his goal of securing a verdict of 'innocent' for his client, not for the purpose of getting at the truth of the matter. Devon studies hard at university for the purpose of getting his degree and then a job, not for the purpose of learning about how the universe works. We are **instrumentally irrational** when we fail to properly use reason to achieve our goals. Datiana thinks that if she belittles her work colleague then she will be more likely to land the promotion, but the boss is actually looking for a positive team player, so her actions result in her failing to land the promotion.

The question is: are we mostly epistemically and/or instrumentally rational or not? We are both instrumentally rational and epistemically rational when we believe something that is true and also improves our well-being. This is the ideal case. Makai researches the leading causes of cancer, which both informs him of the truths about cancer, but also leads him to avoid these dangers. We also have moments of instrumental and epistemic irrationality: Marta's pride makes her think she is the best soccer player on her team, which is not only false but makes her shrug off practices, thereby preventing her from getting better. The more difficult cases involve clashes between these two types of rationality. Sometimes a belief can be epistemically rational but instrumentally irrational: Jin's wife died in a car crash last year, and he insists on dwelling on the awful facts every day, which keeps him locked in his grief. Sometimes a belief can be epistemically irrational but instrumentally rational. Monkeys are afraid of all snakes. This is epistemically irrational, because not all snakes are harmful to monkeys. But it may be instrumentally rational, since it is a quick and effective strategy that protects monkeys from the dangerous snakes too.

Can you believe something for its instrumental benefits alone? Imagine someone offers you $100 to believe something clearly false, namely, that there is an elephant floating in the sky. Can you do it? Imagine someone offers you $100 to believe something that you are uncertain about, namely, that it will rain two weeks from now. Can you do it now?

Self-deception usually involves the case of epistemic irrationality but instrumental rationality. We make mistakes about who we actually are since there are benefits to believing the lies. We mistakenly think we are better drivers than others because that makes us feel good about ourselves. We incorrectly remember a past relationship as better than it actually was because it helps us sleep better at night. So, even cases of self-deception involve a certain type of rationality, namely instrumental rationality.

So, are we more rational than irrational? With the help of philosophy, we can make true the claim that we are more rational than irrational. By studying good reasoning and logical fallacies, we raise the chance that we will reason ourselves to true conclusions, thereby making ourselves epistemically rational. By understanding the upside of the philosophical path (see Chapter 1.4), we can see that our self-interests are often better served by pursuing the truth rather than pursuing personal gain. For example, we mistakenly think we are more sociable than our peers, which makes us feel good about ourselves, but prevents us from improving our social skills. If we saw the truth that we have mediocre social skills, we could work on our listening skills or other virtues of friendship, which would make us have more friends in the end. Thus, practising philosophy can make us more instrumentally rational as well.

Summary

There are numerous possible paths to self-knowledge. We may monitor and revise ourselves as we process information, and we may directly know our own conscious states. We may observe our own behaviour in order to detect our thoughts and feelings, and we may look at material facts to know what we believe. We may interact with others in order to figure out our strengths and weaknesses and to know what we are feeling and thinking. Each of these tactics faces a set of difficulties, but they all remain possible avenues for self-knowledge as well. With the lingering tendency for self-deception, all of these avenues for actual self-knowledge are worth pursuing.

Key Terms in Chapter 9: Self-Knowledge		
Self-Knowledge	Infallible	Paradox of
Inner Sense Model	Luminous	Self-Deception
Introspection	Brie Gertler	Alfred Mele
Privileged Access	Bertrand Russell	Bias
First-Person Authority	Acquaintance	Deception
David Armstrong	Direct	Self-Interested
Theatre of the Mind	Extrospection	Epistemic Rationality
Behaviourism	Gareth Evans	Epistemic Irrationality
Behaviour	Aristotle	Instrumental
Disposition	Attribution Bias	Rationality
B.F. Skinner	Self-Deception	Instrumental
Gilbert Ryle		Irrationality

Philosophy on Television: Self-Knowledge

The Truman Show (1998)

Truman Burbank is a middle-aged man who thinks he has a normal life with a normal job in a normal town, but he is actually the star of a reality TV show centred on his life since birth. Truman grows suspicious of his surroundings, leaving others to wonder what he is thinking, while he also tries to figure out what he is thinking. Several models of self-knowledge are on display in this film, including introspection, behavioural analysis, and social self-knowledge.

Analyze This (1999)

In *Analyze This*, a mafia boss begins to have panic attacks, and consults a psychiatrist to help him figure out why. The psychiatrist helps the mafia boss realize that his anxiety is rooted in the fact that he blames himself for his father's death. This movie, along with others such as *Good Will Hunting* (1997), present a psychiatrist or friend figuring out the beliefs or motives of another person who could not figure it out. These examples support the social model of self-knowledge.

The Office (2005–13)

Several characters in *The Office* exhibit a lack of self-knowledge, and even evidence of self-deception. Pam deceives herself into thinking she does not have feelings for Jim, but she clearly does. Michael Scott deceives himself into thinking his co-workers like him, but most of them do not. Pam and Michael are motivationally biased to not believe true facts about themselves and the world.

Additional Resources

Visit this book's companion resources for additional materials, including video content and an automated tool for planning argumentative essays.

sites.broadviewpress.com/knowing/chapter-9

Chapter 10
Philosophy of Science

THOUGHT EXPERIMENT 10.1

Where Does the Rainbow Smoke Come From?

NASA found a precious resource, rainbow smoke with strange healing properties, on the far side of a distant planet! They want to harvest it. There is only one problem: the rainbow smoke puffs out of a crater at seemingly random intervals. No one can figure out what makes the rainbow smoke puff out. They hire you to figure out how the rainbow smoke appears. How would you figure it out?

Does an apple a day keep the doctor away? Is the Earth flat? Do our personality and future depend on the stars? Do the gods bring the rains? When a log burns, is the flame burning off an invisible substance inside the wood that eventually runs out which then stops the flaming? Is gravity the warping of the fabric of space by heavy objects? Are changes in life forms and geological formations mostly gradual, or are they mostly caused by sudden catastrophes? Are males biologically disposed to prefer things to people, and females biologically disposed to prefer people to things? Do we see by emitting a ray of light out of our eyes onto the target, like a flashlight does? Does smoking cause cancer? Does brain chemistry determine human actions? Do humans contribute to the changing climate of the planet? While these are all vastly different questions, they all share a common theme: they are all questions about how the natural world (or things within the natural world) operates.

How should these questions be answered? The **scientific method** is a particular strategy for finding answers to questions about how the natural world operates. What is the strategy? Answering this question is the central focus of this chapter. Fortunately, the scientific method expands upon several elements discussed in Chapter 7. It begins with observing or experiencing the natural world (Chapter 7.2). Rather than assuming we already know how the world works, or clinging to our wishes about how the world works, it lets the world itself inform us of how the world works, where humans simply observe and then accept what nature reveals itself to be doing. Shanice is wondering whether the geranium in her living room would grow better if it got direct sunshine. She moves it to a very sunny window and sees that it starts to shrivel, so she concludes that it prefers indirect sun. This act of observing what nature does is sometimes called an **experiment**, where the experimenter seeks to answer how the world works, so the experimenter constructs an opportunity to observe nature, and then accepts whatever answer nature provides. In addition to beginning with experience of the natural world, the scientific method also uses reasoning (Chapter 7.1), more specifically a particular type of reasoning called inductive reasoning (Chapter 1.5.3) to derive generalizations from experience. Shanice notices that her plant shrivels in the sun, and from this observation she draws the tentative inference 'All geraniums prefer indirect light.' Such generalizations then become part of a shared body of knowledge (Chapter 7.5) about nature that can be checked and corrected by others, and passed on to future generations. Val tries direct sun for some of her geranium plants, making sure that they get sufficient water given the added drying effect of the sun, and notices that the ones in direct sunlight grow better. This falsifies Shanice's conclusion, and modifies the shared body of scientific knowledge.

More detail to this scientific method will be added as we trace the key developments in, and concerns with, the scientific method over the course of 2,500 years. In order to do so, this chapter follows a chronological order, beginning with Aristotle. As this history unfolds, a central distinction between **scientific realism** and **scientific anti-realism** emerges. Scientific realists argue that the scientific method will yield objectively true answers to the questions we pose about nature, and in time scientific law and theory will mirror nature itself. Scientific anti-realists believe this project of capturing the workings of nature in one objectively true scientific theory is misguided. The philosophers we will investigate take different positions on this issue, which can all be located on the following spectrum:

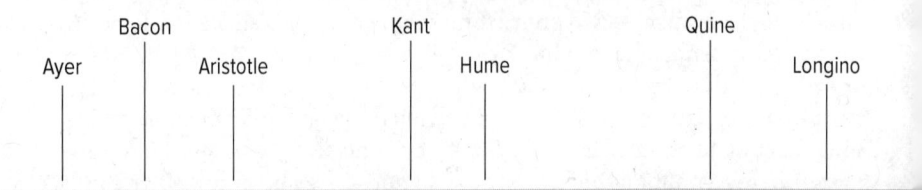

Spectrum 10: Scientific Realism and Anti-Realism

This distinction between scientific realism and scientific anti-realism is similar to the prior discussion in Chapter 2 about the nature of truth, where adherents of the correspondence theory tend to lean toward scientific realism, while advocates of the coherence theory, pragmatic theory, or relativism, tend to lean toward scientific anti-realism.

10.1 Aristotle

Chapter 3 investigated how the earliest philosophers and scientists understood the world. On one side stood the materialists who looked at the material world, or **phusis** (i.e., the natural world as it appears, or the physical) and saw change always occurring. On the other side stood the idealists who focused on the constancy and patterns of the world, or the world's **logos** (i.e., the logic, or the structures behind the changing natural world). Aristotle occupied a middle position between these two in Chapter 3.3, arguing that nature exhibits constancy and change. Aristotle arrived at this conclusion, in part, by developing a theory of knowledge about the natural world that serves as the foundation for the scientific method.

He begins with the regress problem for justification of propositional knowledge, as discussed in Chapter 7.2. Recall the problem: if the claim that 'Socrates is mortal' is justified by the prior premises 'All humans are mortal, and Socrates is human,' then what justifies the prior claim that 'All humans are mortal'? A regress threatens. Aristotle follows the empirical solution to the regress argument, as discussed in Chapter 7.3. Namely, the first premise cannot be justified by prior premises, but rather the first premise must be justified by experience. We know that 'All humans are mortal' by observing hundreds of humans, and noticing that they all die eventually.

The move from observing hundreds of humans that die to the conclusion that 'All humans are mortal' is a form of inductive reasoning, as discussed in Chapter 1.5.3. **Inductive reasoning** begins by observing things, then observing patterns in those things, then making generalizations about those things. For example, Sammi looks at a squirrel and notices that it eats nuts. The next day he looks at a different squirrel and notices that this squirrel also eats nuts. This pattern carries on for several days, so Sammi concludes that all squirrels probably eat nuts. Aristotle thinks this conclusion is reached by appealing to **universals,** which are generalizations that refer to what is true of all the different things that are similar in some respect. The flower is red, the ball is red, and the stop light is red. While each of these things is different, *being red* is true of all of those things, so *being red* is the universal that they have in common. Sammi, then, uses inductive reasoning to go from observing that squirrel *A* and squirrel *B* eats nuts, to the universal generalization 'All squirrels eat nuts.'

This model of knowledge resembles Aristotle's view that nature exhibits constancy and change. The first squirrel busily eats the nuts and then races away, and let us say the second squirrel dies after munching on nuts, and a new squirrel runs onto the scene and eats some nuts as well, so the process of change is clearly observable in nature. But nature has constant patterns to it as well. Namely, these different animals all look the same, so we reason our way to these common patterns, namely, the universal of *being a squirrel* that all these different creatures have in common. And, squirrels follow regular patterns as well that can be noticed through repeated observation, namely, squirrels are furry, and squirrels eat nuts, among other things. These universal generalizations allow Sammi's knowledge to extend beyond the three squirrels he saw. He can predict what will happen tomorrow: if Sammi leaves nuts in the grass near a squirrel, they will disappear. He can explain how things happen: a fourth squirrel ate the nuts, and this is no surprise because by now he knows that squirrels eat nuts. He can figure out the causes of things: a cat and a squirrel are sitting in the grass, and he knows the squirrel caused the nuts to disappear rather than the cat because he knows that squirrels like nuts. Here is a passage from **Aristotle** where he explains this inductive process from observing objects in nature to arriving at universal generalizations:

Posterior Analytics II.19 (Aristotle, 350 BCE)[1]

It would be absurd if we had the principles innately; for then we would possess cognition that is more exact than demonstration, but without noticing it. If, on the other hand, we acquire the principles and do not previously possess them, how could we recognize and learn them from no prior knowledge? That is impossible, as we also said in the case of demonstration. Evidently, then, we can neither possess the principles innately nor acquire them if we are ignorant and possess no state of knowledge. Hence we must have some suitable potentiality, but not one that is at a level of exactness superior to that of the knowledge we acquire.

All animals evidently have such a potentiality, since they have the innate discriminative potentiality called perception. Some animals that have perception (though not all of them) also retain in memory what they perceive; those that do not retain it have no cognition outside perception (either none at all or none about what is not retained), but those that do retain it keep what they have perceived in their souls even after they have perceived. When this has happened many times a further difference arises: in some, but not all, cases, a rational account arises from the retention of perceptions. From perception, then, as we say, memory arises, and from repeated memory of the same thing experience arises; for a number of memories make up one experience. From experience, or rather from the whole universal that has settled in the soul—the one apart from the many, whatever is present as one and the same in all of them—arises a principle of craft (if it is about what comes to be) or of science (if it is about what is).

---

1   Aristotle, *Posterior Analytics* II.19 99b26–100b6, in *Readings in Ancient Greek Philosophy*, 729–30.

Hence the relevant states are not innate in us in any determinate character and do not arise from states that have a better grasp on cognition; rather, they arise from perception. It is like what happens in a battle when there is a retreat: first one soldier makes a stand, then a second, then another, until they reach a starting point. The soul's nature gives it a potentiality to be affected in this way. Let us state again, then, what we stated, but not perspicuously, before. When one of the undifferentiated things makes a stand, that is the first universal in the soul; for though one perceives the particular, perception is of the universal—of man, for instance, not of Callias the man. Again, in these universals something else makes a stand, until what has no parts and is universal makes a stand—first, for example, a certain sort of animal makes a stand, until animal does, and in this universal something else makes a stand in the same way. Clearly, then, we must recognize the first things by induction; for that is also how perception produces the universal in us.

In this passage,

1. *Aristotle says that knowledge does not come prior to experience. Rather knowledge begins with perceiving nature. After perceiving nature, through memory we recognize patterns in nature, and through induction we begin to arrive at universal generalizations.*

What would Aristotle say about the rainbow smoke? He might say that you should observe the crater to see how the rainbow smoke is released. Say you notice that a lightning storm precedes the rainbow smoke for several days in a row. After experiencing these things, and connecting the similarities together via memory, you draw the conclusion: lightning storms probably cause the puff of rainbow smoke.

10.2 Francis Bacon

Aristotle was the dominant scientist until the scientific revolution. As discussed in Chapter 8.3, the scientific revolution was a period of rapid scientific progress and change in the seventeenth century in Europe. One of the key figures of the scientific revolution was the British philosopher and politician **Francis Bacon** (1561–1626). Bacon embraces certain aspects of Aristotle's scientific method, namely, he agrees that experience precedes theory, and that experience leads to universal generalizations about how nature works. But he thinks that Aristotle's appeal to arbitrary experience is prone to human error, and therefore controlled observation of experience through intentionally constructed experimentation is necessary. Arbitrary experience means observing whatever happens to be observable at the moment. Sammi sees a squirrel run by, and there so happens to be nuts nearby that the squirrel eats, so Sammi learns

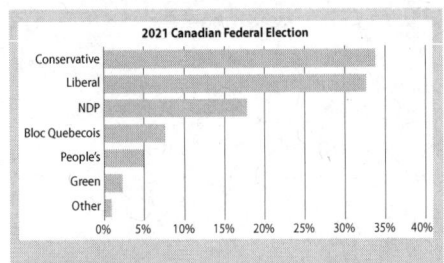

In order to accurately predict (within 2.4%, 19 times out of 20) how 35 million Canadians will vote in an election, polling firms only need to properly poll about 1,600 Canadians.

by experience that squirrels eat nuts. But what if this was an unusual squirrel? What if the type of squirrels in Sammi's country are unusual? What if the nut happened to be salted, and that is what drew the squirrel instead? What if the squirrel would not normally eat nuts, but he happened to be starving at the moment? What if squirrels are willing to eat almost anything, so there is nothing particularly tasty about nuts?

Bacon thinks appeal to arbitrary experience is prone to error. Not only is there no control over these possible contributing variables, but human bias misinterprets the facts to fit what they want to see or happen to notice. Sammi sells nuts for a living, which makes him interpret the squirrel's behaviour as nut-loving behaviour, rather than as salt-loving behaviour. **Controlled experiments** are needed, which are intentionally structured observations that avoid the errors that arise from arbitrarily observing nature. Bacon's strategy for controlled experiments is to remove each possible factor one at a time in order to see which factor is influencing the event, which then provides an explanation for the event. Sammi is not sure if the squirrel likes nuts or salty things, so he offers the squirrel an unsalted nut, and then offers the squirrel a salted pretzel, in order to settle the case. Contemporary scientists typically add several other controls as well. For example, scientists use a **randomized sample**, where the particular subject is selected arbitrarily in order to make the subject likely to be a typical member of the group. Scientists also use a **large sample size**, where many subjects are selected in order to ensure the subjects studied represent the group as a whole. Sammi cannot test only one squirrel, as this squirrel may be an outlier, so he tests one thousand squirrels to see if they all like nuts. Below is a passage from the writings of Francis Bacon.

The New Organon (Francis Bacon, 1620)[2]

1. Man, being the servant and interpreter of Nature, can do and understand so much and so much only as he has observed in fact or in thought of the course of nature. Beyond this he neither knows anything nor can do anything ...

40. The formation of ideas and axioms by true induction is no doubt the proper remedy to be applied for the keeping off, and clearing away of

---

2   Francis Bacon, *The New Organon* (1620), ed. Fulton H. Anderson (New York: Liberal Arts Press, 1960).

idols. To point them out, however, is of great use ... 41. The Idols of the Tribe have their foundation in human nature itself, and in the tribe or race of men. For it is a false assertion that the senses of man is the measure of things. On the contrary, all perceptions as well of the sense as of the mind are according to the measure of the individual and not according to the measure of the universe. And the human understanding is like a false mirror, which, receiving rays irregularly, distorts and discolors the nature of things by mingling its own nature with it ... 42. The Idols of the Cave are the idols of the individual man. For everyone has a cave or den of his own, which refracts and discolors the light of nature, owing either to his own proper and peculiar nature; or to his education and conversation with others; or to the reading of books, and the authority of those whom he esteems and admires ...

82. And an astonishing thing it is to one who rightly considers the matter, that no mortal should have seriously applied himself to the opening and laying out of a road for the human understanding direct from the sense, by a course of experiment orderly conducted and well built up, but that all has been left either to the mist of tradition, or the whirl and eddy of argument, or the fluctuations and mazes of chance and of vague and ill-digested experience ... There remains simple experience which, if taken as it comes, is called accident; if sought for, experiment. But this kind of experience is no better than a broom without its band, as the saying is—a mere groping, as of men in the dark, that feel all round them for the chance of finding their way, when they had much better wait for daylight, or light a candle, and then go. But the true method of experience, on the contrary, first lights the candle, and then by means of the candle shows the way; commencing as it does with experience duly ordered and digested, not bungling or erratic, and from it educing axioms, and from established axioms again new experiments ... Whereas a method rightly ordered leads by an unbroken route through the woods of experience to the open ground of axioms ...

105. In establishing axioms, another form of induction must be devised than has hitherto been employed ... For the induction which proceeds by simple enumeration is childish; its conclusions are precarious and exposed to peril from a contradictory instance; and it generally decides on too small a number of facts, and on those only which are at hand. But the induction which is to be available for the discovery and demonstration of sciences and arts, must analyze nature by proper rejections and exclusions; and then, after a sufficient number of negatives, come to a conclusion on the affirmative instances—which has not yet been done or even attempted, save only by Plato, who does indeed employ this form of induction to a certain extent for the purpose of discussing definitions and ideas. But in order to furnish this induction or demonstration well and duly for its work,

very many things are to be provided which no mortal has yet thought of; ... And it is in this induction that our chief hope lies ...

126. For I do not take away authority from the senses, but supply them with helps; I do not slight the understanding, but govern it.

In this passage,

1. *Bacon says human minds are biased by the following idols: the idols of the tribe (i.e., human biases such as the illusions of human perception and self-deception) and the idols of the cave (i.e., personal biases such as the tendency to notice confirmation of our background beliefs). He also thinks humans are biased by the idols of the marketplace (i.e., social biases such as the fallacies of appeal to popularity and the illicit appeal to authority), and the idols of the theatre (i.e., errors from following poor philosophy). These **four idols** roughly correspond to the biases and mistakes of reasoning discussed in Chapter 1.4 and 1.5*

2. *Bacon says we avoid these errors by letting nature inform us of how it works through controlled experiments. Scientists are humble before nature, believing only and everything that nature shows herself to be like through experimentation, always willing to modify their beliefs about how nature operates if new evidence presents itself.*

3. *Bacon expresses concern with Aristotle's model of inductive reasoning. He thinks there is a temptation to quickly proceed from several observed phenomena to a general conclusion, leaving the generalization susceptible to being proven false by one counter instance. Bacon suggests a slower approach that draws more modest conclusions and repeatedly checks back with nature.*

4. *Bacon rejects accidental experience in favour of experiment. Experiments are structured experiences where each possible cause is removed one at a time in order to track the negative and affirmative instances. The negative instances are often called **necessary conditions**, where we remove the possible cause to see if the effect is removed as well. Sammi offers the squirrel a salted pretzel and a carrot, which removes the nuts from the equation. If the squirrel does not eat those things, then nuts seem to be the necessary factor for the squirrel eating. The positive instances are often called **sufficient conditions**, where we add the possible cause to see if the effect is present. Sammi offers the squirrel unsalted peanuts and almonds, which adds nuts to the equation. If the squirrel eats both, then nuts are what the squirrel eats.*

What would Bacon say about the rainbow smoke? He might not be satisfied with arbitrarily observing the situation. Rather, he may prefer to set up a series of experiments where we gradually delete and restore one variable after another until we find the proper correlation. We should see whether the rainbow smoke appears when the lightning storm does not occur, then we should observe a lightning storm in the absence of other variables, such as the whistling wind and the earthquakes. If the rainbow smoke appears when the lightning storm appears, and doesn't appear when the lightning storm is absent, then the lightning storm may be the cause.

Objection: Hypothesis

Bacon doubted human reasoning ability, so he rejected the idea that scientists should begin or end their investigation with a **hypothesis**, which is an informed speculation on what the results of the study will be or what the results of the study imply. He argued that a hypothesis prior to experimentation can (consciously or unconsciously) bias experimenters into confirming the hypothesis they wish to be true. In contemporary science, hypotheses play a key part, and Bacon's concerns are often avoided by **blinded studies**, where the experimenter is blinded from key features of the study to prevent bias. Dr. Harrow hypothesizes that vitamin D will be effective in treating an illness, so she tests her theory by subjecting some patients to vitamin D and others to no vitamin D, and she does not know who receives vitamin D, thereby avoiding the possibility that her interests will bias the study. Not only are Bacon's concerns alleviated in this way, but the scientific hypothesis is useful. It limits the scope of an experiment to several possible factors, and it also guides the scientist in how to set up the experiment. Dr. Harrow hypothesizes that vitamin D is effective, so she sets up an experiment to test for vitamin D efficacy, which is a more manageable workload than testing every vitamin and nutrient out there.

In addition, the workings of nature are often hidden from plain sight, and require scientists to intelligently speculate on how nature may work. This is the scientific value of novelty, according to which scientists have "eureka moments," where their ingenuity contributes to new scientific knowledge. Consider several scientific discoveries occurring around Bacon's time. On plain sight, the sun seems to revolve around the Earth, but informed speculation proposed and confirmed that the Earth rotates around the sun. On plain sight, the Earth appears flat, but a novel hypothesis that the Earth is round was eventually proposed and established. Just after Bacon's time, **Isaac Newton** imagined for the first time a theory of universal gravitation. The mechanism of gravity, however, was hidden from plain sight and even eluded Newton up to his death. Several hundred years later, the mechanism of gravity was finally imagined by Albert Einstein in another moment of insight.

10.3 David Hume

We encountered David Hume in Chapters 3.4 and 4.2. On both occasions, Hume is skeptical about the rationality of belief in something that lies beyond experience: he doubts the existence of a substratum to substances, and he doubts the existence of a simple unchanging self. In Chapter 7.3, Hume's skepticism finds roots in his empiricism—experience provides justification for claims, and there is no experiential evidence for a substratum or simple unchanging self, so there is no justification for believing these claims. Given, this background, it makes sense that Hume is in some ways a champion of the scientific method, as both emphasize how experience justifies knowledge. But Hume also points out a famous problem at the foundations of the scientific method called the problem of induction.

To see the problem, return to the fact that Aristotle argues that scientific knowledge proceeds from having particular experiences, to having memories that similar things behave in similar ways, to concluding through inductive reasoning that some particular thing always acts in this way. Hume calls into question the inductive reasoning process. His concerns are rooted in his empiricism discussed in Chapter 7.3, where he says that beliefs are justified by experience, so any belief that is not proven by experience is not justified. Not only does the substratum and the simple unchanging self lie beyond experience, but induction yields conclusions that extend beyond experience as well. Sammi sees twenty squirrels eating nuts, so experience only allows him to believe "these twenty squirrels eat nuts." Yet Sammi uses inductive reasoning to conclude "All squirrels probably eat nuts." How does Sammi know this? Sammi never saw the squirrels that lived a hundred years ago, nor can he see the squirrels that will live a hundred years from now, or the squirrels on the far side of the world. How can he be justified in knowing what those distant squirrels eat, given that he has never seen any of them eating anything? This is the **problem of induction**: inductive reasoning draws universal generalizations about natural phenomena, where these universal generalizations extend beyond experience, so cannot be fully justified by experience.

A common way of answering this concern is to appeal to the **uniformity of nature**, according to which nature acts uniformly, or, the same natural objects behave in the same way over time and across instances. The uniformity of nature can be supported by appealing to the existence of the **laws of nature**, where nature behaves in its own law-like manner, regardless of whether humans observe nature or not. Sammi sees twenty squirrels eating nuts, and, since squirrels act the same throughout nature, he is justified in concluding that all squirrels probably eat nuts, even the ones he has never seen before.

Centuries ago, Europeans concluded that all swans were white. They were wrong because they had never observed black Australian swans.

Hume does not approve of this appeal to the uniformity of nature. Why? In order for us to know that nature is uniform, we would have to experience that nature is uniform. We can claim we have experienced this: we have experienced nature repeatedly acting the same for many years in a row. But how do we know that nature will continue to act uniformly? We cannot say: well, since nature has acted uniformly in the past, it will probably continue to act uniformly in the future. Why not? This would be question begging (see Chapter 1.5.4). The question is: "Will nature continue to act uniformly in the future?" So we cannot assume that nature will continue to act uniformly in the future. Sammi sees twenty squirrels eating nuts, so he concludes that the next squirrel he sees will eat nuts too. But perhaps squirrels will start eating crabs or rocks tomorrow? How do we know they won't? We have no experiential evidence that they will not, since we have not experienced the future. The uniformity of nature, therefore, is not empirically verifiable, so the problem of induction remains. Here is a passage from **David Hume** where he explains the problem of induction:

An Enquiry Concerning Human Understanding (David Hume, 1748)[3]

If a body of like color and consistence with that bread, which we have formerly eat, be presented to us, we make no scruple of repeating the experiment, and foresee, with certainty, like nourishment and support. Now this is a process of the mind or thought, of which I would willingly know the foundation ... As to past Experience, it can be allowed to give direct and certain information of those precise objects only, and that precise period of time, which fell under its cognizance: but why this experience should be extended to future times, and to other objects, which for aught we know, may be only in appearance similar; this is the main question on which I would insist. The bread, which I formerly eat, nourished me; that is, a body of such sensible qualities was, at that time, endued with such secret powers: but does it follow, that other bread must also nourish me at another time, and that like sensible qualities must always be attended with like secret powers?

The consequence seems nowise necessary. At least, it must be acknowledged that there is here a consequence drawn by the mind; that there is a certain step taken; a process of thought, and an inference, which wants to be explained. These two propositions are far from being the same, I have found that such an object has always been attended with such an effect, and I foresee, that other objects, which are, in appearance, similar, will be attended with similar effects. I shall allow, if you please, that the one proposition may justly be inferred from the other: I know, in fact, that it always is inferred. But if you insist that the inference is made by a chain of reasoning, I desire you to produce that reasoning ...

---

3 David Hume, *An Enquiry Concerning Human Understanding* (1748), in *The Broadview Introduction to Philosophy*, ed. Andrew Bailey (Peterborough: Broadview Press, 2019), 280–81, 282, 284.

That there are no demonstrative arguments in the case seems evident; since it implies no contradiction that the course of nature may change, and that an object, seemingly like those which we have experienced, may be attended with different or contrary effects. May I not clearly and distinctly conceive that a body, falling from the clouds, and which, in all other respects, resembles snow, has yet the taste of salt or feeling of fire? Is there any more intelligible proposition than to affirm, that all the trees will flourish in December and January, and decay in May and June? ...

But you must confess that the inference is not intuitive; neither is it demonstrative: Of what nature is it, then? To say it is experimental, is begging the question.... It is impossible, therefore, that any arguments from experience can prove this resemblance of the past to the future; since all these arguments are founded on the supposition of that resemblance ... And it is certain we here advance a very intelligible proposition at least, if not a true one, when we assert that, after the constant conjunction of two objects— heat and flame, for instance, weight and solidity—we are determined by custom alone to expect the one from the appearance of the other.

In this passage,

1. *Hume argues that we expect the loaf to be nourishing because our past experiences combined with the idea that the present loaf will be like the past loafs. But for all we know, bread may start making people sick tomorrow.*
2. *Hume says the problem of induction cannot be solved by experimental proof that nature has acted uniformly in the past, for this is question begging. Rather, the problem of induction is solved by appealing to custom or habit. It is just our habit that causes us to think bread will continue to nourish us in the future.*

What would Hume say about the rainbow smoke? He might say we should observe what regularly appears prior to the rainbow smoke. The lightning storm regularly precedes the rainbow smoke, so the lightning storm is probably the cause of the rainbow smoke. But we cannot be sure that the next lightning storm will produce rainbow smoke, as this planet may be completely unpredictable.

10.4 Immanuel Kant

It is worth connecting the background of Hume's problem of induction with the dispute between Descartes' rationalism and Hume's empiricism in Chapter 7.2 and 7.3. The problem of induction is rooted in trying to justify knowledge in experience alone, as Hume does in Chapter 7.3, but experience alone cannot justify induction. If only there were another source of justification! In Chapter 7.2, Descartes proposes another source of justification: knowledge can be justified by reasoning as well, so ideas that are not rooted in experience can be justified as well.

The influential German philosopher **Immanuel Kant** (1724–1804) develops a model of embracing the importance of both reason and experience in a way that offers a possible solution to the problem of induction. To see his model, consider the Google-owned AI system called AlphaGo Zero, who recently became the world's best Go player. How did they program AlphaGo Zero so well? They didn't. The computer taught itself how to play! The computer started from scratch, with no background strategies or game-play examples built in but with only the rules of the game. Then it played itself millions of times, each time learning from prior mistakes, until it became the best in the world. On the one hand, this supports the empiricist doctrine that we acquire knowledge by experience, since the computer only learned by playing itself. On the other hand, this supports the rationalist case that innate cognitive structures contribute to learning as well, since the computer was pre-programmed with algorithms for searching for possible moves, algorithms for evaluating whether a move will improve the chance of victory, and algorithms instructing the machine to repeat moves that lead to victory.

As the Netflix program *AlphaGo* (2019) chronicles, AlphaGo defeated Lee Sedol, the world's best Go player, in 2016. An improved successor named AlphaGo Zero then defeated AlphaGo 100–0; despite this new program having no prior knowledge of the game, "it is able to learn tabula rasa."[4] While AlphaGo Zero only learned the game by experiencing game play against itself, it nevertheless had advanced algorithms pre-programmed in to help it improve through those games.

Kant says that human learning is similar to the type of learning the computer underwent. Before humans ever have sense experience, they know nothing about the world—how could they? They have never seen the world before. After we experience the world, we acquire knowledge of what the world is like and how the world works. But humans are born with innate cognitive structures, including memory and inductive and deductive reasoning abilities, which organizes the incoming sense experience in a way that helps us navigate the world. Sense experience, without the mind's organizing ability, is an inundating stream of raw sense data that never makes sense or gets organized into coherent perception. Sense experience is just raw, unconceptualized brown, green, black, and blue colours and shapes that flood the visual system—which is confusion, not knowledge. The mind, without sense experience, is ready to organize information but no sense information ever comes, so it produces no knowledge. But once

---

4   David Silver and Demis Hassabis, "AlphaGo Zero: Starting from scratch," Oct. 18, 2017, https://www.deepmind.com/blog/alphago-zero-starting-from-scratch.

For Kant, sense experience is like a messy bedroom that needs someone to organize it. The mind is like Marie Kondo (who is a house-organizing expert from the TV series *Tidying Up*), ready to do some organizing work, but having nothing to organize until she enters the messy bedroom. The combination of reason and experience is like Marie Kondo organizing the bedroom.

the mind organizes the sensed colours and shapes, such that they belong to specific recognized objects at specific distances, we know there is a dog barking up a tree behind a black park bench by a river.

For Kant, the problem of induction is one example of how reason combines with experience to generate knowledge. Experience leads Sammi to believe that "All the squirrels I have seen have eaten nuts." As the problem of induction highlights, experience cannot justify the stronger universal claim "All squirrels eat nuts." But we are justified in making this stronger claim. The mind, through inductive reasoning, forms the universal generalization that "All squirrels eat nuts." Here is a passage from Immanuel Kant:

The Critique of Pure Reason (Immanuel Kant, 1787)[5]

That all our knowledge begins with experience there can be no doubt. For how is it possible that the faculty of cognition should be awakened into exercise otherwise than by means of objects which affect our senses, and partly of themselves produce representations, partly rouse our powers of understanding into activity, to compare, to connect, or to separate these, and so to convert the raw material of our sensuous impressions into a knowledge of objects, which is called experience? In respect of time, therefore, no knowledge of ours is antecedent to experience, but begins with it.

But, though all our knowledge begins with experience, it by no means follows that all arises out of experience. For, on the contrary, it is quite possible that our empirical knowledge is a compound of that which we receive through impressions, and that which the faculty of cognition supplies from itself (sensuous impressions giving merely the *occasion*), an addition which we cannot distinguish from the original element given by sense, till long practice has made us attentive to, and skillful in separating it. It is, therefore, a question which requires close investigation, and not to be answered at first sight,—whether there exists a knowledge altogether independent of experience, and even of all sensuous impressions?

---

5 Immanuel Kant, *The Critique of Pure Reason*, trans. John Miller Dow Meiklejohn (1855), Introduction B1 I–II; Transcendental Doctrine of Method, Chapter I, Section 2. 2–4; 465–66.

Knowledge of this kind is called *a priori*, in contradistinction to empirical knowledge, which has its sources *a posteriori*, that is, in experience....

Experience no doubt teaches us that this or that object is constituted in such and such a manner, but not that it could not possibly exist otherwise. Now, in the first place, if we have a proposition which contains the idea of necessity in its very conception, it is a judgment *a priori*; if, moreover, it is not derived from any other proposition, unless from one equally involving the idea of necessity, it is absolutely *a priori*. Secondly, an empirical judgment never exhibits strict and absolute, but only assumed and comparative universality (by induction); therefore, the most we can say is,—so far as we have hitherto observed, there is no exception to this or that rule. If, on the other hand, a judgment carries with it strict and absolute universality, that is, admits of no possible exception, it is not derived from experience, but is valid absolutely *a priori*....

Now, that in the sphere of human cognition we have judgments which are necessary, and in the strictest sense universal, consequently pure *a priori*, it will be an easy matter to show. If we desire an example from the sciences, we need only take any proposition in mathematics. If we cast our eyes upon the commonest operations of the understanding, the proposition, "every change must have a cause," will amply serve our purpose. In the latter case, indeed, the conception of a cause so plainly involves the conception of a necessity of connection with an effect, and of a strict universality of the law ...

For example, if I observe that a piece of wax melts, I can cognize *a priori* that there must have been something (the sun's heat) preceding, which this law; although, without the aid of experience, I could not cognize *a priori* and in a determinate manner either the cause from the effect, or the effect from the cause. Hume was, therefore, wrong in inferring, from the contingency of the determination according to law, the contingency of the law itself ...

In this passage,

1. *Kant blends Descartes' rationalism and Hume's empiricism together by claiming that knowledge occurs when raw sense experience is organized and conceptualized by the mind.*

2. *Kant distinguishes between **a priori** knowledge and **a posteriori** knowledge. A posteriori knowledge is knowledge that comes after ("post") experience. We cannot know that the sun melts wax prior to observing the sun melt wax. A priori knowledge is knowledge that comes before ("prior") to experience. We can know that there is a cause of the melting wax—in fact, every event has a cause—prior to experiencing any causes of the melting wax. Kant here argues that the principle of sufficient reason (i.e., ex nihilo, nihil fit) that we discussed in Chapters 3.2 and 6.1 is an a priori truth—the mind can know, by its own reasoning and without needing experiential confirmation, that all events must have a cause. This issue returns in Chapter 11.1.*

3. *Kant agrees with Hume that experience alone cannot justify universal generalizations, but Kant adds that this proves the mind contributes the necessity or universality to the universal generalization. Kant's position has some similarities with Aristotle's solution to the problem of constancy and change. Namely, Kant agrees that the change in nature is observed through experience, where the constancy of universal law is apprehended by the mind.*

What might Kant say about the rainbow smoke? While travelling to the foreign planet, we cannot know what the cause of the rainbow smoke is, as experience must supply this information. But we can know that the rainbow smoke must have some cause, as it cannot puff into existence out of nothing. After repeatedly observing the lightning storm preceding the rainbow smoke, we conclude 'Lightning storms cause rainbow smoke,' where this conclusion is informed by experience, but is organized into a law of nature by inductive reasoning.

10.5 Logical Positivism

Kant's attempt at reconciling rationalism with empiricism influenced several different movements in the philosophy of science. One such movement was **logical positivism**, which developed as a group of philosophers, called the **Vienna Circle**, regularly gathered in the 1920s in Vienna. They took issue with Kant's doctrine of *a priori* truths. Kant says that *a priori* truths can inform us of how the world is. The logical positivists say that *a priori* truths cannot inform us of how the world is, but they only inform us of the definition of words. It is possible to know in advance of experiencing the world that all bachelors are unmarried men, but this is not because we magically know something about all the unmarried men in the world before we meet them; rather, this is only because 'bachelor' is defined as being an unmarried man, and we can know the definition of a word as soon as we are told the definition of the word.

The logical positivists agree with Kant that sense experience, as it impinges on our perceptual faculties, is raw and unconceptualized. Kant is correct, they say: we do not experience a dog by a river, since the concepts of *dog* and *river* are contributions from the mind as it organizes experience in accordance with our conceptual categories. Rather, we only experience raw and unconceptualized colours and shapes—a moving brown shape and a long blue shape. Hence the statement 'The dog is near the river' is not, strictly speaking, empirically established. All that can be established empirically is that there is a moving brown shape here and now, and a long blue shape. All statements, then, must be translated into **observation sentences**—sentences that mention only raw, unconceptualized, observable states. Experiential verification of these observation sentences constitutes confirmation of more complex statements that are logically derived from, or directly translated from, those observation sentences. Thus, 'The Oreo cookie on the red table' is translated into 'there is a black and white circle and a red square,' which can then be verified as true by experiencing the black and white circle and the red square, which, after translating back, then confirms the original statement about the Oreo cookie.

Some statements, however, cannot be translated into observational sentences—that is to say, there are no possible observations that would count as showing that those sentences are empirically accurate. These include theological statements, as it is impossible to translate 'God is all-knowing and all-good' into observation sentences. Also untranslatable are psychological statements such as 'He feels sad today,' as it is impossible for others to experience someone else's internal feelings. These also include universal generalizations, as it is impossible to make an observation sentence out of 'All squirrels eat nuts,' since no one can ever observe all the squirrels. What should the logical positivists do with these types of statements?

One response to the problem of psychological statements was the introduction of **behaviourism**, which we discussed in Chapter 9.2. Behaviourists translate psychological language into observable behavioural sentences. So, the statement 'He feels sad today' is translated into 'His face is downcast today,' and other such statements capable of observational verification. The positivists said that no such translation is possible for theological statements, so they claimed those statements have no meaning. In making these moves, they introduce the doctrine of verificationism as a test for meaningful statements. **Verificationism** says a statement is meaningful if it can be verified by experience; otherwise it is meaningless. The paradigm of meaningful talk, they thought, was science. Theological statements cannot be verified by experience, so they are not scientific statements. Statements about others' internal feelings cannot be verified by experience, so they are not scientific statements. Behavioural statements can be verified by experience, so they are scientific statements. Universal generalizations such as 'All squirrels eat nuts' cannot be verified by experience either, as Hume points out, leaving the laws of nature under threat of not being scientific statements. Logical positivists solve this problem by saying that observable predictions can be formed from universal generalizations. Thus, 'All squirrels eat nuts' predicts 'Nutty the squirrel, who is approaching the nut, will eat the nut.' This sentence can be verified by observation, so it remains a scientific statement. Here is a passage from **A.J. Ayer** (1910–89), an important figure in the logical positivist movement.

"Verification and Experience" (A.J. Ayer, 1937)[6]

It will simplify our undertaking if we can draw a distinction between those empirical propositions whose truth or falsehood can be determined only by

---

6   A.J. Ayer, "Verification and Experience," *Proceedings of the Aristotelian Society* 37, no. 1 (1937): 137–39.

ascertaining the truth or falsehood of other propositions and those whose truth or falsehood can be determined directly by observation. To the former class belong all universal propositions. We cannot, for example, directly establish the truth or falsehood of the proposition that gold is dissoluble in aqua regia, unless of course we regard this as a defining attribute of gold and so make the proposition into a tautology. We test it by establishing the truth or falsehood of singular propositions relating, among other things, to particular pieces of gold.

We may indeed deduce one universal proposition from another, or even infer it by analogy, but in all such cases we must finally arrive at a proposition for which the evidence consists solely in the truth or falsehood of certain singular propositions. It is here to be remarked that no matter how many such singular propositions we succeed in establishing we are never entitled to regard the universal proposition as conclusively verified ...

Now at last we seem to have reached propositions which need not wait upon other propositions for the determination of their truth or falsehood, but are such that they can be directly confronted with the given facts. These propositions I propose to call basic propositions. If the distinction which we have drawn between them and other propositions is legitimate, we may confine ourselves, for our present purpose, to questions concerning the nature of basic propositions and the manner in which our determination of their validity depends upon our experience.

In this passage,

1. *Ayer distinguishes between statements that are true by definition (i.e., this bachelor is an unmarried man) and statements that are verified by the senses (i.e., there is a green shape here and now).*
2. *Ayer says that universal generalizations (i.e., all robins eat worms) cannot be verified by the senses. However, those generalizations imply statements that can be verified by the senses (i.e., Robbie the robin eats worms), and this adds some degree of verification to the universal generalization, though never conclusive verification.*

What might the logical positivist say about the rainbow smoke? The logical positivist may agree that the generalization 'Lightning storms cause rainbow smoke to puff out of the crater' cannot be verified. But from this generalization we can infer 'The next lightning storm will cause rainbow smoke to puff out of the crater,' and this claim can be verified. This statement, however, still needs to be translated into an observational statement (i.e., light occurs, then red-orange-yellow-green-blue lines appear above a grey circle) before being verified by raw sense experience.

Objection: Problems of Verification

Logical positivism fell out of favour because there are many meaningful and intelligible statements that cannot be directly verified by experience. These not only include theological statements, which, independently of whether they are true or not, are intelligible statements. These also include poetic statements, moral statements, metaphysical statements about minds and free will and the self, and statements referring to internal mental states such as feelings.

In addition, there are ways of constructing non-scientific doctrines that are nevertheless always verifiable by experience. Jan's horoscope reads: "You will feel good today, unless you are having a rough day." This is verifiably true, but only because this can be interpreted as true for every day, no matter what happens. Here is another example: Alfred Adler postulates that all human behaviour can be explained as a response to a sense of inferiority. Jorgé sees a child drowning in the river, and he jumps in to save him, which is explained by his attempt to heroically overcome his sense of inferiority. Jorgé sees a child drowning in the river, and he does not jump in to save him, which is explained by fear that he will fail, which is rooted in his sense of inferiority. Adler's theory is verified as true no matter what happens. The verification criterion fails to achieve one of its main aims, namely, to distinguish between scientific statements and non-scientific statements. That is, while verificationists separate out science from non-science by saying the former are empirically verifiable but the latter are not, it turns out that many non-scientific statements are nevertheless verifiable, so verifiability cannot be the mark of scientific statements. Finding a unique mark that all scientific statements possess but all non-scientific statements do not possess is called the **demarcation problem.**

In response to this over-verifiability issue, the Austrian-born philosopher of science named **Karl Popper** (1902–94) suggests an alternative solution to the demarcation problem. In place of verifiability, he proposes **falsification** as the distinguisher between science and non-science. On this view, a scientific statement—a particular or universal statement, or a whole theory—can be falsified, while non-science cannot be falsified. If Adler cannot describe a situation that would prove his theory false, then Adler's theory is not scientific. If Adler says, "If Jorgé calls 9-1-1 in response to the drowning child, that would falsify my theory," then it is a scientific theory that can be tested for truth or falsity. The principle of falsification has its own solution to the problem of induction as well. On verification, the law of nature 'All squirrels eat nuts' cannot be definitively verified since we cannot observe every squirrel that has ever lived, leaving this law of nature as possibly not a scientific statement. On falsification, however, the law of nature 'All squirrels eat nuts' can be definitively falsified, since locating just one squirrel that does not eat nuts would falsify the theory, leading to the more acceptable result that this law of nature is a scientific statement.

10.6. W.V.O. Quine

Kant introduces the gap between raw sense experience and the mind's conceptualization of this raw sense experience. In the 1950s, philosophers of science took this distinction between raw sense experience and interpretation of sense experience in new directions. Rather than taking the contribution of the mind as involving innate cognitive structures, as Kant does, philosophers took the contribution of the mind to include one's background theories and assumptions, which are informed by upbringing and interests. A background theory is called a **paradigm** or conceptual scheme, which is our model of understanding that we interpret the world by. In the 1500s, the Ptolemaic paradigm located the Earth at the centre of the solar system, with the sun and the planets revolving around the Earth while the Copernican paradigm located the sun at the centre of the solar system with the Earth and planets revolving around the sun. Both paradigms were consistent with the available observations at the time—the sunrise and sunset, and the motions of planets in the sky. The sense experience is the same for both Ptolemy and Copernicus, but they have different paradigms through which they interpret the experience. So, it is true that the mind makes a contribution to scientific knowledge, where the mind's contribution includes the background worldview that one approaches experience with.

The captain of a ship sees a distant light ahead on a collision course. He sends a signal: 'Change your course 10 degrees east!' The response quickly comes back: 'You change your course 10 degrees west!' Angry, the captain sends: 'I'm a navy captain! Change your course!' The response: 'I'm a lighthouse: your call.' The captain shifted his paradigm at that moment: what he thought was a ship, he now thinks is a lighthouse.

It is often the job of science to sort out which of these conceptual schemes is correct, and which is not. After scientific experimentation, it is clear that the sun, not the Earth, lies at the centre of the solar system! But the problem is that there is sometimes an **underdetermination** of theory by data, which means that the observable data is not enough by itself to prove how the world works, which leaves room for different theories to explain the same phenomena in different ways. Here is the data: Téoscar spends ten dollars on fruit, and bananas cost one dollar while plums cost two dollars. There are different ways this data can be true. Téoscar could have bought four plums and two bananas, or he could have bought six bananas and two plums. The data underdetermines the correct theory, so multiple theories can truly explain the same data. A leading figure in this emphasis on the role of conceptual schemes in interpreting sense experience is **W.V.O. Quine**:

"Two Dogmas of Empiricism" (W.V.O. Quine, 1951)[7]

The notion lingers that to each statement, or each synthetic statement, there is associated a unique range of possible sensory events such that the occurrence of any of them would add to the likelihood of truth of the statement, and that there is associated also another unique range of possible sensory events whose occurrence would detract from that likelihood. This notion is of course implicit in the verification theory of meaning. The dogma of reductionism survives in the supposition that each statement, taken in isolation from its fellows, can admit of confirmation or infirmation at all. My countersuggestion, issuing essentially from Carnap's doctrine of the physical world in the *Aufbau*, is that our statements about the external world face the tribunal of sense experience not individually but only as a corporate body....

The totality of our so-called knowledge or beliefs, from the most casual matters of geography and history to the profoundest laws of atomic physics or even of pure mathematics and logic, is a man-made fabric which impinges on experience only along the edges. Or, to change the figure, total science is like a field of force whose boundary conditions are experience. A conflict with experience at the periphery occasions readjustments in the interior of the field. Truth values have to be redistributed over some of our statements. Re-evaluation of some statements entails re-evaluation of others, because of their logical interconnections—the logical laws being in turn simply certain further statements of the system, certain further elements of the field. Having re-evaluated one statement we must re-evaluate some others, whether they be statements logically connected with the first or whether they be the statements of logical connections themselves. But the total field is so undetermined by its boundary conditions, experience, that there is much latitude of choice as to what statements to re-evaluate in the light of any single contrary experience. No particular experiences are linked with any particular statements in the interior of the field, except indirectly through considerations of equilibrium affecting the field as a whole....

Any statement can be held true come what may, if we make drastic enough adjustments elsewhere in the system. Even a statement very close to the periphery can be held true in the face of recalcitrant experience by pleading hallucination or by amending certain statements of the kind called logical laws. Conversely, by the same token, no statement is immune to revision. Revision even of the logical law of the excluded middle has been proposed as a means of simplifying quantum mechanics ...

As an empiricist I continue to think of the conceptual scheme of science as a tool, ultimately, for predicting future experience in the light of past experience. Physical objects are conceptually imported into the situation

---

7   W.V.O. Quine, "Two Dogmas of Empiricism," *The Philosophical Review* 60, no. 1 (1951): 38–43.

as convenient intermediaries—not by definition in terms of experience, but simply as irreducible posits comparable, epistemologically, to the gods of Homer. Let me interject that for my part I do, qua lay physicist, believe in physical objects and not in Homer's gods; and I consider it a scientific error to believe otherwise. But in point of epistemological footing the physical objects and the gods differ only in degree and not in kind. Both sorts of entities enter our conception only as cultural posits. The myth of physical objects is epistemologically superior to most in that it has proved more efficacious than other myths as a device for working a manageable structure into the flux of experience....

Each man is given a scientific heritage plus a continuing barrage of sensory stimulation; and the considerations which guide him in warping his scientific heritage to fit his continuing sensory promptings are, where rational, pragmatic.

In this passage,

1. *Quine rejects the logical positivist view that experience can be given one and only one fully accurate description in observational language.*
2. *Quine argues that experience does not completely determine what the theory (or linguistic description of the experience) must be. Rather different conceptual schemes can describe the same phenomenon differently. Moreover, a theory that appears to contradict experience can be preserved by simply modifying certain aspects of that theory. When the Ptolemaic model faced the problem of retrograde motion (i.e., that the movements of planets in the night sky go back and forth rather than follow the purely circular pattern anticipated by the view that the planets travel around the Earth), Ptolemy simply adjusted his theory to say that the planets travel in smaller circular motions within their larger circular motions around the Earth.*

Can you modify your conceptual scheme while viewing the same sense experience? Next time you watch a sunset, can you see it as the Earth rotating away from the sun, rather than the sun circling around behind it?

What might Quine say about the rainbow smoke? He would point out that the appearance of the lightning storm followed by the rainbow smoke underdetermines, or, does not necessitate, a specific conclusion. Our hypothesis that the lightning storm causes the rainbow smoke is informed by our background assumptions, imported from our knowledge of how the Earth works rather than how this planet works, about how disruptive lightning storms can be to the surface of planets. These background assumptions inform our hypothesis that the lightning storm causes the rainbow smoke to occur. Some other theory, say that 'bright lights cause colors to appear,' is also consistent with the data.

10.7 Helen Longino

While the scientists and philosophers discussed thus far have vastly differing views, they all share one thing in common. Namely, they are all men. Indeed, most of the philosophers and scientists throughout history have been men. Is it possible that a hidden bias, rooted in this pervasive male influence, has been imported into the scientific method? If so, what might that bias be?

In the 1980s, a group of **feminist philosophers**, philosophers who emphasize women's perspectives and issues, began to argue that a male bias exists within the scientific method. What bias might this be? Notice that Aristotle, Bacon, and the logical positivists all developed a scientific method aimed at removing human interests, biases, and perspectives from the equation and instead letting nature reveal its **objective truth** about how it works. Bacon's method brackets humans out of the equation by dodging their self-interested biases and social biases, and simply tests nature to see how it really operates. The logical positivists reduce language to observational statements, which then exactly mirror the sense experience of the world, once again removing various human interpretations from the equation. On these views, science should be **value-free**, or independent of human interests and biases. And, on these views, science involves knowledge of the objective truth, which is truth that is true for everyone regardless of their background or social location. What if this goal of science as value-free knowledge of objective truth is in fact a male bias?

Feminist philosophers of science say this may be the case. Where Quine says our background conceptual schemes inform us how we interpret the world, feminist philosophers note that these male scientists share the background assumption that we can and should bracket human interests out of the equation to arrive at one objectively true science of the world. However, in place of this quest for a value-free and objectively true science, feminist philosophers say it is preferable to acknowledge that our background assumptions necessarily influence our interpretations of empirical data; hence we are **situated knowers**: we interpret data in light of our background assumptions, interests, and social location. Some examples of how our embeddedness in background social and conceptual frameworks is prized in the sciences include the emphasis on **peer review**, where other experts critically review a scientist's results prior to publication. **Collaboration**, which occurs when multiple scientists work together on an experiment, is another example of how social frameworks influence scientific research.

In place of the quest for value-free science, it is preferable to acknowledge the **value-laden** nature of science, or, that human interests necessarily influence scientific processes, and there is nothing wrong with having these specific interests. There are many examples of the value-laden nature of science. The

It is sometimes argued that the emphasis on forces in physics, or on competition in evolutionary theory, is a male perspective evident in these scientific theories (on the assumption that force and competition are typical male traits). Do you agree that these aspects of these scientific theories are informed by male perspectives? What would evolutionary theory, informed by female perspectives as well, posit about how organisms adapt to their environments?

questions that scientists pursue are rooted in human interests. Scientists are disproportionately studying cancer treatments in humans over why bees are dying, since scientists are more interested in preserving human life than bee life. Scientists choose to conduct experiments on issues for which they can receive public funding, or whose results stand a better chance of being published, as this helps their career. Human interests are also involved in funding for scientific research. Governments typically have target areas of research that they fund, while corporations are interested in funding research that leads to profitable products. Thus, money gets funnelled into scientific research involving vaccinations or wireless connectivity, achieving precise scientific knowledge of these areas while other areas of scientific inquiry remain under-researched. Here is a passage from **Helen Longino** (1944–), a leading advocate of feminist philosophy of science.

"Can There Be a Feminist Science?" (Helen Longino, 1987)[8]

Logical positivists and their successors hoped to model scientific inference formally. Evidence for hypotheses, data, were to be represented as logical consequences of hypotheses. When we try to map this logical structure onto the sciences, however, we find that hypotheses are, for the most part, not just generalizations of data statements. The links between data and theory, therefore, cannot be adequately represented as formal or syntactic, but are established by means of assumptions that make or imply substantive claims about the field over which one theorizes.... There is a tradition of viewing scientific inquiry as somehow inexorable. This involves supposing that the phenomena of the natural world are fixed in determinate relations with each other, that these relations can be known and formulated in a consistent and unified way ... the scientific inquirer's job is to discover those fixed relations. Just as the task of Plato's philosophers was to discover the fixed relations among forms and the task

8   Helen Longino, "Can There Be a Feminist Science?" *Hypatia* 2, no. 3 (1987): 51–64.

of Galileo's scientists was to discover the laws written in the language of the grand book of nature, geometry, so the scientist's task in this tradition remains the discovery of fixed relations however conceived. These ideas are part of the realist tradition in the philosophy of science.

It's no longer possible, in a century that has seen the splintering of the scientific disciplines, to give such a unified description of the objects of inquiry. But the belief that the job is to discover fixed relations of some sort, and that the application of observation, experiment and reason leads ineluctably to unifiable, if not unified, knowledge of an independent reality, is still with us. It is evidenced most clearly in two features of scientific rhetoric, the use of the passive voice in 'it is concluded that ...' or 'it has been discovered that ...' ... the scientific inquirer, and we with her, become passive observers, victims of the truth. The idea of a value-free science is integral to this view of scientific inquiry. And if we reject that idea, we can also reject our roles as passive onlookers, helpless to affect the course of knowledge ...

The relevance of my argument about value-free science should be becoming clear. Feminists—in and out of science—often condemn masculine bias in the sciences from the vantage point of commitment to a value-free science. Androcentric bias, once identified, can then be seen as a violation of the rules, as 'bad' science. Feminist science, by contrast, can eliminate that bias and produce better, good, more true or gender free science.... Instead of remaining passive with respect to the data and what the data suggest, we can acknowledge our ability to affect the course of knowledge and fashion or favor research programs that are consistent with the values and commitments we express in the rest of our lives. From this perspective, the idea of a value-free science is not just empty, but pernicious.

Accepting the relevance to our practice as scientists of our political commitments does not imply simple and crude impositions of those ideas onto the corner of the natural world under study. If we recognize, however, that knowledge is shaped by the assumptions, values and interests of a culture and that, within limits, one can choose one's culture, then it's clear that as scientists/theorists we have a choice.... I am arguing instead for the deliberate and active choice of an interpretive model and for the legitimacy of basing that choice on political considerations in this case. Obviously model choice is also constrained by (what we know of) reality, that is, by the data. But reality (what we know of it) is, I have already argued, inadequate to uniquely determine model choice ... I am suggesting that a feminist scientific practice admits political considerations as relevant constraints on reasoning, which, through their influence on reasoning and interpretation, shape content ...

Scientific inquiry takes place in a societal, political, and economic context which imposes a variety of institutional obstacles to innovation, let alone the intellectual working out of oppositional and political commitments. The nature of university career ladders means that one's work must be recognized as meeting certain standards of quality in order that one be able to continue it.... Another push to conformity comes from the structure of support for science. Many of the scientific ideas argued to be consistent with a feminist politics have a distinctively non-production orientation.... The doing of science, however, requires financial support and those who provide that support are increasingly industry and the military. As might be expected they support research projects likely to meet their needs, projects which promise even greater possibilities for intervention in and manipulation of natural processes. Our sciences are being harnessed to the making of money and the waging of war.

In this passage,

1. *Longino rejects the logical positivist view that language can exactly describe sense experience. Instead, she agrees with Quine's argument that theories are underdetermined by experience, so background assumptions play a role in interpreting experience as well.*

2. *Longino argues that value-free science, or, the attempt to dispassionately describe the objective truths of nature just for the sake of knowing the truth about the world, is in fact a male value. She offers value-laden science as an alternative, where background assumptions and interests are acknowledged and embraced. She also says that social relations and processes contribute to the method and output of scientific research.*

3. *Longino provides numerous examples of how values do and should influence scientific methodology.*

What might Longino say about the rainbow smoke? She may notice that the pursuit of the scientific understanding of rainbow smoke (as opposed to other interesting features of the planet) is itself motivated by certain interests, including the interests of NASA, and human health interests in finding a healing product.

Objection 1: Scientific Realism

Scientific realism is the view that scientific theory cuts nature at the joints, or, accurately mirrors the facts of nature. The oxidation theory of combustion says wood burns because of the presence of oxygen in the air, so the scientific realist says that there really exists a substance called oxygen, and it really is present in the air while wood burns. Other theories that interpret the data differently, such as phlogiston theory, according to which the flames burn off an invisible substance in the wood called phlogiston, are simply false. There are not two equivalent conceptual schemes interpreting the same data; rather, one theory is correct while the other is false. Scientific realism is similar to the correspondence theory of truth, as discussed in Chapter 2.1. While scientific realism is endorsed by Aristotle, Bacon, and the logical positivists, both Quine and feminist philosophers of science reject scientific realism, which makes them scientific anti-realists. Instead of endorsing a correspondence theory of scientific truth, they include pragmatic elements, coherence elements, and relativistic elements to scientific truth, as discussed in Chapter 2.2 to 2.4. This means that coherent conceptual schemes and human interests contribute to scientific truths as well.

Scientific realists often deploy a **no miracles argument** in support of scientific realism. Our best scientific theories are very successful. For example, the theory of the electromagnetic spectrum allows us to create wireless networks that effectively transmit signals using the fine details of electromagnetic spectrum theory. What explains the fact that this technology works? On scientific realism, the success of electromagnetic spectrum theory is explained by suggesting that this theory is true, that nature has an electromagnetic spectrum in it, and it has the properties that the science says it has, so of course the technology will work. On scientific anti-realism, electromagnetic spectrum theory does not correspond to the way nature actually is; rather, numerous different theories can explain the data. On this view, it seems miraculous that scientific theories and the technology based upon them would be successful—why would scientific theories work when they aren't actually describing the way the world is? Thus, the success of some scientific theories (and the failure of others) is best explained by the view that scientific theories approximate how nature really is.

Objection 2: When Values Influence Science

At first glance it appears obvious and important that values influence scientific practice and theory. Of course, the sciences should spend more time on vaccine research that can save lives than on studying the mating patterns of spotted frogs! But what happens if the scientific research program is paired with values that are considered wrong? In the 1950s scientists in the USSR instigated a research program rejecting Darwinism in support of Lamarkianism—the view that organisms can pass on traits that they acquired through use or misuse during their lives—since this supported their communist agenda of carrying socially acquired traits into future generations. When values determine scientific acceptability, the scientific method is corrupted. The USSR was conducting bad science, as they were trying to prove something they wanted to be true rather than letting nature speak for itself. As another example, imagine a tobacco company spearheading a research program aimed at demonstrating that cigarettes do not cause cancer. They conduct their experiments in such a way as to prove their point, and they only reveal the studies they perform that prove their point. In this case, the tobacco company is just using—indeed, abusing—science to promote its interests and ideology. It is also possible that good values can impair and influence scientific investigation. What happens if important values such as the specialness of humanity, the equality amongst peoples, the respect for diverse traditions, or the need for economic prosperity, were to conflict with scientific findings?

Summary

The scientific method developed over thousands of years as an increasingly structured attempt to remove human bias and instead let nature inform us of how it works. The scientific method has greatly increased our understanding of nature over many generations—once people thought the gods controlled the weather; now people accept that atmospheric factors control weather patterns. But scientific methodology faces difficult challenges, including the fact that experience alone does not ensure the truth of an inductively derived law of nature, and experience alone is not enough to establish the truth of a theory—either innate contributions from the mind are required as well, or differing conceptual schemes and/or interests inform our interpretations of the data as well. Despite these issues, the scientific method remains an important source of knowledge about the natural world.

Key Terms in Chapter 10: Philosophy of Science		
Scientific Method	Hypothesis	A.J. Ayer
Experiment	Blinded Studies	Karl Popper
Scientific Realism	Isaac Newton	Falsification
Scientific Anti-Realism	Problem of Induction	Paradigm
Phusis	Uniformity of Nature	W.V.O. Quine
Logos	David Hume	Underdetermination
Inductive Reasoning	Law of Nature	Feminist Philosophy
Universal	Immanuel Kant	Value-Free
Aristotle	*A Priori*	Value-Laden
Francis Bacon	*A Posteriori*	Objective Truth
Large Sample Size	Logical Positivism	Situated Knowers
Controlled Experiments	Vienna Circle	Helen Longino
Randomized Sample	Observation Sentences	No Miracles Argument
Four Idols	Behaviourism	Collaboration
Necessary Conditions	Demarcation Problem	Peer Review
Sufficient Conditions	Verificationism	

Philosophy on Television: Philosophy of Science

Black Mirror (2011-)

Black Mirror (2011-) is one of many science fiction television shows. This series examines a variety of different possible scientific technologies, such as artificial intelligence, electronic surveillance, and digital consciousness. Another popular science fiction series is *Star Trek*, where possible scientific technologies, such as space flight, alien species, teleporters, and food replicators, are discussed. These types of shows highlight not only key scientific discoveries and methods, but also reveal what future scientific practice may enable—for good or bad. Other examples of science fiction include *Westworld* (2015-), *Battlestar Galactica* (2005), *Star Wars* (1979), *Blade Runner* (1982), *The Terminator* (1984), and *Interstellar* (2014)—the list is virtually endless.

The Big Bang Theory (2007-19)

The Big Bang Theory is a comedy show that revolves around the lives of several scientists, including a neuroscientist, a physicist, an astrophysicist, and an aerospace engineer. The show captures the scientific conversations, methods, and approaches of these scientists, along with their quirky personalities.

Behind the Curve (2019)

Behind the Curve is a movie that highlights the views of contemporary flat-Earth theorists, as well as criticisms from the orthodox scientific community about the view that the Earth is flat. The film highlights the question of science vs. nonscience or pseudoscience, and differing ways of conducting science.

Additional Resources

Visit this book's companion resources for additional materials, including video content and an automated tool for planning argumentative essays.

sites.broadviewpress.com/knowing/chapter-10

Chapter 11

God and Naturalism

THOUGHT EXPERIMENT 11.1
Something vs. Nothing

Close your eyes. Forget everything you know and remember about reality. Forget that you know that reality even exists. Pretend you don't know whether the universe exists or not yet, so when you open your eyes you are not sure if you will see normal reality or an expansive void of nothingness. Now ask yourself, what is more likely: that the universe exists, or that the universe does not exist? You may immediately say: 'Of course it is more likely that the universe exists!' But maybe that hunch is just biased by the fact that you know the universe does end up existing. Get rid of that bias. Wouldn't it be simpler for nothing to exist? It takes less work for the universe to just not be. It would not be shocking if nothing ever happened at all. It seems quite plausible that nothing is more likely than something.

Have you ever wondered: 'What is the deepest question that could ever be asked?' Leibniz has a suggestion: "The first question we are entitled to put will be—why does something exist rather than nothing? For nothing is simpler and easier than something."[1] Moreover, all the metaphysical questions asked thus far, about the nature of substances, personal identity, mind, or free will, all take for granted that something exists, so it seems deeper to consider this background issue of why something exists at all. Moreover, as all these other metaphysical questions only deal with small corners of reality, such as that part of reality called substances, or persons, or minds, it seems deeper to consider reality in totality by asking: does something exist or not, and if something exists, what is the nature of reality?

To some degree, we've already considered the question of the nature of reality. In Chapter 3, the earliest philosophers divide into two camps: the idealist camp that says that what exists is ideal and constant, and the materialist camp

---

1 Gottfried Leibniz, *Principles of Nature and Grace* 7, in *The Monadology and Other Philosophical Writings*, trans. Robert Latta (Oxford: Clarendon Press, 1898), 415.

that says that what exists is material and changing. In Chapter 4, the idealist camp expanded and was modified to include those philosophers arguing that persons are thinking substances or psychologically defined beings, while the materialist camp expanded and was modified to include those philosophers arguing that persons are bodies or brains. In Chapter 5, the idealist camp was further extended to include immaterial minds or consciousness distinct from the body, or even the view that only mental percepts exist. The materialist camp was further extended to include the view that minds are brains, or even the view that psychological vocabulary is false. In Chapter 6, the idealist camp added the concept of free will to minds and persons, giving minds the power to influence how the universe unfolds, while the materialist camp added the concept that free will is either compatible with a deterministic physical universe, or the deterministic physical universe is what exists, leaving no room for free will.

In this chapter, we consider the addition of another idealist element, namely an all-powerful, all-knowing mind called God that creates the material universe. Those endorsing this view, to the left of the spectrum, are called **theists**, and we shall consider their arguments for why such a being exists, and why there is more to reality than the material universe. We also consider another materialist expansion to include the view that all that exists is the material universe. Those endorsing this view, to the right of the spectrum, are called **naturalists**, and we shall consider their arguments for why the material universe is all that exists, and why there need be no more to reality than the material universe.

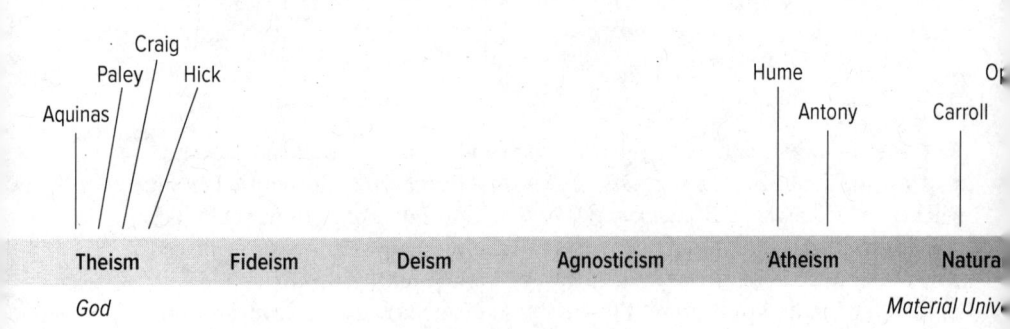

Spectrum 11: God and Naturalism

There are several positions beside straightforward theism and naturalism, though they will not be considered in detail here. **Fideists** believe that God exists, but the existence of God is not proven by reason but rather taken as a matter of faith. We explore several fideist views in Chapter 12.6. **Deists** believe that God exists, but God does not intervene in the universe or human affairs. God created the universe, but then left it alone. **Agnostics** do not know, and perhaps do not care, whether God exists or not. **Atheists** believe that God does not exist. It is possible to be an atheist, but still not a naturalist. Atheism says that God does not exist, but is neutral on the existence of other possible non-natural entities such as numbers, mental states, or moral values. While most atheists are also naturalists, it is worth noting that naturalism goes this one step further by saying that the material universe is all that exists. Having outlined these other positions, let us move on to the contrast between theists and naturalists, beginning with the theists.

11.1 The Cosmological Argument for Theism

Let us begin on the left side of the spectrum, with the theists. Theism comes from the Greek word *theos*, which translates as 'God.' Theists believe that God exists and that God intervenes in the universe and in human affairs, perhaps through performing miracles, speaking to prophets, answering prayers, or providing religious experiences. But what is the nature of this God that the theist endorses? While different religious traditions espouse different divine beings, the Western philosophical tradition usually focuses on the God endorsed by three of the world's major **monotheistic** (i.e., one God exists) religions: Judaism, Christianity, and Islam.

While there are differences between these religious traditions regarding the nature of God, they agree on the following attributes of God. First, God is **omnipotent**, or all-powerful. God can do anything that God wants to do, so long as it is logically possible to do it. Second, God is **omniscient**, or all-knowing. God knows everything that there is to know. Third, God is **omnibenevolent**, or morally perfect. Everything God does flows out of a morally perfect nature, such as an all-loving or all-just nature. Lastly, God is the **creator** of the universe. While God has additional attributes as well, these four attributes are accepted by theists and are central to the arguments raised below for and against God's existence.

Since God is presumed to be the creator of the universe, theists locate particular facts about the universe and argue that these facts are best explained by the existence of God as creator of the universe. The **cosmological argument**, since it contains the word 'cosmos' (which means the universe in its ordered entirety), takes the existence of the universe itself as

The discussion between theists, atheists, and agnostics often brings up the question of the burden of proof, as discussed in Chapter 1.5.4. Some think theists have the **burden of proof**, since theists are claiming something exists while atheists are not. Others think this commits the fallacy of **shifting the burden of proof** onto theists, since both theists and atheists have a burden of proof, as both make a claim (i.e., theists claim God exists, and atheists claim God does not exist). It is the agnostics who make no claim, so have no burden of proof.

Here is an interesting puzzle: could God make a stone so big that God cannot lift it? Presumably, since God is all-powerful, God can make such a large stone. But, since God is all-powerful, God should be able to lift it. Some react to this puzzle by saying that God can do everything that is logically possible. God cannot make a three-sided circle, or a stone heavier than itself, because it is impossible to do these things.

evidence of the existence of God. Imagine that a rabbit appears out of a magician's hat—poof! We wonder what is the cause of the rabbit's appearance? The magician insists that the rabbit appeared out of nothing, by magic, as soon as she shook her wand. But the doctrine of *ex nihilo, nihil fit*, first introduced by Parmenides in Chapter 3.2, speaks against the magician's view. Out of nothing, nothing comes, so the rabbit cannot just magically appear from nothing. Rather, according to the **principle of sufficient reason** discussed in Chapters 6.1 and 10.4, every event that occurs needs a complete cause or reason for its occurrence. So, the rabbit's appearance must have some cause. Here is an obvious answer: it was caused to exist earlier by the rabbit's mother giving birth to him. But what caused the rabbit's mother to exist? Grandma rabbit. But what caused grandma rabbit to exist? Great-grandma rabbit. Much earlier, rabbits evolved from pre-rabbit mammals. But the question keeps tracking backwards until we are finally faced with a dilemma: either the causal processes carry on back in time for eternity, or they come to an end at some first cause.

The first option, that the causal processes trace back infinitely, seems unlikely. Consider the ancient eastern fable where a student asks the teacher what is holding the flat Earth up in space? The teacher replies that the Earth rests upon the backs of four elephants, one at each corner of the Earth. The student asks what holds the elephants up and prevents them from falling down into empty space? The teacher replies that each elephant is standing on a turtle. The child asks: 'what is holding the turtles up?' The teacher replies that it is turtles all the way down. This response is unsettling. Surely, if there is no foundation, no ground that holds up the last turtle that is not itself held up by anything else, then everything will be eternally falling down into empty space. An infinite regress of causes back in time seems likewise difficult to imagine. The remaining option is to say that the series of causes comes to an end at some point in the distant past, at the Creation, when some first cause starts the series of causes, but this first cause itself lacks a cause. This first cause is God. Here is how the medieval Catholic philosopher and theologian **Thomas Aquinas** (1225–74) presents this cosmological argument for God's existence.

Summa Theologiae I, question 2, article 3 (Thomas Aquinas, 1273)[2]

There are five ways in which one can prove that there is a God. The first and most obvious way is based on change. Some things in the world are certainly in process of change: this we plainly see. Now anything in process of change is being changed by something else ... a thing in process of change cannot itself cause that same change; it cannot change itself. Of necessity therefore anything in process of change is being changed by something else. Moreover, this something else, if in process of change, is itself being changed by yet another thing; and this last by another. Now we must stop somewhere, otherwise there will be no first cause of the change, and as a result, no subsequent causes. For it is only when acted upon by the first cause that the intermediate causes will produce the change: if the hand does not move the stick, the stick will not move anything else. Hence one is bound to arrive at some first cause of change not itself being changed by anything, and this is what everybody understands by God.

In this passage,

1. *Aquinas notes that change occurs, where change requires something else to instigate the change, and this change itself must be caused by some prior change. An infinite regress of change is not possible, otherwise there would be no origin of change. So, there must be a first cause that begins the causal process of change, but is not caused to change itself. This first cause is God.*

This argument is one of several cosmological arguments that Aquinas provides for the existence of God. It was a popular argument in support of the existence of God for centuries, but also received criticism. In the following passage **David Hume** provides numerous criticisms of the cosmological argument.

Dialogues Concerning Natural Religion (David Hume, 1779)[3]

I shall begin with observing, that there is an evident absurdity in pretending to demonstrate a matter of fact, or to prove it by any arguments *a priori*. Nothing is demonstrable, unless the contrary implies a contradiction. Nothing, that is distinctly conceivable, implies a contradiction. Whatever we conceive as existent, we can also conceive as non-existent. There

---

2 Thomas Aquinas, *Summa Theologiae* (1273), *Volume 2, Ia.2.3.*, trans. T. McDermott (Cambridge: Cambridge University Press, 2006), 13–15.

3 David Hume, *Dialogues Concerning Natural Religion*, ed. R. Popkin (Indianapolis: Hackett, 1988), 54–57.

is no being, therefore, whose non-existence implies a contradiction. Consequently there is no being, whose existence is demonstrable. I propose this argument as entirely decisive, and am willing to rest the whole controversy upon it. It is pretended that the Deity is a necessarily existent being ... it will still be possible for us, at any time, to conceive the non-existence of what we formerly conceived to exist....

But farther; why may not the material universe be the necessarily-existent Being, according to this pretended explication of necessity? We dare not affirm that we know all the qualities of matter; and for aught we can determine, it may contain some qualities, which, were they known, would make its non-existence appear as great a contradiction as that twice two is five ... and that our mind can at least imagine God to be non-existent or his attributes to be altered. If something is to make his non-existence appear impossible, or his attributes unalterable, it must be some qualities of his that we don't know and can't conceive; but then no reason can be given why these qualities may not belong to matter....

In such a chain too, or succession of objects, each part is caused by that which preceded it, and causes that which succeeds it. Where then is the difficulty? But the whole, you say, wants a cause. I answer, that the uniting of these parts into a whole, like the uniting of several distinct counties into one kingdom, or several distinct members into one body, is performed merely by an arbitrary act of the mind, and has no influence on the nature of things. Did I show you the particular causes of each individual in a collection of twenty particles of matter, I should think it very unreasonable, should you afterwards ask me, what was the cause of the whole twenty. That is sufficiently explained in explaining the cause of the parts.

In this passage,

1. *Hume raises the following dilemma for the theist: if the universe needs a first cause, so does God need a first cause. If God does not need a first cause, then neither does the universe. The former issue raises the child's question of 'who made God' into a philosophical argument. If all things need a cause, then God needs a cause as well. Presumably, super-God made God. But then, super-God needs a cause as well, in the form of super-duper-God. Another regress threatens.*
2. *Hume raises an objection based on committing the **Fallacy of Composition**. Recall from Chapter 1.5.4 that the fallacy of composition is committed when it is assumed that what is true of the parts must be true of the whole. Hume agrees that each particle in the universe requires a cause, and has some other particle as its cause, but this does not mean that the universe as a whole requires a cause. Once*

every particle in the universe is established as having some other particle as its cause, the universe is fully explained.

In recent years a new version of the cosmological argument, called the **Kalam cosmological argument**, has arisen. The argument, which has its roots in medieval Arabic philosophers such as al-Ghazali (1058–1111), not only responds to Hume's objections, but also incorporates contemporary cosmology into its framework. A leading advocate of the Kalam cosmological argument is the American philosopher **William Craig** (1949–), who describes the argument as follows:

Hume says that 'all events need a cause' is learned by observing how the regular objects on Earth work, so is not necessarily true of the universe as a whole. If we experienced rabbits routinely appearing out of nothing, then our minds would easily accept that rabbits can appear from nothing. Others say the claim 'all events need a cause' is necessarily true—it is inconceivable that rabbits or universes could appear out of nothing. Do you think 'all events need a cause' is necessarily true, or do we accept this claim because we are used to seeing events being caused?

"The Kalam Cosmological Argument" (William Craig, 2002)[4]

In my opinion the version of the cosmological argument which is most likely to be a sound and persuasive proof for the existence of God is the kalam cosmological argument based on the impossibility of an infinite temporal regress of events. The argument may be formulated in three simple steps: (1) whatever begins to exist has a cause; (2) The universe began to exist; (3) therefore, the universe has a cause ...

The first premise is rooted in the metaphysical principle that 'something cannot come out of nothing' and is so intuitively obvious that I think scarcely anyone could sincerely believe it to be false.... Does anyone in his right mind believe that, say, a raging tiger could suddenly come into existence uncaused, out of nothing, in this room right now? The same applies to the universe: if there were absolutely nothing prior to the existence of the universe—no God, no space, no time—how could the universe possibly have come to exist?

What evidence is there to support the crucial second premise, that 'the universe began to exist'? ... The standard Big Bang model ... thus describes a universe which is not eternal in the past, but which came into being a finite time ago. Moreover—and this deserves underscoring—the

---

4   William Lane Craig, "The Kalam Cosmological Argument," in *Philosophy of Religion*, ed. W. Craig et al. (New Brunswick, NJ: Rutgers University Press, 2002), 94–113.

origin it posits is an absolute origin out of nothing. For not only all matter and energy, but space and time themselves come into being at the initial cosmological singularity. As Barrow and Tipler emphasize, 'at this singularity, space and time came into existence; literally nothing existed before the singularity, so, if the universe originated at such a singularity, we would truly have a creation *ex nihilo*.' On such a model the universe originates ex nihilo in the sense that at the initial singularity it is true that 'there is no earlier space-time point' or it is false that 'something existed prior to the singularity.' ...

According to the Second Law of Thermodynamics, processes taking place in a closed system always tend toward a state of equilibrium ... the universe is, on a naturalistic view, a gigantic closed system, since it is everything that there is and there is nothing outside it. What this seems to imply then is that, given enough time, the universe and all its processes will run down, and the entire universe will come to equilibrium. This is known as the heat death of the universe.... why, if the universe has existed forever, are we not now in a cold, dark, dilute, and lifeless state? ...

From the first premise—that 'whatever begins to exist has a cause'—and the second premise—that 'the universe began to exist'—it follows logically that 'the universe has a cause.' This conclusion ought to stagger us, to fill us with awe, for it means that the universe was brought into existence by something which is greater than and beyond it ...

The argument does not presuppose that everything has a cause. Rather the operative causal principle is that 'whatever begins to exist has a cause.' Something that exists eternally and, hence, without a beginning would not need to have a cause. This is not special pleading for God, since the atheist has always maintained the same thing about the universe: it is beginningless and uncaused. The difference between these two hypotheses is that the atheistic view has been shown to be untenable ...

In this passage,

1. *Craig puts the cosmological argument in the form of a **modus ponens**. Recall from Chapter 1.5.2 that modus ponens is a valid form of deductive reasoning with the structure: if p then q, p, therefore q. Craig's argument is this: if the universe begins to exist then it has a cause; the universe begins to exist, therefore the universe has a cause. Craig supports premise one through the principle of 'ex nihilo, nihil fit,' which he says is logically necessary, not simply empirically observed.*

2. *Craig supports premise two via the currently dominant model of **Big Bang Cosmology**, according to which the space-time universe began to expand out of a hot, dense state at a finite moment in the past about 13.7 billion years ago, which shows the universe began to exist. (More about this model below.)*

3. *Craig responds to Hume's dilemma that either God also needs a cause, or the universe does not need a cause either. Craig says that only those things that begin to exist need a cause. Since time is part of the universe, the universe begins to exist, so it needs a cause, but God does not begin to exist, so God does not need a cause.*

4. *Craig's argument opens up a response to Hume's view that explaining all the causes of motion in the universe leaves no need to explain the cause of the universe as a whole. Namely, the universe itself exists rather than doesn't, and has an initial moment, both of which require causes.*

What do advocates of the cosmological argument say in response to our question about why something exists rather than nothing? They say that the existence of something calls out for explanation. Even if all the particles in the universe have a complete explanation in terms of causal processes among the particles, we still need to explain why there is a universe at all, rather than nothingness. They conclude that God is the best explanation for the origin of the universe, as it is more likely that the universe was caused by a God than that the universe came from nothing.

Objection: Naturalistic Causes

Beyond the disagreements between Hume and Craig, critics also object to the Kalam cosmological argument on the grounds that we can accept both premises of the argument and still conclude that God does not exist. Namely, it is possible to grant that the universe began to exist, and so the universe needs a cause, but the cause is not some supernatural being called God. Rather, there is a naturalistic cause of the origin of the universe. In the next section we consider this view.

11.2 The Naturalistic Argument for Naturalism

Where theists look at the existence of the universe and say some divine being must have created it, naturalists say that natural causes completely account for the existence of the universe so we should not posit the existence of God. This **naturalistic argument** for naturalism has two premises. First, everything in the universe has a complete natural cause for its existence. Second, we should not posit more causes than needed. If these two premises are true, then we should not posit the existence of God. **Natural causes** are any causes that occur within nature (i.e., any objects or event that occur within the spacetime universe). Why did it rain today? Here is a naturalistic cause: the mountains caused the air to rise, forming clouds, and as the clouds rise the temperature cools in the clouds, which causes water to fall as rain. Here would be a non-natural cause: the gods were angry at all the humans that ignored them, so they made it rain.

What reason is there to suspect that everything that occurs has a complete natural cause? Recall from Chapter 1.1 that ancient Greek mythology posited non-natural causes for many things, such as 'why is there a drought?' and 'why is Helene sick?' and 'why is there lightning in the sky?' and 'why didn't we win the war?' Over time, the sciences provided naturalistic causes for these phenomena. Helene got sick, not because the gods were mad at her, but because she contracted a virus. The lightning did not appear in the sky because the gods were travelling from Mt. Olympus, but because of an electrical discharge between the Earth and the cloud. At the beginning of the twentieth century, it was popular to appeal to a vital spirit, or a life force, animating all living things to explain life. As biology progressed, these life forces were not found, but naturalistic causes of life were found. In Chapter 5.1 we discussed the possibility that everyone has a disembodied mind that explains how we can think, but we also saw in Chapter 5.2 that the neurosciences are finding natural neural causes for these cognitive processes. Given the progress the sciences have enjoyed in providing naturalistic causes for many purportedly non-natural phenomena, it is possible that everything that occurs will ultimately be given a complete natural cause. Indeed, the principle of **physical causal completeness**, as defined in Chapter 5.1, states precisely that all events have a complete natural cause.

Similarly, whereas the theist says that the existence of the universe requires God as a cause, naturalists provide several possibilities of natural causes of the origin of the universe. Some endorse the **Steady State model** of the universe, according to which the universe eternally exists. This view fell out of favor as evidence in support of a new model, called the Big Bang model, increased. This **Big Bang model** suggests that the universe is not eternally existent, but rather that the universe started expanding out of a hot dense single point about 13.7 billion years ago. This model gained prominence because scientists discovered in 1929 that the universe is expanding, which means that it was smaller in the past. By observing the rate of expansion of the universe, scientists calculated that about 13.7 billion years ago all the mass and energy of the universe was densely packed together. The model imagines that the universe began expanding like an explosion, where densely packed matter and energy suddenly began expanding outward.

It is tempting to ask: what then was happening 13.8 billion years ago, before the expansion moment? This question and an answer to it are difficult to imagine. It is like asking, 'what is north of the north pole?'

This raises the question: what brought this initial hot dense state into existence and what made it explode? Naturalists present several possible naturalistic causes for the origin and expansion of the universe. Some endorse the **Oscillating model**, according to which the initial expansion of the universe was caused by the collapse of some prior universe, which was itself caused to expand by the collapse of some still prior universe, and so on back to infinity. The **Quantum Fluctuation model** is another theory about how the universe began to expand. This model appeals to certain peculiarities of quantum physics. Recall from Chapter 6.2 that quantum physics is the study of the behaviour of sub-atomic particles, including some well-established theories about the strange behaviour of these particles. According to quantum physics, due to the effect of quantum tunnelling, particles sometimes appear out of nowhere. The quantum fluctuation model suggests that the universe began as a quantum process resembling a particle appearing out of nowhere.

The second part of the naturalistic argument states that we should not posit the existence of more causes or explanations than needed. Recall the principle of **Ockham's Razor**, discussed in Chapter 5.2. According to Ockham's Razor, we should not multiply entities beyond necessity. In that case, the issue was: if brain processes completely explain our behaviour, we should not posit the additional existence of mental processes causing our behaviour. But now Ockham's Razor applies to everything: if we can completely explain rain by natural processes, we should not add that the gods also cause the rain to occur; if we can completely explain the sickness by being exposed to the virus, we should not add that God also makes the sickness occur. As Isaac Newton's first rule of reasoning says, "No more causes of natural things should be admitted than are both true and sufficient to explain their phenomena. As the philosophers say: nature does nothing in vain, and more causes are in vain when fewer suffice. For nature is simple and does not indulge in the luxury of superfluous causes."[5] Here is an excerpt from Australian philosopher **Graham Oppy** (1960–), who presents this naturalistic argument:

"An Argument for Atheism from Naturalism" (Graham Oppy, 2018)[6]

Some atheists—naturalists—claim that, in an important sense, our universe is all that there is. In particular, naturalists claim that all causal entities have entirely natural constitutions—i.e., all causal entities are composed of nothing but quarks, electrons, protons, neutrons, and so forth—and that all intelligent agents are either entirely natural organisms, or else artificial intelligent agents that are ultimately the creations of entirely natural organisms. According to naturalists, there are no supernatural entities that preceded the universe and were responsible for bringing it into existence ...

---

5 Isaac Newton, *The Mathematical Principles of Natural Philosophy* [1687], trans. Andrew Motte (New York: Daniel Adee, 1846), 384.

6 Graham Oppy, "An Argument for Atheism from Naturalism," in *Philosophy for Us*, ed. Lenny Clapp (San Diego: Cognella, 2018), 4–6.

Although theists differ in the ways in which they depart from naturalism, there is a common feature to theistic departures from naturalism. In every case, theists differ from naturalists by believing in something additional: either believing in one or more additional intelligent agents, or believing in one or more additional forces or powers, or believing in one or more additional non-natural properties of the universe.

Suppose that we are comparing a particular version of theism with a particular version of naturalism. Suppose, further, that these versions of theism and naturalism agree in their beliefs about which natural entities, and natural powers, and natural forces, and natural properties, and natural laws there are. In this case, it's not just that the theist has beliefs in something over and above the things the atheist believes in; it's also the case that the naturalist does not have beliefs in anything over and above the things the theist believes in. From the standpoint of the naturalist, the theistic beliefs of the theist are pure addition; and, from the standpoint of the theist, the naturalistic beliefs of the naturalist are pure subtraction. In short, naturalism is a simpler theory than theism.

A central premise of my argument in support of atheism is the Principle of Parsimony. This general principle states that if there are two competing theories and one is simpler than the other, then, unless the more complex theory provides a better explanation of something than the simpler theory, one should endorse the simpler theory. Since naturalism and theism are competing theories, and, as I just explained, naturalism is simpler than theism, the Principle of Parsimony implies that unless theism provides a better explanation of some relevant phenomenon than naturalism, one should endorse naturalism. And since naturalism implies atheism, it follows that unless theism provides a better explanation of some relevant phenomenon than naturalism, one should endorse atheism.

Some theists might be tempted to argue as follows: Naturalists can give no explanation of the existence of the universe; but theists can explain the existence of the universe in terms of the creative activities of God. So, on this point, theism is ahead.... Whatever range of options is open to the theist to explain the existence of God, exactly the same range of options is open to the naturalist to explain the existence of the universe. If it is open to the theist to say that God exists of necessity, then it is open to the naturalist to say that the universe exists of necessity. If it is open to the theist to say that God's existence involves an infinite regress, then it is open to the naturalist to say that the existence of the universe involves an infinite regress. If it is open to the theist to say that the existence of God has no explanation, then it is open to the naturalist to say that the existence of the universe has no explanation. Insofar as we are interested in explaining the existence of the universe, the postulation of a God who creates the universe does not bring with it any explanatory advantage.

> **In this passage,**
> 1. *Oppy says that theists and atheists agree on the natural facts, but theists add supernatural facts as well. So, naturalism is simpler than theism, in the sense that naturalism says less exists.*
> 2. *Oppy uses the **Principle of Parsimony**, which is another term for the principle of Ockham's Razor, to say that, all things being equal, simpler explanations are better. Since naturalism is the simpler theory, naturalism is better, so we should not be theists.*

What would those endorsing the naturalistic argument for naturalism say about our original question of why there is something rather than nothing? They would argue that cosmologists have a variety of naturalistic explanations for the origin of the universe, and as one will no doubt prove true, we should not posit a God as the creator of the universe.

Objection: Missing Explanations

Theists agree with the principle of Ockham's Razor, that the simplest explanation that explains all the phenomena is correct. But they argue that naturalistic causes cannot explain all the features of the universe, so it is necessary to appeal to a God to explain these additional features. What features of the universe can naturalism not fully explain? Within the discussion on the existence of the universe, theists think that naturalistic causes still do not suffice. The Big Bang model leaves us wondering why there is a universe at all, and why did it begin expanding. The Oscillating model leaves us wondering where the infinite series of universes comes from. The Quantum Fluctuation model leaves us wondering where the quantum states, out of which the universe arose, come from.

There are several other phenomena discussed in this text that may not have complete naturalistic causes. In Chapter 3.1 and 3.2, the material world involved change, where constancy was part of an ideal realm. This issue developed into the contrast between Hume's observation that

The French naturalist Pierre-Simon Laplace (1749–1827) wrote a book calculating how the planets interact with one another and how the moon influences the tides on Earth. When Napoleon Bonaparte met Laplace, Napoleon asked him: "you have written this large book on the system of the universe, and have never even mentioned its Creator." According to reports, Laplace responded: "I had no need of that hypothesis." Another scientist named Joseph Lagrange reportedly replied: "Ah, but that is such a beautiful hypothesis. It explains so much."

the uniformity of nature and the laws of nature extend beyond the world of sense experience, and belong to the realm of constant universals. Ideas, either in the form of Parmenides' unchanging definitions or Berkeley's percepts, were distinct from the natural world as well. In Chapter 5.1, dualists took minds to be distinct from physical brains. Naturalists posit the existence of physical objects and forces only, so the existence of brains makes sense, but why would brains be conscious and full of ideas? Theists posit an all-knowing, unchanging conscious mind called God, so theism makes sense of why conscious minds and unchanging ideas would exist. We shall encounter two further phenomena that may not have naturalistic causes, namely, the design of the universe (Chapter 11.3) and religious experience (Chapter 12.1). There are other phenomena not discussed in this text that may also elude naturalization, such as mathematical objects and moral values. All told, reality may have more to it than nature alone.

11.3 The Teleological Argument for Theism

The mystery of the universe is not only 'why does a universe exist rather than not exist?' but also 'why does this particular universe exist rather than any other type of universe that could have existed?' Why are there complex arrangements of things rather than only barren wastelands of empty space—emptiness would be simpler and easier. Why is the universe immensely large rather than merely containing one atom—smallness would be simpler and easier too. Why are there living beings and conscious beings, rather than only particles? Why is there carbon rather than dipdot? Why are there planets rather than walnuphs?

One peculiar feature of this universe that stands out for theists is its intricate design features. These design features are at the foundation of a second argument for the existence of God, called the **teleological argument**, which is also sometimes called the argument from design, or the fine-tuning argument. The word 'teleology' comes from the Greek word **telos**, which means purpose, design, or end goal. The teleological argument can be put in the form of a modus ponens argument as well: if a thing displays design, then it has a designer; the universe displays design, therefore it has a designer. What reason is there to think the appearance of design invokes a designer? Imagine walking through a forest, and suddenly you stumble upon a set of logs piled on top of each other in a square with a roof of branches on top and an opening that looks like a door. We think: who built this house? Who lives here? We do not think: the wind must have blown all these branches together like this. When we observe the appearance of design, we assume that someone designed it. Here is one famous expression of this point from the British theologian and philosopher **William Paley** (1743–1805):

"The Watch Maker" (William Paley, 1802)[7]

In crossing a heath, suppose I pitched my foot against a stone, and were asked how the stone came to be there, I might possibly answer, that, for anything I knew to the contrary, it had lain there forever; nor would it, perhaps, be very easy to show the absurdity of this answer. But suppose I found a watch upon the ground, and it should be inquired how the watch happened to be in that place, I should hardly think of the answer which I had before given—that, for anything I knew, the watch might have always been there. Yet, why should not this answer serve for the watch as well as for the stone? Why is it not as admissible in the second case as in the first?

For this reason, and for no other, viz., that, when we come to inspect the watch, we perceive (what we could not discover in the stone) that its several parts are framed and put together for a purpose, e.g. that they are so formed and adjusted as to produce motion, and that motion so regulated as to point out the hour of the day; that if the several parts had been differently shaped from what they are ... either no motion at all would have carried on in the machine, or none which would have answered the use, that is now served by it ...

This mechanism being observed, the inference, we think, is inevitable; that the watch must have had a maker; that there must have existed, at some time, and at some place or other, an artificer or artificers who formed it for the purpose which we find it actually to answer; who comprehended its construction, and designed its use.... There cannot be design without a designer; contrivance without a contriver; order without choice; arrangement without anything capable of arranging; subserviency and relation to a purpose without that which could intend a purpose ... Every indication of contrivance, every manifestation of design, which existed in the watch, exists in the works of nature; with the difference, on the side of nature, of being greater and more, and that in a degree which exceeds all computations.... there is precisely the same proof that the eye was made for vision, as there is that the telescope was made for assisting it.

In this passage,

1. *Paley uses the example of a watch to show that things that display design—that is, careful and complex arrangement suitable for achieving a purpose—seem to have a designer.*
2. *Paley says there is evidence of design in the universe, so the universe has a designer, namely, God. What are the design features of the universe? He focuses on the works of nature, such as the human eye and other aspects of living organisms. The eye is so complex and precisely designed for accurately perceiving that it appears to be*

---

7   William Paley, *Natural Theology* (Taylor and Wilks: London, 1802), 1–4, 19.

> designed. The eye, in turn is connected to the brain in such a way as to allow the organism to interpret the sense information, and the brain is connected to the body in such a way as to be able to react to the sense information. These are just small examples of how complex and well-organized life forms are.

Objection: Natural Selection

One of the central premises of the teleological argument is the presumption that the appearance of design is best explained by the existence of a designer. But what if the appearance of design can be present without a designer? Imagine, for example, walking through the forest and seeing rocks in a stream forming a perfect stepping stone path for crossing the stream. We may naturally be inclined to wonder who built this rock path across the stream? But the stones are actually randomly located in the stream by natural forces such as the stream's current over time. And, if lots of stones are distributed at random around long stretches of the river, it is probable that they show up in an arrangement suitable for human crossing at some point. In the same way, it is possible that all living organisms, which is the example of design that Paley emphasizes, has the appearance of design without in fact having a designer.

How is this possible? The processes of **natural selection**—random, unintelligent, and uncaring—can explain this. Here is the explanation from the English biologist Charles Darwin (1809–82), who proposed the theory of evolution by natural selection:

> As many more individuals of each species are born than can possibly survive; and as, consequently, there is a frequently recurring struggle for existence, it follows that any being, if it vary however slightly in any manner profitable to itself, under the complex and sometimes varying conditions of life, will have a better chance of surviving, and thus be naturally selected. From the strong principle of inheritance, any selected variety will tend to propagate its new and modified form.[8]

Imagine that a rabbit has three children: one is stronger, another has greyer hair, and another can jump higher. Suppose the environment these rabbits grow up in happens to favour the rabbit that can jump higher, and thus get at foods on higher ledges. This rabbit will thrive and live long enough to reproduce, and her genetic jumping abilities stand a chance of being passed on to her offspring as well. After successive generations, the rabbits in this environment will be high jumpers. The ability for the rabbits to be able to jump high enough to reach their food has an appearance of design—they can jump

---

8   Charles Darwin, *On the Origin of Species by Means of Natural Selection*, Revised Edition (New York: D. Appleton, 1869), 12.

high enough to reach the ledges where the foods are. But no designer gave them exactly the correct leg strength and agility required to jump to their food. Rather, over time the rabbits that lacked the ability to jump high perished due to lack of food, so of course the rabbits still alive can jump high enough to reach their food, and can reproduce.

While Paley's design argument, which focuses on the design of natural organisms, faces this natural selection objection, contemporary theists often point to another design feature of the universe, a design feature that avoids the natural selection objection. The design feature is the **fine-tuning** of the laws of nature themselves. In recent years cosmologists noticed that the laws of nature have to be

If millions of monkeys typed randomly for millions of years, might one of them eventually type out a Shakespearean sonnet? Theists think it very unlikely, as they think it very unlikely that nature could, through time and chance alone, give rise to complex life forms.

exactly as they are in order for the universe to be hospitable to life developing within it. If even one of many of the laws of nature is slightly adjusted, the universe would collapse back onto itself, or expand too rapidly to permit stars and planets to form. Theists say that the fact that dozens of laws of nature are precisely tuned to allow for life to arise in the universe is best explained by the existence of an all-knowing designer who purposely arranges the laws of nature to allow for the eventual development of life. Here is how William Craig articulates this fine-tuning argument from design:

"Design and the Anthropic Fine-Tuning of the Universe" (William Craig, 2003)[9]

The values of the various forces of nature appear to be fine-tuned for the existence of intelligent life. The world is conditioned principally by the values of the fundamental constants ... a fine balance must exist between the gravitational and weak interactions. If the balance were upset in one direction, the Universe would have been 100 percent helium in its early phase, which would have made it impossible for life to exist now. If the balance were tipped in the other direction, then it would not have been possible for neutrinos to blast the envelopes of supernovae into space and so distribute the heavy elements essential to life ...

---

9 William Lane Craig, "Design and the Anthropic Fine-Tuning of the Universe," in *God and Design*, ed. Neil Manson (London: Routledge, 2003), 155–56.

In investigating the initial conditions of the Big Bang, one also confronts two arbitrary parameters governing the expansion of the Universe: ... related to the density of the Universe and ... related to the speed of the expansion. Observations indicate that at 10^{-43} seconds after the Big Bang the Universe was expanding at a fantastically special rate of speed with a total density close to the critical value on the borderline between recollapse and everlasting expansion. Hawking estimates that even a decrease of one part in a million million when the temperature of the Universe was 10^{10} degrees would have resulted in the Universe's recollapse long ago; a similar increase would have precluded the galaxies from condensing out of the expanding matter. At the Planck time 10^{-43} seconds after the Big Bang, the density of the Universe must have apparently been within about one part in 10^{60} of the critical density at which space is flat ...

The discovery of cosmic fine-tuning has led many scientists to conclude that such a delicate balance cannot be dismissed as coincidence but cries out for explanation. In a sense more easy to discern than to articulate, this fine-tuning of the Universe seems to manifest the presence of a designing intelligence.... suppose Bob is given a new car for his birthday. There are millions of license plate numbers, and it is therefore highly likely that Bob would get, say, CHT 4271. Yet that plate on his birthday car would occasion no special interest. But suppose Bob, who was born on 8 August 1949, finds BOB 8849 on the license plate of his birthday car. He would be obtuse if he shrugged this off with the comment, 'Nothing remarkable about that!'

In this passage,
1. *Craig explains several of the dozens of laws of nature that have to be precisely as they are in order for life to be possible in the universe.*
2. *Craig argues that this fine-tuning of the laws of nature requires an explanation. The theistic explanation that a divine designer adjusts the laws of nature so that life can arise is more likely than the view that it is all just a remarkable coincidence.*

Objection: Naturalistic Causes

Naturalists do not doubt that the laws of nature are as they are. Nor do naturalists usually doubt that the laws of nature have to be remarkably precise in order for this life-permitting universe to be the outcome. But naturalists have several alternative naturalistic explanations for why the laws are precisely tuned for life to be possible within the universe. First, the **coincidence model**, according to which it is a lucky coincidence that the laws of nature are conducive to life developing. Imagine you win a lottery. It is extremely unlikely, granted. But what is the best explanation? Sometimes it is just coincidence. Some set of numbers has to be correct, and you just get lucky this time. Similarly, it is extremely unlikely the laws of nature will be conducive to life developing, but the best explanation is just coincidence.

Appeal to the anthropic principle is another option for naturalists. The **anthropic principle** states that life forms smart enough to ask 'why does this universe exist?' can only exist in universes where the conditions necessary for life are already present. So of course the universe must be fine-tuned to support life, given that life forms presently exist and are asking about the universe.

Many naturalists prefer the **multiverse model** instead of these two options. They say that if you play the lotto once and win, that is too coincidental to be plausible, thereby doubting the coincidence model. But if you play the lotto millions of times and win once, that is quite believable. Similarly, perhaps there are millions of universes, each with slightly different laws of nature (or, perhaps there is one universe with different laws of nature in different pockets of the universe). If one universe out of millions is life supporting, that is quite believable. But is there evidence for the existence of many universes? Theoretical physics allows for the possibility of the multiverse in several ways, so it is theoretically plausible though empirically unverified. The multiverse model is similar to the model of evolution by natural selection. It seems unimaginable how complex living organisms can arise by luck, but given billions of years of chemicals interacting in every possible way, it seems more plausible that life would arise by chance. Similarly, it seems unimaginable that the laws of nature are precisely tuned for life by coincidence, but it seems more plausible that one universe out of billions is life-supporting. Here is a passage from the American physicist and philosopher **Sean Carroll** (1966–), who provides a naturalistic account of the apparent fine-tuning of the laws of nature.

"Does the Universe Need God?" (Sean Carroll, 2012)[10]

The clearest example of apparent fine-tuning is the vacuum energy. The value of the vacuum energy is not greater than (and is probably equal to) that of the dark energy, about 10^{-8} ergs per cubic centimeter. Using techniques from quantum field theory, we can do a rough calculation of what we would expect the vacuum energy to be, if we hadn't already measured it. The answer is quite a bit larger: about 10^{112} ergs per cubic centimeter. The fact that the actual value of the vacuum energy is at least 120 orders of magnitude smaller than its natural value is a fine-tuning by anyone's estimation. Cosmologists don't have a compelling model for why the vacuum energy is so much smaller than it should be. But if it were anywhere near its "natural" value, we would not be here talking about it. Vacuum energy pulls objects away from each other, and a value much

---

10 Sean Carroll, "Does the Universe Need God?," in *The Blackwell Companion to Science and Christianity*, ed. J.P. Stump and Alan Padgett (Malden, MA: Wiley-Blackwell, 2012), 189–91.

larger than what is observed would prohibit galaxies and stars from forming, presumably making it harder for life to exist...

In the face of these apparent fine-tunings, we have several possible options: (1) Life is extremely robust, and would be likely to arise even if the parameters were very different, whether or not we understand what form it would take; (2) There is only one universe, with randomly chosen parameters, and we just got lucky that they are among the rare values that allow for the existence of life; (3) In different regions of the universe the parameters take on different values, and we are fooled by a selection effect: life will arise only in those regions compatible with the existence of life; (4) The parameters are not chosen randomly, but designed that way by a deity ...

Have you ever said to yourself: if only I had done things differently (taken the job, not broken up with the girlfriend, etc.), I would be happier now? According to the multiverse model, there may be another version of you in another universe where you did do those things differently. Perhaps there are millions of versions of you, occupying millions of universes. In some you are murdered, in some you win a lottery, in others you are never born.

The multiverse comes to life by combining inflation with string theory. Once inflation starts, it produces a limitless supply of different "pocket universes," each in one of the possible phases in the landscape of vacuum states of string theory. Given the number of potential universes, it wouldn't be surprising that one (or an infinite number) were compatible with the existence of intelligent life. Once this background is in place, the "anthropic principle" is simply the statement that our observable universe has no reason to be representative of the larger whole: we will inevitably find ourselves in a region that allows for us to exist.

In this passage,

1. *Carroll agrees that the laws of nature are fine-tuned for the possibility of life within the universe, and presents another example of this fine-tuning.*
2. *Carroll provides four possible explanations for this fine-tuning, including the designer hypothesis of the theist and the coincidence hypothesis. He endorses the multiverse hypothesis in combination with the anthropic principle.*

11.4 The Problem of Evil

Whereas theists notice the complex design features of the universe and conclude some all-knowing designer must have designed this wonderfully fashioned universe, atheists notice the chaos and suffering in the universe and conclude some all-knowing designer must not have designed the universe at all. The atheist uses this intuition to fashion an argument against the existence of God called the **problem of evil**. This argument can be put in the form of a **modus tollens**, which, as discussed in Chapter 1.5.2, is a valid form of deductive reasoning with the form: if p then q, it is not the case that q, so it is not the case that p. The problem of evil states: if there is a God, there would be no evil. But evil does exist, so there is no God.

With respect to premise two, what proof is there that evil exists? **Evil** can be defined as the occurrence of gratuitous suffering. Suffering is any harm that an organism capable of feeling harmed endures. But it is easy to imagine suffering that is good and worthwhile: Inga reaches her hands toward a hot fire, and her hands start to hurt from the heat. Here she is suffering. But, as a result of the heat, she stops herself from putting her hands all the way into the fire, thereby saving her hands from burning. So, we must specify that the suffering must be **gratuitous suffering**, which means that the suffering occurs and there is no good that comes from the suffering that makes the suffering worthwhile: Inga is burned in the fire, and no good comes of it: she doesn't learn to avoid fires, she doesn't become a better person because of her injury; only pain and suffering result.

There are three types of evil. First, **moral evil** occurs when a person causes gratuitous suffering. For example, the serial killer Ted Bundy caused needless suffering to his victims and their families. Hitler caused needless suffering to millions of Jews and their families. More trivially, every time we harm others by stealing from them, insulting them, or mistreating them, we are the source of the suffering. **Natural evil** occurs when nature causes gratuitous suffering. For example, a flood causes people to drown, a drought causes people to starve, lighting strikes a tree, causing a forest fire to burn down a house with people in it. A cold spell causes people to freeze. There is also **hybrid evil**, which is the blend of both natural and human causes. Flooding occurs because the ice caps melt because humans released excessive amounts of carbon into the air. Children starve in poor countries because of drought, but also because richer nations

When considering the problem of evil, it is important to avoid the fallacy of **appeal to emotion** discussed in Chapter 1.5.4. While suffering is personally painful, and the horrors of the world are shocking, these emotional reactions are not the basis of disbelief in God in this argument. Rather, the problem of evil calculates the unlikelihood of God having a good reason for suffering.

did not send them enough food, and also because humans in this region did not figure out proper irrigation methods. A reporter is swept away by a tornado, which is the fault of the tornado, but also the fault of the daring reporter who put herself in harm's way.

Why does the existence of evil rule out the possibility that God exists? Here is how the American philosopher **Louise Antony**, a contemporary proponent of the problem of evil, explains the issue:

"No Good Reason" (Louise Antony, 2018)[11]

Theists believe that God, this being who is perfect in all respects, has complete dominion over the world in which we live; most believe he created it. But therein lies a problem: Is this world the kind of world we would expect from a perfect being?

The issue is suffering. Our world is full of suffering; it seems woven into the fabric of life. Every sentient being on the planet suffers, some almost incessantly. Physical suffering is entailed by a natural order that requires some animals to kill others in order to live, and all animals, predator and prey alike, lead lives governed by urgent but frequently unsatisfied biological needs. Much of the physical pain we suffer is the result of disease or injury—to which all animals are constantly vulnerable—but some of it is the natural accompaniment to perfectly healthy processes, like menstruation and childbirth. Creatures who are capable of emotion experience emotional pain: terror, sadness, and confusion. Complex psychologies make available new forms of pain: dread, hopelessness, anxiety, depression, guilt, shame, compulsions, hallucinations, and delusions. The human need for social connection makes nearly inevitable for us the searing pain of loss. How can all of this be squared with the supposition that an all-powerful being set things up with the well-being of His creatures in mind? ...

So let's consider the following argument: an Evidential Argument from Suffering: [1] No morally good being would fail to prevent suffering if he or she were able to prevent it, unless he or she had a good reason to permit it. ["No Tolerance Unless"] (2) An omnipotent being would always be able to prevent suffering. (2.5) *Probably* there is no good reason that a morally good, omnipotent being could have for failing to prevent suffering. ["No Good Reason"] (3) Therefore, if there were a morally good, omnipotent being, then *probably there* would be no suffering. (4) There is suffering. (5) Therefore, *probably* there is no being who is both morally good and omnipotent. Let's see how this argument fares ...

---

11 Louise Antony, "No Good Reason," in *The Norton Introduction to Philosophy, Second Edition*, ed. Alex Byrne et al. (New York: W.W. Norton, 2018), 36–45.

When we confront seriously the amount of suffering in the world (fawns dying in fires, children struck with painful illness, adults enduring pointless depression) and consider the way it is distributed (afflictions heaped disproportionately on the poor and the vulnerable), I think the rational conclusion to draw is that there is no good reason for it. A good reason would have to be one that involved a surpassingly important moral goal, where the achievement of that goal required, in a sense strong enough to constrain an omnipotent being, the mass of suffering we see in the world around us. It's not enough for the theist to insist that there *could* be such a reason or to point out that we haven't proved that there *couldn't* be such a reason: the theist has to show us what such a reason might be. And if the theist cannot? Then the Evidential Argument from Suffering succeeds.

In this passage,

1. *Antony argues that the existence of suffering shows that an all-powerful, all-good God probably does not exist. If God is all-powerful, God is powerful enough to stop suffering. (Moreover, if God is all-knowing, then God knows about suffering.) If God is all-good, God should want to stop suffering, unless there is a good reason for allowing suffering. But, given the amount of suffering in the world, it would have to be a very, very good reason.*
2. *Antony argues that as no strong rationale for the presence of so much suffering has been presented, God probably does not exist.*

Objection 1: Free Will Theodicy

Theists respond to the problem of evil by introducing various theodicies. A **theodicy** is a rational explanation for why God would allow evil or gratuitous suffering to exist. A prominent theodicy is the **free will theodicy**, according to which human free will explains how God can allow evil to exist. Imagine two universes: in Universe *A* there is no gratuitous suffering, but humans do not have free will. Ilya thinks about insulting Adil, but her mouth will not speak the mean words, so Adil is never harmed. Chaznee wants to cheat on her boyfriend, but her arms refuse to remove her clothing, so her boyfriend in never harmed. In Universe *B* there is gratuitous suffering, but humans have free will. Ilya thinks about insulting Adil, and her mouth speaks the mean words, but Adil gets harmed. Chaznee wants to cheat on her boyfriend, and her arms comply, but her boyfriend gets hurt. What is better, Universe *A* or Universe *B*? According to the free will theodicy, Universe *B* is better. It is better to be vulnerable to harm but free than be safe but have no control over yourself. So, an all-good God would give free will to humans, but with that free will comes the ability for humans to hurt each other. So, the existence of free will explains how God can exist while evil exists at the same time. Here is how the American philosopher **Alvin Plantinga** (1932–) explains the free will theodicy:

A world containing creatures who are significantly free is more valuable, all else being equal, than a world containing no free creatures at all. Now God can create free creatures, but He can't *cause* or *determine* them to do only what is right. For if He does so, then they aren't significantly free after all; they do not do what is right *freely*. To create creatures capable of *moral good*, therefore, He must create creatures capable of moral evil; and He can't give these creatures the freedom to perform evil and at the same time prevent them from doing so. As it turned out, sadly enough, some of the free creatures God created went wrong in the exercise of their freedom; this is the source of moral evil. The fact that free creatures sometimes go wrong, however, counts neither against God's omnipotence nor against His goodness; for He could have forestalled the occurrence of moral evil only by removing the possibility of moral good.[12]

Most Hollywood love stories involve struggle: the beloved's family disapproves of the lover but love still finds a way; the lover loses the beloved only to win her back again. Most Hollywood characters also have to overcome difficulties: the woman succeeds despite her difficult upbringing; the man is tempted to the dark side but stays noble. Would we even watch movies where everything is perfect and nothing bad or dangerous happens? How about our own lives? Do we want to live lives worth making movies about? Would you prefer a life/love story that strives to overcome struggle, or one that is pleasant and safe all the way through?

God is good, so God made humans free. With free will we can help or hurt others. If humans choose to hurt each other, then humans are to blame, not God. So, the existence of a good God is compatible with the existence of evil.

Objection 2: Soul-Making Theodicy

Free will may explain moral evil, but it does not explain natural evil. A volcano does not freely choose to erupt and destroy the village below, so appealing to free will cannot explain the suffering that occurs due to the volcano. Why does God make nature with volcanoes and hurricanes and freezing winters, when all of these destructive forces needlessly harm persons? Theists usually appeal to another theodicy, the **soul-making theodicy**, to explain natural evil. According to this theodicy, God can just put everyone in heaven forever, with cotton candy clouds to eat and everyone born smiling at each other pleasantly. But such a place allows no possibility of sacrifice, heroism, courage, forgiveness, or compassion, since everything is perfect all the time. And even their inborn smiles are pre-programmed into them, so they do not develop their own virtue. So, God comes

---

12 Alvin Plantinga, *The Nature of Necessity* (Oxford: Clarendon Press, 1974), 166–67.

up with a better plan. God puts humans into a world where nature can destroy people, but in this world people are capable of caring for the wounded and lifting themselves up as well. The world where humans learn how to overcome and carry each other is a world of deeper good for humans, so God makes this world. Here is how the British philosopher **John Hick** (1922–2012) explains this theodicy:

Evil and the God of Love (John Hick, 1966)[13]

I suggest, then, that it is an ethically reasonable judgement, even though in the nature of the case not one that is capable of demonstrative proof, that human goodness slowly built up though personal histories of moral effort has a value in the eyes of the Creator which justifies even the long travail of the soul-making process ... The question we have to ask is not, is this the kind of world that an all-powerful and infinitely loving being would create as an environment for his human pets? Or is the architecture of the world the most pleasant and convenient possible? The question we have to ask is rather, is this the kind of world that God might make as an environment in which moral beings may be fashioned, through their own free insights and responses, into 'children of God'? ...

Men are not to be thought of on the analogy of animal pets, whose life is to be made as agreeable as possible, but rather on the analogy of human children, who are to grow to adulthood in an environment whose primary and overriding purpose is not immediate pleasure but the reaching of the most valuable potentialities of human personality....

How does the best parental love express itself in its influence upon the environment in which children grow up? I think it is clear that a parent who loves his children, and wants them to grow up to become the best human beings that they are capable of becoming, does not treat pleasure as the sole and supreme value. Certainly we seek pleasure for our children, and take great delight in obtaining it for them; but we do not desire for them unalloyed pleasure at the expense of their personal growth in such even greater values as moral integrity, unselfishness, compassion, courage, humour, reverence for the truth, and perhaps above all the capacity for love.

In this passage,

1. *Hick says that a world where troubles occur and can be overcome is better than a sanitized world where no troubles and no overcoming can occur.*
2. *Hick argues that the soul-making theodicy accounts for natural evil. Volcanoes and droughts occur in order to allow humanity to develop richer character traits, such as the ability to overcome, the ability to help others overcome, and the ability to be grateful to others who help us.*

---

13 John Hick, *Evil and the God of Love* (London: Palgrave Macmillan, 2010), 223.

Summary

Questions about the existence and nature of the universe are the biggest meta-physical puzzles of them all. Why does something exist rather than nothing? Ultimately, the answer was given billions of years ago, and no one was around to see it. And why does this universe exist rather than some other universe? The universe is filled with enough wonders, beauty, and complexity that half of humanity can do nothing but marvel at it while concluding that there must be a designer. But the universe is also filled with enough chaos, barrenness, and suffering that the other half of humanity can do nothing but shake their heads at it while concluding that there must not be a designer. In the next chapter we will consider some of the epistemological issues that arise when considering the possibility of God existing.

Key Terms in Chapter 11: God and Naturalism		
Theism	Kalam Cosmological	Natural Selection
Naturalism	Argument	Fine-Tuning
Omnipotence	Fallacy of Composition	Coincidence Model
Omniscience	William Craig	Anthropic Principle
Omnibenevolent	Big Bang Cosmology	Multiverse Model
Creator	Steady State Model	Sean Carroll
Deist	Big Bang Model	Modus Tollens
Fideist	Quantum Fluctuation	Problem of Evil
Agnostic	Model	Evil
Atheist	Oscillating Model	Gratuitous Suffering
Burden of Proof	Naturalistic Argument	Moral Evil
Shifting the Burden of	Naturalistic Cause	Natural Evil
Proof	Physical Causal	Hybrid Evil
Monotheism	Completeness	Louise Antony
Modus Ponens	Ockham's Razor	Appeal to Emotion
Cosmological Argument	Graham Oppy	Theodicy
Ex Nihilo, Nihil Fit	Principle of Parsimony	Free Will Theodicy
Principle of Sufficient	Teleological Argument	Alvin Plantinga
Reason	Telos	Soul-Making Theodicy
Thomas Aquinas	William Paley	John Hick
David Hume		

Philosophy on Television: God and Naturalism

A Serious Man (2009)

In *A Serious Man* (2009), a Jewish physics professor named Larry endures a series of terrible events, leaving him wondering why God allows suffering. He consults with rabbis, but is left unsatisfied as calamities continue to occur. This movie, along with similar plots in *Tree of Life* (2011), presents the problem of evil as an objection to the existence of God.

Bruce Almighty (2003)

In *Bruce Almighty* (2003) God gives his powers to an average person named Bruce, who thinks he can do a better job of being God than God has been doing. Bruce quickly realizes that God was doing a good job all along. Bruce learns that human suffering often occurs because of free will and often leads to the sufferer becoming a better person in the long run. This movie represents the free will theodicy and soul-making theodicy as responses to the problem of evil. Another movie that connects with these themes is *Pleasantville* (1998).

The Theory of Everything (2014)

The Theory of Everything (2014) follows the life of Stephen Hawking, the leading physicist of our generation, as he uncovers the mysteries of the universe while dealing with a debilitating physical condition. This movie presents the contemporary scientific quest to find answers to the ultimate questions about the origin and nature of the universe.

Additional Resources

Visit this book's companion resources for additional materials, including video content and an automated tool for planning argumentative essays.

sites.broadviewpress.com/knowing/chapter-11

Chapter 12

Religious Experience, Faith, and Reason

THOUGHT EXPERIMENT 12.1

What If You Thought You Saw an Alien?

In *Contact* (1997), the scientist Dr. Arroway enters a spaceship aimed at making contact with an alien species. When the spaceship takes off, she passes out and wakes up on a deserted island. She then meets, and has a conversation with, what she thinks is an alien. After the encounter, she wakes up in the spaceship back on Earth, and her colleagues are certain that she simply passed out. She is certain that she encountered the alien, and though her scientifically minded colleagues ask her for proof, she can provide none. Should Dr. Arroway believe that her alien experience really happened? Should her colleagues believe her testimony that she met an alien?

Have you ever seen something truly mysterious, something that you cannot explain even to this day? Perhaps you felt like a ghost was in your house? Perhaps you saw strange lights in the sky? Perhaps something unexplainable happened, like being healed, or having a near-death experience? For those who haven't had such an experience, perhaps you heard someone speak about such an experience, perhaps a friend, or perhaps on a TV show such as *Surviving Death* (2021) or *Ghost Hunters* (2004–) or *Bob Lazar* (2018). These types of experiences raise difficult epistemic questions: how should we interpret the experience, and should we believe it is veridical (i.e., corresponds with reality)? And, if someone tells us they had such an experience, should we believe their claims?

Religious experiences are similar with these types of mysterious experiences, as they also involve experiencing an unusual and supernatural being. What is a religious experience? As discussed at the beginning of Chapter 8, an **experience** occurs when an event happens to a subject and *there is something* *it is like* for the subject to undergo that event. There are different types of experiences, however. In Chapters 7.3 and 8, the focus was on sense experience, or experiences derived from perceiving the world through the senses. In Chapter 9.1 and 9.3, the focus was on experience of the self through introspection. **Religious experience** is an experience of transcendent or divine reality, of God, or of the gods, or a special connection with nature itself, or of contact with something 'beyond'—something beyond the self and/or beyond the material world.

There are two central questions regarding religious experience. First, if we have a religious experience, should we believe that it is **veridical** or not? No one doubts that people have religious experiences, but the question is whether those experiences correspond to the way things really are or not. Second, if someone tells us they have had a religious experience, should we believe their testimony? To the left of this spectrum stand those that endorse the view that religious experiences are veridical, and that reports of religious experiences should be trusted. To the right stand those who say that religious experiences are not veridical, and that reports of religious experiences should not be trusted.

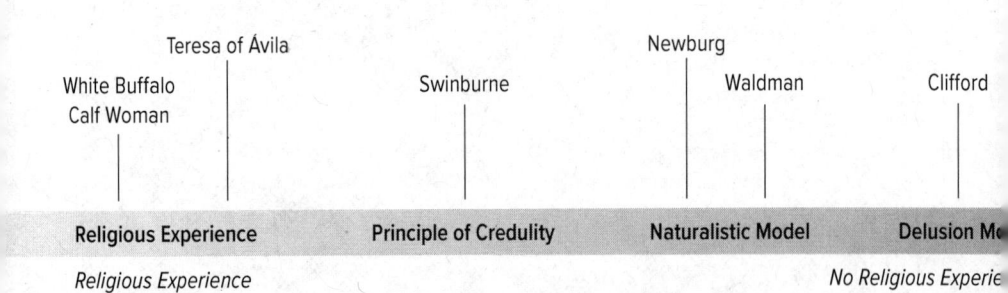

Spectrum 12.1: Religious Experience

In order to get a sense of the subject matter, it is worth beginning on the left side of the spectrum, to define and see several examples of religious experience.

12.1 Varieties of Religious Experience

Various cultures and religious traditions understand God differently, so there are varieties of religious experiences. Some of them are fairly mundane, which means that they may not even involve contact with divinity. American psychologist Abraham Maslow (1908–70) uses the term **peak experience** to describe any moment of self-transcendence or ecstasy, such as a new parent being so caught up in the gaze of their newborn child that their world revolves around someone else, or someone losing track of time because they are effortlessly doing what they are meant to do, or someone feeling like everything is going to be all right and feeling lifted out of their difficult circumstances, or an archaeologist digging up an old cup and feeling connected to the last person who touched it two thousand years ago. These types of experiences might be called, in an extended sort of way, 'religious,' since they involve transcending ourselves and our normal situation; but they do not necessarily involve contact with divinity.

Other religious experiences involve a deity, but do not necessarily include an experience of that deity. For example, a sense of **sychronicity** is a form of religious experience that occurs when it feels as though events just so happen to line up perfectly for us, as though a benevolent being were directing our course. Jasmine suddenly feels thirsty, so she pops into a coffee shop she has never been to before—and she meets her soul mate! The sense of receiving an answer to a prayer or being healed is a similar form of religious experience where a deity is involved, albeit without an immediate sense of the presence of that deity.

There are also religious experiences that involve a deity, and involve an experience of the presence of that deity. **Mystical experiences**, for example, occur when one feels a sense of oneness or unity with all things, natural and/or divine. Mystical experiences can involve deeper awareness of sensory realities, such as concentrating on one's heart beating while considering the life it provides, or sensing one's pure self-consciousness while considering that this is all there is to oneself, or sensing a unity with nature while considering how we come from, and return to, nature. While a mystical experience involves contact with divinity, the distinction between self and divinity is blurred or eradicated. Mystical experiences occur more frequently in Eastern religious traditions, where the divinity is considered an impersonal ground of all being, including our own.

Numinous experiences involve contact with divinity, but the distinction between self and divinity is strengthened. Numinous experience involves a sense of tremendous mystery and fascination in the presence of something wholly other, wholly powerful, and wholly perfect. Imagine standing in the same room as an undetonated nuclear bomb; it may feel awesome and somewhat frightening, due to the weapon's sheer power. Now imagine being told there are ghosts in the room as well. Suddenly you're overcome by an eerie feeling of fascination and mystery due to the unknown. This is what is known as a numinous experience: a powerful (though benevolent) and unknown force suddenly feels present. Numinous experiences occur more frequently in Western religious traditions, where the deity is a wholly other, powerful being with its own personhood.

Here are two different accounts of religious experiences. The first one is from the Indigenous Sioux tradition and involves the **White Buffalo Calf Woman**.

"Ptecincala Ska Wakan" (Eagle Man, 1990)[1]

Before the appearance of the Buffalo Calf Woman, the Indian honored the Great Spirit. But for the Sioux, the coming of Buffalo Calf Woman brought a most important instrument, the pipe, which is now used in all ceremonies. The sacred pipe came into being many, many years ago. Two men of the Sioux tribe were hunting when they saw something approaching in the distance. As the figure grew close, they observed a maiden, attired in white buckskin, carrying a bundle wrapped in buffalo hide. As she walked slowly toward them she sang out and repeated: 'Behold me. For in a sacred manner I am walking.' ...

The good hunter knelt in fear, trembling as the buckskin-clad woman approached. She spoke to him, telling him not to be afraid, but to return to his people and prepare them for her coming. This was done, and the beautiful maiden appeared in their midst, walking among them in a sunwise, or clockwise, direction. She held forth her bundle and said:

'This is a sacred gift and must always be treated in a holy way. In this bundle is a sacred pipe which no impure man or woman should ever see. With this sacred pipe you will send your voices to Wakan Tanka. The Great Spirit, Creator of All. Your Father and Grandfather. With this sacred pipe you will walk upon the Earth, which is your Grandmother and Mother. All your steps should be holy ... All these things are joined to you who will smoke the pipe and send voices to Wakan Tanka. When you use this pipe to pray, you will pray for and with everything. The sacred pipe binds you to all your relatives; Your Grandfather and Father, Your Grandmother and Mother. The red stone represents the Mother Earth in which you will live ...

She walked some distance away from them and sat down. When she rose, she had become a white buffalo calf. She walked farther, bowed to the four quarters of the universe, and then disappeared into the distance. Her sacred bundle was left with the people.

In this passage,

1. *Eagle Man recounts how a sacred woman appears and a Sioux hunter responds with fear and reverence, a reaction that has some of the characteristics of a numinous religious experience.*
2. *Eagle Man recounts how the sacred woman points to the unity of all things, including the unity of the tribe with the land and with their ancestors, which has some of the characteristics of a mystical religious experience.*

---

1   Ed McGaa (Eagle Man), *Mother Earth Spirituality* (New York: HarperCollins, 1990), 3–6.

This second account of a religious experience is from the Christian tradition and involves a first-hand account by the sixteenth-century Spanish Catholic nun and mystic **Teresa of Ávila** (1515–82).

The Life of the Holy Mother Teresa of Jesus (Teresa of Ávila, 1565)[2]

At the end of two years, during the whole of which time both other people and myself were continually praying for what I have described—that the Lord would either lead me by another way or make plain the truth ... I had the following experience. I was at prayer on a festival of the glorious Saint Peter when I saw Christ at my side—or, to put it better, I was conscious of Him, for neither with the eyes of the body nor those of the soul did I see anything. I thought He was quite close to me and I saw that it was He Who, as I thought, was speaking to me. Being completely ignorant that visions of this kind could occur, I was at first very much afraid, and did nothing but weep, though, as soon as He addressed a single word to me to reassure me, I became quiet again ...

Sorely troubled, I went at once to my confessor, to tell him about it. He asked me in what form I had seen Him. I told him that I had not seen Him at all. He then asked me how I knew it was Christ. I told him that I did not know how, but that I could not help realizing that He was beside me, and that I saw and felt this clearly ... I did nothing, in my efforts to make myself understood, but draw comparisons—though really, for describing this kind of vision, there is no comparison which is very much to the point, for it is one of the highest kinds of vision possible.

... One day, when I was at prayer, the Lord was pleased to reveal to me nothing but His hands, the beauty of which was so great as to be indescribable.... Of all impossibilities, the most impossible is that these true visions should be the work of the imagination. There is no way in which this could be so: by the mere beauty and whiteness of a single one of the hands which we are shown, the imagination is completely transcended. In any case, there is no other way in which it would be possible for us to see in a moment things of which we have no recollection, which we have never thought of, and which, even in a long period of time, we could not invent with our imagination, because, as I have already said, they far transcend what we can comprehend on earth.

---

2 Teresa of Ávila, *The Life of Teresa of Jesus*, trans. and ed. by E. Allison Peers (New York: Sheed and Ward, 1960), p. 215.

> **In this passage,**
>
> 1. *Teresa of Ávila reports feeling an experience of the presence of the divine figure of Jesus Christ, and responding with fear and quietness, which has some of the characteristics of a numinous religious experience.*
> 2. *Teresa of Ávila argues that the religious experience cannot be a work of the imagination, nor is it an illusion. She makes this point for, as we will see, some suggest that religious experiences should be interpreted as being illusory.*

What might those supporting the veridicality of religious experience say about Dr. Arroway's claim that she experienced an alien? They may believe her testimony of the experience, and tell her to believe her own experience.

12.2   Religious Experience as Delusions

In Chapter 8.1, the direct realist about perception faced the problem that not all perception is veridical. It may appear to the subject that a dagger is in front of them—but they may be wrong, since they may be hallucinating or suffering from a perceptual illusion. Similarly, religious experience faces the problem that it may not be veridical either. It may appear to the Sioux hunter or Teresa of Ávila that a sacred being is in their presence—but they may be wrong: they may be hallucinating or suffering from a delusion. What reason is there to suppose that religious experience is a hallucination or illusion rather than a veridical experience?

The **diversity of religious experience** counts as an argument against the veridicality of religious experience. Various religious traditions report undergoing different types of religious experiences. The Sioux hunter experiences a sacred woman, while Teresa of Ávila experiences the divine man Jesus Christ. For Buddhists, religious experience involves feeling the impermanence of the self, while Islamic religious experience involves feeling the permanence of the self in an eternal heaven. If different people experience the divine being differently, it seems unlikely they are actually in contact with the divine being. This argument is similar to the relativity of perception argument against our perceptual contact with the material world. Jenn says she met Brad, and he was a sweet man. Angelina says she met Brad, and he was a mean man. The inconsistency in these accounts causes us to doubt that they met Brad at all. The English philosopher and mathematician **William Clifford** (1845–79) raises this objection to religious experience, along with several other objections, in the following passage:

"The Ethics of Belief" (William Clifford, 1877)[3]

The character of Mohammed is excellent evidence that he was honest and spoke the truth so far as he knew it; but it is no evidence at all that he knew what the truth was. What means could he have of knowing that the form which appeared to him to be the angel Gabriel was not a hallucination, and that his apparent visit to Paradise was not a dream? Grant that he himself was fully persuaded and honestly believed that he had the guidance of heaven, and was the vehicle of a supernatural revelation, how could he know that this strong conviction was not a mistake? ...

It is known to medical observers that solitude and want of food are powerful means of producing delusion and of fostering a tendency to mental disease. Let us suppose, then, that I, like Mohammed, go into desert places to fast and pray; what things can happen to me which will give me the right to believe that I am divinely inspired? Suppose that I get information, apparently from a celestial visitor, which upon being tested is found to be correct. I cannot be sure, in the first place, that the celestial visitor is not a figment of my own mind ...

To consider only one other such witness: the followers of the Buddha have at least as much right to appeal to individual and social experience in support of the authority of the Eastern saviour.... If there were only he, and no other, with such claims! But there is Mohammed with his testimony; we cannot choose but listen to them both. The Prophet tells us that there is one God, and that we shall live forever in joy or misery, according as we believe in the Prophet or not. The Buddha says that there is no God, and that we shall be annihilated by and by if we are good enough. Both cannot be infallibly inspired; one or other must have been the victim of a delusion, and thought he knew that which he really did not know. Who shall dare to say which? And how can we justify ourselves in believing that the other was not also deluded? ...

If a chemist tells me, who am no chemist, that a certain substance can be made by putting together other substances in certain proportions and subjecting them to a known process, I am quite justified in believing this upon his authority, unless I know anything against his character or his judgment.... for although I am no chemist, I can be made to understand so much of the methods and processes of the science as makes it conceivable to me that, without ceasing to be man, I might verify the statement ... it is watched and tested by those who are working in the same ground, and who know that no greater service can be rendered to science than the purification of accepted results from the errors which may have crept into them ... Thus it is to be observed that his authority is valid because there are those who question it and verify it ...

---

3 William K. Clifford, "The Ethics of Belief," *Contemporary Review* 29 (1877): 289–309.

No evidence, therefore, can justify us in believing the truth of a statement which is contrary to, or outside of, the uniformity of nature. If our experience is such that it cannot be filled up consistently with uniformity, all we have a right to conclude is that there is something wrong somewhere; but the possibility of inference is taken away; we must rest in our experience, and not go beyond it at all ...

In this passage,

1. *Clifford argues that the diversity of religious experience renders it unlikely that those claiming to experience the divine are correct. He thinks it is more likely that people who have religious experiences are deluded or hallucinating.*
2. *Clifford argues that claims of religious experience fail to meet several other conditions for veridical experience. First, experience is doubted under **non-ideal circumstances**. Chang swears he saw a cow in the field, but it was late at night and far away, so we realize that it could have actually been a horse. Similarly, religious experience sometimes occurs during fasting or under the influence of hallucinogenic drugs, so there is a real possibility that the experience could be mistaken. Second, experience is doubted when **independent confirmation** is not possible. The chemist says he observed salt dissolving in water, and others can verify this themselves, which renders the report of the experience believable. Religious experience, however, is not independently confirmable. A monk has a religious experience of the unity of all things, and Fran does not have that experience, nor does she know how to make that experience happen.[4] Third, the truth of an experience is strengthened when there are **multiple independent accounts** of the same phenomenon. Jared says he went to Australia and saw a kangaroo, and Lyette agrees that she saw a kangaroo in Australia as well, which makes it more likely that kangaroos exist in Australia. Religious experience,*

Psychologist **Sigmund Freud** (1856–1939) argues that religious experience is a delusion based on fulfilling the wishes of the believer: "religious ideas ... are illusions, fulfillments of the oldest, strongest and most urgent wishes of mankind." Many people want to live forever, and many people want there to be an all-loving being, so they posit the existence of God. Do you agree or disagree?

---

4   Sigmund Freud, *The Future of An Illusion* (1927), trans. J. Strachey (New York: W.W. Norton. 1961), 30.

however, does not typically allow for multiple independent accounts of the same phenomenon, as one person may have the religious experience while another has a different experience, or no experience at all, of the divine being.

3. *Clifford says that any experience that falls outside the **uniformity of nature**, or, outside of how nature normally operates, should be met with skepticism. If Fatima reports seeing grey smoke coming from a fire, we do not doubt this experience, as it aligns with the way we understand the world to normally operate. But if Fatima reports seeing rainbow smoke coming from a fire, we doubt this experience, as it contrasts with how we understand the world to operate. Experiences of ghosts or aliens should likewise be doubted, as they involve experiences of unusual beings. Clifford says religious experience should be doubted as well, as we do not usually experience divine beings in the course of daily life.*

What would Clifford say to Dr. Arroway about her claimed experience of aliens? Clifford would say she should doubt that her experience is veridical, since it contradicts what she knows about the world, it cannot be independently verified, and no one else has had a similar experience. She is likely suffering from a delusion, where her mind is playing tricks on her.

12.3 The Principle of Credulity and the Principle of Testimony

While perception faces the problem that not all perception is veridical, there is also reason to believe that experiences of the material world are often veridical, so there is reason to avoid being plunged into skepticism about the material world. Similarly, Clifford is correct that not all religious experiences are veridical, but there may still be reason to believe that religious experiences are often veridical, instead of accepting Clifford's skepticism.

What reason is there to suppose that religious experience is often veridical, rather than merely a hallucination or illusion? The English philosopher Richard Swinburne (1934–) offers up the principle of credulity in support of the veridicality of religious experience. The **principle of credulity** is a general principle about all types of experience, and it states that having an experience that something X is present is evidence that X is present, unless there is some reason to doubt that X is present. This general principle resembles the principle of **phenomenal conservatism** discussed in Chapter 8.2. Shanice experiences the sunshine outside, which is one piece of empirical evidence to support the view that it is sunny outside. Soto experiences his feeling of anger, which is one piece of evidence to support the view that he is angry. Likewise, if the Sioux hunter has a religious experience of the sacred woman, this counts as one piece of evidence that the sacred woman is present. It is possible for religious experience to be false, as it is possible for Soto to not actually be angry, or for Shanice to be wrong about the sunshine. But it now takes evidence to establish that these experiences are false, as there is already one piece of evidence to support their truth.

The principle of credulity has a companion principle called the **principle of testimony**, which says that "those who do not have an experience of a certain type ought to believe any others when they say that they do—again, in the absence of evidence of deceit or delusion. If we could not in general trust what other people say about their experiences without checking them out in some way, our knowledge of history or geography or science would be almost non-existent."[5] The principle of testimony is similar to the nonreductionist view of testimony discussed in Chapter 7.5: that we should trust the testimony of others unless they are proven unreliable. We should trust the testimony of others, or else we lose justification for many of our historical and geographical facts. So, when someone reports having a religious experience, our posture should be to trust that this person experienced a divine being, unless they are shown to be unreliable or deceptive. Here is a passage from **Richard Swinburne** where he not only outlines the principle of credulity, but also addresses some of the concerns raised by William Clifford.

The Existence of God (Richard Swinburne, 2004)[6]

Quite obviously having the experience of it seeming to you that there is a table there is good evidence for supposing that there is a table there. Having the experience of its seeming to you that I am here giving a lecture (that is, your seeming to hear me give a lecture) is good evidence for supposing that I am here lecturing. So generally, contrary to the original philosophical claim, I suggest that it is a principle of rationality that (in the absence of special considerations), if it seems to a subject that x is present (and has some characteristic), then probably x is present (and has that characteristic); what one seems to perceive is probably so. And similarly I suggest that (in the absence of special considerations) apparent memory is to be trusted. If it seems to a subject that in the past he perceived something or did something, then (in the absence of special considerations) probably he did. How things seem to be, that is how we seem to perceive them, experience them, or remember them are good grounds for a belief about how things are or were ...

This principle, which I shall call the Principle of Credulity, and the conclusion drawn from it seem to me correct. It seems to me, and I hope to my readers, intuitively right in most ordinary cases, such as those to which I have just been referring, to take the way things seem to be as the way they are. From this it would follow that, in the absence of special considerations, all religious experiences ought to be taken by their subjects as genuine,

5   Richard Swinburne, *Is There a God?* (Oxford: Oxford University Press, 1996), 133–34.
6   Richard Swinburne, *The Existence of God* (Clarendon Press: Oxford, 2004) 303–04, 315–16.

and hence as substantial grounds for belief in the existence of their apparent object—God, or Mary, or Ultimate Reality, or Poseidon ...

How far are the above challenges available to defeat the claims of those who claim to have experienced God, or Poseidon, or Ultimate Reality? The first challenge may defeat a few such claims, but it is hardly generally available. Most religious experiences are had by people who normally make reliable perceptual claims, and have not recently taken drugs. The second challenge would consist in showing that normally religious perceptual claims were unreliable. If there was a good proof of the non-existence of God or anything similar, then of course that could be done. But the point here is that the onus of proof is on the atheist; if he cannot make his case, the claim of religious experience stands ...

Now, of course, devotees of different religions describe their religious experiences in the religious vocabulary with which they are familiar. But in itself this does not mean that their different descriptions are in conflict—God may be known under different names to different cultures. Likewise a Greek's claim to have talked to Poseidon is not necessarily in conflict with a Jew's claim to have talked to the angel who watches over the sea; it is so only if to admit the existence of Poseidon is to commit one to a whole polytheistic theology, and there is no need to suppose that generally it is ... Admittedly, sometimes the giving of one description to the object of religious experience does carry commitment to a doctrine regarded as false by devotees of another religion. Claiming to have experienced the heavenly Christ commits one to a belief in an Incarnation that an orthodox Jew would not admit. But in these cases, if the opponent of the doctrine can produce good grounds for regarding the doctrine as false, that is reason for the subject of the experience to withdraw his original claim.

In this passage,

1. *Swinburne argues in support of the principle of credulity. If it seems to you there is a table in front of you, this counts as evidence that there is a table in front of you. If it seems to Teresa of Ávila or the Sioux hunter that a sacred being is present, this counts as evidence that the sacred being is present.*
2. *Swinburne addresses several of the concerns raised by Clifford. He rejects the view that religious experience often happens in non-ideal circumstances. Those having religious experiences are not usually attempting to be deceptive or self-deceived, and they are not usually taking hallucinogenic drugs at the time, or under some other poor perceptual environment. Religious experience is independently confirmable, as most religious traditions suggest that all sincere seekers can have a religious experience themselves. Religious experience is confirmed by multiple independent accounts, as many different people within a religious tradition claim to have similar religious experiences,*

and many people around the world claim to have religious experience in general. Religious experience does not violate the uniformity of nature, since many people report having religious experiences, so religious experience is a fairly routine phenomenon of human life.

3. *Swinburne addresses the diversity of religious experience objection. He grants that different people have different types of religious experiences, but he says two different replies are available. First, the **common core** response, according to which all different religious experiences are veridical since they all experience a slightly different portion of one complex divinity. Jenn is correct that Brad is sweet, while Angelina is also right that Brad is mean because Brad is a complex person who is sometimes mean and sometimes sweet. Swinburne notes that this response does not work if the religious experiences are contradictory. Thus, a second response is to say that one religious experience is veridical, while the other is not. Jenn is correct that Brad is sweet; Angelina simply misperceived, or never actually met the real Brad.*

There is a famous Eastern parable of the **Blind Men and the Elephant** that supports this response. Six blind men all touch different parts of an elephant. They all give vastly different reports about what the elephant is like. One claims the elephant is like a snake because he touched the trunk, another claims the elephant is like a spear because he touched the tusks, another claims the elephant is like a tree because he touched the legs. They are all correct, since they are all experiencing different parts of the same elephant.

What would Swinburne say about Dr. Arroway's encounter with the alien? Swinburne would say that seeming to see an alien is one piece of evidence in favour of the view that the alien is present. Since Dr. Arroway appears sincere and credible, she has reason to believe her experience is true, and her colleagues have reason to believe her testimony.

12.4 Naturalistic Accounts

The principle of credulity says that experience of the divinity counts as evidence for the divinity unless there are other considerations calling into question the truth of the experience. One consideration that calls into question the truth of the experience is the possibility that the experience has a naturalistic cause, rather than a super-naturalistic cause. In Chapter 5.2 we considered the view that mental events such as experiences correlate with, or are identical with, brain events. In Chapter 6.1 we considered the view that free will, another mental event, is determined by unconscious brain processes. Perhaps religious experience is likewise caused by, or identical with, brain processing. If religious experience is caused by brain events, this may call into question the truth of the religious experience itself. After all, those having religious experiences believe their experience is caused by the presence of a divine being. If the religious experience is instead caused by brain processing, the truth of the religious experience is questioned.

In recent years, American neuroscientist **Andrew Newberg** and Canadian neuroscientist **Mark Waldman** conducted a series of brain scans on people having religious experiences, including praying nuns and meditating Buddhists. They found that certain areas of the brain activate during reports of religious experience. Here is a passage from their findings:

Born to Believe (Andrew Newberg and Mark Waldman, 2007)[7]

Next to the scanner, a computer screen displays brightly colored images of several cross sections of the brain. Reds and yellows signify areas of intense activity; blues and blacks signify parts of the brain where little activity took place. Although they are not as clear in the black-and-white photographs here, you can still make out the differences in neural activity between the nun's resting state and prayer state. In the accompanying photo, the darker areas in the frontal lobe and language center show increased activity during prayer. Buddhist practitioners and nuns showed significant similarities and differences in neural processing, with the major difference occurring in the language center of the brain ... The nuns and Buddhists both showed greater activity in the frontal lobes, and in particular in the prefrontal cortex, the part of the brain that is just above the eyes. The frontal lobes monitor our ability to stay attentive and alert ...

When I asked the nuns if they wanted to know the results of their scans, I was surprised—they felt no compelling urge to do so. After all, they replied, they did not need scientific evidence to validate their experience—nothing would change their beliefs. They were open to hearing about my findings, nonetheless, so they let me explain. They seemed pleased with my description, but they took the results to confirm that while in prayer they were immersed in the presence of God. I would have worded this differently: while they were in prayer, their sense of God became physiologically real. Clearly, the nuns had a powerful belief system that accommodated scientific data in a particular way. As far as they were concerned, I was taking pictures of the brain 'on God.' The Buddhists, by contrast, used the same information to affirm that their practice helped them to reach a level of pure awareness where they could catch a glimpse of an absolute reality.

---

7   Andrew Newberg and Mark Robert Waldman, *Born to Believe* (New York: Free Press, 2007), 174–78.

This is the interesting thing about our frontal lobes: they can allow a dozen people, all of whom have had the same perceptual experience, to interpret it in a dozen different ways. One reviewer despises a movie; another falls in love with it. A gambler finds pleasure in Vegas; a Puritan finds sin ... Something similar happened to my own research after my previous book was published. Skeptics used my findings to conclude that religious experience was nothing more than a neural confabulation within the brain, and religious practitioners cited my work to confirm that human beings are biologically 'hardwired for God.'

In this passage,

1. *Newberg and Waldman outline how religious experience correlates with brain activity in differing areas of the brain.*
2. *Newberg and Waldman note that this research has different interpretations. For atheists, the interpretation is that the brain causes religious experience, so God is not present during religious experience. In the same way as alcohol or drugs alter brain chemistry and give rise to unusual moods and experiences, or seizures or depression is atypical brain chemistry which leads to atypical psychological states, so atypical brain activity sometimes occurs in other regions of the brain which leads to religious experiences such as feeling the unity of all things, or the presence of some being. But, as drug-induced hallucinations are not veridical, neither are other religious experiences caused by unusual brain activity. For theists, the interpretation is that the divine being causes differing brain activity, which leads to the religious experience. In the same way as sense experience such as perceiving a red balloon or hearing a doorbell ring has corresponding neural activity associated with it without disproving the view that there actually is a red balloon and doorbell present, so the fact that religious experience has accompanying neural activity does not disprove that God is present.*

THOUGHT EXPERIMENT 12.2
Jumping Off a Cliff

During a visit to Africa, you are hiking across rough terrain, and are suddenly aware that a lion is tracking you. You run away, but the lion follows behind you, and your path soon comes to an end at the edge of a cliff! You can see a village on the other side of the cliff. You know you'll be safe if you get to the village, even if the lion jumps over the cliff and follows you. (Lions are good jumpers.) You may be able to jump over the cliff and land safely on the other side, but you are not sure that you will make it. Perhaps you shouldn't try. Should you take the risk, believing you can make it? Or, should you not take the risk, since you are uncertain you can make it?

12.5 Reason and Faith

Another central dispute within the epistemology of religion is whether reason or faith, or some balance of the two, should be preferred. Chapter 1 discussed how philosophers tend to value believing things for reasons, and they seek to provide reasons for the beliefs they hold. A reason, in that context, and in this present context too, means any kind of evidence or proof for a claim, which includes both rational arguments and empirical experience. This emphasis on reasons, as it pertains to the philosophy of religion, leads theists and atheists to provide arguments for and against the existence of God, as discussed in Chapter 11. But perhaps reason doesn't settle the case? After investigating the arguments, theists typically think the arguments for God's existence are persuasive, while atheists typically think the arguments against God's existence are persuasive, showing that consideration of the reasons for/against the existence of God may not settle the issue. Perhaps something else is needed as well. Perhaps faith is needed as well.

One way of characterizing the distinction between reason and faith is to compare the amount of evidence we have for a claim with how strongly we believe the claim. Here is the evidence that Sofia is pregnant: she is two days later for her period than she has ever been in the past, and she has been feeling unusually tired. Here is the evidence that Sofia is not pregnant: she has been trying for two years to get pregnant, to no avail. Sofia, trying to be realistic, decides that this evidence only renders it 20% likely that she is pregnant. Her credence that she is pregnant is 20%, a **credence** being a probability that an individual ascribes to a proposition, where the probability represents how likely the proposition is to be true. While Sofia only thinks it is 20% likely she is pregnant, she nevertheless believes that this time it worked, this time she is pregnant! One week goes by, and her period still doesn't come, so now it is 50% likely that she is pregnant, and she continues to believe that she is pregnant. Three more days go by with no changes, so she gets a pregnancy test which reads "positive," so this evidence makes her 90% sure that she is pregnant. She continues to believe firmly that she is pregnant—and she is very excited by now! In all of these cases there is a difference between the strength of the evidence-based credence and the strength of the belief. This difference is faith. **Faith** usually amounts to going beyond the evidence by believing something is true more strongly than the evidence we currently have for its truth.

Faith occurs in normal circumstances as well as in religious circumstances. The faltering baseball pitcher tells his coach "I can get this guy out," so the coach keeps him in the game despite the coach doubting that the pitcher has any arm strength left. Jen's new friend says "I won't tell anyone your secret if you tell it to me," so Jen trusts her and tells her the secret even though she doesn't yet know if her new friend is reliable. Despite their recent fights, Fernando has faith that his wife is not planning to leave, and his wife has faith that Fernando is not planning to leave. With respect to religion, faith involves believing that God exists, despite not being certain that God exists.

Faith comes in degrees. After two days, the evidence speaks against Sofia being pregnant, but she believes anyway, so a lot of faith is involved. This faith goes against the evidence at this point. After a week, the evidence is exactly mixed, so it makes as much sense to believe she is pregnant as it makes to believe she is not pregnant, so not as much faith is required. After she takes her test, the evidence strongly suggests she is pregnant, so she exhibits very little faith in believing that which is already very likely true. In fact, it would go against the evidence to believe she is not pregnant at this point. The varying degree to which believing by faith beyond the available evidence is encouraged or discouraged is outlined in the following spectrum.

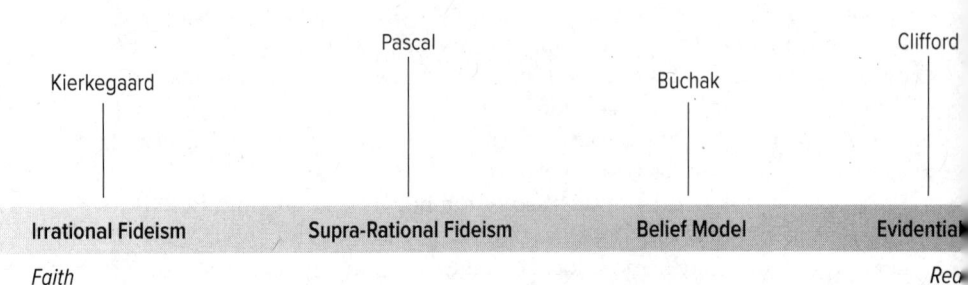

Spectrum 12.2: Reason and Faith

On the left stand those who think that reason is defective in leading to belief in God, so faith must do all the work. On the right stand those who think that faith is defective, and we should never believe anything more strongly than what the evidence supports. In the middle stand several compromise positions, where both reason and faith have a place. Let us begin on the left side of the spectrum, with the fideists.

12.6 Fideism

The term **Fideism** comes from the Latin word *fides*, which means faith, from where the English word fidelity (i.e., faithfulness) also comes. So, fideism is a view that endorses faith in general, and in particular, fideism says that God should be known through faith, in addition to, or instead of, reason. Fideism says that faith is a virtue, so acting on faith is a good thing. Why is faith a virtue? Consider the discussion on phenomenal conservatism. Sally sees a red rose, or hears testimony that koalas live in Australia, or has a religious experience. She can, by default, trust the testimony and believe the experiences are veridical, or, by default, doubt the testimony and doubt the experiences are veridical. The first option reveals epistemic faith or trust. It is not certain that the testimony or experiences are veridical, but Sally defaults to trust. The second option reveals epistemic skepticism. It may be that the testimony or experiences are veridical, but Sally defaults to doubt. Defaulting to doubt makes it difficult to have many beliefs at all and leads to continuous skepticism and suspicion about the truth of everything, so defaulting to trust until there is reason for skepticism may be preferable.

The value of faith is even stronger when considering interpersonal relations. The struggling pitcher says to the coach, "I can get this guy out," and the coach believes in his pitcher, which is considered a good thing. Imagine the opposite case: the pitcher says, "I can get this guy out," but the coach shakes his head and says, "I just don't believe in you." This is not ideal, as everyone wants people to believe in their potential, their promises, their word, or their natural goodness. Or, imagine a relationship founded on doubt rather than trust, where every day both partners must prove that where they went and who they spoke to is acceptable. The relationship would be filled with suspicion and fear, and would need constant re-affirmation that love still exists between them, which is not ideal.

12.6.1 Irrational Fideism

There are two types of fideism. First, **irrational fideism**, which combines the virtue of faith with the rejection of reason. On this view reason is an entirely defective instrument for providing certainty or knowledge, so only faith is useful. Imagine Sofia, who immediately after intercourse just feels like she is pregnant this time, with no evidence supporting her belief. This is belief based on faith alone. Likewise, God, if God exists, abides beyond the universe, so how can human reasoning sort out whether such a being exists or not? Only faith is useful. Here is a passage from the Danish philosopher **Søren Kierkegaard** (1813–55):

Philosophical Fragments (Søren Kierkegaard, 1844)[8]

The idea of demonstrating that this unknown something (the God) exists, could scarcely suggest itself to the Reason. For if the God does not exist it would of course be impossible to prove it; and if he does exist it would be folly to attempt it. For at the very outset, in beginning my proof, I would have presupposed it, not as doubtful but as certain ... I will surely not attempt to prove God's existence; and even if I began I would never finish, and would in addition have to live constantly in suspense, lest something so terrible should suddenly happen that my bit of proof would be demolished ...

As soon as I let go of the doll it stands on its head. As soon as I let it go—I must therefore let it go. So also with the proof. As long as I keep my hold on the proof, i.e., continue to demonstrate, the existence does not come out, if for no other reason than that I am engaged in proving it; but

---

8 Søren Kierkegaard, *Philosophical Fragments*, trans. David F. Swenson (Vancouver: Emerald Knight, 2007), 37–56.

when I let the proof go, the existence is there. But this act of letting go is surely also something; it is indeed a contribution of mine. Must not this also be taken into the account, this little moment, brief as it may be—it need not be long, for it is a *leap* ...

For how should the Reason be able to understand what is absolutely different from itself? If this is not immediately evident, it will become clearer in the light of the consequences; for if the God is absolutely unlike man, then man is absolutely unlike the God; but how could the Reason be expected to understand this? ... In order to be man's Teacher, the God proposed to make himself like the individual man, so that he might understand him fully. Thus our paradox is rendered still more appalling, or the same paradox has the double aspect which proclaims it as the Absolute Paradox ... But can such a paradox be conceived? ... The Reason will doubtless find it impossible to conceive it, could not of itself have discovered it, and when it hears it announced will not be able to understand it, sensing merely that its downfall is threatened.... It comes to pass when the Reason and the Paradox encounter one another happily in the Moment, when the Reason sets itself aside and the Paradox bestows itself. The third entity in which this union is realized (for it is not realized in the Reason, since it is set aside: nor in the Paradox, which bestows itself— hence it is realized in something) is that happy passion to which we will now assign a name, though it is not the name that so much matters. We shall call this passion: Faith....

In this passage,

1. *Kierkegaard claims that reason is defective in knowing God since God is paradoxical. Recall that a paradox is any statement or thing that appears to be contradictory but is not. Since God is so immense, God appears paradoxical to human minds. The paradox arises in the issue of religious experience: different religious experiences appear contradictory to us, so we think they cannot all be true of the same God. Kierkegaard thinks the most obvious paradox involves God becoming human, and God dying, as the Christian tradition espouses. Reasoning cannot grasp such immense truths—as an ant cannot figure out how particles can also be waves.*
2. *Kierkegaard says that in the face of paradox, reasoning falters, so a leap to faith is required.*

What would Kierkegaard say about jumping over the cliff? He would say that we cannot calculate whether we will succeed or fail in the leap. However, safety lies on the other side, so we should just leap, trusting we will make it.

Objection 1: Misplaced Faith

It is virtuous to have faith in someone who truly is the way we believe them to be. But **misplaced faith** is not virtuous, as misplaced faith occurs when we have faith in someone who is not who we believe them to be. The used car salesperson makes a worn-out car sound like the most amazing deal, and Jed just believes him without getting the car checked out. In this case, faith looks like naiveté and foolishness. Similarly, if God does not exist, and people blindly believe that God exists anyway, it looks as foolhardy as believing that Santa exists. One way to discern cases of misplaced faith is to seek out evidence that the person we trust is who we think they are, but this involves the use of reason—which the irrational fideist rejects.

Some theists and atheists, while debating the existence of God, commit the **ad hominem** fallacy discussed in Chapter 1.5.4: atheists insult theists by saying they are delusional or naïve, while theists insult atheists by saying they are immoral heathens. This fallacy is overcome by addressing the opponent's arguments instead of insulting the opponent.

Objection 2: Evidence and Progress

As discussed in Chapter 10, seeking and finding evidence for claims leads to progress in understanding how the world works, which improves our lives over time. To use one example, the miasma theory of disease, according to which disease occurs when one inhales polluted or stinky air, was popular until the nineteenth century. Through scientific investigation and evidence, the germ theory of disease gained prominence, according to which disease occurs because of the transmission of contagious microscopic germs. Without a focus on following the evidence, people would still believe that diseases occur because of inhaling polluted or stinky air. Imagine how the COVID-19 pandemic would have played out without the knowledge that a contagious microscopic virus is causing the disease? People would have taken no distancing precautions, there would have been no one at work developing a vaccine, and many more people would have fallen sick as a result. The immense improvements resulting from seeking out evidence for claims show that the rejection of reason is problematic.

12.6.2 Supra-Rational Fideism

The second version of fideism is **supra-rational fideism**, which combines the virtue of faith with accepting that reason, while limited, is a virtue as well. On this view, considering arguments for and against a proposition is worthwhile but incomplete, so faith is needed as well, as it transcends the limitations of reasoning. Sofia is several days late for her period, so there is some evidence that she is pregnant and some evidence that she is not pregnant, so it is not conclusive. She consults the evidence, but the evidence is not strong enough to prove she is pregnant, so by faith she goes beyond the available evidence to believing she is pregnant. Likewise, the arguments for and against God's existence are helpful, but perhaps they end in a stalemate, with neither result being proven with certainty. This is where faith comes in. The theist uses faith to go beyond the mixed evidence, to arrive at belief in God. Here is a passage from the French philosopher and mathematician **Blaise Pascal** (1623–62):

Pensées (Blaise Pascal, 1660)[9]

Nature presents to me nothing which is not matter of doubt and concern. If I saw nothing there which revealed a Divinity, I would come to a negative conclusion; if I saw everywhere the signs of a Creator, I would remain peacefully in faith. But, seeing too much to deny and too little to be sure, I am in a state to be pitied ...

It is incomprehensible that God should exist, and it is incomprehensible that He should not exist; that the soul should be joined to the body, and that we should have no soul; that the world should be created, and that it should not be created ... Do not draw this conclusion from your experiment, that there remains nothing for you to know; but rather that there remains an infinity for you to know ... If there is a God, He is infinitely incomprehensible, since, having neither parts nor limits, He has no affinity to us. We are then incapable of knowing either what He is or if He is. This being so, who will dare to undertake the decision of the question? Not we, who have no affinity to Him ...

Let us then examine this point, and say, 'God is, or He is not.' But to which side shall we incline? Reason can decide nothing here. There is an infinite chaos which separated us. A game is being played at the extremity of this infinite distance where heads or tails will turn up. What will you wager? According to reason, you can do neither the one thing nor the other; according to reason, you can defend neither of the propositions. Do not then reprove for error those who have made a choice; for you know nothing about it. 'No, but I blame them for having made, not this choice, but a choice; for again both he who chooses heads and he who chooses tails are equally at fault, they are both in the wrong. The true course is not to wager at all.' Yes; but you must wager. It is not optional. You are embarked. Which will you choose then? ... Your reason is no more shocked in choosing one rather than the other, since you must of necessity choose. This is one point settled. But your happiness? Let us weigh the gain and the loss in

---

9   Blaise Pascal, *Pensées* (1660), trans. W.F. Trotter (Mineola, NY: Dover Publishing, 2003), 229–33.

wagering that God is. Let us estimate these two chances. If you gain, you gain all; if you lose, you lose nothing. Wager, then, without hesitation that He is.

In this passage,

1. *Pascal argues that considering arguments for/against God shows some evidence on both sides, and objections on both sides, so neither side is conclusive. Thus, considering the evidence alone cannot settle the matter.*

2. *Pascal thinks the evidential stalemate is solved by what has come to be called **Pascal's Wager**. Does God exist or not? We cannot know for sure, so we are left with betting on what the correct answer is. Should we bet that God exists, or that God does not exist? Pascal thinks that we should wager that God exists.*

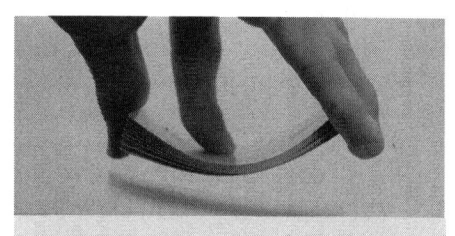

Imagine you are gambling at a casino. Two cards are sitting on the table. One card says "One Million Dollars" and the other says "Nothing." The dealer will point to one of the two cards (he picks each card 50% of the time). If you correctly guess the card he will point to, you win whatever the card says. What card should you guess will be pointed to? Pascal says you should guess the "One Million Dollars" card, because if you are right, you get a million dollars. But if you guess the "Nothing" card and you are right, you win nothing.

What would Pascal say about jumping over the cliff? He would say that we should evaluate our chances of success at jumping over the cliff. However, after evaluating our chances, we will realize that the other side is at such a distance that we may make it, but we may not make it. But, a cost-benefit analysis shows that we should jump. If we jump and fail, we are dead. But if we do not jump, we are dead as well, since the lion will eat us. But if we jump and succeed, we live. So, we should risk taking the jump, as this is the only way to be safe.

Objection: Instrumental Reasoning

Chapter 9.6 highlighted the distinction between **instrumental rationality** and **epistemic rationality**. Epistemic reasons are good, truth-apt reasons to believe a claim is true. Instrumental reasons are self-interested reasons to believe a claim is true. Pascal does not use epistemic reasons to convince us that God exists, but instead uses instrumental reasons when he claims the pay-off is better in betting that God exists.

There are several problems with believing in God for instrumental reasons. First, instrumental reasons for God's existence do not raise the chance that God exists. If Simone believes in God in order to stop her devout grandmother from pestering her, this may be of practical benefit, but it does not show that God exists. Second, theists and atheists often claim that believing in God for solely instrumental reasons is insincere and selfish. Imagine a teenager that only spends time with her parents in order to sweet talk them into buying her a car. The teenager is selfish to think only of how she can benefit from the relationship. The teenager is insincere because she doesn't really want to spend time with her parents: she is just faking it. And how would the parents feel about this when they found out? Similarly, to believe in God for instrumental reasons alone seems selfish and insincere, which God may not wish to reward either. As William James says, "if we were ourselves in the place of the Deity, we should probably take particular pleasure in cutting off believers of this pattern from their infinite reward."[10] Third, as discussed in Chapter 9.6, it is difficult to believe things for instrumental reasons alone. If you were paid $100 to believe an elephant is floating in the air, or that it will rain in two weeks, it is difficult to just believe it for the sake of the money.

12.7 Evidentialism

Given these problems associated with believing despite there being no reasons, or inconclusive reasons, it is worth considering the evidentialist view to the right of the spectrum. **Evidentialism**, as the name suggests, says we should believe a claim only as strongly as the evidence in support of the claim, so it is a mistake to venture beyond the evidence by faith. Sofia is two days late for her period, but she has also failed to get pregnant very often, so her credence that she is pregnant is 20%, and 80% that she is not. She should proportion the strength of her belief to this evidence-based credence, which means she should feel fairly certain that she is not pregnant, but have a glimmer of hope that she is pregnant. After another week goes by, the evidence indicates it is 50% certain that she is pregnant, so she should be equally doubtful and hopeful of her pregnancy. After she has a positive test, the evidence indicates there is a 90% chance of pregnancy, so she should start acting as though she is pregnant but should still have an iota of doubt, as pregnancy tests are occasionally wrong. Once a doctor confirms the pregnancy via an ultrasound, then Sofia should be certain she is pregnant. With respect to God, evidentialism says that we should not use faith to venture beyond the evidence to belief in God. Rather, we should believe in God proportionate to our evidence for God's existence. Most evidentialists argue that the evidence in support of God's existence is inconclusive or weak, so we should either remain uncertain, as agnostics do, or disbelieve in God, as atheists do. In both cases, we should not have faith that God exists.

Arguments in support of evidentialism come from the objections raised against fideism. First, believing based on evidence has a long history of bringing

---

10 William James, "The Will to Believe" (1897), in *The Will to Believe and Other Essays in Popular Philosophy*, https://www.gutenberg.org/files/26659/26659-h/26659-h.htm (2009), 6.

us closer to understanding the world, which helps improve humanity in various ways. Chapter 1.4 outlined numerous personal advantages to believing based on reasons as well, including the fact that what we believe influences our actions, which leads to a happy or miserable life. So, it is best to analyze our beliefs and believe things for good reasons, and abandon beliefs held for poor reasons or no reasons. The case for evidentialism is also strengthened by cases of misplaced faith, where it seems naïve and foolish to mistakenly trust someone or some belief that is untrue. William Clifford provides the following classic expression of evidentialism:

"The Ethics of Belief" (W. Clifford, 1877)[11]

A shipowner was about to send to sea an emigrant-ship. He knew that she was old, and not overwell built at the first; that she had seen many seas and climes, and often had needed repairs. Doubts had been suggested to him that possibly she was not seaworthy. These doubts preyed upon his mind, and made him unhappy; he thought that perhaps he ought to have her thoroughly overhauled and refitted, even though this should put him at great expense. Before the ship sailed, however, he succeeded in overcoming these melancholy reflections. He said to himself that she had gone safely through so many voyages and weathered so many storms that it was idle to suppose she would not come safely home from this trip also. He would put his trust in Providence, which could hardly fail to protect all these unhappy families that were leaving their fatherland to seek for better times elsewhere. He would dismiss from his mind all ungenerous suspicions about the honesty of builders and contractors. In such ways he acquired a sincere and comfortable conviction that his vessel was thoroughly safe and seaworthy; he watched her departure with a light heart, and benevolent wishes for the success of the exiles in their strange new home that was to be; and he got his insurance-money when she went down in mid-ocean and told no tales.

What shall we say of him? Surely this, that he was verily guilty of the death of those men. It is admitted that he did sincerely believe in the soundness of his ship; but the sincerity of his conviction can in no wise help him, because *he had no right to believe on such evidence as was before him*. He had acquired his belief not by honestly earning it in patient investigation, but by stifling his doubts. And although in the end he may have felt so sure about it that he could not think otherwise, yet inasmuch as he had knowingly and willingly worked himself into that frame of mind, he must be held responsible for it....

---

11 William K. Clifford, "The Ethics of Belief," *Contemporary Review* 29 (1877): 289–309.

To sum up: it is wrong always, everywhere, and for anyone, to believe anything upon insufficient evidence. If a man, holding a belief which he was taught in childhood or persuaded of afterwards, keeps down and pushes away any doubts which arise about it in his mind, purposely avoids the reading of books and the company of men that call into question or discuss it, and regards as impious those questions which cannot easily be asked without disturbing it—the life of that man is one long sin against mankind ... Inquiry into the evidence of a doctrine is not to be made once for all, and then taken as finally settled. It is never lawful to stifle a doubt; for either it can be honestly answered by means of the inquiry already made, or else it proves that the inquiry was not complete ...

Are we then to become universal sceptics, doubting everything, afraid always to put one foot before the other until we have personally tested the firmness of the road? ... Shall we steal and tell lies because we have had no personal experience wide enough to justify the belief that it is wrong to do so? There is no practical danger that such consequences will ever follow from scrupulous care and self-control in the matter of belief ... The beliefs about right and wrong which guide our actions in dealing with men in society, and the beliefs about physical nature which guide our actions in dealing with animate and inanimate bodies, these never suffer from investigation; they can take care of themselves, without being propped up by 'acts of faith,' the clamour of paid advocates, or the suppression of contrary evidence. Moreover there are many cases in which it is our duty to act upon probabilities, although the evidence is not such as to justify present belief; because it is precisely by such action, and by observation of its fruits, that evidence is got which may justify future belief.

In this passage,

1. *Clifford introduces the story later known as **Clifford's Shipowner**. A shipowner knows that his ship is worn out, but he ignores his doubts and sends it on a voyage anyway. The ship sinks. Clifford uses this story to argue that it is wrong to believe something on faith that goes against the evidence.*
2. *Clifford describes evidentialism as claiming it is wrong to believe on insufficient evidence. Not only is it an epistemic failing to believe in something more strongly than the evidence suggests, but it is a moral failing as well. What we believe influences how we act, which shapes our friends, family and society, so we have a duty to believe things based on evidence alone. Belief in God is not based on good evidence, so belief in God should be abandoned, which, over the course of time, will purge superstitious beliefs from society and yield a society that reaps the benefits of believing things that are well proven.*

What would Clifford say about jumping off the cliff? There is insufficient evidence that the jump will be successful, so he should wait for more evidence about what will happen—perhaps the lion will forget about the jumper. If the lion does keep chasing, the jumper should jump, though he should not believe he will or will not be successful.

Objection: Life without Certainty

Life often puts us in a position where a choice must be made before enough evidence is available. Should Jasmine go on the blind date with Clifton? She doesn't have enough evidence to know that he is a good man rather than a stalker. If she refrains due to the lack of solid evidence, she will never go on a date in her life. Should Clifton share his feelings for Jasmine at the end of the date? If he hides his feelings, due to inconclusive evidence that she likes him back, then neither one will ever reveal their feelings and they will never fall in love. Should Jasmine marry Clifton? She now knows he is a good man,

Some say that everyone is entitled to their own opinions, since opinions are a personal matter. Clifford disagrees. He says we have a duty to be careful about what we believe since our beliefs affect others. Jones believes "hard work never pays off," but this is not just his own personal belief. Rather, Jones passes this belief on to his children, who also grow up poor due to their belief that work doesn't pay off. Is Jones entitled to his own opinions, or does he have a duty to only hold good beliefs? But perhaps Jones can hold beliefs that don't affect anyone else? Would he have a moral duty to make those private beliefs true as well?

but she still cannot prove that they will have a good life together. If she says no, she loses the chance of having a good life together. Should Jasmine and Clifton have children? They don't know for sure that they will be able to provide a good life for their children, but if they wait, they will lose their chance at parenthood. Should Jasmine return to university? She has to decide before knowing whether there will be a good job at the end, or just a pile of debt. In all of these cases, there is some evidence in support of certain beliefs, but no conclusive evidence.

Evidentialism requires sufficient evidence for belief, but sufficient evidence is not available in these cases, so evidentialism suggests it is wrong to believe on faith in these cases. But this leads to refraining from taking chances that, while they could be mistakes, could also lead to a better life. For these reasons, **William James** argues that Clifford's evidentialism is misguided. He writes:

> *"Do you like me or not?* ... Whether you do or not depends, in countless instances, on whether I meet you half-way, am willing to assume that you must like me, and show you trust and expectation. The previous faith on my part in your liking's existence is in such cases what makes your liking come ... wherever a desired result is achieved by the co-operation of many independent persons, its existence as a fact is a pure consequence of the

precursive faith in one another ... a government, an army, a commercial system, a ship, a college, an athletic team, all exist on this condition, without which not only is nothing achieved, but nothing is even attempted.... There are, then, cases where a fact cannot come at all unless a preliminary faith exists in its coming."[12]

When Clifton's belief, say that his blind date is having a good time, has some but not complete evidence, it would be foolish for him to remain uncertain until all the facts are in. Not only would his hesitation sabotage the date, since his aloofness will dampen the sparks, but the belief that the blind date is having a bad time also lacks complete evidence. If the evidence is somewhat strong but not conclusive, it is more rational to believe than to withhold belief.

12.8 The Belief Model

All of the models discussed so far agree that faith is going beyond the evidence by believing more strongly than the evidence. The irrational fideist thinks we cannot properly evaluate the evidence, so faith involves a leap of trust. The transrational fideist thinks the evidence is mixed, where faith then assents to the claim. The evidentialist thinks that we should follow the evidence rather than have faith. The last model does not think faith amounts to believing something beyond the evidence. Rather, on the **belief model**, faith is a type of belief, where normal beliefs themselves involve accepting a claim that has some support but is not certain.

In order to understand this model, it is helpful to remember what beliefs are. As discussed in Chapter 2.1, **beliefs** are thoughts we have that we agree with or assent to, in contrast with **doubts**, which are thoughts we have that we do not assent to. Jill believes that it will rain, which means that Jill assents to the truth of the claim that it will rain, while Jack doubts that it will rain, which means that Jack assents to the falsity of the claim that it will rain. It is possible to believe some claim while still being less than certain of the truth of that claim. Jill believes that it will rain, but she is not certain that it will rain. Jill's belief that it will rain only requires her to think it is 51% likely that it will rain. Indeed, beliefs are often contrasted with much stronger attitudes toward propositions, such as guarantees. This suggests that beliefs are the kinds of thoughts that we assent to but don't hold with certainty. Jill only *believes* it will rain: she is not certain it will rain, nor does she consider it indubitable that it will rain.

Faith has similar attributes to belief, as both faith and belief involve assent to the truth of some claim where this claim is itself not certain. It is perhaps not surprising that the words 'faith' and 'belief' are often interchangeable. The pitcher's coach leaves the pitcher in the game, saying 'I believe in you, I have

---

12 William James, "The Will to Believe," ix.

faith in you,' which essentially means the same thing. Or, in a religious context, theists are just as likely to say 'I believe in God' as 'I have faith in God.' On the view that faith is belief, faith does not go beyond the evidence to a stronger belief than the evidence suggests. Rather, faith occurs when the evidence itself suggests some state of affairs is more likely than not, but that state of affairs is not certain. Sofia is a week late for her period, which tips the evidence that she is pregnant above the 50% threshold, so she now believes that she is pregnant. Her faith that she is pregnant does not increase the strength of her belief from 51% to 100% certainty, but rather her faith that she is pregnant simply represents the fact that it is likely but uncertain that she is pregnant. Notice that this makes "faith" an everyday and ordinary kind of belief: the belief that your team will win the game tonight, and the belief that vitamin D boosts the immune system. Here is a passage from the contemporary American philosopher **Lara Buchak**:

"When Is Faith Rational?" (Lara Buchak, 2018)[13]

Notice that only certain claims are candidates for faith at all. For example, while it makes sense to say that you have faith that a friend will quit smoking, it does not make sense to say that you have faith that a friend will continue smoking. It is not that you *lack* faith that your friend will continue smoking; rather, this claim is not an appropriate object of faith at all. You can only have or lack faith in a claim that you have a positive attitude towards. Similarly, it does not make sense to say that you have (or lack) faith that 2+2 = 4. You can only have or lack faith in a claim if you're not certain of the claim on the basis of your evidence alone: your evidence must leave it open that the claim is false.

Claims that will be particularly good candidates for faith, then, are claims concerning interpersonal, religious, or moral matters. Take the claim that my friend will keep my secrets. I care a great deal that this claim is true, and my evidence will always leave it open that the claim is false, since she could at any time decide not to keep my secrets. Or take the claim that God exists. Many people have a positive attitude towards this claim—they hope it is true—and while they may have some evidence in its favor ... all of these sources typically leave room for doubt ...

Faith requires a willingness to act on the claim you have faith in without first looking for additional evidence. Furthermore, faith requires a willingness to continue to act, even if counter-evidence arises.... If you have faith that a particular person would be a good marriage partner, you will marry him and you will stick with him even if the marriage isn't what you expected. If you have faith that you will complete your college degree, you will continue in the program even after failing an exam ...

---

13 Lara Buchak, "When Is Faith Rational?" in *The Norton Introduction to Philosophy*, Second edition, ed. Alex Byrne et al. (New York: W.W. Norton, 2018), 116–29.

To be epistemically rational, Anna needs to have degrees of belief that are coherent and supported by the evidence. If Anna's evidence supports a high degree of belief in Bates's innocence, and if her other degrees of belief cohere, then she will indeed be epistemically rational ... Faith does not require either individual to alter their evidentially-supported degrees of belief. More generally, faith does not require you to do anything 'special' with your beliefs: it does not, for example, require you to believe a claim more strongly than the evidence suggests, or believe a claim in the absence of any evidence at all ...

The benefits of the faithful act are apt to outweigh the benefits of waiting for more evidence when you have a large body of evidence in favor of the proposition you are considering taking a risk on, the evidence that you might still encounter is sparse or unreliable, and either postponing the decision is costly or you are risk-avoidant.... We might say: faith guards against unnecessary dithering and misleading evidence ... An individual who commits prematurely is not rational, *but neither is an individual who insists on seeing all the evidence before committing.*

In this passage,

1. *Buchak argues that faith involves belief, where beliefs are assented to because they have some evidence but are less than certain. Faith also involves positive belief, as it is possible to believe, but not possible to have faith, in undesirable things. Kasmir may believe the war will keep waging on, but he cannot have faith that the war will keep waging on. Faith also involves continuing to believe and act on that belief in the face of some counter-evidence. The weather report says it will rain today, so Jill has faith when she continues to believe it will rain today, despite the fact that the morning starts out cloudless.*
2. *Buchak says that faith can be rational, since it is reasonable to believe a proposition is true when the evidence shows that the proposition is more likely than not to be true.*

What would the belief model say about jumping off the cliff? The jumper is 55% sure that he can make it, so it is rational to believe (i.e., have faith that) that he will make it. If, after jumping, the jumper perceives that he may not make it, the jumper should continue to believe that he will make it.

Objection: Openness to Counter-Evidence

On the belief model, faith can persist despite evidence to the contrary, since belief in some claim withstands evidence to the contrary. Eileen continues to publish and search for a job despite repeatedly failing to land an academic position. Despite her present failures, she persists in her wider belief that she will land a job some day. If she does land a job, this becomes a story of perseverance and self-belief through difficult conditions—she kept the faith in herself and her long-term goal, despite the many obstacles. But if she never lands a job, her faith looks foolhardy, given the accumulating evidence against her belief that she will land a job. In religious contexts, Eileen persists in her belief that God exists despite being introduced to the problem of evil at university. So long as she continues to have other evidence rendering the existence of God likely, persisting in her belief remains rational. But if she persists in her belief in God after numerous unanswered questions confront her and her evidence for God's existence crumbles, her faith looks like a stubborn refusal to follow the evidence.

Summary

Fideists take reason to be futile or incomplete, which renders faith paramount, while evidentialists take faith to be foolish, which renders it imperative to proportion the strength of our beliefs with the strength of the evidence. While it is not wise to believe in some claim (whether about God, relationships, or the future) with no evidence for the claim, it is also unwise to refrain from believing in some claim when there is some evidence for the claim. How much evidence the claim that 'God exists' has will depend on where one lands on the arguments for/against God's existence (Chapter 11) and where one lands on the viability of religious experience (Chapter 12).

Key Terms in Chapter 12: Religious Experience, Faith, and Reason		
Experience	Independent	Fideism
Religious Experience	Confirmation	Irrational Fideism
Veridical	Multiple Independent	Søren Kierkegaard
Peak Experience	Accounts	Misplaced Faith
Synchronicity	Uniformity of Nature	Supra-Rational Fideism
Mystical Experience	Principle of Credulity	Blaise Pascal
Numinous Experience	Phenomenal	Pascal's Wager
White Buffalo Calf	Conservatism	Epistemic Rationality
Woman	Principle of Testimony	Instrumental
Teresa of Ávila	Richard Swinburne	Rationality
Diversity of Religious	Common Core	Evidentialism
Experience	Blind Men and the	Clifford's Shipowner
William Clifford	Elephant	William James
Sigmund Freud	Andrew Newberg	Belief Model
Ad Hominem	Mark Waldman	Belief
Non-Ideal	Credence	Doubt
Circumstances	Faith	Lara Buchak

Philosophy on Television: Religious Experience, Faith, and Reason

Contact (1998)
In *Contact* (1998), the scientist Dr. Arroway seems to encounter an alien. Her scientifically minded colleagues question her, and she acknowledges the possibility that she was delusional, but she ultimately remains certain that she encountered an alien. While this movie deals with alien encounters rather than divine encounters, it highlights the difficulty of believing unusual experiences, or the testimony of people claiming to have had unusual experiences.

Game of Thrones (2011–19)
In the TV series *Game of Thrones*, a diversity of gods is involved in the power struggles among different cultures. A variety of religious experiences occur, including the sense of synchronicity (that things are happening for divine purposes), healing, and answer to prayer. Some have faith in the gods, while others think the gods do not exist and that purported religious experiences are delusions. Numerous other movies chronicle how divine forces interact with humans and their affairs, including *Immortals* (2011), *Gods of Egypt* (2018), *Troy* (2004), *Clash of the Titans* (2010), and *The Shack* (2017).

Surviving Death (2021)
Surviving Death (2021) is a docuseries dealing with the religious aspects of near-death experiences. This series explores personal stories of people professing to having had near-death experiences, and discusses the state of the brain during such experiences. This series not only provides examples of religious experiences, but also engages with the question of whether religious experiences have naturalistic causes. Other shows containing near-death experiences include *Flatliners* (1990), *Flatliners* (2017), and *Heaven Is for Real* (2014).

Bruce Almighty (2003)
In *Bruce Almighty* (2003) and *Evan Almighty* (2007), Bruce and Evan, respectively, have a religious experience where they see and hear God. Bruce and Evan both doubt that they have actually had this religious experience—until it becomes obvious that God is speaking with them. Both of their families find it difficult to believe their testimony that the two men have had a religious experience, but they ultimately believe their testimony. These movies not only represent the concept of religious experience, but explore the epistemic attitudes of trust and doubt toward religious experience.

Additional Resources

Visit this book's companion resources for additional materials, including video content and an automated tool for planning argumentative essays.

sites.broadviewpress.com/knowing/chapter-12

How to Write a Philosophy Essay

There are different types of essays. An expository essay aims to just present the facts researched on a particular topic, rather than argue for a certain point of view. A narrative essay aims to vividly recount one's personal life experience or story, rather than present facts researched. A persuasive essay presents facts researched on a particular topic, but also argues for a particular point of view on the topic. Persuasive essays seek to provide the author's reasoned position on a particular topic. Philosophers almost always write persuasive essays, so the goal of the philosophical essay is to convince the reader, through argumentation, of the writer's point of view. Pretend that the reader is neutral and open-minded about the topic: it is your job to convince them that your view is correct. The writer can defend whichever position they wish on the issue, as the professor grades on how well the position is defended, not whether the writer agrees with the professor, or whether the writer endorses the most popular of the available positions. An 'A'-level paper is a paper that excels in all of the following eight components.

1. Thesis Statement

The first paragraph is the most important paragraph in the essay. A good introductory paragraph significantly raises the chance of producing a good paper. An introductory paragraph has three parts: the definitions of the terms that will appear in the thesis statement, the thesis statement, and an unpacked version of the thesis statement called a roadmap. Obviously, the thesis statement is the focal point of all these parts. In fact, the thesis statement is the most important sentence of the entire paper. But what is a thesis statement?

A thesis statement is an encompassing yet concise statement that summarizes the entire paper. It should describe both the issue under discussion, your position on the issue under discussion, and as much of the direction of your argumentation as possible. You may be thinking: how can this be done in one sentence? Fair enough. It can be tricky. But here is one fairly simple formula: "In this paper I argue that _____ (the issue) fails/succeeds because (your _____ main argument)." Here are some examples:

In this paper I argue that Locke's memory criterion of personal identity fails because of the forgetfulness problem.

In this paper I argue that hard determinism succeeds because it aligns with contemporary science and it can overcome the personal responsibility objection.

In this paper I argue that the free will theodicy is a successful response to the problem of evil that theists face.

These examples are all concise (only one sentence) yet encompass the entire paper (the topic, the stance on the topic, some reasons for the stance on the topic). Notice that key terms appear in each of these thesis statements. To use the last example, the terms 'theist,' 'problem of evil,' and 'free will theodicy' all appear in the thesis. For reasons I will describe below, it is important to define every key term before using it. So, your introductory paragraph should have several sentences before the thesis statement defining the key terms that appear in the thesis statement. Here is an example of the beginning sentences of an essay, leading to the thesis:

Theists claim that an all-powerful, morally perfect God exists. According to the problem of evil, God would not allow evil to occur, but evil occurs, so God does not exist. Theists respond with a free will theodicy, stating that human free will is of such importance that it can explain the presence of evil. In this paper I argue that the free will theodicy is a successful response to the problem of evil that theists face.

Since the key terms are defined in sentences prior to the thesis statement, the thesis statement now makes sense to a reader unfamiliar with the issue.

Notice that this format assumes that the essay is a persuasive essay, not an expository essay or a narrative essay. Here is a bad thesis statement, as it outlines an expository essay: 'In this paper I will explain the free will theodicy to the problem of evil for theists.' In a persuasive essay, the author takes a position, and it is important to reveal this position in the thesis statement. Here is another bad thesis statement, as it outlines a narrative essay: 'In this paper I will explain how I have trusted that everything bad happens for a good reason.' In a persuasive essay, the author takes a reasoned stance on the issue, so the reasoning, rather than the emotion or the narrative, should be emphasized in the thesis.

2. Roadmap

If the thesis statement says where the paper will go, the roadmap says how the paper will get there. The roadmap is usually two or three sentences that occur immediately after the thesis statement, still in the introductory section of the paper. The roadmap unpacks the thesis statement, so it actually becomes the structure of the entire paper. A good essay, therefore, not only receives good marks for having the roadmap, but it also ensures that the logical structure (Section 3) is solid. Here is an example of a roadmap unpacking the thesis statement above:

> In this paper I argue that the free will theodicy is a successful response to the problem of evil that theists face. This paper has four parts. I begin in the first section by defining theism, and then I describe the problem of evil (§2). After outlining the free will theodicy in section three, I reply to various objections to the free will theodicy (§4).

Since the thesis shows the several parts that must be present (i.e., parts describing theism, the problem of evil, the free will theodicy, and responses to objections to the free will theodicy), the roadmap shows the logical order to dealing with these parts (i.e., first defining theism before discussing the problem of evil, first defining the problem of evil before raising objections to the problem of evil, etc.). Once the roadmap is complete, the logical structure of the paper is complete as well. You already know that the first section of the paper will deal with theism, the second section of the paper will concern the problem of evil, then you will write on the free will theodicy, and then lastly introduce objections and replies to the free will theodicy.

3. Logical Structure

There is an orderly way to unpack an argument and a disorderly way to unpack an argument. To visualise this, imagine you are flying to the other side of the world with several connecting flights: Halifax to Toronto, then Toronto to Los Angeles, then Los Angeles to Honolulu, then Honolulu to Sydney. A friend asks how you are getting to Sydney, and you say: 'I am getting to Honolulu from Los Angeles.' The friend will be confused. Why are you talking about Los Angeles? Are you going to Los Angeles? How are you getting there? And what happens after Honolulu? There is a correct spatial order to explaining the trip. Similarly, there is a correct logical order to explaining an argument. Unfortunately, it can be difficult to unpack an argument in an orderly way, often because all the ideas make sense together inside the writer's mind, so the writer thinks they will make sense in any order in the paper, or the author has a hard time figuring out which idea relies on which other idea in their mind. It is important to do the hard work of unpacking the argument in an orderly way, as this allows readers to follow along and understand, and also clarifies the writer's view to him/herself.

What is the correct logical order to an argument? One strategy is to pretend the reader knows nothing about the topic—here is your chance to think the professor knows nothing—then explain your view to this naïve reader. With this mind-set, some tactics begin to make sense. First, define a term before using it;

otherwise the reader will be confused about what is going on. This was a key issue in the above discussion of the thesis statement. Second, explain in detail a position before applying that position. Explain the position before objecting to it, otherwise the reader will not understand what you are objecting too. Describe the objection to the position before offering replies to it for the same reason. Provide reasons for why a position fails before stating that it fails.

Fortunately, it should be easy to create an orderly logical structure, as the roadmap already outlines the logical structure of the paper, so you just have to follow the roadmap. For clarity, it may be easier to split your essay into the distinct numbered sections outlined in the roadmap, possibly even adding titles for each section. This helps the reader follow the structure, but also helps the writer stay within that structure. Returning to our example, the paper can be broken into four different sections, each with its own title: (1) Theism (define theism in several paragraphs here); (2) The Problem of Evil (define the problem of evil in several paragraphs here); (3) The Free Will Theodicy (define the free will theodicy in several paragraphs here); (4) Objections and Replies (spend several paragraphs on objections to the free will theodicy, then several paragraphs replying to those objections here).

4. Sentence Structure

Not only should each section, and each paragraph within each section, have an orderly logical flow, but the sentences within each paragraph should also be properly ordered. Each sentence should take one next step in making the argument. For example: 'Theism is the view that an omnipotent, omniscient, morally perfect God exists. Omnipotent means all-powerful, which means that God is able to do anything that is logically possible. God can make rocks float, storms abate, or cancer cells die. Omniscience means all-knowing, which means ...' In this example, each sentence takes the argument one step further. First theism is defined by three attributes, then one of those attributes is defined, then the second attribute is defined, and so on.

It is difficult to make each sentence take the argument one step forward because the argument makes sense all at once inside the writer's mind, so the writer tends to push it all out at once. Here are some common mistakes to avoid. First, do not say more than necessary. You are graded on the accuracy of everything your write, so saying less can avoid penalized mistakes! If a sentence goes off on a tangent (sometimes an entire paragraph is a tangent), then cut these portions out. Imagine travelling to Sydney again. You want to take a straight line to the destination, without wasting time by veering off course. Similarly, when writing an essay, do not veer off course. If your argument is equally strong without an extra sentence, cut that sentence. If a sentence repeats something already said, cut that sentence. If you have already defined a term, there is no need to do so again using different words. Even professional writers often say too much, and this is corrected by editing. Re-reading your paper several times will probably increase your grade by ten per cent, as you will notice many little mistakes that are easily corrected.

Not only must you not say more than necessary, but you must also not say less than necessary. Writers often assume things in their minds without knowing it, so they do not think to write down important steps in the argument. Can you spot the missing assumption here?: 'The availability of shotguns poses a risk to public safety, so shotguns should be banned!' The author assumes that 'anything that poses a risk to public safety should be banned.' This missing premise must be added, then defended, or the argument fails. Another common mistake is to put sentences in the wrong place. If a paragraph focuses on, say, the definition of theism, then that paragraph should house only and all the sentences about the definition of theism. It would be a mistake to define the problem of evil in a paragraph about theism—save the definition of the problem of evil for the paragraph devoted to the problem of evil.

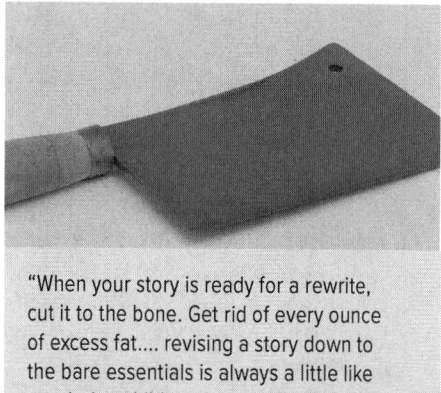

"When your story is ready for a rewrite, cut it to the bone. Get rid of every ounce of excess fat.... revising a story down to the bare essentials is always a little like murdering children, but it must be done."
—Stephen King

Good sentence structure also requires correct spelling, grammar, and punctuation. While texting with friends often involves informal writing and acronyms such as 'LOL' or 'BRB,' more formal writing is required in professional situations such as emails to professors or employers, or written documents. An essay is a chance to practise these formal writing habits. Correct spelling and grammar also make the argument easier to follow, and ensures the argument is read properly. There is a difference between a 'man eating chicken' and a 'man-eating chicken.' There is a difference between saying 'let's eat, grandma!' and 'let's eat grandma!' The sentence 'I love to smell a guy's colon when I hug him' does not mean what the writer thinks—can you spot the spelling mistake? And the sentence 'We will never be apart' is romantic, but 'We will never be a part' is a rejection. Students expect their professor to spell their letter grade correctly, just as professors expect students to spell correctly.

5. Original Ideas

Philosophy essays are persuasive essays, and in persuasive essays students express their own positions on issues, which means that students should formulate their own original positions on issues. This can seem intimidating—how can I, a mere first-year student, have a novel opinion on an age-old philosophical issue? Almost certainly, any arguments you come up with have been written about by philosophers already. But don't let that bother you. Originality is important. In business, an original idea—the touch screen smart phone—can create billionaires. In academia, a paper will not be published if it doesn't state something new and interesting. Similarly, even a first-year essay should contain original ideas. Original ideas (in the context of student papers) are ideas that go beyond textbook readings and classroom material. They're the ones that arise from students thinking through the issues and arriving at their own reasoned positions on issues.

There are several ways to develop original ideas. First, when first confronted with some philosophical view, students usually have a gut reaction in favour of, or against, that view. This gut reaction reveals the student's initial position on the issue. As the professor explains the problem of evil, one student feels this is a strong argument against God's existence, while another student shakes his head all the while. By self-examination, each student figures out why they like or dislike the problem of evil, and then they can write about those reasons. Second, original ideas are also developed through reading about the topic. By reading several different papers on the issue, students figure out exactly what part of some position they have problems with and why. But remember: you must not claim as yours ideas you have read somewhere else. Ideas you obtained from reading them don't count as your original ideas, and their sources must be credited. Otherwise, you commit the academic crime of *plagiarism* (see below).

Originality can take several different forms. Originality often begins with doing some novel research on a topic, such as reading a paper that was not in the course material. Originality can also include developing one's own objection to a position, or developing one's own reply to an objection, or developing one's own strategy for bringing two different positions together. Given the importance of originality, it is acceptable to use 'I' in a persuasive essay, as the writer does present his/her position on an issue. But 'I' should be used formally and in support of the argumentation, rather than informally. And you should be definite, not hesitant, in asserting your position. That is, it is acceptable to state 'I argue X' or 'I will now show that Y.' It is not acceptable to state 'In my experience X' or 'I have felt the truth of Y in my own life.'

6. Accurate Portrayal of Philosophical Positions

A significant portion of every essay simply explains a philosopher's view, or a philosophical doctrine. If the paper argues that the free will theodicy overcomes the problem of evil, then several paragraphs will be devoted to explaining the problem of evil, and the free will theodicy, respectively. If the paper states that hard determinists can overcome the personal responsibility challenge, then several paragraphs will define hard determinism and several other paragraphs will define the personal responsibility challenge.

These paragraphs should accurately describe the philosophical positions engaged with in the paper. The description of the position should be so accurate that an advocate of that position would be satisfied with how you describe it. One way to accomplish this task is to use quotations from advocates of the position described, to ensure that your description aligns with how they define the position. The danger involved in accurately portraying a philosophical view is that it is common to commit the straw person fallacy by describing the position weakly, so it is easier to argue against later. If someone argues that the free will theodicy overcomes the problem of evil, it is tempting to describe the problem of evil weakly and/or unfairly: 'the problem of evil is the ridiculous assertion that God is to blame for everything humans do!' This does not portray the problem of evil accurately or fairly. The portrayal of the philosophical position should be so fair to the position itself that the reader does not know that the author disagrees with it—until they counter the position later.

It is also important to describe the philosophical position in the required depth. It is not enough to spend one sentence describing a position. It is probably not enough to spend one paragraph describing a position. If the position has several premises, separate them and spend a distinct paragraph on each one, providing support and quotations for each premise. For example, spend one paragraph describing the premise 'Evil Exists' and another describing the premise 'If evil exists, then God does not exist.' If the position has key parts that you will disagree with later, be sure to describe those key parts in greater detail at the outset. For example, if the paper argues that the free will theodicy does not apply to natural evil, be sure to highlight the existence of natural evil at the outset.

7. Effective Critiques of Philosophical Positions

After accurately describing a philosophical position, objections to that philosophical position should be raised. Some papers will focus in great depth on one objection, while others will focus in less depth on several objections. Either strategy is fine. In either case, the goal is to hit the target. As an archer tries to take down a target by striking it with an arrow, so the philosopher tries to take down the original position by striking it with a problem. There are several ways of coming up with problems to a position. You can explain how the position leads to an absurd consequence, or explain how the position conflicts with some other truth, or explain how the position is logically inconsistent, or introduce some empirical data that refutes the position, etc.

There are several ineffective ways of criticizing a view. First, it is possible to miss the target by raising an objection that does not pose problems for the view. If someone tries to refute the problem of evil by claiming that the world has lots of good in it, this misses the mark. The problem of evil does not say there is no good in the world; it just says there is evil in the world. It is especially easy to miss the mark if the position has been inaccurately described in prior paragraphs. If someone tries to refute the problem of evil by showing that God is not to blame for everything humans do because they first incorrectly defined the problem of evil as stating that God is to blame for every human mistake, this misses the mark. This is why it is so important to accurately describe the philosophical position at the outset—striking the wrong target is of no use.

It is also possible to miss the target by failing to adequately describe how an objection poses a problem for the view. If someone tries to refute the problem of evil by saying, 'the problem of evil is refuted by the fact that humans have free will,' this does not adequately describe the objection. How does human free will overcome the problem of evil? Which premise of the problem of evil is overcome by the existence of human free will? The author must describe in detail exactly where the objection strikes the position, and exactly how the position fails because of the objection. To return to the archer analogy, it is not enough for an arrow to be properly aimed at the target: the arrow must travel straight to the target and it should be evident that it exactly hits the target.

A position some philosophers have held might seem just silly to you. This may be a sign that you just haven't thought about that position enough—not necessarily enough to make you accept it, mind you, but enough for you to understand how some very intelligent people could have thought that way. Anyway, refrain from calling a position ridiculous or stupid. That doesn't count as philosophical argument: that's just abuse.

8. Quotations and References

An essay is strengthened in numerous ways through the use of quotations. There are two types of quotations. Direct quotations are exact copies of someone else's words placed within quotation marks and properly sourced. Indirect quotations express someone else's ideas in the paper writer's own words, and then properly sources where those ideas come from. Indirect quotations are helpful when summarizing someone's view, while direct quotations should be used when highlighting an important point. There are several types of important points that are worth directly quoting. First, to show that you accurately portray a philosophical position, you can directly quote an author who describes the position you espouse. Second, so that your critiques hit the mark, you can first directly quote an author's view that you later will argue against. Third, any time you plan to interact with an author's view, either by amending or criticizing or endorsing that view, it is useful to directly quote that author's view at the outset.

It can be difficult to integrate direct quotes into your essay. After all, you are suddenly quoting from someone else. How should you show these are not your words? How should you introduce the quotation? Think of a direct quotation as the meat inside a hamburger, surrounded by two buns. The first bun is your introduction of the quotation, where you state the author's name and briefly express what is important about the quote. Next, the meat is the quote, so you write the quotation. Lastly, the second bun is your summary of the important part of the quotation that expresses what you take away from that quotation. Here is an example:

Alvin Plantinga describes the importance of free will as follows: "a world containing creatures who are significantly free is more valuable, all else being equal, than a world containing no free creatures at all" (Plantinga, 1974, 166). In this passage, Plantinga claims that a world with human free will is preferable to a world without human free will.

Quotations should come from peer-reviewed, academic sources, such as books and scholarly articles. There are two online, peer-reviewed academic encyclopedias, the *Stanford Encyclopedia of Philosophy* and the *Internet Encyclopedia of Philosophy*. Most professors accept these sources as well. Internet reprints of peer-reviewed academic publications are also acceptable. Sometimes other Internet sources are helpful and reliable, but because anyone can say anything they please on the Internet, caution is advised. For many professors, unacceptable sources include Wikipedia—which, while peer-reviewed, is not academic—and the professor's class notes and slides, which, while academic, are not peer-reviewed. Print encyclopedias (except for *The Encyclopedia of Philosophy*) are often not accepted—except for gathering facts, such as that Bertrand Russell was born in 1872.

The fact that some renowned philosopher argues for X in a peer-reviewed academic source is *never* an argument for the truth of X that you can give in a paper. This is what makes philosophy writing different from scientific writing, where you can write things such as 'Flisby (2011) shows that all phytoplasmas are gamma-neutral' and that's often enough to establish uncontroversial positions. *All philosophical positions are controversial.* Non-philosophical facts (e.g., 'About 86 per cent of working Americans commute to work in a private car') can be relevant to philosophical arguments, and when they come from a reliable source, they can be taken as established (though they should be properly sourced). Obvious facts ('Pacific island nations contain only a very small fraction of the world population') can be stated without referencing. Don't reference dictionary definitions.

There are several different citation styles, so it is important to correctly cite in the style that the professor requests. Guidelines for various citation styles can be easily found online. Every quotation, whether direct or indirect, requires a proper citation in a bibliography or works cited section at the end of the paper. Different citation styles also come with different bibliographic styles, so it is again important to familiarize yourself with the style the professor requires. It is very important to avoid plagiarism when interacting with the work of others. Plagiarism occurs when the writer uses the *ideas or words* of another person in their essay without referencing that other person. The quickest way to score an 'F' on a paper—and there can be more serious consequences—is to plagiarize, so it should be avoided at all costs. Every university has a detailed plagiarism policy, so it is important to familiarize yourself with your university's policy.

If your paper excels in all eight of the areas outlined above, it will be well on its way to earning an 'A' grade.

Bibliography

Adams, D., and M. Carwardine. *Last Chance to See*. London: Pan Books, 1991.

Anscombe, Elizabeth, and J. Körner. "Substance." *Aristotelian Society Supplementary Volume* 38, no. 1 (1964): 69–90.

Antony, Louise. "No Good Reason." In *The Norton Introduction to Philosophy, Second Edition*, edited by Alex Byrne et al., 36–46. New York: W.W. Norton, 2018.

Aquinas, Thomas. *Summa Theologiae, Volume 2* (1273). Translated by T. McDermott. Cambridge: Cambridge University Press, 2006.

Aristotle. In *Readings in Ancient Greek Philosophy: Fourth Edition*, edited by S. Mark Cohen, Patricia Curd, and C.D.C. Reeve. Indianapolis: Hackett, 2011: *Physics* 714–32, *De Anima* 847–69, *Metaphysics* 796–846, *Posterior Analytics* 714–31, single sentence quoted from *Rhetoric* 65.

——. *Nicomachean Ethics*. Translated by F. Peters. London: Kegan Paul, 1893. https://oll.libertyfund.org/title/peters-the-nicomachean-ethics.

——. *On the Heavens*. In *Complete Works of Aristotle: Volume 1*, edited by J. Barnes, translated by J.L. Stocks, 447–512. Princeton: Princeton University Press, 2014.

Armstrong, David. *The Mind-Body Problem: An Opinionated Introduction*. New York: Routledge, 2018.

Ayer, A.J. "Freedom and Necessity." In *Philosophical Essays*, 271–84. London: Macmillan, 1954.

——. "Verification and Experience." *Proceedings of the Aristotelian Society* 37, no. 1 (1937), 137–39.

Bacon, Francis. *The New Organon* (1620). Edited by Fulton H. Anderson. New York: Liberal Arts Press, 1960.

Baier, Annette. "Cartesian Persons." *Philosophia* 10, nos. 3–4 (1981): 169–88.

Berkeley, George. *A Treatise Concerning the Principles of Human Knowledge* (1710). Edited by C. Krauth. Philadelphia: Lippincott, 1874.

Blanshard, Brand. *The Nature of Thought: Vol. 2*. Norwich: Jarrold and Sons Limited, 1921. https://archive.org/details/in.ernet.dli.2015.149115/.

Bloom, Paul. *The Sweet Spot: The Pleasures of Suffering and the Search for Meaning*. New York: HarperCollins, 2021.

Buchak, Lara. "When Is Faith Rational?" In *The Norton Introduction to Philosophy, Second Edition*, edited by Alex Byrne et al., 116–29. New York: W.W. Norton, 2018.

Carroll, Sean. "Does the Universe Need God?" In *The Blackwell Companion to Science and Christianity*, edited by J.P. Stump and Alan Padgett, 185–96. Malden, MA: Wiley-Blackwell, 2012.

Chalmers, David. *The Conscious Mind*. Oxford: Oxford University Press, 1996.

Churchland, Paul. *Matter and Consciousness*. Cambridge, MA: MIT Press, 1984.

Clifford, William K. "The Ethics of Belief." *Contemporary Review* 29 (1877): 1–5.

Cohen, S. Mark, Patricia Curd, and C.D.C. Reeve, editors. *Readings in Ancient Greek Philosophy: Fourth Edition*. Indianapolis: Hackett, 2011.

Craig, William Lane. "Design and the Anthropic Fine-tuning of the Universe." In *God and Design*, edited by Neil Manson, 155–77. London: Routledge, 2003.

——. "The Kalam Cosmological Argument." In *Philosophy of Religion*, edited by W. Craig et al., 92–113. New Brunswick: Rutgers University Press, 2002.

d'Holbach, Baron (Paul-Henri Thiry). "Of the System of Man's Free Agency." In *The System of Nature* (1770), translated by H.D. Robinson, Volume 1, Chapter XI, 88–102. Boston: J.P. Mendum, 1868.

Darrow, Clarence. *The Plea of Clarence Darrow*. Chicago: Ralph Fletcher Seymour, 1924.

Darwin, Charles. *On the Origin of Species by Means of Natural Selection*. Revised Edition. New York: D. Appleton, 1869.

Descartes, René. Letter to Princess Elizabeth, 21 May 1643. In *Oeuvres de Descartes: Volume 3*, edited by C. Adam, and P. Tannery, 663–82. Paris: Vrin, 1996.

——. *Meditations on First Philosophy*. Translated by Ian Johnston, edited by Andrew Bailey. Peterborough: Broadview Press, 2013.

——. *Passions of the Soul* (1649). Translated by Jonathan Bennett, https://www.earlymoderntexts.com/authors/descartes.

——. *The Philosophical Works of Descartes, Volume 1*. Translated by E. Haldane and G. Ross. New York: Dover, 1955.

Diogenes Laertius. *Diogenes Laertius: Lives of Eminent Philosophers*. Translated by R. Hicks. Cambridge: Harvard University Press, 1991.

Evans, Gareth. *The Varieties of Reference*. Oxford: Oxford University Press, 1982.

Fleming, Noel. "The Tree in the Quad." *American Philosophical Quarterly* 22 (1984): 22–36.

Fodor, Jerry. "The Mind-Body Problem." *Scientific American* 244, no. 1 (1981): 114–23.

Frankfurt, Harry. "Freedom of the Will and the Concept of a Person." *The Journal of Philosophy* 68, no. 1 (1971): 5–20.

Frege, Gottlob. "The Thought: A Logical Inquiry." *Mind* 65, no. 259 (1956): 289–311.

Freud, Sigmund. *The Future of An Illusion* (1927). Translated by J. Strachey. New York: W.W. Norton, 1961.

Galilei, Galileo. "The Assayer" (1623). In *Discoveries and Opinions of Galileo*, translated by S. Drake, 231–80. Garden City: Doubleday, 1957.

Gertler, Brie. "Renewed Acquaintance." In *Introspection and Consciousness*, edited by Declan Smithies and Daniel Stoljar, 89–123. Oxford: Oxford University Press, 2012.

Haack, Susan. "Post 'Post-Truth': Are We There Yet?" *Theoria* 85, no. 4 (2019): 258–75.

Harlow, John M. "Recovery from the Passage of an Iron Bar through the Head." *Publications of the Massachusetts Medical Society* 2, no. 3 (1868): 327–47.

Harris, Sam. *Free Will*. New York: Simon and Schuster, 2012.

Hawley, Katherine. *How Things Persist*. Oxford: Clarendon Press, 2002.

Hempel, Carl. "On the Logical Positivists' Theory of Truth." *Analysis* 2, no. 4 (1934): 49–59.

Heraclitus Homericus. "Homeric Questions." In *Philosophic Classics: Ancient Philosophy, Volume I*, edited by Forrest Baird. London: Routledge, 2019.

Heraclitus. "Fragments." In *Readings in Ancient Greek Philosophy: Fourth Edition*, edited by S. Mark Cohen, Patricia Curd, and C.D.C. Reeve, 19–25. Indianapolis: Hackett, 2011.

Herodotus. *The History of Herodotus*. Translated by H. Cary. London: Henry Bohn, 1848.

———. *The History of Herodotus*. Translated by G. Rawlinson. http://classics.mit.edu/Herodotus/history.3.iii.html.

Hick, John. *Evil and the God of Love*. London: Palgrave Macmillan, 2010.

Hobbes, Thomas. *Leviathan* (1651). In *The Broadview Anthology of Social and Political Thought, Volume 1: From Plato to Nietzsche*, edited by Andrew Bailey et al., 413–90. Peterborough: Broadview Press, 2008.

Homer. *The Iliad*. Translated by S. Butler. New York: Longmans, Green and Co, 1898.

Horsey, Richard. "The Art of Chicken Sexing." *UCL Working Papers in Linguistics* 14 (2002): 107–17.

Hume, David. *A Treatise of Human Nature* (1739). Book 1.1.6 and Book 1.4.6, in *Readings on Human Nature*, edited by Peter Lopston, 365–77. Peterborough: Broadview Press, 1998.

———. *Dialogues Concerning Natural Religion* (1779). Edited by R. Popkin. Indianapolis: Hackett, 1988.

———. *An Enquiry Concerning Human Understanding* (1748). In *The Broadview Introduction to Philosophy*, edited by Andrew Bailey, 276–89. Peterborough: Broadview Press, 2019.

James, William. "The Will to Believe" (1897). In *The Will to Believe and Other Essays in Popular Philosophy*, https://www.gutenberg.org/files/26659/26659-h/26659-h.htm, 2009), 1–31.

———. *Pragmatism: A New Name for Some Old Ways of Thinking* (1907). In *William James: Writings 1902-1910*, edited by Bruce Kuklick, 479–625. New York: The Library of America, 1988.

Kane, Robert. *A Contemporary Introduction to Free Will*. Oxford: Oxford University Press 2002.

Kant, Immanuel. *The Critique of Pure Reason* (1787). Translated by N. Smith. Hampshire, UK: Palgrave Macmillan, 2007.

Kierkegaard, Søren. *Philosophical Fragments* (1844). Translated by David F. Swenson. Vancouver: Emerald Knight, 2007.

Kim, Jaegwon. "What Is Naturalized Epistemology?" In *Philosophical Perspectives, Vol. 2*, edited by James Tomberlin, 381–405. Atascadero, CA: Ridgeview Publishing, 1988.

Kurthy, Miklos, Holly Lawford-Smith, and Paulo Sousa. "Does Ought Imply Can?" *PloS One* 12, no. 4 (2017): 1–24.

Lackey, Jennifer. "Testimony: Acquiring Knowledge from Others." In *Social Epistemology*, edited by Alvin Goldman and Dennis Whitcomb, 71–91. Oxford: Oxford University Press, 2011.

Leibniz, Gottfried. *Principles of Nature and Grace*. In *The Monadology and Other Philosophical Writings*, translated by Robert Latta, 405–24. Oxford: Clarendon Press, 1898.

Libet, Benjamin. "The Neural Time-Factor in Perception, Volition, and Free Will." *Revue de Métaphysique et de Morale* 97, no. 2 (1992): 255–72.

Locke, John. *An Essay Concerning Human Understanding* (1689). London: Routledge and Sons, 1894.

Longino, Helen. "Can There Be a Feminist Science?" *Hypatia* 2, no. 3 (1987): 51–64.

Ma, Xiao-Song et al. "Quantum Teleportation Over 143 Kilometres Using Active Feed-Forward." *Nature* no. 489 (2012): 269–73.

Mahapunnama Sutta. "The Greater Discourse on the Full-moon Night," http://www.suttas.com/mn-109-mahapunnama-sutta-the-greater-discourse-on-the-full-moon-night.html.

McGaa, Ed (Eagle Man). *Mother Earth Spirituality*. New York: HarperCollins, 1990.

Mele, Alfred R. *Self-Deception Unmasked*. Princeton: Princeton University Press, 2001.

Newberg, Andrew, and Mark Robert Waldman. *Born to Believe*. New York: Free Press, 2007.

Newton, Isaac. *The Mathematical Principles of Natural Philosophy*. Translated by Andrew Motte. New York: Daniel Adee, 1846.

Nichols, Shaun, and Joshua Knobe. "Moral Responsibility and Determinism." *Nous* 41, no. 4 (2007): 663–85.

Nisbett, Richard E., and Timothy DeCamp Wilson. "Telling More Than We Can Know: Verbal Reports on Mental Processes." *Psychological Review* 84 (1977): 231–59.

Oppy, Graham. "An Argument for Atheism from Naturalism." In *Philosophy for Us*, edited by Lenny Clapp, 3–14. San Diego: Cognella, 2018.

Paley, William. *Natural Theology*. London: Wilks and Taylor, 1802.

Parfit, Derek. "Personal Identity." *The Philosophical Review* 80, no. 1 (1971): 3–27.

Parmenides. *The Proem*. In *Readings in Ancient Greek Philosophy, Fourth Edition*, edited by S. Mark Cohen, Patricia Curd, and C.D.C. Reeve, 40–46. Indianapolis: Hackett, 2011.

Pascal, Blaise. *Pensées* (1660). Translated by W.F. Trotter. Mineola NY: Dover Publishing, 2003.

Pereboom, Derk. *Living without Free Will*. Oxford: Oxford University Press, 2004.

Plantinga, Alvin. *The Nature of Necessity*. Oxford: Clarendon Press, 1974.

Plato. *Apology*. In *The Apology and Related Dialogues*, edited by Andrew Bailey, translated by Cathal Woods. Peterborough: Broadview Press, 2016.

——. *Cratylus*. In *Plato: Complete Works*, edited by John M. Cooper, translated by C.D.C. Reeve, 101–56. Indianapolis: Hackett, 1997.

——. In *Readings in Ancient Greek Philosophy: Fourth Edition*, edited by Mark Cohen, Patricia Curd, and C.D.C. Reeve: *Phaedo*, 267–319, *Symposium*, 353–54, *Theaetetus*, 11. Indianapolis: Hackett, 2011.

Plutarch. *The Parallel Lives: Volume 1: The Life of Theseus*. Translated by Bernadotte Perrin. Cambridge: Loeb Classical Library, 1914.

——. *Plutarch's Morals: Volume 5*. Edited by W. Goodwin. Boston: Little Brown and Company, 1878.

Quine, W.V.O. "Epistemology Naturalized." In *Ontological Relativity and Other Essays*, 69–90. New York: Columbia University Press, 1969.

——. "Two Dogmas of Empiricism." *The Philosophical Review* 60, no. 1 (1951): 20–43.

Reid, Thomas. *Essays on the Intellectual Powers of Man* (1788). Edited by J. Walker. Boston: Phillips, Sampson and Company, 1857.

——. *Essays on the Active Powers of Man* (1788). Edited by Jonathan Bennett, https://www.earlymoderntexts.com/authors/reid.

Rorty, Richard. "Solidarity or Objectivity." In *Objectivity, Relativism, and Truth: Philosophical Papers, Volume 1*, 21–34. Cambridge: Cambridge University Press, 1991.

Rumi, Jalalu'ddin. *Masnawi*. Edited by Reza Nazari and Somayeh Nazari, translated by Reynald A. Nicholson, www.learnpersianonline.com.

Russell, Bertrand. *The Problems of Philosophy* (1912). Oxford: Oxford University Press, 2001.

Ryle, Gilbert. *The Concept of Mind*, 1949. London: Routledge, 2009.

Schellenberg, Susanna. "The Particularity and Phenomenology of Perceptual Experience." *Philosophical Studies* 149, no. 1 (2010): 19–48.

Searle, John. "Minds, Brains, and Programs." *The Behavioral and Brain Sciences* 3, no. 3 (1980): 417–57.

Sextus Empiricus. *Outlines of Pyrrhonism, Book I*. Translated by R. Bury. Cambridge: Harvard University Press, 1933.

Silver, David, and Demis Hassabis. "AlphaGo Zero: Starting from Scratch," https://deepmind.com/blog/article/alphago-zero-starting-scratch.

Skinner, B.F. *About Behaviorism*. New York: Random House, 1976.

Smart, J.J.C. "Sensations and Brain Processes." *The Philosophical Review* 68, no. 2 (1959): 141–56.

Smilansky, Saul. "Free Will, Fundamental Dualism and the Centrality of Illusion." In *The Oxford Handbook of Free Will*, edited by Robert H. Kane, 489–505. Oxford: Oxford University Press, 2002.

Sokal, Alan, and Jean Bricmont. *Intellectual Impostures*. London: Profile Books, 1998.

Svenson, Ola. "Are We All Less Risky and More Skillful Than Our Fellow Drivers?" *Acta Psychologica* 47, no. 2 (1981): 143–48.

Swinburne, Richard. *Is There a God?* Oxford: Oxford University Press, 1996.

Teresa of Ávila. *The Life of Teresa of Jesus*. Translated and edited by E. Allison Peers. New York: Sheed and Ward, 1960, http://www.carmelitemonks.org/Vocation/teresa_life.pdf.

Thagard, Paul. "Coherence, Truth and the Development of Scientific Knowledge." *Philosophy of Science* 74, no. 1 (2007): 28–47.

Tolstoy, Leo. *Confessions*. Translated by Aylmer Maude. Mineola: Dover Publications, 2005.

van Inwagen, Peter. *An Essay on Free Will*. Oxford: Clarendon Press, 1983.

Vohs, Kathleen D., and Jonathan W. Schooler. "The Value of Believing in Free Will." *Psychological Science* 19, no. 1 (2008): 49–54.

Whitehead, Alfred North. *Process and Reality* (1929). Edited by David Ray Griffin and Donald Sherburne. New York: The Free Press, 1978.

Wittgenstein, Ludwig. *Philosophical Investigations*. Translated by G.E.M. Anscombe. Oxford: Basil Blackwell, 1958.

Yeats, William Butler. *The Collected Poems of W. B. Yeats*. Edited by Richard J. Finneran. New York: Macmillan, 1991.

Permissions
Acknowledgements

Baron d'Holbach (Paul Henri Thiery). From Chapter XI: "Of the System of Man's Free Agency," [excerpted] *The System of Nature, Volume 1* (1770), trans. H. Robinson, Kitchener: Batoche Books, 2001, LXI..

Berkeley, George. From "Of the Principles of Human Knowledge," *A Treatise Concerning the Principles of Human Knowledge* [excerpted, pp. 193–99]. Urbana, IL: Project Gutenberg, https://www.gutenberg.org/ebooks/4723.

Bhikkhu Ñāṇamoli (translator). MN 109: "The Great Full-Moon Night Discourse," [Mahāpunnama Sutta] [excerpted] from *The Middle Length Discourses of the Buddha, A Translation of the Majjhima Nikāya*, edited and revised by Bhikkhu Bodhi, Wisdom Publications, 1995. Copyright © 1995, 2015 Bhikkhu Bodhi. Reprinted by arrangement with Wisdom Publications, Inc., wisdompubs.org.

Blanshard, Brand. From *The Nature of Thought: Vol. 2*, Norwich: Jarrold and Sons Limited, 1921. [excerpted, pp. 264–76]

Buchak, Lara. "When Is Faith Rational?" from *The Norton Introduction to Philosophy, Second edition*, eds. Gideon Rosen, et al., New York: W.W. Norton, 2018. Copyright © 2018, 2015 by W.W. Norton & Company, Inc. [abridged, pp. 116–29] Reprinted by permission of W.W. Norton & Company, Inc.

Carroll, Sean. From Chapter 17, Part IV: Cosmology and Physics, "Does the Universe Need God?," *The Blackwell Companion to Science and Christianity*, eds. J.B. Stump and Alan Padgett. Malden MA: Wiley-Blackwell, 2012. Copyright © 2012 Blackwell Publishing. [excerpted, pp. 189–91] Reprinted by permission of John Wiley & Sons, Inc., conveyed through Copyright Clearance Center, Inc.

Chalmers, David. From Chapter 3: "Can Consciousness Be Reductively Explained?," *The Conscious Mind*, Oxford University Press, 1996. Copyright © 1996 David J. Chalmers. [excerpted, pp. 94–103] Reprinted by permission of Oxford University Press conveyed through Copyright Clearance Center, Inc.

Clifford, William K. From "The Ethics of Belief," *Contemporary Review*, 29 (1877): 289–309 [excerpted]. London: Strahan and Company, Limited, 1877.

Cohen, S. Marc, Patricia Curd, and C.D.C Reeve (editors). Excerpts from "Fragments," by Heraclitus Homericus [pp. 30–40]; from "The Proem," by Parmenides [pp. 43–45]; from Chapter 14: The Sophists, Protagoras (14.1), Prodicus, Hippias (14.4), Antiphon (14.5) [pp. 105–06, 113–15]; from "De Anima," "Physics Book 1," and "Posterior Analytics II.19," by Aristotle [pp. 734–78, 741, 861–62, 864]; of *Readings in Ancient Greek Philosophy: Fourth Edition*, Hackett Publishing Company. Copyright © 2011

Hawley, Katherine. From Chapter 1: "Sameness and Difference," *How Things Persist*, Clarendon Press, 2002. Copyright © 2001 Katherine Hawley. [excerpted, pp. 9–12] Reprinted by permission of Oxford University Press through PLSclear.

Hick, John. From "The Irenaean Type of Theodicy in Schleiermacher," *Evil and the God of Love*, published by The Macmillan Press Ltd (1966, 1977, 1985). Copyright © 1966, 1977, 1985 John Hick. [excerpted, p. 223] Reprinted by permission of Springer Nature, conveyed through Copyright Clearance Center, Inc. http://www.springernature.com.

Hume, David. From *Dialogues Concerning Natural Religion, Second Edition*, ed. Richard H. Popkin, Indianapolis: Hackett Publishing Company, 1988. Second edition copyright © 1998 by Hackett Publishing Company, Inc. [excerpted, pp. 54–57] Reprinted by permission of Hackett Publishing Company, Inc. All rights reserved. From *An Enquiry Concerning Human Understanding* (1748), in *The Broadview Introduction to Philosophy*, ed. Andrew Bailey. Peterborough: Broadview Press, 2019. Copyright © 2019 Andrew Bailey. [excerpted, pp. 280–81, 282, 284] From "A Treatise of Human Nature," *Readings on Human Nature*, ed. Peter Lopston. Peterborough: Broadview Press, 1998. Copyright © 1998 Peter Loptson. [excerpted, pp. 365–66, 367]

James, William. From *Pragmatism: A New Name for Some Old Ways of Thinking* (1907), *William James: Writings 1902–1910*, ed. Bruce Kuklick, New York: The Library of America, 1988, Lectures II and VI.

Kane, Robert. From *A Contemporary Introduction to Free Will*, Oxford University Press, 2005. Copyright © 2005 Oxford University Press. [excerpted, pp. 130–37] Reprinted by permission of Oxford University Press conveyed through Copyright Clearance Center, Inc.

Kant, Immanuel. From *The Critique of Pure Reason*, trans. J.M.D. Meiklejohn (1855), published by G. Bell (1878), Chapter I, Section 2. [excerpted, pp. 2–4, 465–66].

Kierkegaard, Søren [Johannes Climacus]. From *Philosophical Fragments*, trans. David F. Swenson, rev. Howard V. Hong. Originally published by Princeton University Press; reprinted by Emerald Knight Publishing, 2007. Copyright © 1985 Howard V. Hong. [excerpted, pp. 37–56] Reprinted by permission of Princeton University Press, conveyed through Copyright Clearance Center, Inc.

Kim, Jaegwon. From Chapter 5: "Are There Positive Arguments for Type Physicalism?," *Physicalism, or Something Near Enough*, Princeton Monographs in Philosophy, Princeton University Press, 2005. Copyright © 2005. [excerpted, pp. 124–25] Reprinted by permission of Princeton University Press conveyed through Copyright Clearance Center, Inc.

Image Credits

1.1 Office building. Adapted from "Dunder Mifflin." Photograph by Francisco Antunes. Uploaded to flickr.com (https://www.flickr.com/photos/60721972@N00/23743255555) by Francisco Antunes. Image licensed under CC BY 2.0.

1.2 *Socrates and His Students*. Painting by Johan Friedrich Greuter. Cropped from original.

1.3 A McDonald's Big Mac hamburger, as bought in the United States. Photograph by Evan-Amos. Uploaded to commons.wikimedia.org (https://commons.wikimedia.org/wiki/File:Big_Mac_hamburger.jpg) by Evan-Amos. Image licensed under CC0 1.0.

1.4 Hampton National Cemetery, Phoebus Addition. Photograph by David W. Haas. Cropped from original.

1.5 Proposal ("romantic in a springtime"). Photograph by Prayoga D. Widyanto. Uploaded to flickr.com (https://www.flickr.com/photos/8335061@N08/3342632079) by Prayoga D. Widyanto. Image licensed under CC BY 2.0.

1.6 Counterfeit 100 Dollar Bill. Photograph by Osama Shukir Muhammed Amin. Uploaded to commons.wikimedia.org (https://commons.wikimedia.org/wiki/File:Counterfeit_100_dollar_bill,_dated_1974_but_probably_made_later._over-stamped_with_%22Contrefa%C3%A7on%22_on_both_sides._On_display_at_the_British_Museum,_London.jpg) by Osama Shukir Muhammed Amin. Image licensed under CC BY-SA 4.0.

1.7 Birds flying and perched on the wires. Photograph via goodfreephotos.com (https://www.goodfreephotos.com/animals/birds/birds-flying-and-perched-on-the-wires.jpg.php#). Image licensed under CC0.

1.8 Wason Cards.

1.9 Line optical illusion.

2.1 ABBA. Photograph by Bert Verhoeff. Uploaded to commons.wikimedia.org (https://commons.wikimedia.org/wiki/File:Zweedse_popgroep_ABBA_in_Nederland_v.l.n.r._Benny,_Anni-Frid,_Agnetha_en_Bjorn_,_Bestanddeelnr_928-8962.jpg) by Mr.Nostalgic. Image licensed under CC0 1.0. Cropped from original.

2.2 Car wrapped around tree. Photograph by perthhdproductions. Uploaded to flickr.com (https://www.flickr.com/photos/78675950@N03/7981578005) by perthhdproductions. Image licensed under CC BY 2.0. Cropped from original.

2.3 Head and smoke. Image created by Gerd Altmann. Uploaded to pixabay.com (https://pixabay.com/illustrations/face-soul-head-smoke-light-sad-622904/) by Gerd Altmann. Image licensed under the Pixabay License.

2.4 Rabbi ("Tell me the one about the priest and the rabbi again, dear"). Photograph by J Stimp. Uploaded to flickr.com (https://www.flickr.com/photos/128539140@N03/16057491742/in/photolist-qsWQRU-aWdxfk-76YEkG-duADs4-wmUPJ-tBqUCL-6RKdQt-9C3Qu5-bWezEJ-pwCEcP-otcGV4-49xhaJ-s393k9-7Sndns-

3nYNdB-7h3FaG-9W4HJc-7vbFSK-76UGmH-aQPc4T-yLYH7R-6nhbFv-ogzefG-gBUpnU-CtmsaW-e3K4Tn-EymjK-tRcCKu-CZgXFo-MSX11V-y8yb4g-76XVnN-sXL8Rm-a4dYyQ-qyZtRH-yuZfww-xm5t2-4ota5h-m2mt4P-3nYQ6K-y6ZpFQ-fxmj1s-76Yvjd-Q4LQdP-nNWGX3-nPa5Sj-kekkkD-94yCbX-JwMdh-7vdV4V) by J Stimp. Image licensed under CC BY 2.0. Cropped from original.

2.5 Haircut. Uploaded to pxhere.com (https://pxhere.com/en/photo/1072486). Image licensed under CC0.

2.6 Argument. Photograph by rawpixel.com. Uploaded to pxhere.com (https://pxhere.com/en/photo/1452327) by rawpixel.com. Image licensed under CC0. Cropped from original.

2.7 Fake News. Photograph by Marco Verch. Uploaded to flickr.com (https://www.flickr.com/photos/30478819@N08/34969520322) by Marco Verch. Image licensed under CC BY 2.0. Cropped from original.

3.1 Abandoned ship. Uploaded to pxhere.com (https://pxhere.com/en/photo/961394). Image licensed under CC0. Cropped from original.

3.2 *Naval Battle*. Drawing by William Bainbridge Hoff.

3.3 US Navy aircraft from Attack Carrier Air Wing 6 in flight during a sortie over Vietnam. Photograph from the US Navy. Cropped from original.

3.4 *Mona Lisa*. Painting by Leonardo da Vinci.

3.5 Plato and Aristotle from *The School of Athens*. Painting by Raphael. Cropped from original.

3.6 Golden Temple ("Kinkaku ji temple"). Photograph by BriYYZ. Uploaded to flickr.com (https://www.flickr.com/photos/bribri/9977758546/) by BriYYZ. Image licensed under CC BY-SA 2.0. Cropped from original.

3.7 Trojan Horse ("The maquette horse from the 2004 film *Troy*—a present to Chanakkale from Brad Pitt"). Photograph by Edal Anton Lefterov. Uploaded to commons.wikimedia.org (https://commons.wikimedia.org/wiki/File:Brad-Pitt%27s-horse-in-Canakkale.jpg) by Edal Anton Lefterov. Image licensed under CC BY-SA 3.0. Cropped from original.

3.8 Basketball players. Photograph by Chensiyuan. Uploaded to commons.wikimedia.org (https://commons.wikimedia.org/wiki/File:Andrea_bargnani_dunk_2009.JPG) by Chensiyuan. Image licensed under CC BY-SA.4.0. Cropped from original.

3.9 Close up on a pile of screws. Photograph by Marco Verch. Uploaded to flickr.com (https://www.flickr.com/photos/30478819@N08/44560586172/) by Marco Verch. Image licensed under CC BY 2.0.

4.1 Teleportation. Created in Stable Diffusion, Feb. 15, 2023.

4.2 Young and old ("Ricky"). Photograph by Kris Krüg. Uploaded to flickr.com (https://www.flickr.com/photos/kk/64242903/) by Kris Krüg. Image licensed under CC BY-SA 2.0.

4.3 Rope. Photograph by HiveHarbingerCOM. Uploaded to commons.wikimedia.org (https://commons.wikimedia.org/wiki/File:SuperMacro_Rope.JPG) by HiveHarbingerCOM. Image licensed under CC BY 3.0.

4.4 The self. Created in Stable Diffusion, Feb. 15, 2023.

4.5 Forest mushroom. Photograph by Rostislav Kralik. Uploaded to publicdomainpictures.net (https://www.publicdomainpictures.net/en/view-image.php?image=99051&picture=forest-mushroom) by Rostislav Kralik. Image licensed under CC0. Cropped from original.

4.6 Foggy in Leeds. Photograph by Rob Faulkner. Uploaded to flickr.com (https://www.flickr.com/photos/45953381@N05/15899237585) by Rob Faulkner. Image licensed under CC BY 2.0.

4.7 Teleporter. Created in Stable Diffusion, Feb. 15, 2023.

4.8 Anonymous/V for Vendetta/Guy Fawkes Halloween costume mask. Photograph by Marco Verch. Uploaded to flickr.com (https://www.flickr.com/photos/30478819@N08/41224889244) by Marco Verch. Image licensed under CC BY 2.0. Cropped from original.

4.9 Homeless person ("Money, get away. Get a good job with good pay and you're okay. Money, it's a gas. Grab that cash with both hands and make a stash." Pink Floyd, "Money" [1973]). Photograph by Robert Couse-Baker. Uploaded to pxhere.com (https://pxhere.com/en/photo/394595) by Robert Couse-Baker. Image licensed under CC BY 2.0. Cropped from original.

5.1 Mind uploading. Created in Stable Diffusion, Feb. 15, 2023.

5.2 Red carpet. Adapted from "Is Alain Zirah standing on the red carpet with Angelina Jolie? carpet in Cannes." Photograph by Mr Azed. Uploaded to openverse.org (https://openverse.org/image/74f93fca-e12f-4461-af78-06efe2633444) by Mr Azed. Image licensed under CC BY 2.0.

5.3 Moon. Photograph by Patou Ricard. Uploaded to pixabay.com (https://pixabay.com/photos/moon-full-moon-sea-sky-night-sky-2762111/) by Patou Ricard. Image licensed under Pixabay license. Cropped from original.

5.4 *Skull of Phineas Gage*. Drawing from article "Recovery from the passage of an iron bar through the head" by John M. Harlow.

5.5 Night sky. Photograph uploaded to pxhere.com (https://pxhere.com/en/photo/1210959). Image licensed under CC0 1.0. Cropped from original.

5.6 Venice night. Photograph by Iselin. Uploaded to flickr.com (https://www.flickr.com/photos/35279302@N08/3320438680) by Iselin. Image licensed under CC BY 2.0. Cropped from original.

5.7 Ghostly sighting? Photograph uploaded to flickr.com (https://www.flickr.com/photos/31575009@N05/10594484016) by The National Archives UK. Cropped from original.

5.8 Following Apples. Photograph by Richard Revel. Uploaded to publicdomainpictures.net (https://www.publicdomainpictures.net/en/view-image.php?image=178550&picture=following-apples) by Richard Revel. Image licensed under CC0 1.0.

5.9 Artificial intelligence. Created in Stable Diffusion, Feb. 15, 2023.

5.10 Fish ("Smart? No. Hungry? Definitely!"). Photograph by Kalle Gustafsson. Uploaded to flickr.com (https://www.flickr.com/photos/61400543@N04/5676970450) by Kalle Gustafsson. Image licensed under CC BY 2.0. Cropped from original.

6.1 Donkey. ("Santorini's Donkey"). Photograph by Klearchos Kapoutsis. Uploaded to flickr.com (https://www.flickr.com/photos/8383084@N06/4585101978) by Klearchos Kapoutsis. Image licensed under CC BY 2.0. Cropped from original.

6.2 *Pac-Man* (1980).

6.3 Prison cell. Photograph uploaded to pxhere.com (https://pxhere.com/en/photo/1032012). Image licensed under CC0 1.0. Cropped from original.

6.4 Santa Claus. Photograph uploaded to pxhere.com (https://pxhere.com/en/photo/520428). Image licensed under CC0 1.0. Cropped from original.

6.5 Fork in path in park. Photograph by DennisM2. Uploaded to flickr.com (https://www.flickr.com/photos/14674348@N04/1504087870) by DennisM2. Image licensed under CC0 1.0. Cropped from original.

6.6 Spiral galaxy Messier 81. Photograph by NASA, ESA, and the Hubble Heritage Team. Cropped from original.

6.7 Skydive Langar ("AFF Level 1"). Photograph by Tony Danbury. Uploaded to flickr.com (https://www.flickr.com/photos/9678460@N07/7462872188) by wales gibbons. Image licensed under CC BY 2.0. Cropped from original.

6.8 Martin Luther as an Augustinian Monk. Engraving by Lucas Cranach the Elder. Cropped from original.

7.1 Scrabble letters. Photograph by Jonathan Rolande. Uploaded to flickr.com (https://www.flickr.com/photos/110671496@N06/16825148068) by Jonathan Rolande. Image licensed under CC BY 2.0.

7.2 Cocktail in Orrefors Balans martini glass. Photograph by Didriks. Uploaded to flickr.com (https://www.flickr.com/photos/49889671@N03/6217566949) by Didriks. Image licensed under CC BY 2.0. Cropped from original.

7.3 The proposal. Photograph by Mark Guim. Uploaded to flickr.com (https://www.flickr.com/photos/mackarus/2929965867/) by Mark Guim. Image licensed under CC BY 2.0. Cropped from original.

7.4 Computer simulation. Created in Stable Diffusion, Feb. 15, 2023.

7.5 Old man at Canal Bar. Photograph by Robb Todd. Uploaded to flickr.com (https://www.flickr.com/photos/55006168@N06/21237371430) by Robb Todd. Image licensed under CC BY 2.0. Cropped from original.

7.6 *The Unicorn in Captivity* (from the Unicorn Tapestries). Cropped from original.

7.7 Your Popsicle's Melting. Photograph by Kathy. Uploaded to flickr.com (https://www.flickr.com/photos/10129828@N00/3671322447) by Kathy. Image licensed under CC BY 2.0.

7.8 Herd of sheep. Photograph by Johan Neven. Uploaded to flickr.com (https://www.flickr.com/photos/75612671@N03/50539000448) by Johan Neven. Image licensed under CC BY 2.0. Cropped from original.

7.9 Mach bands.

7.10 Coffee. Photograph uploaded to pxhere.com (https://pxhere.com/en/photo/1269179). Image licensed under CC0 1.0. Cropped from original.

8.1 Fallen tree, Achmore wood. Photograph by Ross Angus. Uploaded to flickr.com (https://www.flickr.com/photos/ross_angus/15233155622/) by Ross Angus. Image licensed under CC BY 2.0. Cropped from original.

8.2   Selfie. Photograph by Ádám Fedelin. Uploaded to flickr.com (https://www.flickr. com/photos/150491263@N04/35269383051/) by Ádám Fedelin. Image licensed under CC BY 2.0. Cropped from original.

8.3   Checker shadow illusion. Originally published by Edward H. Adelson, edited by Pbroks13. Uploaded to commons.wikimedia.org (https://commons.wikimedia. org/wiki/File:Checker_shadow_illusion.svg) by Pbrks. Image licensed under CC BY-SA 4.0.

8.4   Meteor. Image by Buddy_Nath. Uploaded to pixabay.com (https://pixabay. com/illustrations/asteroid-space-stars-meteor-1477065/) to Buddy Nath. Image licensed under Pixabay License. Cropped from original.

8.5   Light prism. Image by Joe A. Uploaded to flickr.com (https://www.flickr.com/ photos/187438308@N05/49715450897) by Joe A. Image licensed under CC0 1.0. Cropped from original.

8.6   Specimen of fool's gold or iron pyrites. Image uploaded to sciencestockphotos. com (https://sciencestockphotos.com/free/geology/slides/fools_gold.html). Image licensed under CC BY 4.0. Cropped from original.

8.7   Speeding car ("Blurry Car Strikes again!"). Photograph by Roland Tanglao. Uploaded to flickr.com (https://www.flickr.com/photos/35034347371@ N01/102819201) by Roland Tanglao. Image licensed under CC0 1.0. Cropped from original.

9.1   *The Truman Show*. Created in Stable Diffusion, Feb. 15, 2023.

9.2   Basket of muffins. Photograph by Dana Tentis. Uploaded to pxhere.com (https:// pxhere.com/en/photo/1198266) by Dana Tentis. Image licensed under CC0 1.0.

9.3   *Goldilocks and the Three Bears*. Illustration from *The Book of Knowledge*, edited by Arthur Mee and Holland Thompson (The Grolier Society, 1912).

9.4   Greeting. Adapted from "Handshake between NASA administrator Charles Bolden and JAXA president with Naoki Okumura." Photograph by William Ng.

9.5   Portrait of young woman drinking coffee at home. Photograph by Chevanon Photography. Image uploaded to pexels.com (https://www.pexels.com/photo/ portrait-of-young-woman-drinking-coffee-at-home-324030/) by Chevanon Photography. Image licensed under Pexels license. Cropped from original.

9.6   Seventeenth-century American-made box. Cropped from original.

9.7   Coach and team. Photography uploaded to pxhere.com (https://pxhere.com/en/ photo/1088875). Image licensed under CC0 1.0. Cropped from original.

9.8   Elephant in the sky. Image by Mohamed Hassan. Uploaded to pxhere.com (https://pxhere.com/en/photo/1435433) by Mohamed Hassan. Image licensed under CC0 1.0.

10.1   Smoke. Image uploaded to pxhere.com (https://pxhere.com/en/photo/1362700). Image licensed under CC0 1.0. Cropped from original.

10.2   Canadian election results.

10.3   Black swan. Photograph by TANAKA Juuyoh. Uploaded to pxhere.com (https:// pxhere.com/en/photo/376313). Image licensed under CC BY 2.0. Cropped from original.

10.4 Go game. Photograph by zizou man. Image uploaded to flickr.com (https://www. flickr.com/photos/113856709@N03/12280462513). Image licensed under CC BY 2.0. Cropped from original.

10.5 Teen's messy room. Photograph by woodleywonderworks. Uploaded to flickr. com (https://www.flickr.com/photos/73645804@N00/38787208512) by woodleywonderworks. Image licensed under CC BY 2.0. Cropped from original.

10.6 Hania's lighthouse by night (Crete). Photograph by Alberto Perdomo. Uploaded to flickr.com (https://www.flickr.com/photos/55629889@N00/3156177195) by Alberto Perdomo. Image licensed under CC BY 2.0. Cropped from original.

10.7 Sunset over Lake Washington in Three Acts. Photograph by Michael Seeley. Uploaded to flickr.com (https://www.flickr.com/photos/76093456@N04/28255590309) by Michael Seeley. Image licensed under CC BY 2.0. Cropped from original.

10.8 Lion fight. Photograph by James Sanders. Uploaded to flickr.com (https://www. flickr.com/photos/30516920@N00/32433490003) by James Sanders. Image licensed under CC BY 2.0. Cropped from original.

11.1 Mountain. Photograph uploaded to pxhere.com (https://pxhere.com/en/photo/697867). Image licensed under CC0 1.0.

11.2 Scale, pharmacy. Photograph taken by Naval History & Heritage Command. Uploaded to flickr.com (https://www.flickr.com/photos/41258145@N03/11715228076) by Naval History & Heritage Command. Image licensed under CC BY 2.0. Cropped from original.

11.3 Standing Stone against Tal y Fan, North Wales. Photograph by Stuart Madden. Uploaded to flickr.com (https://www.flickr.com/photos/70056611@N00/9637076871) by Stuart Madden. Image licensed under CC BY 2.0. Cropped from original.

11.4 European rabbit. Photograph by Mathias Appel. Uploaded to flickr.com (https://www.flickr.com/photos/91501748@N07/19618671433) by Mathias Appel. Image licensed under CC0 1.0. Cropped from original.

11.5 The Blue Marble. Photograph taken by the crew of Apollo 17.

11.6 *Pierre Simon Laplace*. Illustration by unknown artist, from the book Les merveilles de l'industrie ou, Description des principales industries modernes, by Louis Figuier.

11.7 Chimpanzee seated at a typewriter. Photograph by the New York Zoological Society. Cropped from original.

11.8 Multiverse. Image by Kevin Dooley. Uploaded to flickr.com (https://www.flickr.com/photos/12836528@N00/5912062168) by Kevin Dooley. Image licensed under CC BY 2.0. Cropped from original.

11.9 Battle scene in a landscape with soldiers on horseback and several fallen men, another group of riders in the background. Engraving by Marco Dente (after Raphael, after Giulio Romano).

11.10 *Romeo and Juliet*. Illustration by F. Dicksee. Cropped from original.

12.1 Outer space. Created in Stable Diffusion, Feb. 15, 2023.

12.2 Sigmund Freud. Photograph by Max Halberstadt. Cropped from original.

12.3 *Blind Monks Examining an Elephant*. Illustration by Hanabusa Itchô.

Index

Page numbers in italics denote figures.